Religious Hatred

Religious Hatred

Prejudice, Islamophobia, and Antisemitism in Global Context

PAUL HEDGES

BLOOMSBURY ACADEMIC
LONDON • NEW YORK • OXFORD • NEW DELHI • SYDNEY

BLOOMSBURY ACADEMIC
Bloomsbury Publishing Plc
50 Bedford Square, London, WC1B 3DP, UK
1385 Broadway, New York, NY 10018, USA
29 Earlsfort Terrace, Dublin 2, Ireland

BLOOMSBURY, BLOOMSBURY ACADEMIC and the Diana logo are
trademarks of Bloomsbury Publishing Plc

First published in Great Britain 2021

Cover design: Ben Anslow
Cover image: *The Inquisition Tribunal*, Francisco Goya (1808–1812)
© incamerastock / Alamy

A catalogue record for this book is available from the British Library.

Library of Congress Cataloging-in-Publication Data
Names: Hedges, Paul (Paul Michael), 1970– author.
Title: Religious hatred : prejudice, islamophobia and antisemitism
in global context / Paul Hedges.
Description: London; New York: Bloomsbury Academic, 2021. |
Includes bibliographical references and index. |
Identifiers: LCCN 2020041826 (print) | LCCN 2020041827 (ebook) |
ISBN 9781350162860 (pb) | ISBN 9781350162877 (hb) |
ISBN 9781350162884 (epdf) | ISBN 9781350162891 (ebook)
Subjects: LCSH: Religions–Relations. | Hate–Religious aspects. |
Christianity. | Islam. | Judaism.
Classification: LCC BL410 .H43 2021 (print) |
LCC BL410 (ebook) | DDC 306.6–dc23
LC record available at https://lccn.loc.gov/2020041826
LC ebook record available at https://lccn.loc.gov/2020041827

ISBN: HB: 978-1-3501-6287-7
PB: 978-1-3501-6286-0
ePDF: 978-1-3501-6288-4
eBook: 978-1-3501-6289-1

Typeset by Newgen KnowledgeWorks Pvt. Ltd., Chennai, India
Printed and bound in Great Britain

To find out more about our authors and books visit www.bloomsbury.com
and sign up for our newsletters.

This book is dedicated to Yuqin Liu, with thanks for her support and being there over the years. I wish her continued health and long life in these troubled times.

CONTENTS

Acknowledgements ix

A brief note on style xi

Introduction: Untheorizing and unpacking 1

SECTION I Why do we hate? 9

1   Dehumanizing humans: Prejudice, identity, and othering 11
2   The hatred unto death: When prejudice becomes killing and genocide 27
Interlude 1: What is religious hatred? 43

SECTION II Bridges from the past 49

3   The oldest prejudice? Christian antisemitism from the Gospels to the ghettoes 51
4   Kafir and Turks: Christians and Muslims through history 67
5   Religious hatred as racial hatred: Enlightenment, citizenship, and racialization 83
Interlude 2: Why did the Holocaust happen? 99

SECTION III Contemporary Western hatreds 105

6   The West's eternal Jewish question? Politics, antisemitism, and Holocaust denial 107

7 'Why do they hate us?' and 'Why do we hate them?': Contemporary Western Islamophobias 125

Interlude 3: Are antisemitism and Islamophobia connected? 141

SECTION IV Prejudice beyond the West 147

8 From People of the Book to enemies of Islam: Islamic antisemitism and Palestine–Israel 149

9 Killing for the Buddha: Islamophobia in the Buddhist world 165

10 Hindutva as hatred: Hindus, Muslims, and the fatherland 181

Interlude 4: Can we regulate religious hatred? (Paul Hedges with Luca Farrow) 195

Epilogue: The good news: Dialogue, civil rights, and peacebuilding 203

Notes 211

Further Reading 281

Index 287

ACKNOWLEDGEMENTS

We stand on the shoulders of giants, and this, as we all know, allows us to look further. As such, in writing this book, I acknowledge my debt to the many scholars, activists, practitioners, and others who have advanced our knowledge of prejudice. I also remember the many victims of prejudice and hatred, deriving from and directed against religion, whose suffering has also, regrettably, given rise to the words I offer herein. Of course, these two groups are not always distinct.

In particular, I must mention the following who in conversations, in teaching and lectures, in offers of help, in reading drafts, or in providing inspiration and impetus to my writing have improved the manuscript enormously. In no particular order: Reuven Firestone, Ari Cohen, Leon Moosavi, Mohamed Imran Mohamed Taib, Abdullah Saeed, Alana Vincent, Irm Haleem, Deborah Lipstadt, David Hirsh, Eve Parker, Terri-Ann Teo, Jeffrey Long, Prashant Waikar, Juhi Ahuja, Nazneen Mohsina, Jude Lal Fernando, Matthew Walton, Laavanya Kathiravelu, Nodirbek Soliev, Mohammed Sinan Siyech, Holly Tipton Hamby, Farish Noor, Todd Green, Carlton Long, Tibi Bassam, (Nur)Sheila Muez, Muhammad Haziq Bin Jani, Charles Asher Small, Ansel Brown, (Nur)Diyanah Yahya, Mohamed Gamal Abdelnour, Iselin Frydenlund and Benny Morris. My apologies for anyone whom I have failed to mention, but my thanks extend to many more whom I am unable to mention.

Finally, three particular people deserve a special mention. First off, Lalle Pursglove, my commissioning editor at Bloomsbury, who has been wonderfully helpful, kind, and responsive. It has been a real pleasure to work with her again. Second, Lily McMahon, the editorial assistant at Bloomsbury, whose efficient and prompt attention have ensured that the whole process has been exceedingly smooth. Finally, Luca Farrow, my research assistant, who has not only co-authored Interlude 4 with me but has fact-checked, chased sources, done research, and smoothed out the manuscript, as well as challenging me to clarify and explain my reasoning or refine what it is that I really wanted to say.

Any remaining failures or mistakes are entirely the author's own.

A BRIEF NOTE ON STYLE

While this is an academic book, I have generally avoided diacritics which many see as exemplifying scholarly standards. This is because it is not a book on specialist linguistics, but is intended to be read widely by scholars and students in many fields, and by those outside academia. As such, the various marks will not clarify particular words or pronunciations but will more likely be off-putting and confusing. I have adopted some diacritics where words are commonly used this way in English, that is, Qur'an. I have put foreign words in italics, unless they are generally used in English, so *hadith* but nirvana. I use foreign/technical terms widely, glossed in the text, but for phrases use English translations, so *ahl al-kitab* will be 'People of the Book', but *dhimmis* is used throughout.

Introduction: Untheorizing and unpacking

Why this book?

Hatred arising from religious impulses, or directed towards a particular religion is not new. But, in our world today, forms of hostility and prejudice associated with religion or directed towards religion are seemingly on the rise.[1] More worryingly, these prejudices have often given rise to genocidal urges. Neither prejudice nor genocide has any particular link to those traditions we typically think of as religions. The former is a very normal way in which we think about, respond to, and react to those around us who, for whatever reason, we see as different. There are rational and irrational aspects to it, some healthy impulses may even lie behind it, but it often results in very unhealthy stigmatization and social vilification of those who have done little or nothing to ask for it. As humans, we often trust those we know and are suspicious of outsiders. This is normal: the unknown other may be hostile, may compete for resources with us, or may be benign. But, before we know which, being suspicious may be the best survival strategy. As a species, we would not have survived if we were not suspicious of potential enemies, rivals, and threats. However, this natural and healthy survival instinct can become a destructive force, even leading us to a desire to wipe out whole other groups of humans to ensure our survival.

I am not discussing religion because I believe it is especially bad or the major cause of such hatred and enmity between people.[2] In recent decades, the voice of strong, so-called New Atheist, critics of religion has derided religion as inherently harmful and a bane on human societies. However, our religious traditions comprise only human beings, who behave as other human beings do in many situations. As such, when we explore religious hatred we see only another subset of human hatred. However, some may still argue that those parts of human culture we call religion are particularly potent sites of hatred, barbarity, and prejudice. There is some element of truth to this, but only some; it is a partial story. One key issue in this regard is, what do we mean by the term 'religion'? I have used it quite a bit so far, and I dare say most readers have known what I meant. However, like so many words we use, it is not so simple. A Christian philosopher, Augustine of Hippo (354–430), once stated that time is a concept that we all know the meaning of, until we stop and think about it. Religion is a bit like that. While we all have a general sense of what it means, we find that we will all actually define it somewhat differently. I do not want to get bogged down by this before we start (see Interlude 1), but we need to keep in mind that 'religion' is not a simple or straightforward term. One more note on how we speak about 'religion(s)' herein may be useful. A religion is not something with agency, only religious actors are. So, for instance, Islam or Buddhism cannot be antisemitic, only individual Muslims or Buddhists may be. However, in title chapters, and some other places we will employ wording about Christianity, Buddhism, Hinduism, and so on that may imply this. It is not to suggest that these traditions – which are always diverse and plural, and so we may speak of the many Christianities, Buddhisms, Hinduisms (which we must bear in mind as we continue) – have only one stance, or that something is inherent to them (they have no essential component beyond that found in the diverse practices of those within the traditions to which we apply these names). Rather, this usage suggests that certain things are embedded within mainstream, authoritative, and pervasive forms. Hence, we may speak of Christian antisemitism or Hindu Islamophobia for reasons which will become clear in the relevant chapters, for prejudices are embedded in substantial ways in these traditions; but we may equally meet Christians, and forms of Christianity, and Hindus, and forms of Hinduism, that are not, respectively, antisemitic or Islamophobic. Importantly, such prejudice is often (or, rather, always) contextually and socially based, rather than something that comes out of the tradition and its teachings as a natural outcome; this will become clear as we discuss what prejudice is and how it arises.[3]

My reasons for writing this book are both complex and simple, and can be broken into five. First, it is a topic that intersects with my research work, even if not my main area, and so has been something of a process of discovery for me. Some scholars take a very narrow focus and spend their whole career diving deeply into a single specialist area. My own trajectory has been somewhat different. In part, this is because my primary focus is interreligious relations, which I have come to realize cannot be understood in a narrow way. While some scholars take a dim view of those who write outside their own narrow disciplinary expertise (and, sometimes, into *their* territory!), it is part of making sense of interreligious relations as a whole. Second, in July 2019, I attended the ISGAP Summer Institute in St John's College, Oxford, on 'Critical Antisemitism', which made me focus deeply on this issue.[4] As I did so, I realized that both antisemitism and Islamophobia need to be understood together as phenomena linked to human identity creation. Third, although my training is in religious studies, especially historical and philosophical issues, I now work in a school of international relations and in a programme focused on contemporary interreligious relations with connections to research centres where religious violence, terrorism, and hatred are highlighted.[5] This partly matches my own research trajectory and interests from more historical issues to more contemporary ones, and from more conceptual encounters to focusing on the social contexts, though the historical and conceptual still interest me and inform the way I approach issues. Fourth, and in connection with the previous three, there is the unfortunate fact that these issues are becoming so pertinent. For a long time after the Holocaust, antisemitism was not a socially acceptable form of prejudice in Europe.[6] Again, prejudice against Muslims, while existing, was part of a generic racism that was not always particularly tied to religion per se. Recent years, as we will explore, have seen this change. As such, I found writing this book a pressing concern. Finally, I found books on Islamophobia, books on antisemitism, and books on prejudice (often focused on race or gender), but rarely were all three drawn together. As such, this book is partly written to fill a perceived hole in the literature. In this regard, I hope it will be useful for teaching, for interested readers who want to see the connections, and as a scholarly contribution to understanding religious hatred as prejudice and the violence it leads to.

I am by origin British but now work in Singapore and have lived in China. This book is written into our globalized world where many of us are mobile, which is part of the nature of religious hatred today. Having said that, I have imagined myself writing primarily for a Western reader because that is where we see both antisemitism and Islamophobia together most commonly. However, these hatreds are not limited to the West, and I hope my journey herein will illuminate people from many corners of our world.

Three further issues also need addressing. First, I have written what is an academic text. Nevertheless, given the pressing enormity of the issues it is one that I have felt compelled to write and must admit to being far from neutral on. However, in the academic study of religion, there is an assumption that scholarship and advocacy (or activism) are always separate. In other words, scholarship is neutral, impartial, and grounded only in secular, facts-based, and reasoned study. However, such a distinction can be challenged on many levels, with feminist, decolonial, and critical theory scholarship all disputing the notion of the detached, rational observer who sits above the fray. In noting reasons why I have written this book, I have already taken account of how autobiography plays into academic study.[7] Nevertheless, I have tried to write a book of scholarship not advocacy, and I believe that the arguments, and evidence amassed, will themselves be compelling. Certainly, I do not wish to impose my views on others and ask readers to make their own minds up. Second, given the scope of the work, I have not been able to address every issue or concern. For instance, the way that prejudice is often gendered, with women often bearing the brunt of discrimination, is only mentioned in passing but could have been a whole book. Again, intersections with racism, while explored, could be taken further. Decolonial issues are also important given how much European norms have shaped the forms of hatred we see but only get passing mention, though informing arguments and approaches within the book. I realize that others would have written this book differently, and my failure to explore certain issues further does not indicate that I think they are not important. Finally, inspired by the writings of Paulo Freire (1921–1997), I understand learning as a journey in which the 'teacher/master' and 'student/disciple' are co-learners.[8] Readers will bring knowledge, experiences, and information which I do not possess. To emphasize that we are always all students in the process of learning together, I will hereon use 'we' rather than 'I' in this book to include readers in this journey. Where I do, on very few occasions, revert to 'I' it is because I am speaking very deliberately as 'the author'.

Terms, concepts, and untheorizing

It would be useful to say something about some of the terms and concepts used in this book. Some of these, such as hatred, prejudice, violence, and genocide, are discussed in the first two chapters that provide a theoretical basis for the book. Meanwhile, race is addressed in Chapter 5 and religion in Interlude 1. However, one particular concept employed is 'untheorizing', which needs unpacking. This is applied to three terms: genocide, antisemitism, and Islamophobia. By untheorizing, we mean an attempt to get away from any overarching grand explanation (the big theory that often makes people famous but is almost always wrong). Rather, we suggest that these terms describe neither discrete things nor unique and special sui generis phenomena. For instance, particularly with antisemitism, some scholars describe it as a unique hate, a particular abstraction that haunts history like a ghost, or even as inexplicable, metaphysical, and defying explanation. Rather, we will suggest, each fits into a wider pattern: antisemitism is prejudice against Jews, Islamophobia is prejudice against Muslims, and genocide is explained by human impulses to violence in particular social contexts. None is a special phenomenon in its own category but part of a wider set of phenomena explained by patterns of human identity creation, prejudice, and violence. (Note: saying that antisemitism and Islamophobia are forms of prejudice is not to theorize them simply as aspects of social dislike, because prejudice can be embedded in political and structural regimes.[9]) However, untheorizing is also to complicate each term, because there is never a single cause, a single type, or single reason for any of them. The nature of antisemitism (prejudice against Jews) has changed over time. Untheorizing implies showing interconnectedness and the local, variable, and contingent factors, rather than supposing an ongoing essence which may be separately theorized.

We also distinguish between analytical and definitional categories. An analytical category is a discrete class of things or a concept that helps us understand other things in relation to them. It can be seen as a Durkheimian 'ideal type' or a particular reified notion which can be contrasted with something else. It is what may be termed a 'higher level' category which encompasses many discrete types of things within it. A definitional category, by contrast, is something that can be usefully delineated from other things but which in and of itself may not be a distinct category or concept. For instance, prejudice is an analytical concept because it refers to a wide range of forms of human behaviour (i.e. antisemitism, Islamophobia, misogyny, racism, classism, etc.). Meanwhile, Islamophobia is a definitional concept because it does not illuminate other things in terms of what it is (prejudice against Muslims) but can be usefully demarcated from other forms of prejudice, for example, gender prejudice, antisemitism, class prejudice, and so on. Being a definitional concept (or 'lower level' category) does not mean that something may not be analytically useful. Indeed, by being able to define discrete areas of human life, whether this is forms of prejudice or spheres of human artistic culture (i.e. poetry, music, fine arts, and pottery are arguably definitional categories within 'artistic culture' as an analytic category), we can better see particular facets of human behaviour and understanding.

Antisemitism and Islamophobia need a bit more unpacking too. Neither has a singular meaning. Indeed, while some distinguish 'antisemitism' as a new phenomenon tied into racial prejudice, from older forms of religiously based anti-Judaism (or Judeophobia),[10] I do not follow this classification. It is not to say that this distinction is incorrect: modern antisemitism is different from medieval antisemitism. However, much contemporary antisemitism is not simply racist but combines older religious motifs. Distinguishing where one form of prejudice transforms into another will always be somewhat arbitrary, as will the definitions. Therefore, we use both antisemitism and Islamophobia in wide and open-ended ways. This will be anachronistic and employs English terms in cultures which may not use them, but by untheorizing these terms (unpacking any specific content beyond simply being prejudice) we would hope not to do undue violence to any context. Partha Chatterjee has warned about 'colonial difference', where a way of understanding is imposed on others (here, neocolonial power manifested in English's omnipresence, and with it particular terms and ways of thinking).[11] Our employment may at first seem alien and distorting, especially when speaking about Islamic antisemitism, Buddhist Islamophobia, and

Hindu Islamophobia (phrases which may seem shocking), but is explained as we proceed. Insofar as we define antisemitism and Islamophobia, we offer a rough and ready definition playing on a joke attributed to Isaiah Berlin that antisemitism is 'disliking Jews more than is necessary', and the same application of the joke (though, it may be said, hardly humorous in its outcome) may be applied to Islamophobia as 'disliking Muslims more than is necessary'. It might seem odd to say this, but as forms of prejudice they represent the types of resentment, dislike, fear, or antagonism that we may 'naturally' have for out-groups in the development of prejudice. As we will see in Chapter 1, prejudice is not (in and of itself) unnatural or deviant but follows the way that we, as human beings, relate to our social world. Certainly, this does not make it inherently positive or useful, rather we develop 'useful' stereotypes (to help us make sense of the world) which become 'negative' stereotypes that lead to excessive dislike and dehumanization of other people and groups.

If any justification is needed for our use of the terms, we offer the following. First, the term 'antisemitism' to mean prejudice against Jews is generally accepted, but we follow the spelling with no hyphen rather than 'anti-semitism'. This follows current preferred usage in antisemitism studies, which notes that as there is no actual 'Semite' (as an ethnic/racial category) against which antisemitism can be posited, it is not actually against Semites. (If it were taken as anti-'Semitism', we may note there is also no 'Semitism' for it to be against.) Further, when first used in the nineteenth century, as (racialized) prejudice against Jews, the term bore no hyphen, which only got introduced and then repeated in somewhat later English usage. To sum up, the hyphen both gives weight to it being something it is not and is an erroneous rendition.[12]

However, there is considerable opposition to the term 'Islamophobia'.[13] Some argue that prejudice against Islam is more about race than religion, so the focus upon religion is wrong. Others suggest the term implies an irrational fear, a phobia, when fear of Muslims is well placed. Again, the term is sometimes said to be a politically correct way to limit criticism of Islam. Some of this is addressed in Chapter 7, so we will not dwell on it at length here. Our usage is based upon it being the currently generally accepted scholarly term for prejudice against Muslims, rather than giving it any particular weight in and of itself. As such, it can cover both racial and religious prejudice. Further, as we also address Islamic antisemitism in this book, it is hardly to stop any criticism of Islam.

Overview

The book comprises ten chapters, four 'interludes', and an epilogue. While the chapters provide the bulk of the material, the interludes discuss some side topics which would not necessarily fit in any chapter but are useful points for discussion. The first section is theoretical and provides a framing context for the book. Chapter 1 discusses prejudice in relation to aspects of human identity creation, showing that while it is a normal and natural process, it can lead to a stigmatization and dehumanization of others. The second chapter discusses what motivates humans to violence in certain circumstances, the processes that lead from words and prejudice into violence and killing. It also argues that what we term 'genocide' represents merely an extreme example of human violence. Interlude 1 asks what may characterize religious hatred, noting that while not distinct from other human hatreds, what we term 'religion' can provide a significant impetus to hatred and violence. It also addresses why we may see hatred towards religion, with this phrase doing double-work within this book.

The second section is historical. Chapter 3 outlines the conceptualization and development of Christian antisemitism from the gospels to the ghettoes, considering how Christianity's division from Judaism led to enmity that became enshrined in various texts and teachings. Chapter 4 covers historical, mainly European, Christian attitudes to Islam and also looks at a two-way interaction considering aspects of how the Islamic attitude to Christianity and other religions developed. Chapter 5 then addresses a key issue in the transformation of antisemitism and Islamophobia into their modern form, which is the development of racism. It discusses theories of race and looks at racism as a form of prejudice with particular attention to the racialization of Judaism. Colonial encounters are also considered. The section ends with Interlude 2 which asks why the Holocaust happened. It seeks to understand some of the connections traced in the previous chapters and how they gave birth to an attempt to destroy Jews.

The third section covers the contemporary Western context, with Chapter 6 surveying antisemitism and looking at themes around Holocaust denial, continued right-wing and Christian antisemitism, and also what is sometimes termed the 'new antisemitism' or left-wing antagonism to Jews via opposition to Israel and support for Palestinian rights. Chapter 7 covers contemporary forms of Islamophobia in the Western context. The roles of the media, politicians, and public perceptions are key. The way that Islam has been racialized, making some Islamophobia a racial hatred, is also considered. Interlude 3 considers connections, and differences, between Islamophobia and antisemitism.

The fourth section takes us on a global survey and begins with Chapter 8 looking at Islamic antisemitism, which covers a broad historical sweep from the way Jews have been regarded traditionally to how contemporary Islamic antisemitism is influenced by Western discourses, including from the Nazis. Chapter 9 addresses how Buddhist Islamophobia has arisen, focusing on how Buddhist notions of violence and a just war developed, both historically and in contemporary times, and how today these have become focused on Islam in such places as Sri Lanka and Myanmar. Chapter 10 addresses both the historical and contemporary aspects of Hindu attitudes to Islam. It shows how a particular form of Hindu nationalism focused on an interpretation of the concept of *Hindutva* ('Hinduness') has led into contemporary Hindu Islamophobia. This chapter also connects some global trends providing something of a conclusion to the book as a whole. Interlude 4 asks whether we can regulate religious hatred and hate speech, looking at legal attempts to delimit and control antisemitism, Islamophobia, and other hatreds in various jurisdictions and in principle.

Given that the book focuses on a deeply distressing set of issues, and reading and research for this book has not always been a pleasant task, and so as to not give the (false) impression that the encounters of Judaism, Islam, Christianity, Buddhism, Hinduism, and the secular world are always negative, we end with an epilogue termed 'The Good News' and discuss various examples and dynamics which lead to dialogue, social action, and reconciliation.

SECTION I
Why do we hate?

CHAPTER ONE

Dehumanizing humans: Prejudice, identity, and othering

Introduction

The foundational study of prejudice remains Gordon Allport's (1897–1967) *The Nature of Prejudice* published in 1954. It helped lay out the way that prejudice is defined, which we can state as follows:

> *Prejudice* is commonly defined as an unfair negative attitude towards a social group or person perceived to be a member of that group and, like other attitudes, consists of three components: affect, cognition, and behavior.[1]

In other words, prejudice is about how we feel (affect), think (cognition), and act (behaviour) in ways that do not fit the evidence (unfair) towards some other person or people. This is social in terms of how we, in society, create in-groups (us) and out-groups (them), and so we will also draw on the Social Identity Theory (SIT) of Henri Tajfel (1919–1982). Prejudice has been heavily theorized in terms of both psychological and social motivations and factors, and this is where we begin to look at the roots of religious hatred.[2]

Prejudice: Some key principles

Building from Allport, psychologists today define prejudice as made of three elements: stereotypes which concern beliefs; prejudice, which is the evaluative and more emotive side; and discrimination, which refers to action based on these.[3] We may argue, though, that we should not neatly distinguish rationalized belief, emotive responses, and actions, as each may build upon – or build up – the others, aspects of which we will see below. Moreover, across disciplines, there is no agreement on terminology and so various authorities will use these terms differently. In general, here, we will employ prejudice as a blanket term; however, when needed we will also use stereotype to refer to particular beliefs, and discrimination to refer to the actions arising from prejudice. We will discuss each of these further below.

Recent studies argue that stereotype and prejudice should be distinguished. Stereotypes are, as it were, a pot of cultural knowledge about certain groups. Everybody in a society will tend to know what the stereotypes about the other groups (and themselves) are; however, not everybody accepts them; this distinguishes prejudice from stereotypes. That is to say, high-prejudice individuals will accept the stereotypes of another group; low-prejudice individuals will typically reject them. Importantly, prejudice means ascribing those generic stereotypes to everybody (or most people[4]) in a whole group. This links back to a key aspect of Allport's work, which is that prejudice is about overgeneralization. However, because we all have knowledge of the stereotypes, in some situations even less prejudiced people can behave in ways that reflect the stereotypes. This relates to what is termed implicit prejudices and explicit prejudices. The former are things we are largely not aware of, while the latter are conscious decisions.[5] So, explicit prejudice may be, for instance, somebody actively discriminating in employment by not given a job to somebody because they do not like Jews, Muslims, Sikhs, or whatever group it happens to be. With the former, when we meet people, we may get certain impressions of them because we have a knowledge of the stereotypes and so will be more likely to classify people in certain ways. As we become aware of this, we can counteract the application of stereotypes.

A further important issue, and a major innovation in Allport's study, is the realization that stereotyping and prejudice are natural.[6] Before Allport, it was assumed in psychology that prejudice was a sign of some form of mental health issue or disorder in our thinking. However, as humans, our senses bombard us with information, and so we naturally categorize the things that we encounter. This applies to objects, animals, and people. We are simply unable to operate without doing this, partly because we need to make quick judgements (or at least our ancestors did) about whether something is a threat or not. However, even threats aside, every day our senses will take in literally thousands, if not millions, of sights, sounds, tastes, and other sensations. The only way our minds can cope is by grouping things together into boxes. This requires a process of generalization. Hence, finding ways to quickly make sense of our interactions with other people is necessary and normal. This leads to stereotyping. Now, many stereotypes might be partially accurate, or based on some facts of our experience. But, they do not work all the time. For instance, in our general category of apples we may expect them to be sweet and crunchy but, of course, not all apples are. When our ancestors were foraging on the savannah, or when we are browsing the supermarket shelves, we simply cannot stop and try to make sense of every individual animal or apple we encounter. Equally, when we see a member of a different 'tribe' (however we determine that) we need to quickly get a general sense of whether we should exchange pleasantries, ignore them, seduce them, treat them as a threat, and so on. Of course, everybody is an individual with their own traits, yet we cannot engage deeply in trying to determine how we make sense of every last person we see; and for our ancestors a good sense of when to run, when to fight, and when to ignore (so you do not waste energy) was deeply important for survival. Stereotyping and prejudice are deeply engrained and natural traits of evolution. Doing it does not make somebody a 'bad' person.

Studies of prejudice suggest that it arises in a spectrum of degrees. These can range from, when we meet or think of the group we have prejudice towards, a feeling of mild discomfort, to disgust, to fear, to anger, then hatred, with Allport describing hate as an extreme dislike.[7] We address Allport's scale for prejudice and hate below, but it is important to note first that we are talking about a wide range of attitudes and behaviour which can go from some mild distaste to the extremes of violence. Moreover, prejudice is not generally understood as being a personal dislike, rather it is a social and collective attitude. Here it links strongly to Tajfel's work on SIT that adds depth to Allport's work.[8] The process of prejudice is importantly connected to how we relate our own group and its identity, our in-group, to other groups and their identities, our out-groups. In other words, prejudice comes to us through what is termed socialization, we learn it as we learn about our other attitudes, social customs, and opinions about the world around us.

We can think more about the three aspects of prejudice: affect, cognition, and behaviour. Prejudice exists as an emotional, affective attitude. We have fear, anger, hate, or disgust towards some other person or group. As such, a strong part of prejudice is not a reasoned and rational thing but more what we may term a 'gut feeling', sometimes pumped up in us by certain rhetoric or group-feeling; it may also come from interactions and encounters where we negatively perceive another (often then applied to a whole group of people). In these terms, it may become an almost instinctive feeling or reaction. However, our prejudices are also cognitive as they come from and inform worldviews, opinions, and rationales. We think out and explain our attitudes – even if the bases for them are not always found in evidential reason – and our wider worldviews often have prejudices embedded within them. Prejudiced ideology may not be known to everyone, at least not in any depth; as with any worldview, few take the time to study and ingest the minutiae of the doctrines and intellectual underpinning, but often – especially for deep-seated and long-lasting prejudices – there will be an elaborate intellectual case built around it. Allport argued that few are really invested in the ideology and, therefore, with changing social contexts, prejudice could quite readily be overcome. However (and this is important), conversely, if people are not heavily invested in an ideology against prejudice it may also

easily return with changing social contexts. Finally, discrimination is prejudice as an aspect of human behaviour. There are actions associated with it.
These can range, as with the variety of levels of prejudice, from simply dis-
tancing ourselves from others, or looking down on people[9] – the glance we
cast upon another can say more than many words – to actual violence or
intimidation. Especially when we consider prejudice as a social construct,
we need to consider all of its aspects. Indeed, in learning prejudice – for it
may be from our peer group or as children that we learn it – it is often the
last aspect, behaviour, where we first, or most strongly, observe and imitate
patterns that internalize the prejudice in us. Importantly, behaviour, far more
than abstract concepts, is the thing that embeds prejudice in both social and
individual ways of being. Sometimes our prejudices may not be carefully
thought through in cognitive terms, though we may (later) rationalize it to
ourselves at some level, but we have habits that instil prejudice in ourselves
and those around us. Behaviour can, generally, clearly signal to those we
have prejudice against that they are other than us, despised, looked down
upon, or are simply not welcomed. We should spell out a key aspect of this
clearly: prejudice is not always built from ideas or worldviews into actions
but our actions (perhaps implicitly learnt from what others do) may instil in
us prejudices. If our parents always crossed the road to avoid people with
different skin pigmentations then we will learn that they are people to be
avoided and develop some aversion to them, even if racist ideas are never
stated to us overtly.[10] Judith Butler's notion of performativity may be noted
here, which speaks of the way that particular forms of behaviour express a
worldview (and reinforce it by performing it, especially in public). As such, in
countering prejudice, a battle of ideas is not enough, rather an anti-prejudice
performativity which challenges established norms of prejudice is needed.[11]

A scale of prejudice

Here, we return directly to Allport's classic study. We have mentioned above
the fact that prejudice may manifest in various degrees, and relating to this
Allport notes that

> It is true that any negative attitude tends somehow, somewhere, to express
> itself in action. Few people keep their antipathies entirely to themselves.
> The more intense the attitude, the more likely it is to result in vigorously
> hostile action.[12]

In relating the various degrees of prejudice, he sets out what he sees as the
behaviours, based on attitudes, that may go alongside them. This he presents
as a five-point scale. It is not, he notes, a strictly mathematical demarcation
with the numbers representing – as it were – points on a Likert scale from

least to most, with each being roughly equal from each other. Rather, the five points merely give us what we may term a variety of actions. Moreover, he suggests that these are simply heuristic markers that indicate a far more numerous range of activities, behaviours, and states of mind which help us conceptualize the variety of what is encompassed by prejudice. Allport's fivefold categorization of prejudice is as follows:[13]

1. *Antilocution*. Most people who have prejudices talk about them. With like-minded friends, occasionally with strangers, they may express their antagonism freely. But many people never go beyond this mild degree of antipathetic action.

2. *Avoidance*. If the prejudice is more intense, it leads the individual to avoid members of the disliked group, even perhaps at the cost of considerable inconvenience. In this case, the bearer of prejudice does not directly inflict harm upon the group he dislikes. He takes the burden of accommodation and withdrawal entirely upon himself.

3. *Discrimination*. Here the prejudiced person makes detrimental distinctions of an active sort. He undertakes to exclude all members of the group in question from certain types of employment, from residential housing, political rights, educational or recreational opportunities, churches, hospitals, or from some other social privileges. Segregation is an institutionalized form of discrimination, enforced legally or by common custom.

4. *Physical attack*. Under conditions of heightened emotion prejudice may lead to acts of violence or semi-violence. An unwanted Negro family may be forcibly ejected from a neighborhood or so severely threatened that it leaves in fear. Gravestones in Jewish cemeteries may be desecrated. The Northside's Italian gang may lie in wait for the Southside's Irish gang.

5. *Extermination*. Lynchings, pogroms, massacres, and the Hitlerian program of genocide mark the ultimate degree of violent expression of prejudice.

We should note that this is not simply a scale which everybody moves along. Somebody at the first level, where prejudice is simply talk, will not necessarily proceed to have done enough talking and move then to further forms of action. Many people, or prejudices, will often – and for long periods – stay at one level. Nevertheless, each may be a stimulus to a higher level of prejudice. Indeed, prejudice may not necessarily develop through each of the stages outlined here. Strong words may inspire some into direct violent action, and Allport notes Hitler's rhetoric as a case in point:

It was Hitler's antilocution that led Germans to avoid their Jewish neighbors and erstwhile friends. This preparation made it easier to enact the

Nürnberg laws of discrimination which, in turn, made the subsequent burning of synagogues and street attacks upon Jews seem natural. The final step in the macabre progression was the ovens at Auschwitz.[14]

We may, at this stage, note that while legal regulation against hate speech may seem to some to be a violation of free speech, violence, or even genocide always begins somewhere. That somewhere is more often than not words. Hence we need regulation against prejudice as hate speech (see Interlude 4). For those who may be on the receiving end of hatred, we must remember that one *man's* free speech may be the incitement that leads another to kill *his* fellow human beings. (We break with gender-neutral language here because, all too often, we see male orators stoking hatred with young men responding in violence to it, but this is not to say that women cannot equally be fitted to either task.[15]) The prejudice manifested is often predicated on the lines of perceived racial, gender, religious, and class identities among others: the non-white, non-male, non-Christian, and non-elite often being those on the sharp end of verbal, and consequently physical, abuse arising from prejudice, though, of course, this may be different in non-Western contexts and the matrix is contextual. Furthermore, prejudice is often intersectional. Here, this is taken to mean at least two things: first, it often hits hardest at the intersection of various such groupings, so Black women may be particularly affected; second, those with strong prejudices are not often prejudiced against only one group but multiple ones, so the person prejudiced against Muslims may well also dislike Jews, Blacks, socialists, intellectuals, and look down on women.[16]

It is also worth noting that Allport's usage of the word discrimination differs from the current sociological usage, which sees it as enacted prejudice, that is, an action or state of affairs that excludes or disadvantages someone based on perceived traits. For him, discrimination is a stage between mild antipathy and violence. Nevertheless, his stages remain useful as they help demonstrate the range of prejudice and point towards a potential continuum. One aspect of this is a recognition that what may seem relatively mild forms of prejudice are not simply innocent. As Allport said, 'From the point of view of social consequences much "polite prejudice" is harmless enough – being confined to idle chatter. But unfortunately, the fateful progression is, in this century [the 20th century], growing in frequency.' There is, in other words, no 'benign bigotry', especially as this may be manifest in forms of privilege for certain groups which may result, for those less privileged, in what has been termed by Alvin Poussaint '*death by a thousand nicks*'.[17]

Hate

While we know what we mean when we say, 'I hate X,' digging further down shows that although 'hate is thought of as a single emotion … there is reason to believe that it has multiple components that can manifest themselves in different ways on different occasions'.[18] Robert and Karin Sternberg elucidate this in a 'duplex' theory of hate, noting five key elements.[19] First, hate is closely linked, psychologically, to love. One can turn to the other. We may suggest that it is because of some closeness, or even attraction, that we come to really hate some other. It is a recognition that they may have what we admire in some way, or are related to some other love we have. Importantly, the Sternbergs note, it is perceptions rather than any reality per se that are behind this. Second, hate and love are not opposites, neither is one the absence of the other. Their relationship is 'multifaceted' and is composed of three distinct elements (intimacy, passion, and commitment) in each case. How these elements relate varies, so one person may experience hate, or the combination of hate and love, differently from another. Third, the structure is triangular, so hate has three corners: negation of intimacy, negation of passion, and negation of commitment; this mirrors love's triangular structure: intimacy, passion, and commitment. Fourth, both hate and love come from narratives. We hear stories about other people, and we tell ourselves stories about others. These stories, and how we experience them, mean that hate and love manifest inside us, again in ways that may differ from how others hear and retell the narratives. Fifth, 'hate is one major precursor, although certainly not the only precursor, of some instances of terrorism, massacres, and genocide'.

While accepting the narrative told here, we should depart from one aspect of the Sternbergs' theory. This is that they place their theory in relation to 'humanistic psychologists' such as Erich Fromm (1900–1980) and Abraham Maslow (1908–1970) for whom 'love represents human maturity and fulfilment, whereas hate represents a perversion of the positive possibilities for humankind. Hate is not something we are born with – it is something we acquire'.[20] While this may be, as they say, humanistic, it does not seem to fit within an understanding of humanity based on perspectives from evolutionary biology and anthropology. Allport countered prevailing trends of his day by arguing that prejudice was not a mental abnormality but a normal part of how we understand the world. We extend this by noting the evolutionary background.[21] The same applies to love and hate. As complex evolved beings interacting with the world, anger and hatred are as integral to our survival as are empathy and love. As social apes, both the more 'positive' and more 'negative' emotions are key to who we are. To deny them, or to suggest they are not part of being fully human, is problematic. Now, this is not to deny that our hatred of any specific human groups is not learnt, for prejudice is always social. Neither is it to deny that learning empathy and love for others will help us flourish as human beings, nor that uncontrolled hatred is harmful (but is uncontrolled love not also harmful?).

Given their characterization of hate as having three corners, the Sternbergs suggest that various degrees of hatred are possible. Their analysis is, notably, supported by other studies which observe the bases of hate as multiple, though they may be termed somewhat differently, for instance as 'feelings of *disgust*' (negation of intimacy), 'feelings of *fear* and *anger*' (negation of passion), and 'feelings of *contempt*' (negation of commitment), which we align with the Sternbergs' conceptions as noted in parenthesis.[22] The Sternbergs define degrees of hate in the following terms: cold hate or diminution of another; cool hate or disgust; simmering hate or loathing; hot hate based in anger/fear; boiling hate or revulsion; seething hate based in anger/fear and a diminution of another; and burning hate where we want to annihilate another.[23] They suggest that we can see a 'danger level', gauged from 0 to 3, depending upon how many of the components of hate are present (the negation of intimacy, passion, and commitment). At 0 there are no hate components, and then at 1 we have one component, at 2 two components, and at danger level 3 all 'three of the components of hate are present', and this is when 'massacres and genocides are much more likely to result. ... They are also a product of stories'.[24] Killing and genocides, however, are a concern of Chapter 2, where we will also note other contributing factors.

In terms of what hatred involves, the Sternbergs note its multiple nature, with manifestations (here within relationships) as diverse as acting coldly; yelling and throwing things; walking out; physically hurting their partner; behaving as usual.[25] Relating it to religion, they note, 'members of one religion or religious sect may be taught to hate members of another religion or religious sect, who are characterised as "infidels" or "traitors"'.[26] This highlights that while hate will manifest differently in each person, we must not neglect the social aspect of hate and other emotions, and how they manifest in group contexts.[27] The 'hate-based propaganda' which the Sternbergs understand as supporting hatred 'typically depicts the [hated] individual [or group] as subhuman or inhuman, or otherwise incapable of receiving, giving, or sustaining feelings of closeness, warmth, caring, communication, compassion, and respect'.[28]

Before proceeding, we may profitably consider debates in the humanities and social sciences between two dichotomous poles which, for ease of reference, we can gloss here as relativists and universalists. Relativists believe that every cultural group and its human experience is different, universalists that essentially common human experiences unite all cultures. Both sides have strong arguments, but often these days the relativist side is seen as the most theoretically sophisticated, with universalists seen as being naïve or beset with a colonial superiority complex (given that, often, it is Western norms that are claimed to be universal). We may assert a path between the two, following such thinkers as Boaventura de Sousa Santos who notes: 'All cultures are relative, but cultural relativism, as a philosophical posture, is wrong. All cultures aspire to ultimate concerns and values, but cultural universalism, as a philosophical posture, is wrong.'[29] Indeed, the argument that we must prefer relativism over universalism as the latter is colonialist is itself an assertion that can support Western superiority by making it unchallengeable in the face of postcolonial critique; if no culture's notions of justice, equality, or fairness are anything but their own contextual narrative then they have no valid critique of the norms of our own culture. It is important to note that, in terms of the operation of prejudice, we see fairly stable cross-cultural patterns of human othering and in-group and out-group formation taking place. As Achille Mbembe has argued, 'The deep structure of our world is the same everywhere ... because we share in a common humanity.'[30] While the dynamics are always particular and culturally specific, if we wish to understand human hatred towards other humans the pursuit of a strong relativist position leads us into misunderstanding rather than providing, as it may in some circumstances, insights into human cultural diversity.[31]

In-group, out-group, and stereotypes

Stereotypes are our ideas of the other; they are not simply found in a cognitive/psychological framework but relate to social identity formation. This is because these ideas, while the way we process them is unique to each of us, are always formed as part of a wider set of social and group relations. The group aspects of this are therefore key. A fundamental feature of our identity is that it is never something that we claim in isolation. Indeed, very often, our sense of identity (as an individual or group) is primarily posited on what we are not, rather than what we are.[32] We are continually creating in-groups and out-groups which pit 'us' against 'them'. Studies highlight three key things for our purposes. First, these identities are never stable or clear-cut, they are inevitably arbitrary. In considering religious identities, we can consider the following scenario:

> A Christian and a Muslim sit down together to talk. They may see them-selves in differing in-groups based upon theology: the Christian believes in the Trinity and that Jesus is the 'Son of God'; the Muslim asserts a strict singular monotheism. However, when joined by a Buddhist, the Christian and Muslim are united into an in-group of 'believers in a crea-tor deity' against the Buddhist. The fourth person to join this group is an atheist, but now the in-group of the 'religious believers' is composed of the Buddhist, Christian, and Muslim who characterise the non-religious atheist as part of their out-group.[33]

While entirely hypothetical, our various in-group and out-group permuta-tions above reflect actual positions that real people take as they position themselves against those they perceive as outsiders. Whether our in-groups and out-groups are based around class, gender, religion, race, or any other category, each of them is created as a socially imagined category in human discourse. They are not actual things which exist, no matter how perma-nent, rigid, or structured they may appear to be; there are many studies and examples of this, for instance, in terms of the Irish not being considered part of 'white' society in the United States until it became useful to distance them from African-origin slaves.[34] Following Benedict Anderson (1936–2015), we may speak of our group identities as essentially imagined.[35]

The fact that our in-group and out-group constructions are socially variable and shifting does not make them either any less real in their consequences or any less certain as 'actual facts' about the world for those who hold them (i.e. perceptions). Therefore, we need to consider the consequences of holding them. Our second point then is the creation of in-group salience norms. That is to say, we imagine that whatever we consider the unique factors that hold our in-groups together are more unique than they are. We typically insist that what marks us as different from our out-groups is a vast chasm, rather than seeing potential connections. For instance, Christians – when perceiving Christianity as the shared in-group – will typically argue that the Trinity is fundamentally unique and conceptually distinct from any form of Trinitarian belief in other religions.[36] Differences among Christian conceptions of the Trinity will be minimized in such identity construction to contrast with, for example, Muslims. Conversely, if Muslims and Christians find themselves stressing their common belief in deity against, for example, atheists then their differing forms of monotheism will be downplayed. We can pay attention to Rogers Brubaker's observation that ethnic groups (we may posit that this applies equally to other groups, e.g. religious, sectarian, etc.) do not have any natural affinity except that espoused through some discourse, and that the kind of concerted in-group and out-group formation discussed here needs an organization to create and promote those interests.[37] Against Brubaker, though, we may suggest that this seems to apply to fairly large-scale social formations, and that in small-scale settings (e.g. family/tribal groups or in new sub-cultures) what he terms organizations may be somewhat coterminous with groups. (Though specific individuals may carry undue weight, and hence the interests served in small groups may be those of the charismatic leader in place of the organization, though a more democratic group formation is plausible.) We will note, in subsequent chapters, the role of specific organizations in fomenting prejudice.

Our third point is, perhaps, the most significant, and this is the tendency to create stereotypes. These are of two types: positive stereotypes of our in-group; negative stereotypes of our out-groups. Our in-group is honest, smart, upright, kind, brave, noble, and just; yet our out-group is dishonest, dumb, deceitful, unkind, cowardly, debased, and unjust. Study after study underlies the way that we imagine those we see as different from ourselves as being lesser, and at worst even subhuman. None of this is based on facts as such, but simply the way that we as humans imagine the world around us as a place of binaries. There may well be useful evolutionary traits behind this, where we bond with our families, tribes, and hunting or war groups, and are suspicious of those who come from elsewhere – some may be trustworthy, others may not, and it is safest to err by assuming the worst. It is not, however, a good way to actually understand what other people are like. Nor, in more complex societies, is it necessarily a helpful way to make assumptions about and inform interactions with those who may be different from us.

Psychologists use the term 'stereotype activation' for when stereotypes become accessible to us cognitively.[38] This goes back to the fact that we all have the social knowledge of these, but for those who are more prejudiced it is more likely that these will be invoked or even automatically triggered. However, the processes by which stereotypes get triggered, as it seems they need to be recalled from our long-term memory, may vary. Certainly, creative thinking or other memory-active processes may prevent them from rising to the surface and can even mean they become disrupted. Our identification with particular social groups at any specific time can also have an effect on this, in terms of which identities or stereotypes are salient to us, as our social identities and in-group and out-group identification are fluid.[39]

Othering and deindividuation in majority–minority contexts

A term used to speak about the process by which some become stereotyped or made strange, different, or not normal, in a way that creates distance and opprobrium, is 'othering'. This is not distinct from the formation of in-group/out-group dynamics, but thinking separately about this can help reflect on it. A key figure in thinking through some of these dynamics is Stuart Hall (1932–2014), who focuses on the notion of representing 'difference' while he stresses that identity creation is always a 'process':

> Identity emerges as a kind of unsettled space, or an unresolved question in that space, between a number of intersecting discourses. … Identity is not a fixed point but an ambivalent point. Identity is also the relationship of the Other to oneself.[40]

A key point of stereotyping the out-group is the way that its 'difference' to the in-group is represented (which may be pictorial and not just verbal). But representing the difference, we learn from Hall, is itself about creating a relationship; the difference is significant for the prejudice. Moreover, in situations of majority–minority dynamic (though in other situations too), this representation creates a norm. Of course, some in-group identities are very specifically sub-cultures within a society, or may even be antithetical to the social norms of society, but when we come to questions of discrimination the majority norm often matters because it is typically the majority (occasionally a minority may be invested with power) that determines the standards and pattern of a society. To be othered in such a context is not simply to be part of one group and not another, it is to be outside the mainstream. It is to have an identity that may be considered exotic, strange, or even dangerous (and hence may be securitized[41]). Notably, it may be a sub-group that most intensifies such othering and stereotyping, for instance, in far-right violence against Muslims or Jews, including in vigilante action, but the stereotypes they invoke are typically those of the wider majority culture.[42]

Deindividuation is a term that describes Allport's notion that an individual is deprived of their identity as an individual and treated generically as part of an out-group. It is often linked to being dehumanized, or what may be termed objectification whereby somebody is treated only as an object, or a means, rather than a person in their own right.[43] It is also key to discrimination because it is by being no longer an individual but part of a group about whom prejudicial attitudes exist that an individual finds themselves othered.[44] We can also link it to stigma and the internalization of negative stereotypes by the othered individual. Allport assumed that, over time, stereotypes would be internalized and acted out; however, current studies suggest something more contextual where we find situational predicament, in which there may be times that performing to stereotypes may be a salient behaviour, a trade-off against one's own identity, and other times where it may not be.[45]

Such deindividuation, or objectification, of outsiders is not simply something which we do to castigate another as a prejudiced group but exists along a spectrum from what may be termed 'mild' to 'extreme' levels. At the mild level, we simply fail to relate to the individuality of another in an encounter, or maybe we have a casual indifference to what another tells us, but deindividuation extends to an utter and complete dehumanization of another at the extreme level. Given the busyness of life and the sheer volume of incoming information, it is almost impossible that we do not all, at some point, engage in mild objectification of other people, or even whole groups. We cannot attend the same way to every account of suffering we hear on the news; after a long, hard day of work we find it difficult to hear our partner's, friend's, or children's complaints about their day; rushing in and out of a shop, we treat the cashier simply as a means to an end rather than as a human being with their own needs, frustrations, and expectations.[46] Indeed, it is worth bearing in mind that such objectification happens to many social groups: women, the poor, bankers, the 1 per cent, lawyers, the unemployed, Romanies, Blacks, Chinese, immigrants, and so on.

We may also note that some forms of deindividuation, or stereotyping, are fairly common motifs found globally and across time. One of these is the assumption that our in-group is 'civilized' while the out-group is 'uncivilized'. This may not be the specific term used, but *we* are moral, trustworthy, and noble, while *they* are immoral, untrustworthy, and undignified will be typical motifs. Again, cleanliness and dirt are motifs that are commonly used. Those who are envisaged as filthy may be seen as polluting or sullying to the purity that one imagines for oneself and one's own group (or country). This may be related to Mary Douglas's notion of dirt as 'matter out of place', whereby danger lurks in the out-group when they are 'dirt' (a totally dehumanized classification) existing where you believe purity and cleanliness should be.[47]

An important aspect of objectification of another is discrimination and the perception of discrimination. While discrimination is prejudice enacted, this may occur in more or less overt ways and may be more or less recognized as such, both by the one doing and the one on the receiving end. For instance, second-generation immigrants in the UK report a higher perception of discrimination than their parents, which may be because while their parents compare their situation to that of the place from which they came, their children have an expectation of equal treatment.[48] Certainly, today, when prejudice exists but discrimination might be illegal, it can manifest in what Kristin Anderson has termed 'benign bigotry' where people with racial, religious, or other biases may not be willing to openly vent their views and it may be 'covert and unconscious'.[49] This relates to the lower end of Allport's scale of prejudice noted earlier. Moreover, depending on the context, discrimination may be blatant, subtle, or covert and can occur between individuals, in organizations, or may be systemic.[50] We return to some of these questions in future chapters, but may note that certain forms of enacted prejudice or discrimination which are illegal today have often been legal, even accepted social norms. What is accepted within a society changes over time, and the line between what is socially accepted or not, and what is legal or illegal, is a thin and porous one. Today, we live in an age where it seems certain forms of prejudice may more readily be voiced than even a decade ago.

Scapegoating

A concept that Allport develops to explain the way that a minority may become the target of pent-up frustrations by some in-groups is the scapegoat:

> The term *scapegoat* originated in the famous ritual of the Hebrews, described in the Book of Leviticus (16:20–22). On the Day of Atonement a live goat was chosen by lot. The high priest, robed in linen garments, laid both his hands on the goat's head, and confessed over it the iniquities of the children of Israel. The sins of the people thus symbolically transferred to the beast, it was taken out into the wilderness and let go. The people felt purged, and for the time being, guiltless.[51]

Allport notes that the theory of prejudice alone will not account for who becomes the scapegoat, and that there is no 'all-duty scapegoat'.[52] He argues that they may be ad hoc, although some longer term scapegoats exist, which may be based on religion, race, or ethnicity as these seem to provide the basis for a more stable identity. Though, in reviewing the long history of the Jewish people as a scapegoat, he notes that both history and psychology (we may add sociology and perhaps other disciplines) are needed to determine why, in particular times and places, they have become the scapegoat.[53]

We may also look at the work of René Girard (1923–2015) on scapegoating. For Girard, the concept of the scapegoat is related to his theory of mimetic desire, which concerns not only imitation but also competition.[54] Girard sees mimesis as not simple imitation but a copying of the 'negative' or 'darker' traits and behaviour of others, rather than their 'positive' behaviour; we do not simply imitate what may be seen as laudable. He sees it as instinctive and not something we necessarily think about. Mimetic desire also relates to competition (desire for the same things, perhaps competition over resources or power) where an escalating conflict emerges between the parties. This cycle of competition may even result in violence. However, for Girard, an innocent sacrificial victim on whom the growing inherent violence of mimetic desire is played out may be substituted. This is the scapegoat. The potential communal violence is enacted, though on a lesser scale (but perhaps remarkably destructive for those it affects) on a third group. This common act becomes something which allows the other groups to reaffirm their shared social bond; though this is never rationalized, the killing of an innocent life assuages their own conflict. Stemming from Allport's work, this was classically seen as 'frustration-aggression-displacement theory' where frustration leads to aggression which is then levelled against some other group. However, studies have found no evidence for it. But 'ideological theory', which starts with notions of a perception of relative deprivation, explains the dynamic well. According to this, the chosen scapegoat will typically have little power, be physically recognizable, and usually already stereotyped negatively in some ways such that it can be believed that they are responsible for the group's perceived deprivation.[55] Importantly, here, we can raise another point which is the way in which those with political force, or those seeking political or social prominence, may manufacture an enemy, in a process that has been termed 'manufactured consent', where constructing a (real or imagined) common enemy forms part of the process of creating a strong in-group identity. It can help instil obedience to the leadership (often of an organization, *pace* Brubaker), and its ideological premises, to resist the external force or enemy. This common enemy could be Communists, immigrants, terrorists, colonialists, capitalists, or others.[56]

Overcoming prejudice?: Intergroup contact thesis and respect for the other

Often attributed to Allport, Intergroup Contact Thesis suggests that, under the right circumstances, one of the best ways to reduce prejudice is simply to bring people into interpersonal encounters: getting to know the other.[57] This has to be appropriately done, with enough time to overcome any tensions. Further, various criteria need to be met for this to take place, which include: the equality of status in the encounter of those engaged, so they have similar knowledge levels, background experiences, and so on; there should be some shared purpose between them, perhaps a task or some reason to pool resources; there must be intergroup cooperation, so both groups need to work together without competing; and there must be some backing for what they are doing coming from their traditions and customs or authorities which are respected and can support the venture.[58] While there is some evidence of its success, its benefits often seem to be only moderate in nature.[59] We will turn to more discussion on what may be termed 'positive' news in the face of the naturalness of prejudice in the Epilogue. However, we may briefly note here the thought of the philosopher Emmanuel Levinas (1906–1995). A Lithuanian Jew who lived through the Holocaust, which took an estimated 95 per cent of his Jewish compatriots, Levinas believed that we must stand before the 'Face of the Other'. By this he meant to see them as an Other (note the capitalized 'O'), as a human being whose face and eyes speak to us. Levinas held that, seen in this way, the bottom line would be that they say to us: 'Do not kill me.' This is, Levinas believed, the desire, the plea, of all humans to other humans. To stand against prejudice is therefore not to simply be among others, who may be othered, but to see every other human being as an Other. To stand in relation to them as owing a duty to their life, integrity, and dignity.[60] It certainly offers a way of seeing our fellow humans that is opposed to prejudice.

CHAPTER TWO

The hatred unto death: When prejudice becomes killing and genocide

Introduction

We all know that prejudice does not necessarily, even normally, lead to the killing of another human being. Whether it be the attitude we (our societies) have towards Romanies (Gypsies), Hispanics, South Asians (Bangladeshis, Pakistanis, and Indians – often lumped together in popular British pejorative slang as 'Pakis'[1]), or any other group (Japanese, Irish, Catholics, etc., etc., etc.) they can be socially excluded, mocked, or hated without any direct desire to kill them. Yet physical violence often follows. Whether it be people being picked on in the school playground, stones thrown through the windows of a residence or place of worship, people being jostled or harangued on the street, violence is the daily experience of many minorities. While it is generally hard for us to envision killing another human being, even one we detest or despise, we know that the move to this is actually readily taken. As the so-called third species of chimpanzees, humans retain many of the traits of our primate cousins and the desire, even thirst, to kill is often not far below the surface. It has been remarked that civilization is only two meals away from anarchy, and, when threatened, physical violence is a normal human response. We will explore below some of the mechanisms and factors that are at play as prejudice and discrimination lead into enacted violence and even intentional killing. However, we will also go a step further and discuss, given its relationship to religious hatred, genocide. Genocide is not simply self-defence – which may include the killing of another single, or even a number of, human being(s) – the term speaks about the intentional and wilful desire to eliminate an entire group of people. It is seemingly the destruction of life at a whole other level. Given our interest in religious hatred, that the term 'genocide' is a result of an effort to eradicate Jews also leads us to consider what takes people beyond the far more mundane, even everyday, act of murder to develop a genocidal intent.

In this chapter, we will proceed by several steps. First, we will discuss what we mean by violence, because in contemporary scholarship besides simply physical violence, forms of social and cultural violence are included. Second, we will look at definitions of genocide and also attempt to untheorize it, which is to say to take away mystification about it as a special or analytically distinct sphere and show how it fits within 'normal' human patterns of murder. Finally, we will survey the history of the concept of genocide and instances of what may be termed genocide to help elucidate our discussion.

Understanding violence and mechanisms of violence

Violence is commonly associated with physical brutality. However, the scholarship of violence understands it more broadly with social, psychological, and verbal assaults all captured by this nomenclature.[2] While it is acts of physical killing that concern us here, we will consider violence within this broader remit. This is because, at least as resulting from prejudice, physical brutality and killing do not occur in a vacuum but are based upon words and ways of life that alienate and distance us from those against whom physical violence will be meted out. Therefore, to understand the framing and process that leads to killing, we must see it as part of a wider pathway of brutalization in social, cultural, and linguistic terms. Indeed, Gyanendra Pandey argues, 'The routine ordinary practice of violence' from beatings and rape to 'general humiliation on the streets, in public buses, in films, and so on' can allow 'considerable tolerance (not to say celebration) of such violence'.[3] This broader conceptualization of violence stems from the work of Johan Galtung in the 1960s.

Galtung first describes personal (or, direct) violence. This is direct somatic harm to another, which for Galtung deprives the victim of some form of self-actualization, a key aspect of his theory of violence.[4] Next comes structural (or, indirect) violence, the way that society is structured so that not everyone has equal access to resources, political influence, education, and so on. This, Galtung says, may be worse than direct violence – it is not simply a step to physical violence – as people may lead miserable lives and die early from oppression. Slavery is, perhaps, the extreme expression of this,[5] but socio-economic differences within neighbourhoods can lead to radically different life chances and life expectancy.[6] Finally, there is cultural violence, things which legitimize direct and/or structural violence, that is, justifying worldviews, attitudes, and ideologies. In whatever form, violence is something that negates or hinders self-actualization of the person who suffers it, their fullness as a human being cannot be realized.[7] Furthermore, physical violence is often employed for its cultural impact: 'Violence also includes assaults on the personhood, dignity, sense of worth or value of the victim. The social and cultural dimensions of violence are what give violence its meaning and power.'[8] As noted, while understanding violence broadly, this chapter focuses on physical brutality, though, as we will see, there is always a structural or cultural context for murder and genocide.

Social exclusion and the creation of in-group and out-group dynamics comes naturally to humans, which leads us to ask: is physical violence inherent to us as a species? In response, scholars have advanced radically differing conclusions. Some look at our evolutionary heritage through chimpanzees and gorillas and, based on how commonplace violence is in their societies, suggest that we are biologically driven to physical violence.[9] However, as the third species of chimpanzees, we share as much in common with bonobos as we do with chimpanzees, and bonobos are generally more peaceful and employ sex as a conflict resolution technique.[10] While we have the potential for violence within us, we also have 'mirror neurons' which allow us to be aware of pain in others (these are found in humans and, seemingly, other animal species) which leads to empathy,[11] something which seemingly manifests strongly in bonobos.[12] Moreover, Siniša Malešević provides a very convincing overview of evidence to show that before around 12,000 BCE there was remarkably little evidence of human brutality, and after this violence often seems linked to particular social structures. Indeed, many forager communities have systems of society that seek ways to avoid unnecessary physical violence.[13] What this means is that, for most of human history, our species has quite possibly tended to live in ways that culturally seek peace rather than physical violence and to avoid killing if possible. Indeed, evidence of ancient battles suggests – despite the rhetoric of glorifying manuscripts – remarkably few deaths, while many instances of recorded tribal group aggression may be responses to Western colonial incursions that destroyed previous ways of life.[14] Therefore, as a species, we may not be overtly prone to violence. But neither are we primarily peaceful.

Structures for warfare have advanced as a process of human organization.[15] Indeed, *contra* Stephen Pinker's assertions of a dramatic decline in human violence, with some scholars contesting Pinker's 'preposterous'[16] estimates of ancient deaths, the period from about the seventeenth century till the twentieth century has been the most violent and brutal in human history, with techniques and ideologies for mass killing reaching unprecedented proportions.[17] Only in the second half of the twentieth century till the early twenty-first century have mass killings declined, but rather than being due to any supposed civilizational feats, or Enlightenment values, the presence of mutually assured destruction (MAD) via nuclear capability has arguably often prevented tensions from escalating into outright warfare.[18]

Moreover, suicide, disease from pollution, and incarceration have become more predominant features of modern societies in these decades, while the intersectional nature of what counts as a crime and who is imprisoned are causes for concern.[19] Building from the work of Michel Foucault (1926–1984), it can be noted that with increasing forms of social surveillance and control, the actual state implementation of physical coercion by violence (the guarantee of control) can be replaced by self-policing. For instance, declines in certain forms of criminal activity are often related to increased CCTV coverage, and also no-tolerance-policing, rather than a civilizing impetus in society.[20] However, whether humans are more or less prone to violence, or whether modern or pre-modern societies are more violent, is somewhat immaterial to our arguments. What is important is that, given the right circumstances, motivations, and social contexts, humans can easily be led into acts of violence and genocide. In other terms, violence may become 'normalized' within particular social and cultural contexts, which is what Pandey termed 'routine violence'.[21] This may be in contexts of war or simply in situations where the state, or other actors, can socialize us into seeing physical violence as 'routine', 'normalized', or acceptable. This can also heighten levels of brutality to be enacted against outsiders (or 'traitors'). For instance, among those 'radicalized', into militant neo-Islamic jihadism in groups such as ISIS, a petty criminal background – where violence was already accepted behaviour – made framing extreme violence as normal less difficult, especially in a warzone context.[22] Importantly, while every act of violence is contextually different, we see common patterns and deep structural aspects.[23]

Stathis Kalyvas distinguishes between the outcome and process of violence.[24] A key point is that only studying manifestations (the outcome) of physical violence is limited, giving rise to perceptions that violence is random, irrational, or based in primitive impulses, whereas it is often the result of a process that is rational, planned, and instrumental, that is, to instil fear.[25] Moreover, Kalyvas points out that a focus on the process may also break down what he terms 'a dichotomous worldview populated only by victims and perpetrators', which in the context he explores, civil wars, often distorts study of the deep dynamics.[26] It may, though, be politically expedient to speak of 'victims' and 'perpetrators' in terms of Gayatri Chakravorty Spivak's 'strategic essentialism', where a generalized term may be a powerful motif even if analytically inadequate.[27]

The process of violence involves the way that dehumanization occurs as part of the apparatus by which humans may overcome their tendency not to harm others, what Albert Bandura terms 'moral disengagement'.[28] Excepting perhaps a few cases, Bandura tells us that 'people do not usually engage in harmful conduct until they have justified, to themselves, the morality of their actions'.[29] Moreover, he argues that these processes are part of socialization into society (certainly modern Western ones). This form of socialization, he argues, is common in, for instance, the ways boys develop, the way some men mistreat women, and is what lies behind the tobacco industry.

Key factors for Bandura are: *moral justification* where we frame our actions in terms of what is good or just, that is, as self-defence or 'holy war'; *euphemistic labelling* whereby we avoid saying what we have done, so the killing of civilians becomes, for example, 'collateral damage'; *advantageous comparison* by saying the harm was better than alternatives; *displacement of responsibility* by, for instance, claiming to be only carrying out orders; *diffusion of responsibility* where multiple people participate in parts of an operation so nobody takes the full burden on themselves, that is, where the roles of bomb maker and bomb-planter are separated; *disregard or distortion of consequences* where perpetrators do not think about what happened, or tell only one version of events; *attribution of blame* by saying that the victims were the aggressors or 'brought it on themselves'; *dehumanization* in which the victims are seen as less than human or are 'savages' or 'demonic'.[30] Yet, while people are socialized to behave in these ways, Bandura notes that we also have a 'power of humanization' which often keeps tendencies to violence in check. This can manifest in a sense of empathy with another group or person or a more ideological commitment that opposes violence.[31] Nevertheless, it is clear that moral disengagement is not a facet of some pathology or abnormal psychology but is common in human beings, and various studies of those who have committed political violence have not shown pathological traits.[32] Indeed, groups such as Al-Qaeda have sought to weed out those with psychotic traits because such individuals were a hindrance to the kind of long-term plans and operations it enacted.[33] Rather, we see something akin to Hannah Arendt's 'banality of evil' in that the perpetrators of atrocities are not the inhuman monsters of our imagination but rather ordinary human beings no different from the rest of us.[34] As Philip Zimbardo argues of the Stanford prison experiment (where students were given the role of prisoners and guards, and which needed to be cancelled midway because the guards, ordinary students days before, were becoming increasingly cruel), the descent into dark forms of human behaviour can come with great rapidity in certain social situations.[35] Likewise, if people see themselves as 'following orders' from a legitimate authority, those orders may override their normal sense of morality.[36] This is not to say that we do not see psychopathic traits in some instances, and studies of military personnel who committed atrocities (e.g. Abu Ghraib) show some were more prone to 'dark' tendencies (e.g. Machiavellianism, narcissism, psychopathy, the dominance facet of social dominance orientation, and right-wing authoritarianism).[37]

Two final aspects of violence should be noted. First, violence is often sexualized. While male on male violence is common, male violence against women, including rape as an act of war, domination, or submission, is unfortunately also common. Many organizations or traditions which support strong prejudices often extol particular versions of masculinity and femininity in which the male is valorized as the defender of the (innocent, defenceless) female, often posited against a hypersexualized or predatory stereotype of the out-group.[38] Second, is it easier to kill those close to us or strangers? Much discussion on warfare suggests that the depersonalized and unknown enemy can be attacked with fewer inhibitions, but criminology shows that many violent crimes (murder or rape, for instance) are most frequently committed against those we know.[39] We see acts of violence and genocide in both cases: former neighbours, even relatives, may be murdered as much as strangers.

Defining and untheorizing genocide

From 1946, genocide was recognized as a crime under international law by the United Nations General Assembly (A/RES/96-I). This was given weight by the 1948 Convention on the Prevention and Punishment of the Crime of Genocide (CPPCG) which stated that genocide could happen in war or peace (Article 1) and defined it as

> any of the following acts committed with intent to destroy in whole or in part, a national, ethnical, racial, or religious group, as such:
>
> a. Killing members of the group;
>
> b. Causing serious bodily or mental harm to members of the group;
>
> c. Deliberately inflicting on the group conditions of life calculated to bring about its physical destruction in whole or in part;
>
> d. Imposing measures intended to prevent births within the group;
>
> e. Forcibly transferring children of the group to another group.[40]

Scholars have also noted social classes as groups against whom genocide may occur. Genocide, in its strict legal–political definition, exists alongside other delineated crimes which include ethnic cleansing, crimes against humanity,[41] and war crimes. While these distinctions practically define specific crimes which may be tried, they arguably hinder understanding of the wider dynamics. These various 'crimes' are not always analytically distinct and a sociological analysis, while not neglecting distinctions, will see commonality in the contributing factors.[42] Indeed, various definitions of genocide, war crimes, and so on exist. Moreover, precise definitions, or theorizations, of what *exactly* 'genocide' is typically fixate upon a specific context, often for political or apologetic purposes (i.e. to accuse others of genocide, to claim a particular status, or to deny that one's own group committed it).

Just as we untheorized antisemitism and Islamophobia by suggesting that they are simply patterns of prejudice within human social contexts (see Introduction), so too we must untheorize genocide. This is not to suggest we abandon the word; there have certainly been attempts to consciously annihilate entire identified groups (to use a rough, ready, and dirty definition), but we should not imbue it with too much weight. Rather, we will see that genocide is simply a contextualized form of human killing which, in certain ways at least, is not specifically different from many other forms of murder in terms of its basic impetus and drive. Genocide is not a distinctive and unique phenomenon, rather it is within the remit of wider mass killings,[43] though we will note how genocide may be definitionally distinguished below.

Let us distinguish here, for heuristic purposes, between three forms of killing: hunting, self-defence, and murder.[44] All three, let us posit, typically work on one principle: self-/group survival (widely construed). Let us define each one. Hunting: predatory carnivores hunt for food, and the killing is simply done for basic sustenance in accordance with Abraham Maslow's (1908–1970) hierarchy of needs.[45] Self-defence: just as the hunter hunts, so the prey seeks to elude the hunter, which may be by speed but also by force such as when a giraffe kicks a lion. It is direct force against an immediate threat. Murder: here, the intentional killing of another creature outside the realm of direct hunting and self-defence. It is done because some other, a rival, is seen to pose a threat, either existential (to 'my/our' culture or way of life) or physical (to 'my/our' life or body), to our group interests, our gene pool, ourselves, and so on. This, seemingly, occurs among primates more widely, with recorded cases of murder among chimpanzees.[46] It includes what we do not normally call murder, that is, as a legal term (hereafter, I use 'homicide' to mean legally defined 'murder'). For instance, warfare and execution are (legalized) murder, carried out because of some perceived threat from those it is deemed correct to kill. (We do not, here, use murder to denote who holds legitimate rights to life and death, which is a separate debate.[47]) Like chimpanzees, humans may conduct such murderous killing over resources (land, mates, etc.) or for reasons of existential angst (cultural continuity, purity, etc.). All, however, boils down to survival. An exception is the potential for ('psychopathic') killing for pleasure. However, I suggest this falls outside the 'normal' realms of human social behaviour (it may, though, be 'natural' in that aggression is needed for primate survival, and extreme cases of aggression might have been evolutionarily beneficial, while some psychopathic traits may be socially useful[48]). Murder, as defined here, is limited to intelligent species: it requires planning and foresight, as well as what (in legal terms) would be termed mens rea, the volitional intention to kill. Legally, this may distinguish 'homicide' (as used here) from manslaughter (accidental or reckless killing), but here it distinguishes murder from hunting and self-defence.

Murder is a continuum from the killing of a single person, perhaps a mating rival or unknown outsider perceived as a threat, to genocide, though the latter is definitionally distinct, requiring a set of social, cultural, and ideological factors to justify (however inadequately) the annihilation of entire groups. In as far as it is not possible to distinguish, with analytic clarity, genocide from other forms of political mass murder or ethnic cleansing, or, for that matter, mass murder from terrorism or state violence, we see a continuum. But this is not to say they are undifferentiated. In the terms of this book: murder operates here as an analytical category, but we can clarify definitional categories within this meta-category. We can, for many reasons, meaningfully define different types of murder. From single murders, to group murders, to mass murders, to genocide, there are meaningful distinctions. But the differences, analytically, are only ones of degree, for the killing is performed with merely more complex reasoning and social formations distinguishing them. We may also typically distinguish between legally acceptable and unacceptable murders, on the one hand warfare, typically taken as the legitimate actions of a state, and on the other homicide, as being a crime by a person or group. Some murder is socially (politico-legally) justified in some situations, other murder is not socially (politico-legally) justified. What may fall into the socially justified camp will vary contextually. Here, we will not enter into any moral justification for making such distinctions. Rather, our focus is simply upon mechanisms and categorization. Here, murder categorizes a type of killing by certain animals, such as chimpanzees and humans. Indeed, warfare is, arguably, seen in such diverse species as whales, ants, chimpanzees, and humans. But we may suspect that genocide is a peculiarly human preoccupation, it requires certain reasonings and social formations. As such we may assert that (in our current situation) genocide is something done by intelligent apes. To this we may add, for fullness, intelligent and social apes capable of symbolic thinking, but to some extent this is only an extension of intelligent apes.[49] There is no reason why, if social systems prevailed, that chimpanzees or other primates, even other intelligent species, may not commit genocide. However, it remains at present, as far as we are aware, the preserve of the most intelligent ape.

Our argument may seem shocking. Is not genocide an almost unimaginable horror? The outcome of totalitarian thinking or deriving from specific moral or social evils? Even a distorted by-product of modernity and the nation state? But we must demystify 'genocide'. As we will see below, there is no specific totalitarian ideology, distinct modern worldview, or anything else that links, historically or conceptually, all acts we may classify as genocide. It certainly involves some belief in the superiority, or rights, vis-à-vis the victim, of one's own group, but there can be a variety of rationales. If we untheorize genocide, then it is necessary to place it firmly within the context of murder as a type of violence committed by intelligent and social apes. Perhaps, a necessary caveat is that intelligence or sociality does not lead to murder or genocide: both these acts humans can rationalize as wrong, while sociality requires cooperation.[50] As humans, we are prone to commit violence and murder in some contexts, but averse to killing in other social contexts. Nevertheless, given the nature of the beings we are (evolutionarily and biologically), and the social dynamics which shape our societies, it is unavoidable to conclude that we could even call genocide 'normal' (no matter how abnormal it is to most of us most of the time!) in that it arises from the ways we behave, socialize, and interact. None of this makes it the only human response, the best human response, and certainly not a desirable human response. But if we want to stop genocide, we do ourselves no favours to mystify it as an almost unfathomable phenomenon. Recent scholarship shows us that violence, even grievous inter-ethnic slaughter, is neither irrational nor primitive but has its own internal rationality and processes.[51] Violence, murder, and genocide do not come from extreme ideological notions or figures, it is too normal for that. For instance, Zygmunt Baumann's discussion of genocide as a manufactured facet of modernity and its depersonalization (he compares Auschwitz to a factory) ignores how the organizational systems underlying it were laid thousands of years earlier and disregards the often face-to-face brutality both in the Holocaust and in other episodes of genocide.[52]

Accepting that genocide exists on a continuum with other forms of murder does not mean that it may not be meaningfully distinguished. Warfare and genocide are, for instance, distinct.[53] It is a definitionally meaningful category even if not an analytically meaningful category. As noted, attempts to circumscribe it precisely are problematic, but we may construct a general definition that combines both ideological and structural aspects. To start it is 'the persecution and destruction of human beings [or other species] on the basis of their presumed or imputed membership in a group rather than on their individual properties or participation in certain acts'.[54] Alongside this, from the CPPCG definition, we can add that it is 'committed with intent to destroy in whole or in part' that group. Furthermore, genocidal desire requires a particular fixation upon an entire out-group that is so extremely othered that it is determined to be incapable of ever having in-group belonging. They may be stereotyped as inherently hostile, filthy, lascivious, subhuman, or demonic. Importantly, while about narratives, iconography often vivifies stereotypes with art, poetry, literature, and music all potentially involved.[55] Moreover, the group is ideologically framed as a threat to survival, hence the framing may be: kill or be killed. It may be perceived as an eternal/omnipresent threat and to be so utterly existentially dangerous that their existence requires their annihilation; they cannot simply be persecuted, segregated, humiliated, or ostracized. It may be that attempts at eradicating them by pushing them beyond the borders of one's own group/territory have failed and so annihilation becomes a necessary resort. Normally, this occurs in periods of turmoil, social upheaval, warfare, or crisis, and though the CPPCG notes genocide may occur even in peacetime, seemingly genocide generally requires fraught social moments.[56] This may involve a battle for survival over scarce resources.[57] These genocidal impulses will partake in cultural and symbolic violence within a process leading up to an act of genocide. It will require the building of a narrative of justification in which othering, deindividuation, and stereotyping build the sense of existential threat, which very often is far more imagined than real; often, the victims may be a tiny minority but one imbued with vast symbolic significance. However, as Max Bergholz has shown, these narratives need not be widely accepted for violence to begin, and he speaks of violence as a 'generative force' which compels actors to take on (in his case) ethnic identities and polarized worldviews lest they too become victims, with violence inscribing the need for such identities.[58]

Importantly, many perpetrators are not psychotic but otherwise ordinary human beings.[59] As such, in preparing the ground for genocide, it is generally necessary that a rationale for the destruction of the target group is present: the history of the other may be erased in books, artefacts, and memories; their cultural productions belittled, derided, or dismissed; their presence made invisible or problematized in various ways. Though, as noted above, violence may be the generative force in certain contexts, the erasure of the other overlaps with justifications for slavery, colonialism, and warfare.[60] Indeed, colonialism can be a ripe seedbed for genocide.[61] The rationale may be built as a conscious effort or may, in some circumstances, arise from the ground, but in many cases it seems that the genocidal impulse and activities arise mostly from the connivance of certain elites and organizations, including those seeking power, to find a common enemy.[62] Though those engaged in killing may not always be acting on these ideological presuppositions, opportunities for economic gain or revenge may motivate a number of those recruited for, or simply carrying out, the killings.[63] The narratives created must, in some way, normalize violence, that is to say, make it appear that the infliction of physical harm and acts of murder are not only justified but have become part of the way of society and are a necessary, even beneficial, thing.[64] Genocide always follows words.

We have, above, outlined a set of factors that provide a multifaceted definition based around the various ways in which genocide may arise and be justified. Against essentialist definitions, it does not neatly encapsulate a single rationale or feature, but untheorizes it as a complex social phenomenon.

A conceptual history of genocide

The term 'genocide' arose directly from the Holocaust, and that stands as a paradigmatic instance. The term 'genocide' and its legal instantiation are directed to ensuring that no comparable events may take place. The term was first used by a Polish lawyer, Raphäel Lemkin (1900–1959), in *Axis Rule in Occupied Europe* (1944), while he almost single-handedly campaigned for its recognition by the UN as an international crime. He had previously implored the UN's predecessor, the League of Nations, to recognize crimes of 'barbarity' and 'vandalism', respectively cultural and intellectual destruction, to castigate Nazi action against Jews.[65] Despite the passing of the CPPCG, many subsequent instances of genocide have occurred, while others have argued that there were also numerous examples of genocide before the Holocaust. These examples are extensive and explored in detail elsewhere,[66] rather, our exploration here of particular instances will examine the ways typical theories of genocide fail. These theories will be placed into a few specific types, rather than looking at the arguments of individuals per se. I will classify these as follows: first, theories that the Holocaust showed something unique within Nazi ideology; second, related to the first, seeing genocide as emerging from totalitarian ideologies; third, attributing genocide to the dynamics of the ethnocentric nation state; fourth, relating genocide to the spirit of modernity, often tied to capitalist consumption or colonialism; and fifth, seeing it as only a recent phenomenon. This list may not be comprehensive but encapsulates many of the most significant theories. Notably, we do not wish to dismiss the value of these theories, for they highlight key dynamics in genocidal impulses and specific outbreaks of genocide. However, we cannot attribute all genocide to a single specific theoretical explanation. I will move thematically through this section, not directly following the outline of the five types above.

Starting with the Nazis, because where else does one begin a survey of genocide, some have argued that what happened to the Jews was symptomatic of a very specific ideological and structural discourse unique to its context. Certainly, previous antisemitism, around two thousand years' worth with a distinct precursor in Martin Luther, does not explain the Holocaust. Prejudice does not automatically lead to physical violence, let alone killing (though Christian animus towards Jews had often led to murder), and certainly not the need or desire to annihilate an entire group. It seems plausible to posit that Hitler first wished simply to expel all Jews from the realm of the Teutonic people. Only later did the Final Solution with the gas chambers become the modus operandi, with the resultant deaths of around 6 million Jews, over 70 per cent of all Jews under Nazi occupation in this period, which at the end of the war was an unfinished programme of annihilation. We discuss the reasons for the Holocaust elsewhere (see Interlude 2), so do not expand on it here. However, while philosophers such as Hannah Arendt (1906–1975) have argued that antisemitism, as exemplified by the Nazis, was far more than simply a hatred of Jews, being a more brutal call for genocide, her equation of genocide only with Nazi ideology seems problematic.[67] The enthusiastic murder of Jews, and a willing engagement in the Nazi extermination programme, was seen in the mass slaughters undertaken by, for instance, Poles in Nazi-occupied areas and in Romanian support, almost without the need for Nazi promotion, to organize and assist in the mass deportation of Jews to the extermination camps.

If we discuss ideology, while religion is often ignored as a motive – with assumptions that genocide is always ethnic, economic, or political – or just seen as a cover for these other motives, it may be important. For instance, it has been compellingly argued that the ideological narrative of the genocide against Bosniak Muslims in places such as Srebrenica and the bombardment of Sarajevo, during the Balkan wars of the 1990s, were deeply seated in a Serbian Orthodox identity that looked back to the medieval period for its basis.[68] Moving chronologically further back to, perhaps, the first advocacy for genocide we come to the Hebrew Bible. In taking occupation of the 'promised land', there are directives for the Israelites to kill every man, woman, and child of the resident groups.[69] It is doubtful if this is evidence of an actual genocide. The texts comprising this portion of the Hebrew Bible were heavily edited in the exilic and post-exilic period around the fifth and sixth centuries BCE, with a particular focus on reinforcing both certain priestly temple traditions and the Israelite tradition of monotheism (which was not the only Israelite devotional tradition, as the repeated injunctions against polytheism and the worshipping of deities besides Yahweh show). Therefore, we are not reading primary historical texts about the period in question (which was perhaps around five hundred years earlier, if the Israelites did indeed come from elsewhere). Moreover, the archaeological evidence is not consistent with a genocide having occurred. It would have involved the brutal suppression of groups that had a superior civilizational complexity compared to the nomadic Israelite tribes. Nevertheless, the desire for the utter annihilation of an entire group of people was clearly expressed, to eradicate them from the territory that another group wishes to possess and claim as its own. When these texts were edited, a concern about ritual purity may have played a part, alongside a damning dehumanization. As such, arguments that genocidal ideology is wholly modern need to deal with the presence of such texts and historical accounts. It may be noted that, for militant religious Zionists today, these texts act as something of a blueprint in their desire to drive the Palestinians from their homelands, because the Palestinians are declared to be the equivalent of the Amalekites who have no place in a land gifted by God to the Jewish people and so are perceived as the eternal enemies of Jews and Israel.[70] To some extent, therefore, it radicalizes the secular Zionist narrative in which the Palestinians were to be simply forcibly removed to make way for the Israeli nation as envisioned by Theodore Hershel (1860–1904) in his papers and enacted in the *Nakba* (see Chapter 8).

For some theorists, genocide is inherent in modernity, sometimes specifically the ideology of the modern nation state. This has been argued by such scholars as Baumann and Mark Levene, and relates to the nation state being tied to the identity of a particular ethnolinguistic group. Mono-ethnicity was not the only ideological option for the creation of the nation state. In the French Republic after the Revolution a new conception of citizenship arose in which all people in France, regardless of ethnicity, were linked by their participation within, and commitment to, the ideology of the Republic and its Constitution (but here within a mono-cultural framing). As discussed in Chapter 5, this became problematic in relation to the 'Jewish Question'. But, for many, the nation state was envisaged as a homeland for a singular cultural and linguistic identity posited in relation to a perceived racial/ethnic identity. This was certainly part of the rationale for revolts against the Ottoman Empire, with Greeks, Armenians, Kurds, and Arabs seeking their own homeland. Within Europe, German nationalism was typically posited upon this ethno-national model, while Winston Churchill (1874–1965) mythologized British nationhood and identity around an imagined Anglo-Saxon heritage. In part, therefore, modernity was a move from an age of empires which flourished as religiously and ethnically diverse cosmopolitan entities towards nations composed of religiously and ethnically monolithic blocks. In creating these new national units, those deemed to fall outside the remit of the nation's identity were oftentimes either forcibly evicted or murdered. This was seen when Greeks and Turks were pushed out of each other's territories, and sometimes massacred. Or in the Armenian Genocide of 1916, when around 500,000 Armenians were slaughtered by Turkish troops and civilians, comprising perhaps half the Armenian population of Anatolia.[71] The late nineteenth to the mid-twentieth century is a period drenched in blood through the search for ethno-racial national purity. This ideology has played a role in global violence from the nineteenth through to the twenty-first centuries. In certain ways, the Holocaust fits this pattern.

Another key aspect of modernity's association with genocide is colonialism. The destruction of native life in the Americas was partly accidental, the collapse of empires allowing European rule was often due to exposure to new diseases from Eurasia to which indigenous populations had no immunity. However, deliberate mass murders of native populations occurred. One case was the intentional distribution of blankets infected with smallpox by the US government to indigenous Americans.[72] Moreover, the use of concentration camps and the removal of whole populations was first tried in African colonies, with links between those involved in 'vengeful' genocide[73] in South West Africa and later Nazi troops.[74] The stereotyping and dehumanization of native populations, as savages lacking civilization and religion,[75] was part and parcel of the regimes which allowed them to be killed or enslaved en masse. Nelson Maldonado-Torres, building on the work of Frantz Fanon (1925–1961), sees coloniality as part of a project of modernity involving not only the justification of war but also '*the naturalization of extermination, expropriation, domination, exploitation, early death, and conditions that are worse than death, such as torture and rape*', and so being a project that could lead towards 'genocidal tendencies'.[76] Achille Mbembe also argues for a logic in Western modernity, stemming from coloniality and the logic of rationalization, towards what he terms necropolitics where 'in our contemporary world, weapons are deployed in the interest of maximum destruction of persons'. This has created '*death-worlds*' which he describes as 'new and unique forms of social existence in which vast populations are subjected to conditions of life conferring upon them the status of *living dead*' and which he links back to the situation of slaves in plantations and the progression to the Holocaust and beyond.[77]

Nevertheless, problems arise when we envisage genocide simply as a product of modernity's ideological schemata. First, as noted already, we can see a justification for genocide from around two and a half thousand years beforehand. The desire for purity is, *pace* Mary Douglas (1921–2007), not a dynamic only known to modernity. Second, if genocide is linked, as Baumann argues, to a post-Enlightenment and capitalist rationalism and industrialization, it does not account for the racialization of religious difference developing in early modern Spain which underlies Europe's colonial regimes, modern antisemitism, and the Holocaust (see Chapter 5). Third, as Levene has noted, it is not clear what differentiates earlier mass political killings from genocide.[78] The Jewish pogroms of nineteenth-century Russia were arguably genocidal in nature, certainly they seemed to aim at times for the elimination of entire populations of Jews, but arose with different dynamics (in a pre-modern, peasant society). Fourth, Malešević has noted how civilization and brutality are linked – we see mass violence and warfare arising with organization (of formalized social structures), (urban) settlement, and centralized (governmental) authority. If we see a rise of more formalized forms of killing it is more to do with the mechanics of organized societies and the possibility for mass killings of whole groups, rather than any ideological factors[79] (notwithstanding that primitive weaponry can achieve the same effect, as seen for example in Rwanda where machetes were the weapon of choice for an act of genocidal ethnic cleansing[80]). Organizational power, inherent in any civilization, is also the means for mass killing. While some scholars have contrasted civilization with the brutality of non-civilized peoples, in the ancient world 'the first known civilisations' are distinguishable from those around them in 'their ability to use organised violence and fight wars of conquest', while genocide is also linked to this ability to organize violence.[81] The connection of posited civilizational advance to brutality and control (often indistinguishably interlinked) may be a factor in certain contexts of genocide.[82] Finally, Western colonialism is neither the first nor the only imperial regime, and brutality has typified many attempts to destroy enemies or strike fear into them, with some seeing genocidal episodes in the Roman destruction of Carthage (146 BCE), the Mongol destruction of whole populations (thirteenth century), and the First Crusade against the Cathars (thirteenth century).[83]

Notwithstanding this, the modern nation state has often claimed for itself the sole right to use violence, something which Max Weber saw as being a potential source of conflict between nation states and religion.[84] Coupled with this, its insistence upon its civilizing vision and the ability to enforce its version of purity raise the possibility for systemic state violence. The French Republic's brutal suppression of rural inhabitants of the Vendée, as anti-revolutionary and therefore deserving of being wiped out without mercy, is often seen as symptomatic.[85] However, whether this is distinct from the display of force by any ruling polity throughout history to those who challenge its sole jurisdiction and ideology is questionable. From the Chinese

Qin Emperor's conquest of the surrounding kingdoms, to the Roman suppression of revolt, we see this occurring. Of course, this may be different from how we are speaking of genocide as an attempt to annihilate an entire identified ethnic, religious, racial, or social class (these are modern Western terms, and so we need to see what the relevant terms would be in other contexts). Nevertheless, we have seen the ideological foundation in the Hebrew Bible, and historical potentially genocidal incidents were noted above. The further back we go in history the harder it is to assess the evidence, so the appearance of genocide as modern may relate to the availability of reliable sources. Following Malešević, it may also relate to the organizational capacity to destroy entire populations.

The choice of violence

The above discussion has been more conceptual than descriptive. Given the very quantity of episodes that could be described as genocides – a depressingly large number – any attempt at comprehensive description, even listing, would not be possible. Far more could be said about the Holocaust, the Rape of Nanjing (1937), the Srebrenica Genocide (1995), the Cambodian Genocide (1975–9), the current Rohingya crisis in Myanmar, and many more.

There are specific dynamics to every genocide, but by untheorizing genocide we have seen it not as being tied to any particular context but as arising in the way that intelligent apes create social and ideological narratives tied to dehumanization of an out-group. The inclination to murder is natural to us, in socialized contexts. However, counter-instincts also exist in us as humans. In the same socialized contexts some choose to murder, others to save lives. Human agency is (almost) always a factor.[86]

INTERLUDE 1

What is religious hatred?

Introduction

The argument of this book is that antisemitism and Islamophobia are best understood as types of prejudice. No more, no less. In Chapters 5 and 7 we will see how both, respectively, may often be forms of racism. Does this mean that there is nothing special about religious hatred? For some scholars, religion is nothing but an arbitrarily pared-off aspect of culture. However, despite its wide and varied usage over time, religion does help us delineate aspects of culture that we struggle to speak about otherwise. In the terms of this book, it is a meaningful definitional category even if not an analytic category. Moreover, religious hatred – signifying both hatred stemming from religion and hatred provoked by (a specific) religion(s) – may show particular, even if not unique, characteristics. But, first, we need to ask what we mean by 'religion'.

What is religion?

The borders between those things we term 'religions' and those things we classify in other ways are not watertight but full of grey areas.[1] Some scholars therefore argue we should abandon the term as effectively meaningless, while they also note that modern, Western, and Protestant (Christian) conceptions have dominated how we think about religion.[2] This is related to a set of problematic characterizations often termed the 'world religions paradigm' (WRP). Here, we will argue that religion remains meaningful as a definitional category, following the distinction outlined earlier. We cannot enter the voluminous debates on religion's definition, classification, and genealogy, but five key points pertaining to the way that religion is employed herein and how it is typically represented will help us see how it feeds into forms of prejudice.

First, as used herein, 'religion' categorizes aspects of human cultural activity orientated towards the 'transcendent', that is, spheres of a posited reality beyond the mundane, somatic world. Against the claim that it is simply a modern, Western scholarly imaginary we can note that those traditions we categorize as 'religions' have been classified as related phenomena over millennia and cross-culturally.[3] Indeed, even critics who argue we should reject religion seek synonyms to replace it.[4] Second, nevertheless, we must be aware that we are employing a particular modern English term which does not have direct equivalents either historically or geographically. This means we are often engaged in acts of translation. Yet this is true of almost every term. For instance, ancient Greeks had no term for slavery, but we readily talk about slavery in ancient Athens. But we must decolonize our usage, so it does not privilege the WRP as 'correct'. Third, the WRP separates 'religion' from 'politics' (among other categories). But 'religion' and 'politics' have not traditionally been distinct. From the 'divine right' of European kings, to the *tianming* ('Mandate of Heaven') of Chinese emperors, religion has been political, and the political religious. In many periods and societies, separating them leads to conceptual distortion. Notably, the previous two points are not per se arguments against employing 'religion', as similar issues apply to 'philosophy', 'art', 'politics', 'furniture', and 'literature', that is, these are equally terms which do not have direct translations or equivalents in many languages, while each blurs categories that would be found elsewhere. Fourth, a direct corollary of the last point is to question the categories of 'religion' and 'secular'.[5] While normalized in the modern, Western social imaginary, even supposedly representative secular nation states conflate the two. For instance, the United States has a 'firewall' between church and state, but celebrates itself as 'one nation under God', while presidents hold 'prayer breakfasts' and appear (even obligatorily) alongside priests and pastors to highlight their 'Christian credentials' to the electorate. Note: we are not arguing that religion and politics should be combined nor that the secular–religion distinction needs dismantling (though it may do), we are simply highlighting the social situation. Fifth, if we assume a WRP bias we will fail to understand religion's dynamics. To take four common WRP claims:[6] religion is based in core texts; beliefs and doctrines are central; syncretism is a distortion of religion; and, you can only belong to one religion (at a time). Religion is often taught this way in schools and universities, and it is how politicians, the media, and many religious leaders talk about it. It is, however, almost entirely wrong. Space does not permit this to be explored in depth, but some examples should dispel these as 'norms': at first, Buddhists did not write their teachings down, believing that oral transmission was superior, so early Buddhism was not reliant on texts; Judaism is typically seen as prioritizing orthopraxy (correct practice) over orthodoxy (correct belief), that is, having 'correct' 'theological thoughts' is less important than, for instance, Shabbat observance; mainstream Christianity is syncretic with 'Pagan' Christmas trees and Easter eggs, Zoroastrian resurrection beliefs (this was adopted by Judaism then passed to Christianity and Islam), and Indic rosary beads (originally Buddhist and Hindu, then adapted by Muslims and transmitted to Christians); in the Chinese cultural world people would readily engage Confucian, Buddhist, Daoist, and folk practices without seeing them as incompatible.[7] These issues are important in terms of prejudice towards what is regarded as 'proper' or 'improper' religion, with terms such as 'superstition', 'cult', or 'primitive religion' being used by some to designate religious practices or traditions they do not approve of. What we must note is that what counts as 'religion' changes, as human categories are contingent and flexible.

Religious hatred and the sacred

Mark Juergensmeyer argues religion may lead to a 'cosmic war'.[8] If we fight for 'secular' ends then peace may be settled when enough is done to satisfy our honour, or when whatever material goals we have are achieved as far as needed. But, if God is on our side, we may castigate our opponents as the children of Satan. In a cosmic war, the saints battle the demons, and absolute good opposes absolute evil. In such cases, Juergensmeyer suggests, it may be harder to reach a compromise and easy to justify annihilating our opponents. After all, they are less than human, even demonic. A 'crusade' or 'holy war' may even be its own good. Hatred justified by religion may, therefore, be particularly chilling and unrelenting. However, while Juergensmeyer has a strong case, at least four counter-points need to be considered: religion's ambivalence as capable of promoting both war and peace-making; human interpretation; our models of the 'sacred' which may extend beyond 'religion'; and actual practice.

While many critics point out that militant 'scriptural' texts, sometimes termed 'texts of terror', may justify war, even in the most brutal fashion, there are also texts that advocate nonviolence,[9] peace, tolerance, and love. Scott Appleby talks about the ambivalence of the sacred to describe religion's capacity to be used for both war and peace, while Perry Schmidt-Leukel has spoken of the way that religion has both the characteristics of 'oil' and 'water', that is, when thrown onto the flames of violence and hatred it may cause a greater conflagration, but may also put out those very flames.[10] In other words, the same texts or teachings which justify unrelenting war may also be the source to end that war. This is related to human interpretation. Even if somebody supposes that their scriptural texts are a divine and infallible revelation from a deity, they still need to read and interpret them. Hermeneutics, or textual interpretation, will always play a part. Some critics of religion suggest that certain texts literally and directly justify extreme violence; for instance, in relation to Islam, Frederic Raphael argues that Muslim violence against Jews is inevitable because: 'It's in the text.'[11] However, such a suggestion disregards many pertinent facts: Muslim tradition categorizes Jews as *dhimmis*, or 'protected people', not as people to kill; Islamic hermeneutics does not use a literalist 'it's in the text' approach, but says the Qur'an must be read through the traditions of the Prophet (*sunnah*), and as interpreted by the *ulama* (jurists) who endorsed seeing Jews as *dhimmis*; moreover, there are passages where we can say 'it's in the text' praising Jews and telling Muslims not to dispute with them. Which parts of texts people decide to read, or prioritize, or read in the light of other parts, or in relation to other factors change over time.[12] Today's enemies may be tomorrow's friends (and vice versa). Texts, traditions, and teachings are tricky things tending to transformation.

Next, we may associate the term 'sacred' with religion, but it has a sociological usage as the absolute values of a society or culture.[13] These are the taken-for-granted, non-negotiables, which we hold as absolute truths. From free speech to democracy, human rights to the rule of law, such sacred values are not simply 'religious'. These are values for which people fight and kill, and recent wars between the United States and various militant neo-Islamic jihadis[14] have exemplified a clash of 'sacreds', with each side unwilling to compromise, and justifying the destruction of the other as 'evil' because they have differing 'sacred' values.[15] From nationalism to the defence of human rights, we have absolutes for which we will kill and will not compromise. 'Secular' contestations, as much as religious ones, may lead to Juergensmeyer's 'cosmic wars'. Revisiting our discussion of religion, we may suggest that, in this usage, 'sacred' is an analytical category with 'religion' as a definitional category within its remit, alongside such non-negotiable worldviews as nationalism, Marxism, human rights, or secularism.

Finally, we need to measure the concept of the 'cosmic war' and a total unwillingness to compromise with what actually happens. History may be our guide. A case-in-point is the 'crusades'[16] launched by the 'Christian West' ostensibly to free the 'Holy Land' from Islam and also to defend Christians in the East from the same threat. However, across the centuries, and at various junctures, many 'crusader' leaders, despite the clear 'cosmic war' potential, were ready to negotiate and find common ground with Muslims, while the actual reasons for fighting were often more complex. A pure 'cosmic war' may, in principle, be intractable, but the actual battles of real, complex humans in negotiated and contextual practice tend to be open to interpretation and compromise.

This discussion of rationales does not say everything that may be said about religious hatred, but it has highlighted a number of key principles for us, suggesting that religious hatred may be distinctive in some ways, but is not sui generis and distinct from other forms of human hatred. Indeed, in as far as religion is something humans do, religious hatred cannot be entirely distinct from other hatreds, because such hatred (as any hatred) is always and only enacted by humans against other humans (sometimes other animals too) in relation to the way we perform prejudice and violence as social behaviours.

The hatred of religion

Likewise, the hatred of specific religions will find its origins in human prejudice as a general category. Elsewhere, we will discuss the origins and nature of particular religious hatreds, but it may be useful to say something about the contemporary hatred for religion as a whole expressed by those known as the 'New Atheists'. This term often indicates four specific people: Richard Dawkins, Sam Harris, Christopher Hitchens (1949–2011), and Dan Dennett. But it also includes such figures as Ayaan Hirsi Ali, Stephen Fry, and Lawrence Krauss among others. While each is distinctive in their approach, they tend to share a disdain for religion as a whole (though Harris is sympathetic to Buddhism), which is especially manifest for the so-called Abrahamic religions (Judaism, Christianity, and Islam), with Islam often especially singled out as the worst offender. We could even suggest they promote religionophobia. But what accounts for it? Why does religion itself inspire hatred from certain non-religious people or groups?

There is undoubtedly no single answer as to why religion is hated in contemporary society. Nevertheless, we can point to at least five contributing factors, though how far these influence any individual will vary. First, certainly since 9/11 if not before, religion – especially Islam – has been associated with violence and seen as the [main] cause of warfare and terrorism. This is clearly not so if one examines the relevant statistics (see Chapter 7). However, it is widely touted by some in the media and a good number of more or less credible public intellectuals. Second, various scandals from corruption to child sexual abuse have rocked religious institutions, with the Catholic Church being most hit by the latter. Combined with the first point, it is suggested that religion is the root of most evil in the world and 'poisons' (a metaphor from Hitchens) everything it touches. While such a suggestion would be very hard to prove – how one would even set about it is unclear – it is nevertheless a popular shibboleth among New Atheists.[17] Third, religion may be seen as an offence to reason. The false narrative of an age-old battle between science and religion is often wheeled out in these debates; the facts deny this, but prejudice never stops to look too closely at evidence, and confirmation bias and implacable stubborn assuredness in well-worn tropes does the rest.[18] Fourth, religion may be an offence to a secular certainty that some see associated with modernity, especially as we face a situation where religion is increasingly dominant on the global political stage,[19] ignoring the complexity and cultural conditioning behind how we envisage these issues. This may be reinforced as we see what is often termed 'fundamentalist' religion on the rise. This is often associated with the three so-called Abrahamic monotheisms of Judaism, Christianity, and Islam, but this usually just reflects the knowledge and Western context of such critics.[20] Finally, in relation to Islam, a form of racialized prejudice is directed against traditions, beliefs, and behaviour seen as alien (see Chapter 7). None of these reasons may be unique to New Atheist hatred of religion, and they manifest in the religious hatred of one religion towards another religion, but they point towards some key issues.

Today's religious hatreds

While distinctive, religious hatred is not unique, but it is certainly worth isolating and exploring, especially given the global proliferation of antisemitism and Islamophobia. For much of history, in what we may broadly term the West, Judaism has been the most reviled religion, but today Islam often fills that space, which is not to deny the continued deep undercurrents (even upsurge) of antisemitism today. We also see new, or rekindled, hatreds in global contexts towards both religions.

Bridges from the past

CHAPTER THREE

The oldest prejudice? Christian antisemitism from the Gospels to the ghettoes

Introduction

It would be too simplistic to trace a straight line from the Christian scriptures to the Holocaust and the deaths of around six million European Jews. However, to deny that the teachings and heritage of Christian antisemitism played a part in contributing to that trajectory would also be wrong. For the best part of two thousand years, Christian religious leaders and texts fed into a situation where Jews were, arguably, the most reviled group in European society. They were subject to periodic pogroms and singled out for opprobrium. We will trace the situation through a largely chronological exploration but noting some special themes along the way.

The Gospels as sources of antisemitism

For Christians, it is hard to admit that their sacred texts may be sources of hatred and terror. Yet, when it comes to Jews, this is the situation. Let us first start with some context. Jesus was Jewish. All of Jesus' immediate disciples and followers were Jews. Saul of Tarsus, better known as Saint Paul, was a Jew. The Gospel writers would have seen themselves as Jews or writing in the Jewish tradition. As such, we cannot straightforwardly call early Christianity and its texts antisemitic. However, that they became so, or were used to support a narrative of antisemitism, seems undeniable. Let us begin by noting a few texts that have been particularly problematic in the heritage between the Jewish and Christian communities:

'His blood be on us [Jews] and on our children' (Mt. 27.25).

'You [Jews] are from your father the devil' (Jn 8.44).

'the doors of the house where the disciples had met were locked for fear of the Jews' (Jn 20.19).

These three brief quotes set out three problematic motifs, though others could be counted, that have haunted the relationship of the two traditions. First, the quotation from Matthew's Gospel is taken from Jesus' trial. As the Gospels tell the story, though tried before the Roman Governor Pontius Pilate, it was certain Jewish leaders and people who called for Jesus' death, though he died a Roman traitor's death.[1] As such, a charge laid before all Jews has been deicide: Jews are 'God-killers'. This is then linked to the second quote, from John's Gospel, where Jews – though the quote is directed at Jewish leaders – are seen to be in league with the devil. Some Christians up until at least the mid-twentieth century (and maybe some still today?), actually believed that Jews had horns and cloven hooves instead of feet – traditional signs of devilry. I have been told by Jewish friends of their relatives who, as the first Jewish people met by some Christians (including highly educated ones), were actually asked if they could show them their horns! This was not figurative, but a literal belief. This helped to explain a wider complaint about Jews as a 'stiff-necked' people who had deliberately not recognized their Messiah. We shall return to this point below. Third, again from John, a natural enmity is spelt out between Jews and Christians, with Jesus' early disciples having to hide due to 'fear of the Jews'; of course, in later centuries, it was more often Jews who would hide for fear of Christians. I would add a fourth point here, brought to my attention by Reuven Firestone,[2] that (drawing from biblical language) we regularly speak of 'the Jews' while we generally say 'Christians' (rather than 'the Christians'). This seemingly innocent definitive article is problematic in various ways: it helps us conceptualize Jews as a single collective; it therefore acts as a form of othering and deindividuation in which a non-dominant group is signalled as 'the X' rather than as individuals. From a religious studies perspective, it plays into the way that religions are problematically portrayed as monolithic systems, such that we can ask what (the) Jews, (the) Buddhists, or (the) Muslims and so on *all* believe (or should believe).[3] In reality there is no singular group of 'the Jews' (nor 'the Blacks', 'the Irish', 'the Chinese', etc.), but this definitive article does the work of fixating this notion in our language and worldview.

These texts need to be understood in context. As noted, they came from a predominantly Jewish community and Jewish writers (though they were subsequently redacted). As such, they were partly about intrareligious contests. This is also true when we see Jesus making criticisms of groups such as the scribes and the pharisees in the Gospels, saying, for instance:

> You serpents, you brood of vipers, how are you to escape being sentenced to hell?[4] Therefore I send you prophets and wise men and scribes, some of whom you will kill and crucify, and some you will scourge in your synagogues and persecute from town to town, that upon you may come all the righteous blood shed on earth. (Mt. 23.33-35a)

In later Christian polemics, this was understood as a criticism of Judaism as a system. However, as a Jewish rabbi from Galilee, a rural peasant area, Jesus was presumably making a critique of what was the largely more metropolitan priesthood and rabbis of Jerusalem and the bigger cities.[5] Likewise, recent studies place Paul within his Jewish context. Therefore, his criticisms of Judaism as a tradition of 'the law', which Christians have typically seen as a systemic critique of Judaism as a whole system/religion, are actually part of an internal Jewish debate about how Jewish tradition should be understood. Furthermore, Paul is arguing in traditionally Jewish terms, in what might be termed *midrash*, or rabbinical commentary.[6]

It is only really in the last Gospel of the New Testament, John's Gospel,[7] that we actually see a category of 'the Jews' being castigated. This is read, by later Christian commentators, back through all the Gospels and in Paul's writing as an inherent contrast between two distinct blocs: Jews and Christians. However, while the term 'Christian' as a label appeared quite early – we are told it was first used in Antioch (Acts 11.26) – we must understand what it originally meant. The term 'Christ', from which we get Christian, is the Greek version of the Hebrew term 'Messiah'. In other words, the term 'Christian' identifies followers of a Jewish Messiah; it is a signifier of Jewish identity. Therefore, in the context of the New Testament, Jew and Christian do not stand as members of different traditions. Such a move is found only as we move beyond the age of these texts to the Church Fathers who developed the tradition.

Adversus Judaeos: The Church Fathers

It is common to refer to the major figures who developed the Christian tradition as the 'Church Fathers'. These bishops, priests, and theologians may be said to be primarily responsible for inscribing the words of the New Testament with the antisemitic sense with which we have come to read them. This was not necessarily intentional, but, as the renowned historian of Christianity Jaroslav Pelikan (1923–2006) argued, in the first century it was obvious that Jesus was Jewish, in the second century it was an embarrassment, and by the third it had become simply obscure.[8] This generalizes more complex trends, but it helpfully demarcates stages. As noted above, the burgeoning Christian movement largely had Jewish leaders (Jesus' direct disciples and other early leaders) and its rationale was directly based in Jewish tradition. For instance, Mark's Gospel begins by referencing various texts of the Hebrew Bible and so appeals to Jewish sources for legitimacy.[9] Indeed, given that Jews were exempt from making sacrifices to the imperial cult of emperor worship, being Jewish would be beneficial for Christians and gave them a place where they were understood in society. However, following various rebellions, notably that in which the Jerusalem temple was destroyed in 70 CE by the Romans as punishment, and then the massive Bar Kokhba Rebellion of 132–135 CE, rather than giving a somewhat privileged place in society, being Jewish was a sign that somebody was a troublemaker and potentially a traitor. Hence, Christians tried more and more to distance themselves from Judaism. Further, we know that relatively few Jewish converts were made, and soon the Christian leadership and rank and file were predominantly from Gentile (i.e. non-Jewish) backgrounds. As such, by the third century, the leadership of the community and context in which the Gospels and Paul were read was not principally Jewish: to call Jesus a rabbi would have made little contextual sense to many Christians. We need, therefore, to understand the world and words of the Church Fathers in relation to this, though it would not be till at least the fourth century that a division between Christians and Jews, church and synagogue, can clearly and definitively be demarcated.[10]

From the second century, a new writing form developed among the Church Fathers: *Adversus Judaeos* literature.[11] This Latin term means, more or less literally, 'against the Jews'. Indeed, some Church Fathers wrote texts or delivered sermons to which this name was given directly. To some extent it continued the logic of John's Gospel. Considered by most scholars to be among the last of the New Testament texts, the writer(s) of John wrote in a context in which increasing polemic between 'Christian Jews' and 'mainstream Jews' was found in the synagogue and beyond. As the Acts of the Apostles (*c.*75–85 CE), which records incidents from a much earlier date, makes clear, the Christian teaching was often not welcomed in the synagogues. So there were, in effect, two parallel Jewish communities in many places: an offshoot of devotees claiming Jesus as messiah, Christians; and the mainstream Jewish community, increasingly led by the rabbinic scholars who would define later Judaism, especially after the temple in Jerusalem was destroyed and they were in exile from Jerusalem. How did the younger sibling understand itself in relation to its older cousin? The answer was often bitter and polemic, with the *Adversus Judaeos* literature testifying to this.

Justin Martyr (*c.*100–165 CE) was one of the first to write such a work, and in his *Dialogue with Trypho* he details a debate with a Jewish figure in which he argues: 'The law promulgated at Horeb is already obsolete, and was intended for you Jews only, whereas the law of which I speak is for all men [sic].'[12] This continues the work of Paul, in that the older covenant which God is seen to have made with the Jewish people alone is now considered broken and null and void, with a new covenant being made through Jesus, making Christians the heirs to the promises to Abraham and Isaac. Hence Christian scripture has two parts: the older record of the first covenant(s), termed the Old Testament; and the texts of the new community proclaiming Jesus, the New Testament. This actually highlights a problem with an anachronistic understanding of Judaism and Christianity as two distinct 'religions' in this period – indeed, the terminology and conception of religion that we have today is a very modern one.[13] Only recently can we speak of two separate 'religions'. Christians, then, saw themselves as the 'real Judaism', with Jews being those now rejected by God and cut off from this covenant. The Christian church calls itself the new Israel. It also reflects a Christian reading of *an* old and *a* new covenant, for the earlier Jewish tradition had at least three covenants, but Christianity focuses only upon that with Abraham which it sees itself superseding.[14] This teaching is still found in many Christian churches, which continues a problematic trope in Christian antisemitism, that Judaism is an illegitimate and dead tradition.

However, much as Justin helped to delegitimize the traditions of Jewish people, other Church Fathers furthered the demonization of Judaism. In his *Adversus Judaeos*, Tertullian (*c*.155–220) argued that Christianity was the tradition of love to be contrasted with the dead law of Judaism. However, perhaps the most polemical was the much revered John Chrysostom (*c*.347–407). Writing from Antioch, he made the following claims, fully elucidated in eight sermons:

> You will learn that they ['the Jews'] are abominable and lawless and murderous and enemies of God. ... I shall first demonstrate that even if they had not been deprived of their ancestral way of life, even so their fast would be polluted and impure. ... And I shall demonstrate that not only the fast, but also all the other practices which they observe – sacrifices and purifications and festivals – are all abominable.[15]

In terms of demonizing the Jewish people, Chrysostom, though not alone, was an influential voice. According to Walter Laqueur, Chrysostom used the 'most violent language', comparing the synagogue to a brothel and calling it 'a temple of devils', saying that he hated it and the Jews.[16] Another saint, bishop, and theologian, Ambrose of Milan (*c*.339–397), also painted a picture of Jews as ardent opponents of Christianity who had tried first by killing Jesus and also, subsequently, to put a stop to Christianity. The single most influential voice of the Western Christian tradition, however, would be one of its towering figures: Augustine of Hippo (354–430).[17] Augustine's contribution is interesting because he sought to protect Jews from harm. While Augustine argued, in his later writings, that heretics should be killed and persecuted by the state – his rationale was that they put souls at stake, hence it was better for a few to die than leave open the chance of many more people being sent to hell if they too became heretics – Jews, he said, should be kept alive. It would not be a life of anything like toleration, however, for he believed that they should be a reviled and ignominious people. Their role, though, would be a warning or sign to others of the truth of Christianity, and as such they should be allowed to remain. Outsiders to society and with no home, for after the destruction of Jerusalem by the Romans it was decreed that no Jew should be allowed on pain of death to set foot inside the precincts of the new city built in its place, they would be a moral reminder and an eternally cursed people wandering the earth.

With the Church Fathers we see a full set of charges that exist in later antisemitism that Ronald Miller has termed the ABCs of antisemitism and which are traceable to Christian scriptures. The Jews are: (a) *accursed*, for committing deicide; (b) *blasphemous*, for they know the truth but deny it (if Hebrew prophesy points to Jesus as the Messiah, it must be wilful for those who know that scripture best to deny it); (c) '*contemptible* in their perfidy'; (d) *diabolical*; and (e) *excluded*.[18] We shall see more examples of this as we proceed.

Blood libels and calumnies

On 27 August 1255, a young boy was found dead in a well in Lincoln, England. Known to posterity as (Little) Hugh of Lincoln he became a Christian saint with his festival day celebrated on the date of his death. This is because his death was understood to be martyrdom, somebody who had died because of their Christian faith, and legends of miracles associated with his body made his cult famous. He is of interest here because his death was blamed on Jews, nineteen of whom were executed in the days following. His story is even mentioned in Geoffrey Chaucer's (1343–1400) *Canterbury Tales* (*c*.1387–1400) as part of the story of the prioress. But why were Jews blamed for his death? The answer relates to a medieval superstition: Jews need Christian blood, specifically children's blood, for their sacrifices and rituals. This related to the belief that Jews were in league with the devil, with human blood being a common ingredient in supposed sorcery and witchcraft.[19] The blood libel charge goes back to pre-Christian times; indeed, allegations were made that Christians themselves killed children as part of their rituals and relates in part to accusations and fears of unknown and seemingly dangerous groups (because of their outsider status).[20] However, it was from the twelfth century that these charges arose against Jews in Christian countries.

Sometimes these accusations were linked to a sacrilegious re-enactment of the crucifixion, and the charges often seemed to arise around Holy Week. This is, perhaps, not a coincidence. It was on the Sunday before Easter, the start of Holy Week, that accounts of 'the Jews' taking Jesus' blood upon themselves and their descendants were highlighted in Gospel readings in Church. This culminates liturgically on Good Friday with Jesus' crucifixion, raising the issue of Jews as guilty of deicide. That Jesus' death upon the cross is generally seen as the atoning sacrifice of Christian theology, and so a necessary component of God's plan in medieval theological speculation, remained unconnected to the prejudice against Jews (whose supposed role in ensuring the crucifixion seemed necessary for God's plans to be fulfilled presumably). Numerous accusations of the blood libel in various forms can be counted in the following centuries. A further charge arose with the Black Death (which reached Europe in the mid-fourteenth century), when various waves of bubonic plague swept Europe, that this was also the responsibility of Jews. Often they were accused of poisoning wells and, despite the fact that they died alongside Christians, many Jews were accused and slaughtered with the near apocalyptic fervour that gripped European society. In some places half or more of the entire Jewish population were wiped out by the plague, so clearly they were not immune.[21] As an aside here we may note that illnesses, particularly plagues or epidemics, have often been blamed on minorities or outsiders, a fact as much true today as then.[22]

An important note about these allegations is that they were often refuted by the church hierarchy. Popes and church leaders investigated, and taking an evidence-based approach, decreed that allegations of the blood libel or Jewish responsibility for the Black Death were entirely unfounded. An example is Pope Gregory X's (1210–1276) 'Letter on Jews' of 1272 which declares that Christians have falsely accused Jews and that any Jews held under these accusations should be released.[23] However, despite such official condemnations, priests and church leaders at the local level were often part and parcel of the allegations and killings. Even as late as 1881, a Jesuit organ named *La Civilta Cattolica* claimed 'that ritual murder was ... an integral part of the Jewish religion', with blood libel charges continuing into the twentieth century.[24]

Jews in the Middle Ages: Crusades, massacres, and life

As is discussed in Chapter 8, for much of the medieval period – indeed, until quite late in the modern period – Jews found a far more congenial home in Muslim-majority polities than in Christendom. As *dhimmis* ('protected people') in Islamic law, they could go about their daily business and conduct their own affairs with far more freedom and less potential uncertainty. It would be wrong to suggest that constant blood libels and massacres were the lot of Jews in Christendom, but they lived under fear of potential threats. While Augustine's powerful voice meant that they were at least partially exempt from attacks (though this did not stop periodic assaults), their position in society remained insecure to say the least. In Christendom, Jews had no legal status and existed only at the largesse of monarchs or nobles who offered protection, though this could be withdrawn as readily as it was given. They were also, in various ways, socially excluded. For instance, from at least 1215, Jews (like Muslims) were expected to wear particular clothes to differentiate them from Christians, as decreed by the Fourth Lateran Council. This was put into effect by varying laws in such countries as England, France, Spain, and beyond with yellow (or other coloured) badges, hats, or belts being variously required. Moreover, regulations determined both the permissibility, or otherwise, of interfaith marriages and also when and where who could eat with whom.[25]

Certainly, in many places, Jews were successful and sometimes valued citizens. Indeed, when Charlemagne (c.742–814) founded new cities he, like some other medieval rulers, actively invited Jews to come and settle. This was primarily a matter of business, with Jews having a reputation as merchants who could increase the affluence of regions. One reason for this was that Jews often worked closely with Jews elsewhere in mercantile endeavours. Indeed, at a time when tensions often ran high between Christians and Muslims, it was Jews who became the middlemen and could reach the more affluent markets of the Islamicate world through local Jewish connections. Internecine Christian strife often meant that Christian rulers or their emissaries could not travel to other Christian territories, so Jewish traders were a practical necessity. The other thing for which Jews were known was moneylending. The Hebrew Bible forbid usury, or lending money for profit. According to medieval Christian teaching, this meant that Christians could not loan money for profit to other Christians. Jews, likewise, were forbidden from this practice, but in the legal clarification of this in the medieval period it was decreed that it was permissible for Jews to lend money to non-Jews. While, in the medieval period, as through most of history, it seems that the majority of Jews were poor and scraping a living, there was also a perception of 'the rich Jew', 'the greedy Jew', and especially given their role as moneylenders to Christians, Jews who profited – unfairly – from Christians. Understanding the trajectory of this for further potential violence is hardly rocket science. Indeed, how far attacks upon Jews in the medieval period were inspired by more theological motives or socio-economic gain is hard to say. Certainly, whether for rich prelates seeking to free themselves from debt or rampaging peasant hordes, attacks on persons perceived as the mercantile or moneylending Jew could be seen as an easy source of income.

A number of the most serious attacks on Jews were associated with what have become called the 'crusades'. Launched from the eleventh until the seventeenth centuries, the crusades were a series of attempts by Christians in Europe primarily to liberate Jerusalem and the rest of the Christian 'Holy Land' from Islamic rule; though some crusades were launched against smaller heretical groups within Europe, and one notorious crusade ransacked and pillaged the Orthodox Christian city of Constantinople, then possibly the world's richest metropolis. While Jews were not a direct target of any crusade, they often became victims, with prejudice, as discussed elsewhere, often being intersectional against various inter-related groups.[26] The First Crusade, launched in 1096, is estimated in various attacks across Northern Europe, on its way to Jerusalem, to have taken between five and ten thousand Jewish lives. There were, of course, no census figures and with much indiscriminate slaughter it is hard to estimate. Nevertheless, the number of deaths probably accounted for the destruction of one third of all Jews in Northern Europe at the time.[27] The entire Jewish population of the cities of Cologne, Mainz, and Worms were massacred in seemingly spontaneous attacks that may have been theologically or economically motivated; Jews in certain places were spared in return for payment.[28] Elsewhere, local leaders tried, with greater or lesser success, to protect 'their Jews', including in the Papal States.

At the start of the Second Crusade, Bernard of Clairvaux (1090–1153), another prominent Christian saint, tried to ensure that such massacres would not occur again, yet he seemingly faced an uphill struggle. In popular opinion, killing Jews was something that gained remission from sins on the crusades, as much as killing Muslims. While Rosemary Radford Ruether notes that despite the theological injunction enshrined by Augustine that they should not be killed, this period seems to mark the beginning of more systematic pogroms, as mobs learned that often their violence against Jews would be tolerated and sometimes condoned; little legal protection stood between them and Jews, whether Jews were targeted for theological reasons or financial gain.[29]

Despite the general terms of this overview, medieval prejudice against Jews was often complex and contextual. Outbreaks of violence in one place existed alongside more placid arrangements elsewhere.[30] Indeed, attacks on Jews were sometimes related to prevailing local political and economic circumstances, while David Nirenberg contends that violence, rather than simply being about persecution, was an act of boundary marking that could even, in the medieval context, be seen as a way of stabilizing community relations, and he notes of the often annual Holy Week violence: 'To treat Holy Week riots as signs or symptoms of a linear march towards intolerance is to deny their character as repeated, controlled, and meaningful rituals, and to ignore the possibility that violence can bind and sunder in the same motion.'[31] Nirenberg may be correct that a pseudo-Girardian scapegoating (where the victims are one of the parties in the contestation that alleviated tensions) may have helped underline the status of the underdog by the perpetrators, but we may question Nirenberg on how far victims of the violence would understand this as creating a meaningful bond with the perpetrators.

The Jews and Their Lies: Luther's legacy

If we were to trace a line through the theological development of Christian antisemitism from the Gospels through the Church Fathers and up till the Holocaust, a key node along that trajectory would be the writings of Martin Luther (1483–1546). While fiery polemic in figures such as Ambrose and Chrysostom may have, if it were not for Augustine, provoked more direct violence, which was indeed a threat for medieval Jews, Luther effectively turbo-charged the logic and discourse of hatred and potential violence.

The early Luther was a very different figure. His works were initially marked by a sympathy towards Jews, and he was the first figure for around a thousand years to very directly point out that not only Jesus but also most of the early disciples were Jewish. This recognition may well have, in part, been related to the rising historical consciousness and linguistic learning arising from the Renaissance, which was a strong impetus behind the Protestant Reformation.

Luther believed through his reading of Paul, strongly marked both by his reading of Augustine and the impetus of late medieval Catholic piety, that he was returning to the fountainhead of Christianity. In Protestant rhetoric, medieval Catholicism had lost sight of the true teachings of Jesus and his disciples, especially Paul, and had cloaked it over with a tradition that masked its radical teachings about humanity, sin, and the need for salvation through pure grace.[32] Like early Christians, Luther believed that what he taught was prefigured in the Hebrew Bible, and therefore he was supremely optimistic that once Jews heard his teaching they would flock to the banner of reform. This was not to be the case. Whether it was simply because his early, even naïve, optimism that Protestantism would be the pathway to Christianity for all Jews was dashed or for more complex reasons, Luther became more vehemently opposed to Judaism throughout his later life. Indeed, he wrote one of the most deeply antisemitic tracts of the Christian tradition shortly before his death: *The Jews and Their Lies*. Thus, between 1523 when he wrote *That Christ Was Born a Jew* and 1542 with the publication of *The Jews and Their Lies*, Luther's attitude performed an almost complete reversal.[33]

To place Luther in his context, Germany was a place where severe condemnation of Jews and Judaism was common. Some quotes from his contemporaries will illustrate this.[34] A certain city burgher Peter Schwartz stated:

> The Jews have been punished severely from time to time. But they do not suffer innocently; they suffer because of their wickedness. Because they cheat people and ruin whole countries by their usury and secret murders, as everyone knows.

Meanwhile, the Renaissance humanist Johann Reuchlin (1455–1522) declared:

Everyday, they outrage, blaspheme and sully God, in the person of his Son, the true Messiah Jesus Christ. They call him a sinner, a sorcerer, a criminal.

Although along with figures such as Erasmus of Rotterdam (1466–1536), the noted humanist scholar, Reuchlin, and others of the Renaissance period did argue for some level of tolerance.[35] But more militant currents were running elsewhere, and a convert from Judaism to Christianity by the name of Johannes Pfefferkorn (1469–1523) had written an influential book, *Der Judenspiegel* (*The Mirror of the Jews*), claiming that Jewish texts outraged Christian decency and contained calumnies against Christians. Pfefferkorn even sought the permission of the Holy Roman Emperor Maximilian I (1459–1519) to destroy the Talmud. It is worth stopping briefly to contextualize this. Throughout the medieval period, Catholic Christians had employed a Latin version of the Bible, termed the Vulgate, translated by (saint) Jerome (*c.*347–419/20). As noted above, the Renaissance saw a revival of linguistic learning and part of this involved reading the New Testament texts in their original Greek which challenged Jerome's work. But, also, the Hebrew Bible was read in Hebrew, offering further challenges. As part of this, learned rabbis were sought out as Hebrew tutors, and thus it came to light that the accepted Christian Hebrew Bible differed from that used by Jews at this time, in that it had extra texts. This played into Protestant hands as it added grist to the mill that Catholics had illicitly added to Christian tradition, especially as support for prayers for the dead (which Protestants opposed) drew strongly on these texts. The additional texts were actually ones which had widely circulated among Greek-speaking Jews when Christianity first developed and so were adopted by the church as its Old Testament, while Rabbinic Judaism in due course took a narrower range of texts, accepting, many argue, only those books seen as originally written in Hebrew. However, a further realization was that, for Jews, the Hebrew Bible was in certain ways not as central to learning as the Talmud. The Talmud is a voluminous text, or set of texts, which records the teachings of significant rabbis, acts as a commentary on the Bible, and provides the practical legal outworking of biblical laws, explaining how the teachings of Moses should be understood and obeyed in everyday life. Much Jewish learning is debate and discussion on the Talmud rather than, as in much of Protestantism, direct study of the biblical text. Moreover, for Jews, the Pentateuch, the first five books of the Bible attributed to Moses, are given such a central role that, in Protestant eyes, Judaism underplays the significance of the theological teachings they find elsewhere in the Hebrew Bible.

Three key points, for us, lead from this. First, in Protestant Christian polemics, Jews could be accused of betraying the biblical text because of their focus on the Talmud as the interpretive lens. This dovetailed with anti-Catholic prejudice. But, also, the Talmud had, over the centuries, picked up quite a bit of anti-Christian polemic, some of which was insulting to Jesus and Mary. As Christians gained access to this, the kind of accusations made by figures such as Pfefferkorn became another part of the tradition of antisemitism, though awareness of the Talmud had surfaced periodically before this time. Second, the focus on the Pentateuch which Christian traditions term the 'laws of Moses' as opposed to the Jewish terminology of the 'teachings of Moses', played into the stereotype that had arisen via Paul that Judaism was essentially legalistic, in ways which caricature Jewish adherence to biblical injunctions. Third, and an aside to our discussion here but significant, is that a continuing problem in most Christian (and academic) representations of Judaism is that it is a religion that can be understood by reference to the Hebrew Bible; the Talmud is sometimes simply ignored. For instance, Jews often find themselves scripturally represented, in textbooks and elsewhere, by the Hebrew Bible as if this summed up their main teachings and ideas. Such representations may be made in reference to a common Judeo-Christian tradition, which typically asserts that both religions share many central texts from which they similarly draw. This misrepresents the integrity of Rabbinic Judaism, the strand of Jewish tradition which has grown up over the last two thousand years and which draws heavily upon the traditions which stretch back before then. Jewish tradition is composed primarily of forms of interpretation of the Torah (here meaning the Jewish Hebrew bible, though it can indicate only the Pentateuch, or even all Jewish teachings and tradition) through rabbinical commentary and argumentation as found in the Talmud and then in subsequent interpretation. This, more than the Hebrew Bible, represents Judaism in its own integrity. Continuing misrepresentations of Judaism (as noted, even in academia) reveal a continuing trope of Christian antisemitism: that Judaism is a dead tradition in that it has not developed since biblical times and can be read primarily through a Christian lens. Without reading the Talmud and other rabbinic texts it is not always clear how Jewish interpretations of the Hebrew Bible differ from Christian ones. This was something of a detour away from our discussion of Luther, but it is an important side note about the way that a Christian theological reading of Judaism still continues to distort our perception of that tradition, while it helps us understand part of Luther's criticisms of Judaism.

Luther asserts that Jews are 'the children of the Devil', indeed he states that they even 'accuse God of lying and proudly despise the whole world' while their schools are 'nothing but the Devil's nest'.[36] Further, relating to what we have noted about the Talmud, Luther takes direct aim at this, arguing that it says: 'It is no sin to kill if a Jew kills a heathen. ... It is no sin if he [a Jew] does not keep his oath to a heathen. ... And they are the masters of the world and we are their servants, yea, their cattle!'[37] Indeed, Luther asserts that the Talmud is 'worse than heathen philosophy'.[38] Alongside this goes his claim that Jews 'pervert the Word of God, are avaricious, practice usury, steal, commit murder (wherever they can do so) and on and on teach their children to do such'.[39] Throughout the text of *The Jews and Their Lies*, Luther further adds other accounts of the Talmud insulting Jesus and Mary, as well as recounting how Jewish moneylending helps them enslave Christians.

Many tropes from the Christian tradition of antisemitism are found paraded through Luther's work, but he also adds certain new parts, in particular about how Jews are the masters and Christians the servants. Nevertheless, Luther has a solution to the situation of 'the Jews', and in a series of acts of revenge, or 'remedies', he sets out what is noted below. In the light of what we know happened afterwards this may seem quite chilling. Indeed, one time I taught a class in Germany on Lutheranism and interfaith dialogue which included the legacy of what Luther had said both about Muslims and Jews, which left my audience of young German students quite aghast for they had never been told the exact details of how Luther had set out his 'remedy' for 'the Jews':

> First, their synagogues should be set on fire, and whatever does not burn up should be covered or spread over with dirt. ... And this ought to be done for the honour of God and Christianity. ... Secondly, their homes should likewise be broken down and destroyed. ... Thirdly, they should be deprived of their prayerbooks and Talmuds. ... Fourthly, their rabbis must be forbidden under threat of death to teach any more. ... Fifthly, passport and travelling privileges should be absolutely forbidden to Jews. ... Sixthly, they ought to be stopped from usury. ... Seventhly, let the young and strong Jews and Jewesses be given the flail, the axe, the hoe.[40]

Ghettoes and pogroms: Jews in Christendom in modernity

The Jewish populations were expelled from territories in Europe at various times in history. In 1492, under pain of either conversion or death, they were expelled from the Iberian Peninsula after a new Christian monarchy was declared. But they had previously been expelled from England in 1290, a pattern seen in many other places. Where they remained, they were often forced into special areas, which had been normal in many medieval cities. Partly for protection, partly from in-group solidarity, but also because they were ostracized from the wider society, Jews lived together. In Eastern Europe, the shtetl (Jewish village) became the norm for living. However, first in Italy and then elsewhere, this became more formalized, with the ghetto being a particular walled area of a town, or area outside the town, where – with its own curfew – Jews were locked in at night. This physically enforced the social, and with it theological, exclusion of the Jew. To some degree it offered protection from random mobs, being under guard and protected, but it reinforced an insular and inward-looking attitude.[41]

Notably, in 1084, Jews were offered, as a kind of privilege, a walled enclosure by Rüdiger Hutzmann (or, Hußmann), the Bishop of Speyer (1073–1090) seeking to entice them to his territory. Hence it was not, at first, entirely negative as we will discuss below. But it certainly became seen as discriminatory, and the situation in ghettoes often deteriorated. The critique of ghettos arose in the Enlightenment period, with the ghetto (enforced segregation) system ending in Western Europe in the nineteenth century but only in the twentieth century in Eastern Europe (though there it was not typically in a formally walled area).

We can say more about the ghetto, which has long resonated in the imagination. It has become a more widely used term applying to areas not simply set aside for Jews, but slum areas associated with particular ethnic communities, often Black Americans, leading to some contestation between them and Jews on the ownership of this word.[42] It has even been used by Palestinians to describe their context.[43] The term itself, despite some dispute on origins, simply refers to a neighbourhood in Venice termed the Ghetto Vecchio which was the site of a disused foundry which in 1516 was set aside by the Venetian Senate as a temporary site for Jews. It would last for 281 years, but was initially simply a way to balance Venice's self-image as a pure Christian city (and so not inhabited by Jews) with its mercantile need for a Jewish community.[44] As an institution, it was the Papal States that would formalize this arrangement for Jewish life, and on 14 July 1555, Pope Paul IV issued a bull entitled *Cum nimis absurdum* ('Since it is absurd') that stated: Jews should not live alongside Christians; any city should have no more than one synagogue; Jews should wear 'a hat or some obvious marking' to be clearly recognized; and that all Jews should live in one place, or if needed several, with 'one entry alone, and one exit'.[45]

As well as providing some protection, the ghetto was at first not seen as wholly negative and other groups, such as Turks in Venice, requested their own distinctive site such as the Jewish ghetto. This had some utility for the city state given the need for taxation and tracking of goods. Protests against the ghetto primarily took off in the late eighteenth century, and in terms of being an area wholly separated and walled off, it was a feature only of the Italian peninsula and lasted until the Ghetto of Rome was finally dismantled in 1870.[46] But, it was in this time of its disappearance, in the late nineteenth century, that the ghetto really began to figure as a feature of the Jewish and wider literary imagination. It represented the segregated nature of Jewish life in particular quarters, or in shtetls,[47] with claims that attempts to break it down were foiled by antisemitism.[48] Certainly, it was seen as going against Enlightenment values of emancipation (see Chapter 5), and tearing down the ghetto was often assigned some importance for the French when invading Italy.[49] We must also realize that in the Papal States the ghetto was not simply the somewhat pragmatic, if argued on Christian grounds, ghetto of

Venice. Rather, it was a 'component of a concerted assault on Jewish life designed to make Jews thoroughly miserable and reduce them to penury'.[50] This was posited upon Augustine's idea that Jews should not be wiped out, but they should be brought to see their wretched existence as those who had refused their God, which was also a means to encourage conversions. The ghetto, in this form, was therefore a distinctly theological endeavour.

Prejudice and the Jews

Theories of prejudice could be related to Judaism in various ways. Gordon Allport (1897–1967) saw Jews as a typical scapegoat. Indeed, possibly René Girard's (1923–2015) reading of this concept may help us understand the massacres during the crusades in German cities, if encounters between locals and the considerable masses of crusaders passing through led to tensions which found their outlet in a third-party scapegoat, though ideological theory (see Chapter 1) would explain this. Of course, hatred also plays a large part. Given the theory that love and hate are related, we could consider the fact that some have seen the very kinship of Christianity and Judaism, as siblings in strife, playing into the enmities.[51] We also see clear examples of stereotypes of 'the Jews', alongside definite prejudice, and many examples of discrimination, with Jews often excluded and vilified, even when outright violence is not enacted. Importantly, some writers have seen antisemitism as an almost unique phenomenon, but in at least its manifestation in Christian tradition it accords fully with mainstream theories of prejudice, as we have untheorized it. While antisemitism would morph into a more racist strain in modernity, arguably, the concepts of Christian antisemitism remain a potent feature of subsequent antisemitic thought and have certainly helped justify modern vilification of Jews.

CHAPTER FOUR

Kafir and Turks: Christians and Muslims through history

Introduction

The history of the encounter of Muslims and Christians is not one solely marked by antagonism and conflict, but neither could it be claimed to be irenic and peaceful. Moreover, at different times and in varying contexts, we have seen very diverse dynamics shaping the encounter and relationship. Here, our aim is to focus on some of the tensions, but we will also not overlook the more positive encounters to give a holistic picture. We will also ask how far debates are shaped by religious rivalries and theological issues, and to what extent we have seen the clash of empires and imperial ambitions as Deepa Kumar argues.[1] Samuel Huntington once remarked that Islam is marked by 'bloody borders';[2] however, that blood was often spilt where Islamic borders met Europe's Christian borders, which are equally blood stained, especially as they expanded with imperialism.

The earliest records and encounters in Muhammad's lifetime and beyond

Records of Muhammad's (571–632) life suggest that one of the first people to validate his visions and position as a prophet was a Christian monk in the Arabian desert. This certainly puts a positive spin on the early relationship and places a direct connection between the religions, which we will discuss further shortly. Moreover, various incidents in Muhammad's early career suggest a positive relationship. For instance, while being persecuted in Mecca, Muhammad told some followers to flee to Ethiopia because its Christian king was wise and just and would protect them. Indeed, an important note is that even after Muhammad established what could be termed an 'Islamic state' in Medina, he told his Muslim followers elsewhere they had no need to migrate (*hijra*) as they could be just as good Muslims where they were and were free to follow their practices and beliefs under non-Muslim rulers. In another example, Muhammad let a group of visiting Christians pray in his mosque at Medina, arguing that they had this right in Islam. Again, Saint Catherine's Monastery in Sinai still holds a document, believed to come from Muhammad, that grants Christians protection and has – pretty much – ensured their continuity and religious freedom under Islamic rule for around fourteen hundred years.

However, the last example suggests a certain tension: that protection was needed in the context of the burgeoning military conquests and expansion that began under Muhammad and continued apace with his successors. Within decades of the establishment of Islam, Muslim conquerors had taken Jerusalem and smashed many of the Asian holdings of the Byzantine Empire – the last vestige of the Roman Empire – and had gone further across North Africa. The early logic of Islam, established by Muhammad in the face of military opposition, was to expand Islam's borders, and – as the early Islamic rulers saw it – to bring peace to the world through the spread of Islam. Having united the various Arabic tribes from centuries of internecine warfare, a fairly familiar pattern to students of history unfolded, of mounted warrior tribes becoming a formidable fighting force that carved their way with relative ease through more settled and established civilizational and urban societies. For the urban groups, this typically unleashed a sense of bewilderment and anxiety, even worries about the world's end, as they came under new rulers. However, we must stress that the early conquests were, while of course brutal as they involved warfare, conducted in a spirit of tolerance across religious borders. When Muhammad's successor, Caliph Umar (*c.*584–644), took Jerusalem in 638, he first met the Patriarch of Jerusalem on the Mount of Olives dressed as a 'humble nomad, with a patched cloak' and promised protection to the Christians and their holy places, something which also applied to the Jews, while he also prayed outside the Holy Sepulchre to ensure zealous Muslims would not try to take possession of the church.[3] Indeed, it has been argued that a logic of tolerance was built into early Islam.[4]

Nevertheless, the context for future Muslim–Christian relations in what became the two perceived blocs of a European Christendom and an Islamic Middle Eastern and North African (MENA), or Arab, world was set in place through these early conquests, or more particularly through perceptions of the differences that followed. The motif of Islam as threat was born for Christians. Franco Cardini argues that, at least in many parts of Europe, this was not initially perceived as a threat arising out of religious difference or warfare, but these aspects became established by around the eleventh or twelfth century, and much of it was the consequence of myth-making. For instance, a Frankish military leader Roland (d. 778) who almost certainly died when other Christians attacked the rearguard of the Frankish army, became mythologized as a brave warrior falling to treachery and Muslim aggression.[5] Indeed, the notion of 'holy war' often attributed to Islam via the concept of jihad, which simply means striving,[6] is arguably a Byzantine Christian concept. It was later adopted by Catholic Christians in the offering of indulgences for those fighting against the 'Saracen' in the 'crusades'.[7] Yet European Christians framed the crusades as violence coming from Muslims rather than themselves.

One other aspect of this early period that needs mentioning is the Islamic innovation of the *ahl al-dhimma* (often *dhimmis*) or 'protected people'. This was a legal juridical principle of governance created by the burgeoning Islamic empire to safeguard the position of certain groups under their rule. These people, generally those deemed the 'People of the Book' (*ahl al-kitab*),[8] were allowed to govern themselves in terms of community law and religious worship within the Islamic state. In return for payment of what is generally termed a poll tax (*jizya*), they were exempted from military service and protected by the ruler of the Islamic polity, the caliph or sultan. We discuss some aspects of this further in later chapters, but within the early Islamic polity, Christians (and Jews) had a relatively stable position, providing they did not engage in warfare against the rulers or support others in this. It was a position that has often been described as being a 'second-class citizen', but Christians were generally not directly persecuted nor subject to sporadic violence.

Theological debates and rifts between the traditions

It is worth asking to what extent theological questions played into the dynamic of tensions. While differing views of deity, or the place of Jesus, did not lead to outbreaks of violence in the early conquests, we know of early debates.[9] Meanwhile, theological differences were later utilized by each side to help explain the situation encountered and to draw a battle of cosmic proportions between the two traditions. Indeed, while at times the two traditions lived in peace, at other times theological disputes and questions were employed to suggest a natural enmity and to help envisage the other as a threat that could not be tolerated.

The theological disputes are numerous and wide ranging. Some key ones, which have perhaps caused the most tensions on both sides, can be noted here.[10] The first concerns the two foundational figures of each tradition, Jesus and Muhammad, though the issues are very different. For Muslims, seemingly early on influenced by a strict Jewish monotheistic impetus, the divinity of Jesus was denied. If God is strictly *One*, then no notion of the Trinity could be entertained – a matter which has led to accusations of 'association-ism' (*shirk*) against Christians, arguably the most grievous religious offence in Islam, which means putting something else alongside or equal to God. For most (but not all) Christians, the Islamic view of Jesus provides the greatest difficulty, for it undermines a key basis of their faith: that of Jesus as the second person in the Trinity and God incarnate. In Arabic, Allah means '[The] God' and is how Arabic-speaking Jews and Christians say 'God', as such it is rendered here simply as God, as there is no separate Islamic name for God beyond that known to Christians and Jews; all claim to worship the God of Abraham. But, Jesus being placed alongside God convicts Christians, in the eyes of Muslims, of *shirk*. However, for Muslims, Jesus is not derided, but is highly respected and held as one of the greatest of the prophets. Indeed, for Muslims, Jesus is held as the Messiah, meaning the person who will in the Last Days lead God's armies against those of Satan (Shayṭan/Iblis). This leads into the problem with Muhammad, for Muslims assert that while they give all respect to Jesus, mutual recognition of Muhammad is not forthcoming from Christians. It is often held by Christians that prophethood ended with John the Baptist foretelling Jesus, hence even if one admires Muhammad as a man or leader it is hard for many of them to call him a prophet (although various theological arguments have been advanced to show that giving Muhammad the status of a prophet is possible within Christianity). Muslims feel rebuked by this and, at the very least, misunderstanding and ill-will is often generated in discussion on this topic.[11]

Alongside this, the vast majority of Muslims deny the crucifixion of Jesus. For many, given the elevated Islamic view of prophethood, it is inconceivable that a prophet could have been crucified; Muslim tradition has generally held that Judas was given Jesus' visage by God so that he would suffer in Jesus' place, with Jesus escaping and living elsewhere. (Historically, the evidence is fairly incontrovertible: Jesus was crucified by the Romans as a traitor.) This standpoint offers a serious dispute with mainstream Christian theology. We may note, though, that recently a number of Muslim scholars have argued that the interpretation against the crucifixion is not as clear-cut as often presumed.[12]

Again, central for Muslims is the Qur'an, believed in orthodox Sunni thought since the eleventh century to be the uncreated co-eternal Word of God. The most serious Christian polemic against the Qur'an as being, in effect, the rantings of a deranged fanatic that defame God, plagiarism from the Christian and Jewish sacred texts alongside other folk tales, or simply incoherent nonsense, deeply offends Muslim sentiments. Christian scholars who have studied the Qur'an do not hold these views, and we are talking about prejudiced stances; however, especially as accessed through more or less biased translations from the Middle Ages onwards, these attitudes became standard fare in much – but far from all – Christian apologetics against Islam.[13]

The final issue we will mention is the problem of supersessionism. In Chapter 3, we discussed how Christians held that they had superseded Judaism, making it an obsolete system. Coming later, Islam has often presented itself in supersessionist terms as the final, complete, and uncorrupted revelation from God. According to this viewpoint, while the Hebrew Bible and New Testament are understood as scriptures from God, it is believed that they have become corrupted and it is alleged that Jews and Christians, especially the latter, have either tampered with the original texts or distorted the meaning.[14] Muslims hold that the New Testament was originally Jesus' own text, the *Injil* (Gospel), which Christians deliberately changed to insert their own teachings contrary to Jesus' words. On the one hand, the Qur'an and Muhammad's traditions suggest that Christians (also Jews, but see Chapter 8 on that) were 'People of the Book' and much praise is found in the Qur'an for the People of the Book. Yet, on the other, given the many years over which the Qur'an was written and the changing political relations with various Peoples of the Book, in other parts the language is harsher. Christians are said to have false teachings, corrupted revelation, and are best avoided. Depending upon how one reads it, which *hadiths* (sayings of Muhammad) one reads, and which interpretations one follows, Christians can be both those closest to Muslims or deadly enemies. All this leads from the logic of supersessionism, and the social and political – alongside ideological – context in which it is read.

From the Christian side, in terms of supersessionism, we may note that Islam has always posed a problem. From around the nineteenth century, in Protestant missionary theology (though much earlier related traditions are found, arguably even back to the scriptural foundations), the logic of supersessionism, or fulfilment, that applied to Judaism has at times been read into other religions and traditions.[15] Just as the Jewish law is seen as 'stepping stones' to Christianity, it has been argued that Hinduism, Buddhism, Confucianism, and other religions can be seen in a similar way. They provide, Christians have argued, the moral framework for life and intimations towards a divine reality which, correctly interpreted, will lead people to Jesus and Christian teaching. However, Islam is different. Not only does it postdate Christianity, and so the logic of it looking forward to Christianity makes less sense, but its foundational documents are seen to explicitly reject Christian teachings, and even to be a polemic against Christian orthodoxy. In these terms, Christianity has struggled to make positive theological sense out of Islam. Compared to other religions, a positive reading of Islam has simply been harder. This is not to say that it is not possible, and various theological rationales for Islam's teachings and what it contains have been put forward; sometimes that Muhammad did not truly understand Christianity and so rejected a false version. Certainly, Islam's rejection of the Trinity does not equate to what most Christians would understand by the Trinity, while its accusation that the idea of Jesus as God's Son entails a literal mating of divine and human shows a lack of knowledge of Christian teachings. However, for much of Christian history, Islam has been read as anti-Christian.

With regard to what we have said so far, two key terms may be briefly discussed: 'kafir' (often translated as 'infidel') and 'heretic'. Each represents a polemical slur against the other tradition in certain usages. First, *kafir*, which is a complicated word with no singular meaning.[16] Sometimes translated as 'infidel' or 'unbeliever', though these could relate to other terms too, it has been used to brand Christians the ultimate outsiders in Islamic thought. In standard polemic usage, to be a *kafir* is not simply to be somebody who does not accept Islam, which could be down to ignorance or lack of opportunity to encounter Islam. Rather, the *kafir* actively rejects God, and so becomes an enemy of Islam. Somebody who, in some militant readings of Islamic tradition (or, for some, in certain times of tension), may and should be killed by devout Muslims. Given the reading of Christians as those who have actively tampered with Jesus' revelation, the accusation is not just a mistaken following of teachings, but a wilful desire to pervert God's word. Hence, the Christian may be considered *kafir*. This is certainly not the standard reading of Christians by the *ulama* (jurists, or Islamic legal scholars) who have defined how the tradition understands the Qur'an and Muhammad's traditions in terms of *shariah* (Islamic legal and social practice). However, in times of conflict, it becomes one way to frame the enemy.

Meanwhile, an early Christian tradition to explain Islam, which became widespread in medieval Europe, was that Islam was simply a Christian heresy. It was held that Muhammad was an embittered ex-cardinal who, having failed to become pope, fled eastwards to establish his own deviant teachings. Coming from a Greek term indicating 'choice', heresy had, by about the third century, become the standard accusation against rival Christian sects. Hence, applying this to Islam at a time when the Western end of the Eurasian landmass had become Christendom – a perceived monolithic Christian society – made sense both in terms of Christian tradition and also how to deal with other 'religions'. As discussed in Interlude 1, 'religion', as the concept is typically understood, did not exist until modernity, and so Islam and Judaism were not seen as separate 'religions'; rather, Judaism was understood as a 'failed' version of Christianity, and Islam was heresy. European Christians had no cognitive map to make sense of what we would term religious diversity except in terms of orthodox Christianity (Catholicism), heretical Christianity (Orthodoxy and other Christians), Paganism, and failed Christianity (Judaism). Augustine had determined that killing heretics was desirable in Christian states, and so killing Muslims followed this logic. This is not to say that no positive medieval images of Muslims existed, and against such diatribes, even from figures such as Thomas Aquinas (1225–1274), we see Nicholas of Cusa (1401–1464) giving a much more nuanced and sympathetic understanding.[17]

While we cannot simply see the conflicts of Muslims and Christians as religio-theological ones, each tradition contained perceptions of the other that made justifying enmity and even righteous killing of the other a logical, even desirable, end.

The Middle Ages and the crusades: A decisive and lasting schism

The term 'crusade' is heavily invested with meaning. From the Christian side, it is typically understood to refer to the 'holy wars' undertaken to free the Holy Land from Muslim rule that allegedly kept Christians persecuted and prevented the free exercise of pilgrimage, though the term was not current when the first such war was launched.[18] From the Muslim side, it is typically understood as the aggression they experienced from Christian invaders who attacked without provocation and sought to destroy Islam. It is, therefore, a weighted term. In the First Crusade (1096–1099), announced by Pope Urban II (c.1035–1099) at the Council of Clermont (1095), there was papal backing for the defence of their fellow Christians in the East. (At this time, Catholic and Orthodox Christians widely perceived each other as heretics, but this out-group status was transformed into an in-group identity in the face of a new commonly perceived out-group threat.) Further, there was the granting of indulgences for those who went to fight against Muslims. This was in the context of a developing sense of the dynamic of a battle between the 'world of Islam' and a nascent sense of a 'Christian Europe'.[19] In relation to what was noted above about Islam as heresy, we can quote Bernard of Clairvaux (c.1090–1153) in one of his sermons (c.1145) seeking support for the Second Crusade (1147–1150): 'The demon of heresy has taken possession of the chair of truth, and God has sent forth His malediction upon His sanctuary.'[20] Bernard, we may note, did not even see Muslims as objects for potential conversion, rather they were to be killed mercilessly.[21]

We should also contrast Umar's dialogical and relatively peaceful entry into Jerusalem, with protection for Jews and Christians, with the arrival of the crusaders who slaughtered the vast majority of Jews and Muslims they found in Jerusalem (the Orthodox Christians were spared probably only because they had previously been exiled). If there are perceptions of violent and uncivilized aggressors, Western Christians are in no place to point fingers at Muslims.

Some points need noting. First, Muslim rule over Jerusalem and the area that is today Israel–Palestine did not prevent pilgrimage, and indeed it was often fully supported. Only under one caliph, al-Hakim (985–1021), a Shi'ite Egyptian ruler, were Christian holy sites desecrated, but he equally persecuted Sunni Muslims and Jews.[22] As a rationale, or excuse, for the wars, it therefore holds no water. Many see the rationale for the wars based in the logic of economics, partly related to the feudal system. As younger sons did not inherit, there were many landless knights and some social unrest. These potential mercenaries were up for grabs and there was a promise of rich plunder.[23] However, Cardini argues that the huge response to the call for crusading cannot be understood without the apocalyptic expectations of the time and the religious fervour gripping European Christian minds, many of whom believed that this crusade would allow them to be in Jerusalem for the end of the world.[24] The crusades, or more particularly the mythology of the crusades, has helped create a mythos of the clash between Islam and Christianity.

Second, for Christians in Europe, there was generally little direct knowledge of Islam, so much relied upon imagination.[25] We have noted this already. But one example is that Islam was often perceived as a monolithic threat, which did not acknowledge diversity nor internal divisions. There has, of course, never been an 'Islam' or a 'Muslim world' at war with 'Christendom' or a 'Christian Europe' because these are imagined communities, not realities. But events like the crusades have helped enforce this imagined reality, alongside the events and social imaginary associated with such places as the shrine of St James at Compostela in Spain which Cardini argues is key to the imagination of Europe, distanced from a hostile and threatening Islam.[26]

In the crusades, and elsewhere, a more nuanced view will never show us Islam and Christianity as diametrically opposed. Rather, we see differing exchanges, and often irenic meetings. Notable is the meeting in 1219 of Francis of Assisi (c.1181–1226) with Sultan al-Malik al-Kamil (1177–1238). Walking across the battle lines, Francis's peace mission saw him engaged in what seems to have been a deep dialogue over several days with the sultan.[27] This was very much a one-off, but we see a wider pattern of Christians who lived among Muslims being generally (but not always) more sympathetic to Islam.[28] Certainly, during the crusades, the Christian settlers in the region seem to have integrated and seen local alliances as natural, in ways that were not true of those arriving from Europe.[29]

Some contexts and cameos: Al-Andalusia and Christians in Muslim lands

We have spoken of the interpretation of Muslim–Christian relations between what would become perceived as 'Christian Europe' and 'the Muslim world'. However, for many centuries and still today, numerous Christians have lived under forms of Islamic rule or in Muslim-majority states.[30] Their experience has often been dramatically different from that imagined by those in Christian-majority lands. As we may expect, and has been inherent in what has been said above, the experiences in differing times and places were distinct: we cannot simply generalize to a one-size-fits-all situation. Both fairly irenic coexistence and fierce persecution could be found, while fierce polemic arose at times in Arab Christian responses to the Qur'an.[31] Yet, at other times, Islam was presented as being '"on the way" to the truth ... even ... fulfilling some biblical promises'.[32] Again, in social terms, the experience of *dhimmis* varied, and there were relatively few martyrs.[33]

Perhaps the best known and most remembered period is the experience of Al-Andalusia, the Arabic term for the Iberian Peninsula, which is used to describe the period from the eighth to the fifteenth centuries (711–1492) when there were Muslim rulers in the region. Like much else in the history of Christian–Muslim relations it is variously imagined, or mythologized. On the one hand, Maria Rosa Menocal (1953–2012) has romanticized it as a haven of coexistence under the phrase *The Ornament of the World*, while others have suggested it was a period of brutal conquest and oppression.[34] As is so often the case, the truth is more interesting and more complex, being something of both, neither, and a little of each.[35] Under the Iberian Umayyad dynasty, there was a fair degree of peaceful coexistence, as was typical of early Islamic rule following what was seen as the example of Muhammad and his successors. Indeed, the Umayyads had, it seems, been invited to Al-Andalusia by both Jews and Christians who had found themselves persecuted by other Christians (in connection with debates about what was deemed 'orthodoxy' and 'heresy') and who, rightly, believed they would live more freely under Islamic rule. As such, we do not see an aggressive Muslim conquest as such, but Muslims and, primarily, some Christians forming an alliance against other Christians. After the collapse of centralized Islamic power, Al-Andalusia was primarily factional, with various Muslim and Christian leaders engaging in strategic alliances with other Muslim and Christian leaders, with no real concern for religious supremacy of one side over the other. This is not to say that such rhetoric did not occur, but much of the later legend of a Christian reconquest resulted from the propaganda of the final victors, Queen Isabella (1451–1504) and King Ferdinand (1452–1516), who sought to promote unity underneath themselves among the rival potential claimants to thrones and territories.

It is certainly telling that Spain's great Christian knight of the legend of reconquest is remembered by his Arabic name El Cid ('the Lord', *c.*1043–1099). Indeed, one of his great victories, the siege of Toledo (1085), was partly a revenge attack for the death of his lord who had been the Muslim ruler of that city, the *malik* al-Qadir, though it was also motivated by self-interest as he took control of the city as his fiefdom.[36] He fought for both Christian and Muslim sides, and this crossing of borders is perhaps more representative of what is termed the '*convivencia*', or 'living together':

> The term *convivencia*, or living together, is often used to describe the coexistence of these three religious communities [Islam, Judaism, Christianity] in Islamic Spain. ... [It] has come to represent the romanticized vision of a uniquely tolerant and symbiotic pluralism ... especially attractive to those striving to improve interreligious relations.[37]

Certainly, there was a strong tradition of living alongside each other, and via Al-Andalusia much culture, literature, philosophy, and science found its way to Europe. Indeed, Europe's twelfth-century Renaissance can be traced to this route, as can the troubadour tradition, the passage of Aristotelian philosophy, and developments in science.[38] However, there were also those who resented or resisted Islamic rule. In Al-Andalusia, the most famous are the martyrs of Cordoba.[39] However, it would be wrong to see this as general dissatisfaction. While about fifty Christians were put to death in 850, they were strongly opposed by their community leaders, and it appears to be a rather striking event by its lack of consistency with the general situation (that such a group of martyrs is something of a one-off across many centuries is notable). The historical records show us that bishops and others tried to stop what became something like copycat acts when the caliph, who tried hard not to have to kill anyone in this context, found that some were willingly insulting Muhammad to purposefully be martyred.[40]

Muslims and Christians in modernity: Elizabeth I, Napoleon, and the Ottomans

In contemporary contexts, many speak of the battles and wars between the 'Muslim world' and the 'Christian world'. However, the actual history is more complex. After Henry VIII (1491–1547) separated the Church of England from Rome and subsequent monarchs found themselves in antagonism with countries such as Catholic Spain, alliances with the Ottoman Empire proved attractive.[41] Under Queen Elizabeth I (1533–1603), an alliance with the Turkish sultans meant that Muslims were often welcomed, and there are records of Muslims praying in the streets of London in the Tudor period (though resentment towards them arose in due course and the 'Turks' were banished). Indeed, a number of battles which are often portrayed as examples of Islamic aggression against Christendom were actually related to alliances between Christian and Islamic powers in conflict with other Christian groups.[42] Much of this dynamic interaction between the Islamic and Christian worlds, where we see both conflict and alliances, was forgotten in subsequent centuries where colonial dynamics altered perceptions.

Often perceived as pivotal was Napoleon's (1769–1821) expedition into Egypt. This was of immense symbolic importance because, for centuries, Muslim empires – most recently the Ottomans – had threatened Europe militarily and existentially. Napoleon showed the new strength of Europe against the comparative weakness of the Ottomans, unable to defend one of their heartlands. To give some context to this, we need to turn back a millennium to earlier battles.

In 732, Muslim soldiers from Al-Andalusia were turned back from Northern France at the battle of Poitiers; though this was certainly not an invasion repelled, it was a raiding party at a time when internal tensions within the Islamic world meant that expansion was curtailed.[43] This marked the furthest extent of Islamic excursions into mainland Europe, and after this no such extensive raids took place, as the Sunni Umayyads of Spain competed with the Shi'ite Fatimids of Cairo, who in turn competed for territory against the Abbasid dynasty in Baghdad, with many later internal rivalries and smaller dynasties and local rulers in the mix.[44] However, with the Ottomans taking Constantinople in 1453, we see a date that for some historians marks a pivotal movement. It was the end of the Roman Empire in any form and, for some, marks the transition from the Middle Ages to Early Modernity. Symbolically, the once greatest city of Christendom, Constantine's city, the Christian capital of the Roman Empire, had fallen to Islam.[45] Later renamed Istanbul, it became the capital of the Ottoman Empire as the Turkish horsemen who were behind it became a more urban and settled community; we may note that these horsemen were not Muslims when their campaigns started, but first taking many Muslim-majority lands they adopted the religious beliefs of those they had conquered.

Beyond the existential shock of the loss of Constantinople (sometimes termed Byzantium), in the decades following, Ottoman armies would reach further into Europe and threaten the gates of Vienna in 1529, then again in 1683. Only a shock victory for the defenders saw the Ottoman advance stopped, while various internal disputes meant they would not again seek such military ventures into the Western section of the Eurasian landmass. Nevertheless, until the nineteenth century, much of South Eastern Europe – from the Balkans to Greece – remained staunchly Ottoman territory. We should stop to note that the battles at Vienna were not Muslim–Christian conflicts. In 1683, the Polish king who defeated the Ottomans brought with him his Polish Tartar (Turkic Muslim) troops who were crucial, while the Ottomans were allied with Louis XIV of France (1638–1715), the famous Catholic Sun King.[46] Christian–Muslim alliances were the norm, despite often polemic diatribes that Christian Europe was at war with the Turks. We may note here that European terms for, and perceptions of, Muslims have shifted from (to simplify) Saracens (medieval), to Turks (early modernity), to Arabs (contemporary).

These Islamic advances meant that, for Europeans from the fourteenth to at least the eighteenth century, an awareness of this huge – and generally culturally superior – Islamicate Empire to their East was a constant cautionary note. Indeed, throughout this period and after, the term 'Turk' was in many European languages a standard term to mean Muslim, with little or no differentiation made between different Muslims or forms of Islam. In terms of how they were viewed, the German reformer Martin Luther (1483–1546) is an often-cited source. In 1530, fear of the Turks was widespread in Europe, with much wartime propaganda circulating. Noting that he had read only two polemics, Luther remarked: 'I have eagerly desired for some time to learn about the religion and customs of the Muhammadans.'[47] By 1542, Luther had acquired a translation of the Qur'an in Latin and read it. His concern was to counter the theological dangers he saw, and he urged the Council of Basel in 1543 to publish it widely, noting that

> It amazes me ... that long ago no one rendered the Qur'ān into the Latin language, even though Muhammad had ruled and caused great harm more than nine hundred years ago. ... They were merely satisfied to know that Muhammad was the enemy of the Christian faith.[48]

His writings on Islam were more extensive than those on Judaism, including: *On War against the Turk* (*Vom Kriege wide der Türken*, 1528), *Army Sermon against the Turk* (*Eine Heerpredigt widder der Türken*, 1529), and a German translation of Ricoldus de Montecrucis's (1242–1320) *Refutation of the Qur'an* (Latin: *Confutatio Alcorani c.*1300; German: *Verlegung des Alcoran*, 1542). He described what he knew about the Turks, which he equated to Islam as a whole. In contrast to his attitude towards Judaism which became harsher over time, as his knowledge of Islam grew his earlier harsher polemics softened. Nevertheless, after he had read the Qur'an in 1542 he concurred with most other medieval writers that it was an abominable book, stating: 'what a cursed, shameful, and dreadful book it is, full of lies, fables, and every abomination'.[49] His main criticism was what he saw as lies about God and Christians, particularly in terms of Islamic denial of such things as Jesus' divinity, and he alleged that it is 'the Devil speaking through Muhammad'.[50] But, on the 'Turks' themselves, he had a very dichotomous picture. On the one hand he stated the benefits of Islam, as he saw it, which he said made Turks 'very pious ... abstemious ... [and] faithful, friendly, careful to tell the truth', yet at the same time he claimed that they were also 'depraved' and the 'Devil incarnate' (*der leibhafftige Teuffel*).[51] Luther's ambivalent attitude can be said to be not entirely unrepresentative: Turks were Christians' fiercest enemies, yet for those with some acquaintance with Muslims an admiration for their piety and way of life was often gained. Muslim representations of Christians in wartime situations do not reflect much better.

To return to Napoleon, Muslims started to develop a new attitude with his expedition into Egypt and the rise of Western colonialism. From the early days of Islam until the decline of the Ottomans, the story of Islam had been (to a large degree, or was remembered as) one of expansion, conquest, and victory.[52] Though, where it did not align with imperial power, Islam spread through Sufi itinerant preachers and Muslim traders. Across much of Central Asia and into China, as well as through South East Asia, Islam's spread was largely through peaceful encounters and exchange. Its numbers in these territories attest to its widespread appeal, with Indonesia today being the most populous Muslim nation in the world. However, the rise of Western colonialism brought a new period of Islamic self-doubt. Why was it that they, once mighty and advanced, now declined? Why was poverty and lack of learning perceived as typical of Islamic societies? Why did the once backward and weak Christians now represent progress, learning and both economic and military power? This perception, found on both sides of the encounter, led to a dynamic of polarizing views. The history of the crusades, with the motif of the European Christian as an inherently hostile aggressor, shaped Islamic views of Christians, entangled with bitterness in struggles against colonialism and regret at the lost golden days of Islamic glory. Meanwhile, the Muslim as threat and a constant danger to the Christian lurked within the mind of Western Christians, as well as later secular Europeans. A patronizing and dismissive view of Islam was also often reflected in this, as the sorry state of contemporary Muslim societies was read into history and ideology as the inherent state of what Islam would lead to.

This is not to say that other attitudes did not exist. Despite the decline of Islamic power, in the late nineteenth and early twentieth centuries when Christian (mainly Protestant) missionaries believed in the 'evangelisation of the world in this generation' (i.e. that an almost total conversion of the world to Christianity was within their grasp), Islam was still held to be the greatest 'spiritual' threat facing them, with other religious traditions often being seen as spent forces.[53] Likewise, Muslims perceived Christians as the chief threat against which they needed to defend their tradition, although secularism became seen increasingly as an equal foe for many (though, for some Muslims, secularism has been seen as beneficial).[54] Again, as the modern study of religion developed, an increasing number of Christian scholars became enamoured of the charms and power of Islam. Through the early twentieth century and beyond, figures such as Louis Massignon (1883–1962), Kenneth Cragg (1913–2012), and Huston Smith (1919–2016) became sympathetic interpreters of Islam to a Western, and often Christian, audience. A role taken up more recently by John Esposito and Karen Armstrong.

Some notable Muslim converts in Western contexts can also be noted, showing that in very recent times Islam per se was quite socially acceptable and not threatening in certain contexts. Among these is Alexander Russell Webb (1846–1916), the first prominent American convert to Islam in 1888. His conversion came while he served as the US Consular Representative in the Philippines where he had been appointed in 1887 by President Cleveland. He was the only Muslim speaker at the Parliament of the World's Religions (1893). Other notable Muslim converts have included Mohammad Ali (formerly Cassius Clay, 1942–2016), Yusuf Islam (professionally known as Cat Stevens), Vinnie Paz (Vincenzo Luvineri), Mike Tyson, and Timothy Winter (also known as Abdul Hakim Musad).

The contemporary legacy of Christian–Muslim encounters

Today, among mainstream Muslims and Christians, we are more likely to see dialogue and appreciation rather than antagonism and hostility. Discussions in dialogue of such things as the position of Jesus are widespread.[55] However, it would be wrong to suggest that fear and animosity have been left behind. Moreover, more widely in the societies where these traditions have long been traditionally embedded, memories, and fears of each other often do more than linger and can break into violence. We discuss this further in Chapter 7, but it is worth noting how the legacy discussed here remains by picking out three motifs: crusades, Europe, and imagination.

The motif of the crusades has been a recurring theme. The term is a reading back onto history to classify and term a whole range of wars by that name. As Christian military expeditions, moreover, crusades were not simply against Muslims but were also launched against those perceived as heretical Christians in Europe. On the Christian side, though, they have become part of an imagined battle with what is seen as an Islamic world threatening Christian Europe, and so the need for a crusade may be seen as justified. For Muslims, however, the notion of the Christian West as the aggressor savagely seeking to attack, even destroy, Islam has become potent. As such, events like the 'war on terror' have been seen by some Muslims, in as far as it primarily involved Christian majority/heritage nations attacking Muslim majority nations, as part of a pattern of crusading aggression against them.

Our identities are primarily claimed not by who or what we are but by what we define ourselves against. Europe is a case in point. How we now envision Europe is a creation defined in large part against Islam. Europe has never been Christian, indeed, for hundreds of years, Muslims have been majority or significant populations in many parts of it. There have been resident Muslim populations and mosques in Poland since the sixteenth century, across the Balkans Muslims have been present for hundreds of years, were a significant presence in Spain and Portugal for around 800 years, and as occasional traders and settlers the Muslim presence has been known in virtually every part of Europe. Indeed, the common imaginary of Europe stemming from Greco-Roman roots ignores the fact that the Greeks saw the European mainland as barbaric and looked to Persia, India, or Africa as cultural centres, while the legacy of science and learning from the classical world was mediated and passed back only as it had been substantially enhanced through centuries of advances by Muslims. Europe, whether as an idea or cultural concept, is reliant and indebted greatly to Muslims.

The third point is inherent in the previous two, for it is in how we imagine such things as the crusades and Europe that they have their power. Imagination is core to the discourse of both these concepts: Muslims and Christians remember the other as the aggressor and themselves acting in (self-)defence in the crusades. Whatever the facts – and questions arise as to how we would establish them – how events are remembered, and therefore imagined, is far more pertinent to their role in influencing relations between Muslims and Christians. Developing from this here, though it is pertinent throughout this book, such encounters (Christian–Muslim, Jewish–Muslim, etc.) rarely, even never, happen in isolation. There is normally another (imagined) party in these encounters. The relationship to this other is never static, for it is variously imagined, and so operates as what may be termed a 'shifting third'. Typically, in Christian–Muslim relations either, or both, Judaism or secularism has been part of the imaginary which relates to how each envisages, and interacts with, the other party. (Naming this as a 'shifting third' is not a numerical signifier, for there may be multiple other parties in such relationships.) This will also be involved in the wider nexus, such that, today, a perceived secular Europe may affect how Muslims and Christians relate to each other in, for example, Germany or the Netherlands. We will not expand on this here, but we need to be aware that Muslims and Christians have never met in a vacuum.[56]

Two-way attitudes and perceptions

Identity theory can help us understand the shaping of historical perceptions. We have focused very much upon a particular context, that of Europe and the relationship with Muslims across MENA. This is not to suggest that this is the only or most significant relationship or encounter between Muslims and Christians. Across the Eurasian landmass and out to China, Muslims and Christians have over the course of almost 1500 years had many and varying interactions. Moreover, encounters have occurred in such places as Indonesia and across Africa. However, for geopolitical reasons the shaping of identity and prejudice in the context discussed here has become an aspect of the global relationship in the contemporary period. Each has envisaged the other as an aggressive adversary. 'The Turk', 'the Saracen', and 'the Arab' as stereotypical tropes have become embedded in Christian minds, while 'the crusader' is a stereotypical trope in Muslim minds.

CHAPTER FIVE

Religious hatred as racial hatred: Enlightenment, citizenship, and racialization

Introduction

Today, when prejudice is discussed, people may think of racism against 'Blacks',[1] 'Chinese', 'South Asians', or others. This may seem distinct from antisemitism and Islamophobia if these are understood as 'religious' and not 'racial' prejudices. However, as prejudices, they share common aspects, and although some resist classifying racism, antisemitism, and Islamophobia together, racialization as a process elucidates them all.[2] Moreover, both antisemitism and Islamophobia have been racialized in the modern world, with older religiously based prejudice giving way to, or fusing with, racist narratives. Here, we will focus on Jews (on Muslims, see Chapter 8). Four further important notes can be made before we begin: first, racism is often credited to the Enlightenment[3] but has roots in early modernity;[4] second, racialization is not a novel modern Western innovation (even if modern racism is) as it is based in patterns of prejudice found historically and globally; third, claims that race is a scientific category are unfounded and come from misperceptions developing since the late eighteenth century; fourth, we will see that racism and prejudice are malleable and intersectional with categorizations often fusing ethnic/racial, national, conceptual/ideological, and religious markers.

Race, racism, racialization

Race and racism, while separable for analytic purposes, are deeply entwined; categories of race lead into racism, and racism needs race. But race is a fiction, a socially constructed category:[5] skin colour, often a marker of 'race', is based on melatonin in skin pigmentation and demonstrates no fundamental difference between humans, but can be remarkably persistent as a perceived marker.[6] The standard differentiation of species in biology is the possibility of breeding across the species, making humans clearly one species; race as a subspecies is also demonstrably wrong,[7] partly because all humans are 99.9 per cent genetically identical.[8] Meanwhile, tracing genetic descent has shown that people who appear 'white' may hold considerable African ancestry, normally indicative of being 'Black'.[9] The fact that the supposed differentiator does not exist does not make prejudice any less real: 'Prejudice is a complex subjective state in which feelings of difference play the leading part, even if the differences are imaginary.'[10] Furthermore, Gordon Allport (1897–1967) reminds us that the use of an ' "enemy race" … is especially serviceable' for demagogues 'who wish to unite their followers' because it provides a 'common enemy' but is also 'vague'.[11] Race is a powerful social reality, therefore Ibram Kendi remarks: 'I still identify as Black. Not because I believe Blackness, or race, is a meaningful scientific category but because our societies, our policies, our ideas, our histories, and our cultures have rendered race and made it matter.'[12]

Allport's notion of stereotypes helps explain the imagination of race and the simplicity of thinking that all Jews, all Blacks, all Muslims, all white people, and so on can be readily grouped together, and is why this device readily supports discrimination.[13] But what accounts for it? Kendi argues that it does not come naturally to the human mind,[14] and in one sense this is true, with evidence showing that young children play happily with others with no regard to racial markers and would seem to learn racism.[15] However, in-group and out-group formation are natural to the human mind. Moreover, racism per se is also not simply a European product but has been present in China, India, and Japan for centuries,[16] while occidentalism exists as much as Edward Said's (1935–2003) orientalism.[17] However, as discussed below, the current standard markers of race only attained their current form in the last few centuries in a lineage stemming from Europe. Importantly, the signifiers of race, or ethnicity – an equally problematic term[18] – have changed: who gets to count as 'Black' or 'white' varies. Therefore, we will discuss 'racialization' to discuss the processes by which 'race' is ascribed onto particular groups,[19] though such markers are not only ascribed but are sometimes claimed by the in-group as 'self-racialisation'.[20] Racialization helps us see that race, ethnic groups, or religious identities are largely processual and contextual in their ascriptions, not fixed distinct markers of agency and identities, and so fit within what Rogers Brubaker terms 'groupism'.[21]

Indeed, insider claims of distinct identities are often matters of disputation, for example, who counts as a 'Jew' is about boundary marking and is policed by various 'authorities'.[22]

Kendi argues that we cannot have 'non-racist' policies, ideas, or people, only racist or anti-racist ones.[23] As we may read his argument, adding our own lens on identity and prejudice theory, it is part and parcel of being human that we form in-groups and out-groups, and so all our thinking will be bound up within systems informed by othering. It is necessary, therefore, to seek to actively counter racism and prejudice. Therefore, something which presents itself as neutral or simply 'non-racist' may be part of such a system, though we may ask whether such an attitude may enforce unnecessary polarization?[24] Nevertheless, a question raised is what does this mean for the study of racism: is this book racist or anti-racist, if it cannot simply be 'non-racist'? Certainly we find that a systemic racism underlines many aspects of our world, with criminologist Biko Agozino noting that, in the UK, the vast majority of Black women in jail are there for a single crime: possession of marijuana, something which white women are not typically imprisoned for.[25] We could therefore argue that the criminal justice system is itself racist, requiring anti-racist readjustment. The study of racism in relation to antisemitism and Islamophobia therefore alerts us that the question may not be whether something is antisemitic or Islamophobic, or not antisemitic or Islamophobic, but whether it promotes/contains these prejudices or is 'anti' these prejudices. Processes of racialization and prejudice may be built into systems and need to be fought against if we wish to overcome them.[26]

The foundations of race and racism

Discussing the foundations of modern, pseudo-scientific racism may invoke a chicken and egg conundrum: which came first: race or racism? But Francisco Bethencourt convincingly argues that the answer is racism: systems of prejudice against certain groups had been in operation for centuries before these were codified as races.[27] Race became a way of making sense of differences and perceived existing out-groups, whereby 'The visible point of physical difference is made a magnet for all sorts of imaginary ascriptions.'[28] Spain and Portugal are central in the story of the creation of race for two reasons. One is the 'European discovery' of the 'New World' around the sixteenth century where race became central for differentiation. The other was the ideological linking of purity to blood. In 1449, in Toledo, Jews who had converted to Christianity ('conversos' or 'New Christians', sometimes 'morranos') were barred from holding public office under a series of statutes named *limpieza de sangre* (purity of blood). The 1492 conquest of the Kingdom of Granada by Queen Isabella (1451–1504) and King Ferdinand (1452–1516) saw Jews and Muslims banished or forcibly converted to Christianity across Spain. However, conversion did not bring these former Jews or former Muslims ('moriscos') into the Christian mainstream, as they were considered liable to backslide into Judaism or Islam.[29] Jewish or Muslim descent was seen as an impurity that lingered through generations. Conversion alone could not erase the tendency to revert to the former religion, and this seems linked to later thinking about specific 'racial types'. Key in this is Carl Linnaeus (1707–1778), who classified animal species in his *Systema Naturae* (1735), including a hierarchical ranking of the human 'races' as white, yellow, red, and Black.[30] Immanuel Kant (1724–1804) and David Hume (1711–1776), among others, made similar, but differing, hierarchies, with the former asserting that the white race 'contains all incentives and talents in itself', the 'Hindus' finally 'acquire culture in the highest degree, but only in the arts and not in the sciences. They never raise it up to abstract concepts,' while the 'Negro race … acquire[s] culture', but only a culture of slaves; that is, they allow themselves to be trained', though he seemingly repudiated such views in his final work.[31] However, such ranking systems almost invariably saw the 'white race' as the highest, with the 'Black race' at the bottom. While, today, especially in the United States, this differentiation is often simplified to 'Black' and 'white', 'colourism' theory stresses that the perceived darkness or lightness of skin tone remains important.[32] But across many parts of the world, European colonial regimes created 'races' and ascribed characteristics to them for the benefit and legitimization of their ventures.[33]

This systemization came before Charles Darwin's (1809–1882) theories of evolution which, like modern technologies of genetics and DNA testing, suggest that we share, if not a single common heritage,[34] then species identity. However, evolution did not lead to the disappearance of racism and instead was used to justify notions about the evolution of the supposed 'races', which sometimes led to eugenics programmes. Notably, not only does contemporary science not support the ideology of human races, it even challenges the distinctiveness of *Homo sapiens* as a species. What separates us distinctly from the other higher primates is unclear, and the designation of humans as the third chimpanzee sets our species alongside chimpanzees and bonobos.[35]

In the nineteenth century, aspects of pseudo-science such as craniological measurements supposedly showed how different skull structures indicated both 'human races' and their respective intelligence levels. Claims of differing intelligence remain part of racist ideology, often tied to perceptions of superior morality and a higher civilization, with 'biological' or 'scientific racism' naming these delegitimated claims.[36] Especially in the United States, studies showed that 'Blacks' had lower IQ levels than 'whites'; however, differences in socio-economic status and access to education were generally not factored into the results. Indeed, recent studies showing the differences in IQ narrowing significantly strongly indicate that the differences are environmental and not innate, but the debate still has traction in some circles.[37]

Christianity and commerce as markers of 'Black' and 'white'

Biblical interpretation has been another resource used to justify racism. Those racialized as 'Black' have been regarded as descendants of Noah's son Ham.[38] This claim, tied to white supremacist narratives, was used to justify the slave trade, legitimize the KKK, and in South Africa to support apartheid.[39] This leads us to consider the extent to which race is actually a religious marker. This may seem counter-intuitive: surely race is about scientific, ideological, or political claims. However, the markers of whiteness and Christianity often go hand-in-hand: 'Historically and conceptually, there is no cordon sanitaire between history, culture, nationality, ethnicity, and race. Race is a motley crew, and that motley crew includes religion. Religion is constitutive of race.'[40]

Returning to the Iberian Peninsula, only those classified as Spanish-blood Christians were seen as pure Christians. Before this, race was not tied to Christianity. During the crusades, medieval Christendom longed for the mythical Prester John, a powerful Christian king believed to live beyond Muslim lands, to come and save them. Often envisaged in India, later myths saw him based in Ethiopia or elsewhere in Africa: the saviour Christian could therefore be 'Black'. In traditional iconography of the Three Kings/ Magi, one was always portrayed as Black, as images of power, wealth, and royalty were associated with Black skin. However, the Spanish Reconquista and the Spanish voyages of exploration which followed found once mighty African kingdoms in decline. With the systematization of the African slave trade, the notion of Black skin lost its positive connotations in Europe and became associated with poverty, degeneration, and inferiority. Religion was sometimes claimed as the answer to perceived racial differences, with Christianity becoming associated with Europe, whiteness, and civilization. Many argued that in South America, as in Africa, the indigenous people were destined for slavery and fit only for servitude to Europeans; whether they were even fully human was itself a debate. But Christianity was also a counter-hegemonic force, with figures such as the friar Antonio Montesinos (1475–1540) arguing that the indigenous peoples of South America were fully human and could be Christianized. As such, the religious card could be played two ways: to promote or resist discrimination and prejudice towards non-Europeans ('non-whites').

By the eighteenth century, it was well established that various races were innately inferior. Therefore, even if Black African slaves could be converted to Christianity, they remained inferior following the blood-lineage logic. While some argue this was a process led by elite intellectual ideologues, rather racial ideology systematized an already hegemonic world view that had been driven by commercial interests. The development of ideology and practice is entwined, with the ideology of 'racial regimes' sanctioning the political and economic privilege of existing elites at the expense of subalterns.[41] Perceptions of race, civilization, and religion were also tied into these systems, with religion often seen as part of a hierarchy that matched racialized categories. Some religions were seen as the 'highest' (i.e. Christianity) or 'lowest' (i.e. polytheistic or animist beliefs) with a hierarchical range in between. As Tomoko Masuzawa makes clear, what counted as a 'world religion' was fluid and could fit the prejudices and presuppositions of the classifier. Nevertheless, it would be wrong to see a too tight connection between the discourse of race and religion, and the influential scholar of religion Friedrich Max Müller (1823–1900) rejected race as a scientific category, because as a philologist it made no sense in terms of the families of language he encountered.[42]

To note some ways that race, whiteness, and religion were connected, we can note the Irish who came to North America as indentured serfs. While legally distinct from Black slaves, their situation was in many ways materially and socially indistinguishable. They were tied to landowners, indebted, and forced to work. It has therefore been argued that they were in effect 'Black'. The stigmatization of the Irish is nothing new, with the Statute of Killenny (1336) forbidding the cohabitation or marriage of English and Irish lest English habits 'degenerated' towards the Irish model.[43] However, it is argued that the Irish were made 'white' in the period when African slaves came to America, as part of a divide and rule policy, so that they would not find a natural alliance with the Africans as fellow oppressed workers but would see themselves as sided with the landowners as fellow 'whites'. Nevertheless, the US Naturalization Law of 1790 which gave naturalization rights to 'free white persons' still meant that certain 'whites'/Caucasians, such as the Irish and Italians, were not as readily accepted as were Anglo-Saxons.[44] This partly reflected not only Protestant–Catholic prejudices but also intra-white racism, with Germans also prejudiced against. Some Caucasian Christians were perceived as 'free white persons' more readily than other Caucasian Christians. Such prejudice applied also to Jews and Muslims, though where they fitted into the schemata of race and religion varied contextually.

Philosophy and the myth of white European civilization

Hume asserted that

> I am apt to suspect the negroes to be naturally inferior to the whites. There scarcely ever was a civilized nation of that complexion. ... On the other hand, the most rude and barbarous of the whites ... still have something eminent about them, in their valour, form of government, or some other particular.[45]

His claim signifies a pivot of worldview that occurred around this time. Today, we find it normal to imagine (erroneously) that 'Western civilization' developed in an unbroken chain from the ancient Greeks and Romans, through to the Renaissance and Enlightenment, and to us today. At most, some who hold to such an (outdated) narrative may concede that during the 'Dark Ages' the learning of classical antiquity was preserved by the Islamic world. In this perspective, civilization, science, democracy, human rights, the arts, and so on are the possession and invention of a white, European lineage standing as a shining beacon in a world of darkness (light/white and dark/Black being linked). It is a view that is almost entirely wrong and marked by a historical and geographical myopia.

Prior to the eighteenth century, Europeans saw philosophy originating, variously, in the Middle East, South Asia, or Africa.[46] The Greeks, despite portraying themselves as *the* civilized people, were aware of their debts to Persia, India, and Egypt. However, in the Enlightenment, a new genealogy of philosophy was imagined: Greece was the foundation with a direct lineage to modern Europe. Philosophy became solely white and Western, with non-Europeans written out or invisibilized.[47] For instance, Latinized/Anglicized names are used for Ibn Sina (980–1037, Avicenna) and Ibn Rushd (1126–1198, Averroes). Yet the Enlightenment was global. Knowledge from China was passed back by Jesuit emissaries, and it was often seen by Europeans as a superior civilization. The philosopher Gottfried Leibniz (1646–1716) claimed that Emperor Kangxi (1654–1722) was the greatest living prince, and figures such as Voltaire (1694–1778) looked with some awe upon Confucianism and Buddhism as humanistic moral systems devoid of a deity. Philosophy, here, is just taken as an example, but almost universally the European debt to the rest of the world (in science, the arts, etc.) was hidden, dismissed, distorted, or simply forgotten.[48]

The timing of this world view pivot is not accidental. Up until the late eighteenth century, but really until the nineteenth century, Europe remained the poor cousin on the global scene: the so-called twelfth-century Renaissance in Europe was spurred by the culturally superior Islamic presence in Al-Andalusia, while the later European Renaissance of the fifteenth to sixteenth centuries happened first in the trading cities of Italy because of direct trading routes with the Islamic world and beyond. Advances in astronomy, including the work of Copernicus (1473–1543) and Galileo Galilei (1564–1642), were possible only because of the imports of superior Ottoman optical lenses. Indeed, the supposedly ground-breaking astronomical observations of Tycho Brahe (1546–1601) had been surpassed around fifty years earlier by Taqi al-Din Muhammad ibn Ma'ruf (1526–1585), a Muslim astronomer and mathematician from the Ottoman Empire. Yet, in science textbooks, Copernicus, Brahe, and Galileo, not Taqi al-Din, are included. This is merely indicative. The medical textbook of Ibn Sina, the *Canon of Medicine* (1025), was used in Europe until the eighteenth century. Indeed, before the nineteenth century, most of the European colonial ventures in Asia were small coastal trading posts entirely dependent upon the goodwill of local rulers. The case of the Dutch in Japan, where they retained a limited presence on the island of Dejima and were not allowed inland by order of the Shogun, was typical. While the Dutch managed to control the nutmeg trade from Southeast Asia, at the height of European colonial power, European countries only accounted for around 10 per cent of the spice trade in South India.[49] Much of Asia, Africa, and the Middle East had been an interconnected trading and cultural region for centuries before the Europeans supposedly 'opened up' these routes. Europe's marginal presence before this period has been forgotten, as have the dynamics that saw it expand and grow in power: gold coming into Spain and Portugal from South America, conquered primarily by Eurasian diseases with death rates often over 50 per cent within a few years of contact; the ongoing collapse of the Mughal Empire in India allowing gradual British incursions; and silver from British mercantile opium trade in the Chinese empire. The details of Europe's rise from the bottom to the top need not detain us.[50] However, they are key in understanding the imaginary claims of white racial supremacy, and how Europeans and their heirs, including Americans, have constructed their place in the world. They also have ongoing consequences today in terms of global economic imbalances and the relative inequality/ impoverishment experienced by minority groups in Western nations.[51]

Jews and Enlightenment citizenship, nationhood, and race

The foregoing survey of the development and ideology of race and racism may seem to take us some way from antisemitism and Islamophobia; however, they provide the mechanism by which these prejudices become expressed in the modern period. Here, as noted, we focus upon Jews as they were the quintessential internal outsider.

The Enlightenment is the period in which Europe moved from primarily being composed of feudal monarchies into modern nation states. This saw the transformation of subjects into citizens. These dynamics deserve our particular attention in terms of five spheres: the differentiation of secularism and religion; the birth of the nation state; citizenship; rights and freedom of belief; and public life.

However, first it is necessary to consider the ideological transformations of Jews in this period.[52] David Nirenberg sees the philosophers of the Enlightenment translating 'Christian ideas about Jewish error and irrationality into secular terms', noting Benedict Spinoza (1632–1677) as one example for whom the Hebrew Bible represented the pre-eminent example of blind faith, dogmatism, and irrationality.[53] In John Locke's (1632–1704) *Letter Concerning Toleration* (1685), intolerance was exemplified by Jewish law, with intolerance transcended by Christian freedom from the law (hark-ing back to readings of Paul via Luther), an interpretation also found in Voltaire (1694–1778) and Kant. Therefore, while the Enlightenment was foundational for modern conceptions of religious liberty, citizenship, and equality, and saw equal rights given to Jews, and in figures such as Moses Mendelsohn (1729–1786) Jews found the opportunity to partake in its intel-lectual life, this revolution was also based in paradigmatic polemics against Judaism. Indeed, Nirenberg suggests the Enlightenment retained aspects of Augustine's antisemitism.

Returning to our five dynamics, first, secularism entails the separation of the mechanics of the state from the hands of religious institutions, which meant primarily the Christian churches; though the conception of secular-ism can mean far more than this, with simple distinctions between public/secular and private/religious distorting complex and contested realities.[54] In principle, if not in practice, a secular state does not legislate on the accept-able religion of its citizens. Hence, whether a citizen is Catholic, Protestant, Muslim, Jewish, or Buddhist is not the concern of the state per se. However, Judaism was contentious and moved between being a marker of ethnicity/race, nationality, religion, and concept/ideology.

Second, stemming from the Treaty of Westphalia (1648), we see a new conception of what a country is: the nation state. To simplify contrary and changing dynamics, this period saw a move from absolute monarchies into constitutional monarchies and the growth of republics, with newly formed strict and bounded borders. Nationalism was also asserted against imperial-ism, and national autonomy was often linked to racial/ethnic lineages as a natural right. For instance, when the Greeks rebelled against the Ottoman Empire, the notion was that the Greek people deserved a nation as a right. However, 'lesser races' were often deemed incapable of governing themselves (or to need tutelage before they would be ready), justifying European impe-rialism.[55] The notion of ethnic groups as national groupings also affected Judaism, as the Jewish people were sometimes called a nation, and it was asked if a nation could exist inside another nation, with suggestions that Jews were inherently disloyal or unassimilable.

Third, while citizenship was the status of those within nation states it was not, at first, universal. In the French Revolution, women and slaves were not enfranchised, and only in 1792 were the poor; however, Jews were the most contentious category. If citizens needed to be free and active participants engaged with the new law and constitution and not simply subservient to legal restrictions, it was asked whether 'all humans were capable by nature of achieving this conversion'.[56] If Judaism exemplified obedience to the law, in contrast to Christian freedom, then could 'the Jewish type' be a real citi-zen? Speaking of the way Edmund Burke (1729–1797) applied 'Judaism' even to non-Jews who exemplified such perceived traits, Nirenberg reminds us that conceptions of human freedom, social relations, and our relation to the law were issues 'two millennia of pedagogy had taught Europe to ask in terms of "Judaism"'.[57] In France, from September 1791 Jews were emancipated, but often remained excluded socially. Judaism could be both an ethnicity and a conceptual marker.

Fourth, what later became enshrined in human rights legislation as freedom of religion and belief (FoRB) was a key Enlightenment concern. In the United States, a foundational principle is that government shall not legislate for an established religion. Many of the Pilgrim Fathers were Protestant dissenters fleeing persecution from the established (Anglican) Church of England, but their toleration did not extend beyond Protestants. Catholics and Jews were initially not tolerated in New England.[58] Thomas Jefferson's (1743–1826) plea for Jewish toleration was an exception in the early period. Furthermore, the traditions of indigenous Americans were excluded, as the 'superstition' of 'savages', from protection under FoRB until 1978.[59] Religion, civilization, and race were often conflated.[60] Here, Judaism was a religion but not an acceptable one.

Fifth, the proof of the pudding is in the eating. As such, we need to look at the entry of Jews, alongside Catholics, into the various spheres (politics, law, universities, military) from which they had long been excluded. A few indicative examples are chosen here. In the UK, the first Jewish MP, Lionel de Rothschild (1808–1879), was elected in 1847 but could not sit in the House of Commons until 1858 as doing so required a Christian oath before then. Later, Benjamin Disraeli (1804–1881), of Jewish descent, became prime minister in 1874, yet despite having been baptised as an Anglican as an infant and having been an MP since 1837, he still faced accusations from his great rival William Gladstone (1809–1898) about his character based on antisemitic stereotypes. The 1871 Universities Tests Act allowed those of any religion to become members of the universities (meaning Oxford, Cambridge, and Durham), whereas previously they were closed to non-Anglicans, though people of all religions were previously admitted to University College London, founded (1826) as a secular institution, while St David's College (SDC), Lampeter, a Welsh institution founded in 1822, had no religious test according to its 1828 Royal Charter.[61] Only in the late nineteenth century could Jews be commissioned as officers in the armed forces.

In the United States, Jews technically had legal equality through such laws as the Plantation Act (1740), the Virginia Act (1785), and the First Amendment (1791) to the US Constitution (1789). Article IV of the Constitution abolished any religious test as a qualification for office, but restrictions against Jews (and Christian dissenters) continued in Maryland until 1826 and North Carolina until 1868. In New Hampshire, no non-Protestants could hold office until 1877. Only in a 1940 Supreme Court ruling was it stated that the First Amendment applied equally to federal government positions. In terms of entry of Jews into the legal profession, Louis Brandeis (1856–1941), a Jewish lawyer, entered Harvard law school in 1875, and in 1916 became the first Jewish Supreme Court Justice. Canada meanwhile issued an Emancipation Act in 1832, following a case in 1804 when a Jewish member was elected in Quebec but was later debarred from office for not saying the Christian oath.

It was not always a one-way street of increasing emancipation, however, and while French conquests under Napoleon brought some equality for Jews across much of Europe, this was later reversed. This reversal occurred in 1815 in Germany. A German Jew, Gabriel Reisser, during the 1820s, tried and failed to get a university lectureship in jurisprudence and was banned from practice as a notary in Hamburg.[62] Jews were restricted by law from holding administrative and juridical positions until 1869, and full emancipation only came across the German empire in 1871. However, Jews often faced de facto exclusion even if not de jure exclusion. For example, Jews were systematically failed at the Emory University dental school in the 1950s and 1960s by an antisemitic leadership.[63]

While the new notion of the nation state provided Jews with the possibility of entry into modern society as equal citizens, no longer stigmatized as the religious outsider, two major factors prevented their full emancipation. First, the representation of Judaism as an ideology meant that they were normally the primary other which was negatively portrayed as the opponent of modernity, secularism, reason, and the new freedom of citizenship. Second, there was a sense that Jews remained 'a nation apart', so they were ethnically excluded as not being part of the primary populace. Moreover, while recognized as human, questions still remained as to whether they could be fully integrated; was 'the Jew' some form of 'brute beast', like 'the Black', who was incapable of being fully integrated into society? Legally, they were normally accepted as capable of inclusion, but socially we often find a different story.

We have noted the history of Jews and Catholics being legally or socially excluded from society, though the matrix may be Jews and Muslims, or all three groups, or others including Blacks, LGBTQI people, Asians, and so on. This exemplifies the intersectional nature of hatred. As Frantz Fanon (1925–1961) reported being told by his philosophy teacher in Martinique: 'Whenever you hear anyone abuse the Jews, pay attention, because he is talking about you.'[64] Furthermore there may, perhaps, be a hierarchy of prejudice, and some former victims of prejudice may become part of an alliance against another minority. However, Fanon's words alert us to be wary; occasionally, in fourteenth-century Aragon, Muslims would join Christians in attacks on Jews, but this did not mean that Muslims became an accepted group.

In the United States, some theorize that because Jews were excluded from elite universities and a number of elite professions in the early twentieth century, they were not regarded as 'white'.[65] Skin colour is not an absolute marker of 'race'; however, the notion of Jews as 'Black' perhaps reflects the way that US race relations have fixated on Black–white lines. In Linnaeus and others, a much wider range of racial markers existed, with the Semitic language group often seen as a distinct ethnic/racial marker. Nevertheless,

Ansel Brown has spoken about what he sees as 'profound' commonalities in the experience of the African diaspora and the Jewish people as both were enslaved, exiled, and fought for their freedom.[66] Their experience is certainly not identical, with – in at least the early twentieth century – Blacks being legally and explicitly barred from various parts of society, while for Jews it was often implicit. So, for instance, a golf club with no Jewish members often meant they were not welcome, rather than banned from joining.[67] Furthermore, many Blacks experienced Jews as 'white' oppressors,[68] and Jews do not today face the dangers that particularly young Black Americans do (at least if they remove the markers of their Jewishness). This highlights how racialized identities are contextual, and Jews in the same country, in the same period, even in the same city could be sometimes 'white' and sometimes 'not-white'.

The nineteenth-century Jewish question: Pathologies, pogroms, and protocols

The nineteenth-century pogroms and repression that Jews in Eastern Europe and Russia faced were often associated with traditional Christian prejudice, though sometimes they were economically motivated as some Jews were used as tax collectors by nobles and so were severely resented. Nevertheless, the vast majority of Jews lived in relative poverty in the Shtetl, small village communities, made famous in depictions such as *Fiddler on the Roof*.[69] The pogroms and repression raised tensions across Western Europe and in the United States, as vast numbers of poor, unskilled, and culturally distinct Jews from the Ashkenazi communities of Eastern Europe migrated en masse to these areas, further raising questions about whether Jews could actually integrate into Western liberal democracies: the so-called 'Jewish Question'. Indeed, those Jews now enculturated into Western Europe were often equally prejudiced towards those they saw as their uncouth co-religionists with whom they shared little, showing an internal prejudice arguably akin to colourism. The Jew as impoverished, unskilled, and unassimilable migrant was therefore one image of the late nineteenth and early twentieth centuries.

But, with emancipation, 'The success of [some of] the Jews [sic] was undeniable, particularly in finance and the liberal professions, although many of their artisans (the majority of the community) were [negatively] affected … by the Industrial Revolution.'[70] Resistance, resentment, and pogroms were not unusual as this once oppressed group became another challenger in the marketplace, with traditional Christian prejudices justifying hostilities. One notorious instance in France was the Dreyfus Affair. Alfred Dreyfus (1859–1935) was an exceptionally talented young artillery officer who had risen rapidly to the rank of captain and entered the army's General Staff but was falsely accused of spying for the Germans. The media excoriated him, partly for his Jewish background, but his origins in Alsace – near the French–German border – also played into this. A huge public outcry arose, with some backing him – including major figures of French intellectual life such as Émile Zola (1840–1902) and Georges Clémenceau (1841–1929) – but public opinion generally was deeply suspicious of Dreyfus. The courts at first also ruled against him, and he was imprisoned on Devil's Island from 1855 to 1859. However, it became undeniable that the allegation was malicious with no supporting evidence.

Dreyfus's case is widely discussed as just antisemitic, with crowds protesting against Dreyfus shouting 'down with Judas', but the situation seems more complex. His Alsatian background remained one factor in his vilification, with the tension between Jews having an 'ideological status as aliens' yet also having a 'legal status as citizens' playing into the issue.[71] Others have noted that a wider collection of groups were often stigmatized together including

> Jews, women, primitive peoples, proletarians, the insane, and mass culture, constituting a cultural matrix in which specific threats were conceptualized with reference to the others. Based upon tacit concerns about race, gender, sexuality, class and disease, this cultural imaginary pervaded fin-de-siècle society and framed many of the polemics of the Dreyfus Affair.[72]

We see again an intersectional prejudice. Moreover, pseudo-scientific and medicalized taxonomies were used by both Dreyfus's detractors and supporters, some treating Jewishness as a pathology, others speaking of the 'contagion' or 'social disease which is anti-Semitism'.[73] This raises the question of how Jews (and other outsiders) were, and are, represented, with tropes of pathology and disease.

One key addition to antisemitism in this era is manifested in the notorious *The Protocols of the Elders of Zion*.[74] The notion of a vast Jewish conspiracy to control not only the financial markets but also global governments seemingly began as the plot of a novel.[75] However, in due course, the fictional story of the secret meeting plotting this global takeover started to circulate on its own. It gave life to new versions of tropes and developed alongside contemporary prejudices. For instance, in 1879 Wilhelm Marr (1819–1904) published a lengthy pamphlet suggesting the connection of Jews with finance and portraying them as exploiters of the common people, entitled *Der Sieg Judenthums über das Germanenthums* (*The Way of Judaism over Germanicism*). He is credited with coining the term antisemitism. In the *Protocols*, Jews are not just avaricious and driven by greed, but 'the Jew' is the controller of world finance, the ultimate banker. Moreover, Jews become the mastermind behind the global stage, the puppet master pulling the strings to which politicians and world affairs dance.[76] The exact origins of the story are debated – either France or Russia – but it was soon circulating widely throughout Europe in various guises and versions. Debunked and shown to be a fiction, it nevertheless still has a great following today among antisemites. This text developed from stereotypes of the Jew as moneylender and fed into the discourse associating Jews with capitalism but expanded into conspiracy theories of global domination that would allow Jews to become the ultimate enemy.

Nazi ideology, the Aryan race, and the metaphysics of racism

We end this chapter with the racialization of Jews in Nazi ideology and propaganda. Importantly, this is not distinct from what had gone before. But Nazism systematized and radicalized trends developing since the Iberian categorization of blood lineages. Officially, a Jew was a person 'descended from two full Jewish grandparents', and those partially Jewish were termed a '*Mischling*' or mixed race (mestizo) person.[77] But, picking up on earlier trends, Nazi ideology extended Judaism beyond a race to an essence, with Joseph Goebbels's (1897–1945) display of 'degenerate art' including only six artists who were actually Jewish,[78] playing on notions of Judaism polluting society. Indeed, some scholars have argued that this shows that race is not simply an ideological issue but also a metaphysical one.[79] The fear of contagion resides in the ethnicity and the blood. Among white supremacists, there is talk about the one-drop rule, that even one drop of Black or Jewish blood is enough to make somebody 'non-white'. In Nazi terms, this meant that conversion out of Judaism was not enough; in this it drew from the Iberian 'blood lineage' ideology of modern racism. Nazi antisemitism also developed the Enlightenment reinvention of Christian tropes, seeing in Judaism some deeper malaise, and fearing that imagined Jewish cultural forms, ways of thinking, and tendencies could seep into the wider culture. As another example, when news about the genocide started to come to the UK, the House of Lords of the British Parliament observed a few minutes of silence, and the notion of pollution can be seen in Goebbels's reaction to this with these words from his diary: 'Astonishing, how much the English people, above all the upper classes have become Judaized and scarcely have the English character anymore' and have become 'infected'.[80] Purity, therefore, had to be enforced far beyond religious or ethnic borders. It is in these terms that racialized categories become understood as metaphysical as they exert an ontological threat, a threat of being and existence, to the supposed white/Aryan race/culture. But this was not new per se in Nazism.

One figure much cited was Arthur Gobineau (1816–1882), who expounded upon Aryan superiority.[81] Notably, Nazi Aryan Race theory was a distinct strand; it focused upon a white North-Western European ideal, with Adolf Hitler (1889–1945) seeing it exemplified in the Germans,

English, Scandinavians, Dutch, and North Americans (the 'Teutonic peoples'). However, figures such as Müller had a different notion of the Aryan (sometimes Arian), which followed the linguistic families he had traced. The Aryan people were traced, if anywhere, to Central Asia and found a lineage through North Indian Sanskrit roots into Greek, Latin, and then various European languages. It was a linguistic group differing from the Semitic languages, with the ethnolinguistic Aryan of such theory being radically distinct from the imaginary Aryan Race of the Nazis.[82] Furthermore, the Nazi ideology developed previous thought which de-emphasized the religious character of Judaism and stressed the financial aspect, harking back to the legacy of Marr and the *Protocols*. A key theorist in this was Houston Stewart Chamberlain (1855–1927), a Briton who took German nationality during the First World War and had published the book *Die Grundlagen des Neunzehnten Jarhundert* (*Foundations of the Nineteenth Century*, 1899). He believed the Jews were not a pure race and deplored their emancipation. Purity was key for the Nazis and so intermarriage was frowned upon, and it was forbidden for Germans either to marry or have sexual relations with Jews after the 1935 Nuremberg Laws (this was later extended to include Blacks and Romanies). Certainly, Adolf Hitler's (1889–1945) *Mein Kampf* (1925) made heavy use of Chamberlain. For Hitler, as with the *Protocols*, Jews were the main enemy, and one whom it seemed necessary to eradicate from Europe, which also harks back to antisemitism becoming almost a metaphysical principle, as the contagion he imagined was utterly threatening to the existence of Hitler's ideal. Indeed, purity was so central that Hitler's colonial ambitions did not extend to other continents; to preserve the purity of the Teutonic people, their homeland must be founded within the traditional territories of the Aryan people.[83] Hitler's approach moved from boycotts and rhetoric, through segregation, to targeted attacks and eventually the implementation of the Final Solution. Exactly when Hitler's thoughts moved from the removal of the Jews to their extermination is not clear, but Bethencourt sees genocide as fitting the early logic of Hitler's thought, and in 'Nazi Germany', we see 'the most complete case of political application of racial theories'.[84]

In creating the idealized perfect human race it was not just Jews, though, who were killed by the Nazis, with the disabled being targeted, and Romanies also facing genocidal extermination when the opportunity arose.[85] Rarely do we see only one group targeted.

The reach of race-based religious hatred

We typically associate racism with bias based on perceived skin colour, or ethnic markers, but as we have seen it is a far more complex nexus of prejudices and ideologies. While racism may target skin colour, it may be based upon ideologies of purity or blood lineages which can reach metaphysical heights with the very nature of the stigmatized group being seen as an existential threat. This is, arguably, seen today in the title of Douglas Murray's *The Strange Death of Europe* (2017) where the metaphysical racialized threat is transferred to Muslims who are seen to be 'invading' Europe and threatening the imagined white, European civilization.[86] In terms of discrimination, we see shifting patterns of racialization around in-groups and out-groups as socially constructed and malleable categories. Ideal Christians can be 'Black' or 'white', while Jews have been racialized as 'Semitic', 'Black' and 'white', though this risks oversimplifying the complicated nexus of relationships. Elie Wiesel observed that while it often 'begins with the Jews, it doesn't end with the Jews', with racism and prejudice being intersectional, necessitating the need for an intersectional response – perhaps a reason why many Islamophobes and antisemites deride the concept of intersectionality as a liberal mish-mash, for it cuts to the core of ideological racism and its octopus-like tentacles.

INTERLUDE 2

Why did the Holocaust happen?

Introduction

The Western zenith, or nadir, of antisemitism occurred with the Holocaust. As genocide it is discussed in Chapter 2, but here we are concerned with joining the dots, though without giving a single or clear-cut answer as to why it happened. In a context imbued with Christian tradition, antisemitism streamed through the veins of German and European culture. Despite the moves towards citizenship for Jews in the Enlightenment period, antisemitism as racism was still rife. So, we may ask a number of questions. Was the Holocaust simply the end point on a trajectory beginning with Christian antisemitism and racialized modern antisemitism, through earlier pogroms, to this event? Was the Holocaust a rupture, for despite earlier episodes of violence, no attempt to exterminate Jews had been made? Was the Holocaust specific to the German trajectory of antisemitism where, for instance, Luther's invective and Aryan nationalism were crucial aspects? Was it something simmering within the wider Christian–European antisemitic ethos waiting to erupt and events in Germany were simply the catalyst? Was it unique to Adolf Hitler's (1889–1945) ideology and Nazism? We will explore some answers that have been given.

The Holocaust and Germany

Roger Ballard argues that the fact that the apogee of antisemitism can be found in Germany is not coincidental but relates to the German drive towards nationhood as distinct from, for example, the French model. For the Germanic speakers, the goal was not common citizenship – based on something like French laïcité – but a notion of a common racial bond, founded in the German romanticism of the nineteenth century which valorized the myth of their Aryan roots as an Indo-European ethnolinguistic group. Within this ideology, Jews were perceived as the most prominent threat to purity, and following the earlier racial logic stemming from the Iberian Peninsula this meant that the integrity of the German Aryan stock was at risk. With that, what set the Germans apart and justified their unity as a people was imperilled.[1] In this reading, therefore, the Holocaust was distinctive to Germany. Indeed, we may add that Luther's earlier rhetoric, as we have seen, added fuel to the flames. In advocating the burning of synagogues and the Talmud, and chasing Jews from their homes, it may be suggested that what was enacted on Kristallnacht (1938) was nothing other than Lutheranism in practice, and certainly a number of German Lutheran bishops understood it this way.[2] However, while this might justify the expulsion of Jews from Germany, it did not necessarily justify their elimination. Indeed, sometimes the Holocaust was not something that Germans enforced on other Europeans, for those other Europeans enthusiastically partook in its violence. The evidence suggests that from France to Hungary and Poland, locals were very willing to help round up Jews and send them on their way, seemingly with some knowledge of what was happening, and in some cases brutally killed a good number of Jews on their own when they believed they could get away with it.[3] We may therefore posit that we cannot locate the Holocaust in some peculiar Germanic angst: either national identity or a specific Lutheran zeitgeist.

The Holocaust and antisemitism

Then, we may ask, was the Holocaust the result of a European antisemitic fervour that was building up through the ages? David Nirenberg suggests that this is not the case, and having traced the ideological foundations of antisemitism he suggests that 'I do not believe that the history of thought I have attempted to sketch in these pages *determined* why Germany moved from Anti-Semitism to genocide, and other nations did not (setting aside the question of collaboration).'[4] While he specifically focuses on Germany here, and so reinforces that it was not a specific German issue, his work more widely traces Western European thought. What role, then, did the previous two thousand years play? Here, again, I believe that Nirenberg is on the money when he says, 'But I do believe that the Holocaust *was inconceivable and is unexplainable* without that deep history of thought.'[5] We can identify enemies relatively quickly – evolutionary adaptation to ensure human survival means that we can readily respond to threats, and even perceive them when they do not exist – and killing may follow. But the scapegoating of Jews gestated for a long time, with many tropes suggesting their threat and menace to society. Deborah Lipstadt says that it took her many years to link the prejudice she saw as part of her life as a young American Jew with what was enacted by Adolf Eichmann (1906–1962) and others, but once the dots are joined, we see that genocide and a long-seated sentiment of prejudice are not distinct.[6] But this still raises the question of why the Final Solution? Why there and then, as hatred of Jews had existed for a long period. Moreover, ghettoes to segregate Jews would have dealt with any sense of them polluting the surrounding culture; expulsion would also have served that role; pogroms or periodic massacres might satisfy the mimetic desire for a scapegoat as René Girard (1923–2015) postulated. So why genocide?

Planning the Holocaust

The Final Solution was some time in planning and gestation, and is often seen to involve a number of stages: first, legislation, separation, expulsion, or ghettoization; second, concentration and labour camps; finally the stage of killing and genocide; though these were not always chronologically distinct.[7] From the early 1930s, while antisemitism was a cornerstone of Nazi propaganda, there was no indication that genocide of Jews would eventually become their ideology. Notably, Romanies, the disabled, resisting Poles, and others were all at times either majorities in the concentration camps or slated to be killed and wiped out alongside Jews. In terms of planning, Hitler, it seems, even discussed a mass evacuation/expulsion of Jews during the 1930s as he thought about how to solve the Jewish Question that plagued him. At Belsen and other camps, it seems that the plan at first was simply to round Jews up. While there is some indication that the idea had already formed, it was not until 1942 that the Final Solution was put into effect in earnest. Though we may note that a speech by Hitler in 1939 from the Reichstag is often cited where he states that 'the consequences [of an international world war] will be ... the destruction of the Jewish race in Europe'.[8] In enacting the Final Solution, SS paramilitary so-called Death Squads, the *Einsatzgruppen*, were first employed, but it soon became apparent that this was not efficient, and so in Auschwitz and elsewhere the concept of the death camp was employed. Regardless of the mechanics, what impelled this? As discussed in Chapter 2, the act of genocide while shocking, even almost unimaginably horrific, is unfortunately an aspect of human behaviour within a particular socialized context where violence is normalized, when the victims are sufficiently demonized and othered, such that their death counts for nothing, or more especially when their death is deemed an inherent good in and of itself.

This last point raises a curious question. Certainly, the Nazis were deeply antisemitic, and from Hitler to Eichmann to Hermann Göring (1893–1946), to those carrying out the killings, many believed that this work was noble and decent, yet they also sought to dissimulate their actions. This is seen in the infamous Wannsee Conference of 20 January 1942, where the Final

Solution, it seems, was planned and plotted. Writing to Reinhard Heydrich (1904–1942), who convened the conference, Göring spoke about the Jews being subject to 'emigration and evacuation', in the 'execution of the intended final solution of the Jewish question'.[9] Likewise, the conference minutes show talk of 'transit ghettos' before people are 'to be transported from there farther to the East', noting only that 'Jews employed in essential war industries could not be evacuated for the present, as long as no replacements were available'.[10] We could hypothesize why such euphemistic language is used.[11] Albert Bandura's analysis that lessening the consequences is part of the psychology of enabling violence is one idea. Again, euphemistic labelling, especially in transmitting the orders, may have been useful, for while the police may have been happy to 'evacuate' Jews to transit camps they may have balked at sending them to death camps. Maybe senior Nazis were aware that history would judge them or that their words may be leaked, and so sought to minimize their own complicity. How far everyone knew what was going on is debatable, even Eichmann used it as a defence in his trial;[12] it seems to be something which people could have seen plainly had they wanted to, but was perhaps so terrible that people turned a blind eye.[13] It was certainly impossible to keep something like the Holocaust a secret. Perhaps it was simply too awful for people to acknowledge that it could be true? But true it was, and while Holocaust denial is discussed in Chapter 6, we must note here that the facts are incontrovertible. Although Eichmann claimed ignorance in some cases, in others he could not deny his complicity in gassing and killing. Moreover, at the Nuremberg trials at the end of the war nobody denied that the killings and genocide had taken place, rather many tried to pass the buck, claiming they were only following orders. The physical evidence that was uncovered, despite attempts to destroy such things as the gas chambers in the death camps, was compelling. Finally, there is testimony from survivors.[14]

The Holocaust: Ideology, motives, and genesis

But, even if we can trace a development, what was the catalyst? One answer may be the individual: was Hitler the reason? While, as Nirenberg suggested, Hitler's desire to enact the Final Solution on Jews would be inconceivable without the background of antisemitism, it needs a directive to turn even pogroms into a more programmatic objective: to kill every Jew. The answer here is that we cannot be sure. Hitler was, most certainly, a product of his times[15] and perhaps hated his own Jewish ancestry compared to the Aryan ideal he extolled. But was it his personal evil that led from these bases to the Final Solution? No doubt he played a part, but Hitler's own formation in the nexus of narratives and events at this time also needs to be considered. Certainly, the focus on the Final Solution was not designed to enhance

Nazi war aims, as the manpower and resources used were much needed at the time. It was a specific ideological agenda in and of itself that almost transcended everything else that Hitler and the Nazis aimed at. If the Final Solution had been conceived in advance, then arguably ongoing warfare gave Hitler the confidence to carry it out, perhaps believing that the crime would be hidden within the savagery and confusion of war.

While Hitler as an individual is undoubtedly part of an explanation, he lived within a social context. A context in which hatred and suspicion of Jews had been normalized in discourse and practice. The legislation and physical violence had much support from the churches, with Lutheran Bishop of Thuringia, Martin Sasse (bishop 1934–42), exulting that on Kristallnacht: 'On 10th November 1938, on Luther's Birthday, the synagogues are burning in Germany.'[16] Hitler himself had invoked Luther who 'with one blow, heralded a new dawn ... He saw the Jew as we are only beginning to see him today.'[17] Days later, on 15 November, Sasse issued a pamphlet on Luther's writings on the Jews entitled *Martin Luther über die Juden: Weg mit ihnen!* (*Martin Luther on the Jews: Away with Them!*). While there was opposition to the violence against Jews from some Christians, this was often limited, and even some leading thinkers seen as being opposed to Nazism, and even sympathetic to Jews, were hardly free from antisemitic sentiments: Dietrich Bonhoeffer (1906–1945), a Lutheran theologian, executed for his involvement in a plot to kill Hitler, stated in 1933 that 'The state's measures against the Jewish people are connected ... in a very special way with the Church. ... [T]he "Chosen People" that nailed the Savior of the world to the cross, must bear the curse of its action through a long history of suffering.' Meanwhile Karl Barth (1886–1968), perhaps the most influential theologian of the twentieth century, stated as late as 1942 that 'The Jews of the ghetto ... have nothing to attest to the world but the shadow of the cross of Christ that falls upon them', declaring Judaism to be 'outmoded and superseded'.[18] As such, the ideology that justified such demonization of the Jew was found even among Nazi critics, even among people who later opposed the actions against Jews as being too harsh. Certainly, as far as we can make out, Hitler was not acting alone and many enthusiastically helped in the extermination of Jews, even those outside Nazi territory, and while it has often been held that the Italians refused to cooperate in the Final Solution, with Jews under Italian control remaining relatively safe while those under Nazi control died, at least from 1943 to 1945 many Italians 'were, in fact, responsible for genocide'.[19]

Local and individual context needs to be considered, and surely not everyone involved bought into genocide, or even consciously acknowledged their complicity. As Philip Zimbardo and Stanley Milgram suggest, many may have found following orders to override their normal moral barriers. Perhaps an interesting case is the doctors who worked on human experimentation at Auschwitz, who Robert Lifton found were marked by their 'ordinariness. ... Neither brilliant nor stupid, neither inherently evil nor

particularly ethically sensitive, they were by no means the demonic figures –
sadistic, fanatic, lusting to kill – people have often thought them to be.'[20]
While some were more extremely enthusiastic, others unsure, and some at
first refused – one even managing to avoid it altogether – they were socialized
by those already within the system, often with heavy drinking and a bond-
ing camaraderie, such that it just became like another day at the office.[21]
Jews had been dehumanized and othered, seen as polluting the German race,
and were enemies of the Reich.[22] None of the above precisely answers why
the Holocaust happened. However, we see a nexus of ideology, deep-seated
prejudice, and the creation of a dehumanized enemy where the logic to kill
them and a normalization of violence permeates the system. Whatever the
cause of the Holocaust, a system that allowed it was in place.

Resistance

Of course, against any argument of the Holocaust's inevitably, or its foundations in Western and Christian antisemitic traditions, we must also remember that there were those who resisted it. This was true of both Christians
and others who in many cases risked their own lives to save and hide Jews
who had been neighbours, or were simply strangers in need.[23] Of those
saved, Anne Frank (1929–1945) is undoubtedly the best-known example
through her diary and house, which is now a tourist pilgrimage site, but she
was far from alone. We must not, therefore, see prejudice as an unconquer-
able force even when embedded so deep in society and culture, and certainly
the tendency to humanize and have empathy with the Other also marks us
out as human beings. If we ask why the Holocaust happened, then without
being too simplistic we may speak about the constant struggle between the
best and worst urges of human nature: because of what humans do we may
despair, but also despite what humans do we may hope.

SECTION III

Contemporary Western hatreds

CHAPTER SIX

The West's eternal Jewish question? Politics, antisemitism, and Holocaust denial

Introduction

In terms of Western traditions of antisemitism, there is no doubt that the Holocaust is a landmark. Many vowed that such an atrocious event could never happen again, while Western Christian and secular people had seemingly recognized the error of their ways and would no longer speak disparagingly of Jews and Judaism.[1] Sociologist David Hirsh discusses that when doing a master's degree in antisemitism in the 1990s, the focus was purely historical. Yet, while it took a long time, antisemitism in public and acceptable forms has resurfaced, meaning we must, as Deborah Lipstadt insists, face up to *Antisemitism Here and Now*.[2] Today, right-wing and neo-Nazi groups are emerging from the dark shadows into prominence, including in deadly attacks on synagogues and individual Jews, while the so-called new antisemitism sees left-wing rhetoric on the State of Israel[3] merging with antisemitic tropes.[4]

We will start by dealing with right-wing antisemitism. At heart, this is not new but sometimes takes new forms. Next, and contributing a sub-theme, will be continuing Christian antisemitism, which is often tied to right-wing narratives but not always. We then turn to Holocaust denial which primarily draws from the extreme right-wing but, as we will discuss, partly via Islamic forms of Holocaust denial (discussed further in Chapter 8) can also cross over into left-wing discourse. This will then lead us to the new antisemitism.[5] This is often linked to support for the Palestinian cause in Israel–Palestine and an attitude sometimes termed anti-Zionism, indicating opposition to the legitimacy of the State of Israel. A useful note before we begin is that while I am demarcating right-wing and left-wing antisemitism, we see places where these cross over, with some tropes or groups having appeal across these boundaries, so while we use them as heuristic markers, we should not imagine that everything falls neatly into this divide.[6]

Right-wing antisemitism: The return of the dark

Antisemitism is so deeply embedded in Western culture that it seems doubtful it will be eradicated any time soon. While, with the demise of the Nazi regime, such views largely went underground, they never disappeared entirely. Meanwhile, in explicit neo-Nazi movements, in what is often termed the alt-right, and in some right-wing nationalist movements, such as the Front National in France under Jean-Marie Le Pen, antisemitism has been a key part of the ideology. Of course, we may debate how mainstream such views are, and certainly under Marine Le Pen, Jean-Marie's daughter, the Front National has tried to improve its electability by eschewing antisemitism; indeed, Jean-Marie was expelled from the party in 2015 for his antisemitism. Nevertheless, Jewish people in Europe feel increasingly unsafe as graves have been defaced with Nazi imagery, though both Islamic antisemitism (Chapter 8) and antisemitism from the left are concerns there,[7] while in the United States a number of right-wing shooting attacks on synagogues have taken place.[8]

While we might distinguish Neo-Nazis, the alt-right, and right-wing nationalists, for they are not homogeneous, we should note shared narratives across these movements. The riots at the 'Unite the Right' rally in Charlottesville, Virginia, in August 2017 which saw the alt-right clash with counter demonstrators saw the former carrying banners declaring that 'Jews are Satan's children', while they chanted 'Jews will not replace us'. Importantly, this march was not simply about Jews because across the United States' far-right spectrum we see that 'hatred of Muslims, utter contempt for African Americans and Latinos ... and deep-seated antisemitism are essential to all of them'.[9] This follows standard right-wing racism, with elements – especially in the United States – of Christian antisemitism mixed in.

Five distinct things may be noted. First, what has perhaps allowed these very disparate groups to unite and grow in strength has been the Internet and social media.[10] While not adding a distinct feature to antisemitism, the mobilizing power to bring often isolated and frustrated young men (these groups often more overtly appeal to males) together should not be overlooked. Second, while hard to pin to the right alone, popular conspiracy theories have many antisemitic tropes. For example, David Icke, a former British television football commentator who gained notoriety as a claimed prophet of a new religious dispensation, now tours to packed-out auditoriums in which he expounds that a secret cabal of (primarily) Jews (his preferred term is 'Rothschild Zionists') run the world. This is not new material, though that this cabal may be lizard people is a new twist.[11] However, with conspiracy theories of many types gaining traction, it allows a potential channel for such views to become more mainstream, with QAnon being one example that appeals to both those we may traditionally envisage as right wing and left wing.[12] Third, some right-wingers have eschewed antisemitism and homophobia; both were previously defining aspects. If 'hatred of Muslims' becomes central, Islamic homophobia and antisemitism become what right-wingers define themselves against, and may even be used to assert a popular zeitgeist with liberals, progressives, and the mainstream, which has also included making links with environmentalism.[13] Importantly, though, the far-right is fundamentally antagonistic to Western liberal values, and it may be wise to exercise a certain suspicion that such attitudes have entirely disappeared. Fourth, because antisemitism is often seen as unacceptable, and what was once embraced as a badge of honour (being an antisemite) is now disavowed, various other terms are used to avoid mentioning Jews directly, for example, in the United States, Walter Laqueur notes the use of 'East Coast' or 'New York'.[14]

Finally, antisemitism has tried to normalize itself. While the Front National has moved away from antisemitism because it is aware that it makes them seem like extremists, another ploy has been used by the alt-right in the United States. One thing that a number of commentators noted about the Charlottesville event was that the demonstrators did not look like the KKK, nor neo-Nazis, nor even crazed zealots. Rather in khaki trousers and smart shirts they looked like regular guys or college students, as many were. Certainly as one alt-right leader Richard Spencer had previously noted: 'We have to look good.'[15] If these figures had looked like extremists, then the antisemitism (and other forms of racism) would have been easy to spot, and for those looking they are there – like the cries of 'blood and soil' which is an old Nazi chant[16] – but today's antisemites may not look like Nazis and may pass off as just ordinary folk expressing justified concerns about their nation: that is certainly how they want to come across. Just because antisemitism is out from the shadows does not mean it is always clearly seen in the light of day.

Christian antisemitism (after the Holocaust)

Antisemitism has been rejected by almost all mainstream churches, exemplified by the Catholic Church at the Second Vatican Council (1962–5) overturning almost two thousand years of teaching that God's covenant with the Jewish people was null and void after Jesus. Catholicism now teaches that there are two valid covenants, that with the Jews and that with Christians, hence missions to Jews are no longer required.[17] One particular instantiation of this was the removal of the wording in the Good Friday prayer calling for the conversion of the 'perfidious Jews' (offered in the week before Easter, a traditional time for attacks on Jews), though wording to similar effect was temporarily reinstated by Pope Benedict XVI.[18] This notion that Christianity replaced Judaism, known as supersessionism, is apparent in the traditional language used by Christians to describe their biblical texts: the Old Testament (the record of the covenant with the Jews) and the New Testament (the new covenant with God through Jesus). To avoid antisemitic connotations, some theologians now, therefore, speak of the First (or, Older) and Second (or, Newer) Testaments, which may even seemingly give priority to the Jewish covenant. But, for many Christians, little has changed: the language of the Old and New Testaments persists in daily usage, while the Bible still tells them that the Jews killed Jesus and that the Jews and the synagogue, the 'vipers', are the enemies of Christians and the church.

Especially among evangelical or fundamentalist (literalist) wings of biblical interpretation,[19] what is often taken to be a 'straightforward' reading of the biblical text will win out over the niceties of what may be seen as political correctness. But views that Christianity replaced Judaism in God's plan, or that the Jews are the 'devil's children', are also found in mainstream churches as people read their Bibles often with little direction from their more theologically literate pastors who may simply assume that we live in a post-antisemitic world. One example from fairly recent popular culture would be Mel Gibson's film *The Passion of the Christ* (2004), which portrayed 'the Jews' as responsible for Jesus' death and as shady devious figures. Certainly, some critics have portrayed this as an antisemitic film, but for Gibson it was just telling the Gospel story as he understands it.[20] Telling the Gospel story, as often understood, and antisemitism are not necessarily distinct.

Finally, especially in the United States, a dislike of Judaism may be mixed into an apocalyptic worldview in which the Jews play an important role, though this view is certainly not held by most Christians nor all evangelicals. The political aspect of this worldview may manifest as support for Israel, in the belief that the return of Jesus as Messiah will occur once all Jews have returned 'home' to Israel, ushering in an apocalyptic war centred on the Middle East. The stories of war and disasters within the Book of Revelations are taken literally. Some (mainly American) evangelicals thus believe that supporting Israel and destabilizing the peace process may be a way for their ultimate fulfilment. That many Jews will be killed is expected, even considered beneficial, within this worldview. It appears also that some Jews who support a militant Zionism find congenial bedfellows with these evangelicals despite disliking, even detesting, each other.[21]

Holocaust denial

The Holocaust happened: period. While many historians, and various critical scholars, today suggest that there are no facts and everything is interpretation, that perhaps at most we can have 'evidence', it is a simple historical fact that the Holocaust occurred. Now, whether it was closer to 5 or 6 million Jews who were killed, whether the initial plan was genocidal or whether this developed at some later point, and how the killings of Romanies, the disabled, and homosexuals were linked to the Holocaust are, arguably, debatable. Perhaps, the landmark proof of the Holocaust came when the populist historian David Irving started a libel campaign against Lipstadt in the UK courts for accusing him of being a Holocaust denier. In her defence, Lipstadt had to prove that Irving distorted and misrepresented the evidence on the Holocaust. Her defence team dismantled and destroyed all of Irving's claims and evidence, while the defence evidence is now open access online, making the facts that prove the Holocaust publicly accessible.[22]

Though Irving's work became famous through the trial, he is relatively marginal, with significant figures in developing the ideology of denial including Robert Faurisson (1929–2018) in France, a former professor at the University of Lyons-2, Harry Elmer Barnes (1889–1968) in the United States, Richard Verrall (pen name Harwood) in the UK, who wrote a very influential pamphlet, and Arthur Butz, a professor of electrical engineering at Northwestern University in Evanston, Illinois. Butz is particularly influential in the chain of events, as he is perhaps the first person to have made Holocaust denial seem like serious scholarship.[23]

Despite differences between the deniers, Lipstadt notes various things in common. Ideologically, all are antisemitic, and many seek to rehabilitate National Socialism. Methodologically, they typically use a range of devices such as selective quotation, misquotation, and distortion. Some examples may be noted. First, deniers claim the International Committee of the Red Cross (ICRC) released death figures post-war that undermined the Holocaust; however, these figures are purely fictitious as the ICRC never released any numbers: their aim was to 'help war victims not to count them'.[24] Second, it is asserted that 6 million Jews could not have been killed, quoting a reputable source to claim there were only 6.5 million Jews in pre-war Europe; however, the source is misquoted as the 6.5 million figure was the number of Jews under land dominated by the Nazis in 1939.[25] Third, the claims of Margarete Buber's book *Under Two Dictators* are distorted to portray a positive remembrance of life in the concentration camp, although she explicitly talks about executions, gas chambers, and horrific conditions.[26] Fourth, the existence of the gas chambers is frequently contested, but this involves ignoring vast amounts of evidence and distorting actual records, while the main denier source is a report given by somebody with no credentials to assess the evidence.[27] Fifth, deniers note the absence of the single piece of evidence they claim would be required to prove the Holocaust: a written order by Adolf Hitler (1889–1945) to kill all Jews. But single documents do not constitute historical proof, while abundant documentary, physical, and oral evidence exists. Finally, some have suggested that the evidence of the Nuremberg trials is forged or inadequate, or that a German perspective is ignored. Such claims are not credible: documentary evidence from the trials is vast; in guilty pleas many argued they were just following orders rather than denying being involved in the extermination; we also have victim and other eyewitness testimony. For all this to be false requires many (tens of) thousands of people being involved in a vast conspiracy across decades.

If it is so black and white, why are we discussing it? Because Holocaust denial is increasingly widespread. Irving was a well-known historian of the Nazi period, and Lipstadt noted that sometimes his claims were not adequately critiqued by mainstream historians (like a number of pseudo-scholarly claims about Islamic antisemitism in history, see Chapter 8).[28] While Irving was disgraced, and reputable historians now recognize his bias, in groups such as the alt-right Holocaust denial is virulent. As an indication, reading the comments under the trailer for the film *Denial* (2016) on YouTube will show quite how many people feel able to openly express their denial of the Holocaust.[29] Sometimes the argument is made in terms of free speech. If Holocaust denial is seen as a form of denied (illegal) speech, deniers argue that powerful interests (invoking age-old antisemitic tropes about Jewish influence) have banned discussion because they know the Holocaust did not happen. As noted, the trial evidence is available, but deniers know that few people will actually check the sources. Holocaust denial has even found a space in some left-wing groups.[30]

Some important aspects of the discourse of Holocaust denial should be noted. First, Lipstadt in her book about her trial against Irving was careful in the title: *History on Trial*. She was clear that it was not the Holocaust itself on trial. But, for the far-right, it is about creating an alt-fact universe. As Lipstadt argues, advocates of Holocaust denial want it discussed as just another side of history,[31] as though they are engaged in respectable discussion of various interpretations or viewpoints. But it always masks antisemitism and is not simply another interpretation.

Second, a seemingly odd aspect of the discourse of the extreme right, especially neo-Nazis, is that the Holocaust did not happen, but that it would be legitimate. Because Holocaust denial is never separated from anti-semitism, this strand of thought paints Jews as a group of people who are pernicious or demonic, and argues that the Holocaust would have been justified. This both contests standard discourse and acts to diffuse potential responses: does one counter the argument that it is right to kill Jews, or that the Holocaust did not happen?

Another issue, and not necessarily involving direct Holocaust denial per se, is changing the argument about what it was and who was behind it. For some, the argument is made that the Holocaust was actually part of a

Jewish/Zionist plot to create the sympathy that was needed for the foundation of the State of Israel. This goes back to older tropes of antisemitism, that everything that happens in the world is part of a plot by an all-powerful Jewish cabal in their bid for global supremacy. The illogical aspect, that this was engineered by destroying approximately one third of the whole of world Jewry, is not something that conspiracy theorists are concerned with. This argument is also a way for the Holocaust to enter left-wing discourse as a critique of Zionism/Israel (see below).

Finally, a trope which comes up in some Holocaust denial related material is that 'Nazi antisemitism [was] Germany's legitimate response to attacks on it by "international Jewry"'.[32] This plays into the old narrative of the immense power of 'the Jew' as a danger but also throws antisemitism back into the face of the persecuted group because 'they brought it on themselves'. This familiar narrative links to the new antisemitism where it is sometimes claimed that hatred of Israel/Jews is justified because of the actions of Israel.

Can 'anti-racism' be antisemitic?

We address the topic of left-wing antisemitism last partly because it is the most recent phenomenon and also because it is the most controversial and hardest to understand. To some extent, however, left-wing antisemitism is not new. The association of Jews with a banking cabal that runs society has long been a trope, and the left can buy into this. Figures such as the Rothschilds, a prominent and influential Jewish banking dynasty, play into a discourse which links Jews with capitalism and as enemies of the working people. But Jews have a long association with left-wing politics, while many on the left see themselves as anti-racist and therefore opposed to antisemitism: a famous incident in left-wing British history is the Battle of Cable Street (1936), where, in London's East End, the working class and socialists took to the streets to fight Britain's fascist black shirts, partly in defence of their Jewish neighbours. It was a symbolic end to fascist claims in the UK to represent the working people and signalled the left's alliance with Jews against fascism. However, the Soviet Union's antisemitism, especially under Stalin, inspired some on the left, especially in critiques of Jews as capitalists.[33]

One incident, which made headline news, was the support which the then UK Labour Party leader, Jeremy Corbyn, gave to an artist who produced what was held to be ostensibly an anti-capitalist mural. It depicted a circle of bankers around a monopoly table with images of the oppressed working masses below them. Other symbolism included an eye in a pyramid referencing the illuminati or masonic movements, tied in some conspiracy circles into antisemitic notions of Jewish global domination. Some of these bankers were seemingly identifiable. One was Mayer Amsched Rothschild

(1744–1812), while another was J. P. Morgan (1837–1913); the former Jewish, the latter not – though some commentary cast all the bankers as Jewish.[34] Seemingly stereotyped notions of 'the Jew' were evident in the crooked noses and hunched figures; arguably, the most 'stereotyped' figure is Morgan whose visage fits the Jewish stereotype, but he is not Jewish and is identifiable because it is a recognizable portrait. Meanwhile, the illuminati symbolism is not always tied to antisemitism, but can signify any cabal with global power; it is linked to conspiracy theories of a small elite controlling the world. Therefore, we see a mural with antisemitic tropes, but which arguably could be read as an anti-capitalist message. We are told that after a more careful examination, Corbyn agreed it contained antisemitic imagery – which it does – and publicly repudiated antisemitism.[35] The arguable ambivalence of this picture is notable: left-wing antisemitism may arise from anti-capitalism, or opposition to Israeli oppression of Palestinians, but can become statements about 'the Jew', may unduly target Jewish people more than others, or may employ antisemitic tropes and imagery. It may also result in the demonization of at least some Jews, and the creator of the mural, Kalen Ockerman, noted that he was aware that some Jews were uncomfortable with his mural which showed Rothschild and Paul Warburg as, in his words, 'the demons that they are'.[36] This is not to deny antisemitic dislike of Jews on the left, but institutional antisemitism rather than personal animosity to Jews may be the more typical instantiation of the new antisemitism.

The Boycott, Divestment, Sanctions (BDS) movement is often said to typify left-wing antisemitism. The aim of this movement is to impose sanctions on Israel to curtail its oppression and extreme policies in relation to the Palestinians; note, we are using the terms 'oppression' and 'extreme policies' whereas others may speak more strikingly of 'apartheid' and 'genocidal policies' – we will come to some of this in due course. Here, scholars of antisemitism diverge on whether BDS can be termed antisemitic: Hirsh argues that it is inherently so;[37] Lipstadt suggests that 'it depends'. Certainly, there are a range of motives in BDS: some want to pressure Israel to cede control of the West Bank, allowing a Palestinian state in alignment with UN resolutions for a two-state solution; others want a new single state, thus ending Israel as a Jewish state; yet others argue that Zionism is inherently racist and Israel must be destroyed.[38] Hence BDS, and its supporters, cannot be treated as a monolithic movement. Furthermore, how far the kind of views noted may merge with animosity to Jews varies. Many BDS advocates see themselves as committed anti-racists with the campaign against the State of Israel being founded in a desire for the liberation of an oppressed group, the Palestinians. However, the meaning of racism and, therefore also, anti-racism has shifted over time, and indeed proclaiming oneself an anti-racist is not the same as being anti-racist in practice. Virulent antisemitism exists in certain parts of the BDS movement, including in key spokespeople, but assuming good motives on the part of many in BDS does not mean it may not manifest as structural antisemitism. Certainly, BDS acts primarily against Jews and directs criticism solely at Israel in a way that seemingly overlooks similar, or worse, human rights abuses by other nations.[39]

It is necessary, here, to consider how Israel fits into left-wing discourse. From 1948, many saw Israel as a progressive anti-colonial movement that resisted Western imperialism (Jewish terrorist/liberation groups had attacked British interests in Palestine when it was a British mandate).[40] Many also admired the kibbutzim – collective farming communes – as essentially left-wing. Discontent with Israeli policy and practice began in the 1960s, with the six-day war of 1967 being central,[41] but into the 1980s the left was predominantly pro-Israeli, and Anthony Julius suggests the new antisemitism only 'became hegemonic in the 1990s and 2000s'.[42] Two factors were central in this shift. First, a move from class issues to identity politics and single-issue campaigns.[43] So the Palestinian cause, or LGBTQI, became key framing leftist concerns rather than class per se. Second, a change of focus to 'Third World' revolution during the 1960s and 1970s[44] where the white Western world is seen as inherently oppressive. Jews became racialized as 'white' and therefore could not be an oppressed group; instead, the Palestinians are oppressed, so Israel's framing shifts from being anti-colonial to being a white, European, colonial settlement. As an example of how Jews are racialized as 'white', a suggestion for a focus on Jewish women during International Women's Day was dismissed as inappropriate because it was stated by an organizer that Jewish women (framed as 'white') cannot understand oppression.[45]

With the failure of the Oslo peace process in the 1990s and the rising dominance of the Israeli right-wing since 2000, with more oppressive policies against Palestinians, the left has increasingly demonized Israel. Indeed, a sense of betrayal is felt by some on the left, alongside a growing sense of the Palestinians as not just oppressed but even facing apartheid or genocide. Hirsh suggests that the changing stance of the literary theorist Judith Butler between 2006 and 2013 on BDS, or more specifically on an academic boycott of Israeli universities, is indicative. In 2006, Butler opposed the boycott on the grounds that academic freedom meant that it was important to be in contact with Israeli academics, many of whom opposed government policies and the treatment of Palestinians, but by 2013 she was in favour of an institutional boycott of Israeli universities. Hirsh suggests a key motivation is that to appear progressive, to be part of what he calls the 'community of the good', necessitates supporting BDS.[46]

Considering an oft-drawn BDS parallel about sanctions because of the claimed Israeli 'apartheid' (discussed below) and sanctions on South Africa during apartheid, will help show how some argue we see slippage into structural antisemitism resulting from BDS. Sanctions on South Africa affected primarily one group: white South Africans, or the Afrikaners. However, in that case, it was seen as justified because they were the oppressive group. Likewise, BDS and boycotts of Israeli universities, while not directed at Jews per se, have the net result that Jews are predominantly affected. But many (Israeli) Jews oppose the acts of militant settlers and are part of the political opposition, a matter we take up further below. As discussed in relation to prejudice and racism, we see both personal bias and structural discrimination. Lipstadt usefully notes that BDS advocates may not be personally anti-semitic, although Hirsh seems to suggest that because the effects of BDS are racist/antisemitic, its advocates are racist/antisemitic. Nevertheless, Hirsh seems correct that the BDS movement slips into structural antisemitism by effectively targeting one particular group.[47]

Turning to accusations that Corbyn is antisemitic, and antisemitism is rampant in the British Labour Party, we need to see what is being discussed. Seeking to uncover alleged overwhelming Labour Party bias, in 2017 the Campaign Against Antisemitism conducted a poll with YouGov, a British polling organization. It found that antisemitism in the British Labour Party more or less mirrored national averages, with 32 per cent of supporters endorsing at least one antisemitic trope (examples of these included: Jewish people chase money more than others; and that Jewish people use the Holocaust for political ends).[48] However, figures in other parties were similar or higher: in the nationalist right-wing UKIP party 39 per cent; in the mainstream right-wing Conservative Party 40 per cent; in the centre-ground Liberal Democrats 30 per cent. (That is to say, antisemitism is apparently more prevalent on the mainstream political right, but this is rarely discussed in the UK media, or raised as an issue the mainstream political right needs to deal with.[49]) Notably, prejudice was higher among men than women (42 per cent vs 29 per cent) and increased with age (over 65: 46 per cent; 18–24: 27 per cent). Nevertheless, many more complaints were made against Labour than other parties, with 1,283 complaints about antisemitism received between January and June 2019. The majority of complaints were not levelled against Labour Party members, but following investigations eight members were expelled and over one hundred other lesser disciplinary measures were brought against individuals.[50] Allegations rumbled on after an investigation by a senior human rights lawyer, Shami Chakrabarti, found that there was a visible problem, stating: 'I am not saying that this [Antisemitism] is endemic, but any seasoned activist who says that they are completely unaware of any such discourse must be wholly insensitive or completely in denial.'[51] Critics such as Hirsh described it as a whitewash, and the fact that Corbyn nominated Chakrabarti for a peerage within months did seem suspicious. However, Hirsh is forced to concede that 'neither [Jan] Royall nor [David] Feldman, however, criticized or distanced themselves from the [Chakrabarti] report';[52] Royall and Feldman had done their own reports on instances of Labour antisemitism (which many regard as more robust) but both had decided that, despite some evidence of antisemitism, it was not systemic. However, this is not to dismiss it as insignificant, both because there are ideological reasons to suspect it is widespread,[53] as we discuss here, but also because what may be seen as the most definitive report – by the Equalities and Human Rights

Commission (EHRC) – has suggested institutional failings in tackling anti-semitism by, for instance, not taking complaints seriously.[54] Indeed, while noting some positives, overall the EHRC report was quite damning:

> While there have been some improvements in how the Labour Party deals with antisemitism complaints, our analysis points to a culture within the Party which, at best, did not do enough to prevent antisemitism and, at worst, could be seen to accept it.[55]

As with the BDS movement, we appear to be looking at (at least) two separate issues: personal prejudice against Jews and animosity against Israel which may spill over into antisemitic tropes or practices. Certainly, for many, it is fantastical that a lifelong anti-racist campaigner such as Corbyn is accused of antisemitism, but whether or not he or other Labour figures harbour antisemitic prejudices is somewhat irrelevant to the possibility of structural antisemitism existing. To explore this further, we turn next to discuss anti-Zionism, but before that we may note Hirsh's analysis that 'Today's antisemitism is difficult to recognize because it does not come dressed in a Nazi uniform and it does not openly proclaim its hatred or fear of Jews. In fact … It stands in the antiracist tradition', and moreover 'is a … phenomenon whose very existence is angrily contested'.[56]

Demonizing or criticizing Israel?

Hirsh uses the phrase 'the Livingstone Formula' for those who argue that accusations of antisemitism are used to block legitimate criticism of Israel.[57] This has become a key area of debate. A recent definition of antisemitism (see below, and the longer discussion in Interlude 4) includes (unfair) criticism of Israel as an indicator of antisemitism.[58] Clearly, a lot of criticism of Israel is not antisemitic. However, while some instances are more clear-cut, it can be hard to delineate what is and what is not acceptable. Also, how far do Israel or Jewish groups seek to control what is said about it? To briefly address this second point, accusations about Israel as an all-powerful Jewish cabal controlling the world replicates older antisemitic tropes drawing from *The Protocols of the Elders of Zion*. This is not to say that, in various ways, Jewish groups do not try to control or monitor criticism of Israel, and Lipstadt notes: 'Some Jewish organizations have compiled lists of professors who have signed BDS resolutions and have urged Jewish students to boycott the classes of these teachers.'[59] Such activities are clearly, though, very far from a controlling cabal, so any accusations of such activities as showing Jewish attempts at control may become antisemitic.

In terms of when criticism of Israel moves from being legitimate political commentary to antisemitism, in general, we can say that when critiques move from specific issues, policies, or groups to being monolithic claims about Jewish/Israeli influence/character, or 'the Jews', in stereotypical ways, then they have become antisemitic. One way this particularly manifests is in criticism of Zionism which leads into vilification of Israel and almost inevitably into disparagement of Israelis (meaning Israeli Jews) but slips into attacks on any Jew who is not explicitly anti-Zionist.

The definition of antisemitism aforementioned is that of the European Union Monitoring Centre on Racism and Xenophobia (EUMC, now the Agency for Fundamental Rights), which developed the definition used by the International Holocaust Remembrance Alliance (IHRA). We may quote the IHRA definition in full:

> Antisemitism is a certain perception of Jews, which may be expressed as hatred toward Jews. Rhetorical and physical manifestations of antisemitism are directed toward Jewish or non-Jewish individuals and/or their property, toward Jewish community institutions and religious facilities.

But most important is the description around this, which states:

> Manifestations might include the targeting of the state of Israel, conceived as a Jewish collectivity. However, criticism of Israel similar to that levelled against any other country cannot be regarded as antisemitic. Antisemitism frequently charges Jews with conspiring to harm humanity, and it is often used to blame Jews for 'why things go wrong.' It is expressed in speech, writing, visual forms and action, and employs sinister stereotypes and negative character traits.

Criticism of Israel can slip from focusing on the actions of the government, which clearly does not represent all Israeli Jews, to generic claims about Jews, especially their support for Zionism. Zionism often stands in for a monolithically represented support for militant religious settlement,[60] which at its most extreme may countenance taking all land perceived as promised to the Israelites in the biblical text, which can even include Jordan and beyond. But the meaning of Zionism has changed and is open to diverse interpretations. At base, it refers to the belief that the Jewish people – like other peoples, stemming from modern Western theories of nationalism (see Chapter 5) – deserve their own nation state. Theodore Herzl, often seen as the key theorist, believed that either Argentina/Patagonia or Palestine would be somewhere to found the secular nation state he envisaged.[61] Notably, even as it became clear that Palestine was the desired destination, the vast majority of Orthodox Jews opposed it because they believed that only the Messiah could restore a Jewish homeland. The Balfour Declaration (1919) in which the British suggested Palestine should be a homeland for the Jews was a step towards it, while the Holocaust gave the impetus, with many Jews believing that the establishment of a nation state would finally make them safe. The vast majority of early Jewish immigrants were refugees who had been displaced from Europe, and they were soon joined by many Jews forced from their old centres in the Middle East, as well as a global influx including many fleeing repression in the Soviet Union.

While founded as a Jewish nation, the State of Israel saw itself as providing a secular equality for all its citizens. However, tensions were inherent, and changes would occur. Was Israel a homeland only for Jews, or also for the Palestinians whose ancestral lands were there? What role would Jewish religious authority have? Being a Zionist may describe several different stances. A Zionist may believe that Jews have a right to a homeland, but in a nation open to all who live there, including Palestinians, and accept the two-state principle. A Zionist may believe that Israel–Palestine should be cleared of Palestinians to make way for a Jewish homeland; this view was clear in Herzl's own private writings, where he stated that the indigenous inhabitants would need to be cleared out, but surreptitiously.[62] Finally, a Zionist may have a militant religious vision, and from around the 1980s, some Orthodox Jew suggested that they had God's mandate to return, while Palestinians, cast as Arabs, were understood as analogues to the biblical enemies of the Jewish people such as the Amalekites or Philistines. In other words, the argument is that in driving Palestinians out, which some may see as even requiring genocide, Jews are being obedient to God's commands.[63] These three options represent idealized poles, with various shades of thought existing. With the rise of those favouring the last interpretation of Zionism, sometimes termed the Israeli religious right, and the ascendancy of anti-peace militant right-wing governments for well over a decade, Israeli government policy has become harsher and more brutal towards the Palestinians. Indeed, religious Zionist settlers increasingly take Palestinian land, attack homes, and destroy the olive trees that are key to the indigenous Palestinian people.[64] The settlers are protected by the Israeli army, though the army at times also tries to keep them in check.

Increasingly, this latter vision is understood by critics of Israel as representing Zionism. It leads directly into claims that Zionism, and therefore the Israeli state itself, is inherently racist. From this comes the accusations about apartheid. We need, therefore, to assess the debate as to whether Israel is an apartheid state, with some suggesting that: 'It is possible, given their primary focus on different sides of the green line [i.e. inside Israel where Jews and Arabs can both vote, attend university together, etc., or within the occupied Palestinian territories], that there are varying degrees of validity in both sides' arguments.'[65] Certainly, key figures such as Desmond Tutu have accused Israel of practising apartheid,[66] while a former UN special rapporteur Richard Falk issued a report, with Virginia Tilley, that made this accusation.[67] As a professor of law emeritus at Yale, and with his previous UN role, Falk's views carry weight. However, he is a controversial figure who has received criticism from, for example, the UN in the person of Ban Ki Moon in relation to 9/11 conspiracy theories,[68] and from the British government in relation to the publication of an antisemitic cartoon.[69] We can perhaps only say that some laws or policies are 'apartheid-like', which would not meet the requirements for a condemnation of the whole system of the State of Israel as being an 'apartheid regime'. Moreover, Israel is a democracy with groups that actively oppose the extreme policies the right-wing Likud party has adopted and the settlements which Likud has implicitly, if not explicitly, supported, and as such it is hard to define the State of Israel per se as an 'apartheid regime'. However, it has moved further in that direction in recent years and could conceivably become one. Recent moves, under the so-called Trump 'peace plan', to annex large sections of land are certainly worrying in this regard.[70]

It is in this context that we have seen the rise of anti-Zionism. It may mean several things, just as Zionism may mean several things. Globally, most Jews will identify as Zionists insofar as they believe that it is right and necessary that Jewish people have their own nation state (like other national/ethnic groups) and that it needs to be strong to protect Jews should another Holocaust appear on the horizon and also to keep its local enemies at bay. Having said this, many Jewish Zionists are deeply critical of the policies of the State of Israel vis-à-vis the treatment of the Palestinians. They are appalled at what has happened. However, as discussed, many in the anti-Zionist movement see Zionism as equated with the recent government policies and as implicated in the religious right settler Zionist movement. We see here why anti-racist, anti-oppression activists may come to characterize not just Israeli Jews (many of whom do not support the current government policy[71]) but also all Jews – except those who entirely denounce Zionism – as the enemy, which is not to say that this jump is legitimate, but the (problematic) assumption made is that those not openly denouncing must implicitly endorse what is done. But to ask Jews who understand Zionism more inclusively, and who we may say have a justified concern to have their own nation state, to renounce the very existence of the State of Israel is deeply problematic. It is in this climate that Jews become perceived as oppressive, white, colonial settlers. Jews become, en masse, the bad guys in the narrative. Notably, the UN General Assembly passed a resolution in 1975 declaring Zionism a 'form of racism and racial discrimination'; however, this was rescinded in 1991. Nevertheless, it has been 'an article of faith for Israel's left-wing opponents that Zionism is a racist ideology'.[72] Indeed, in line with the UN, the British National Union of Students (NUS) passed anti-Zionism motions in the 1970s, and when in 1985 there was a ban on the Jewish Society by the Sunderland Polytechnic Students' Union this was deemed not antisemitic because the society was openly Zionist and it was held that Zionism is inherently racist.[73] As discussed, support for a legitimate homeland for the Jewish people need not be a racist belief, and many Jewish, and non-Jewish, Zionists are very critical of the extreme, 'apartheid-like' policies, of certain governments within Israel. Nevertheless, the perception of Zionism as racist has led to a quandary on the left: if general left-wing principles are followed (and if Jews are a people who suffer from prejudice) then it should be possible to allow Jews to be Zionists and define antisemitism as they see it, but to allow this is seemingly to be complicit in a racist programme.[74]

Allying with those who stand against Israel has, therefore, become normal on the left. For instance, in support of the Palestinians, Corbyn has characterized two movements, Hamas and Hezbollah, as 'friends' and shared platforms with them and given them his support, leading some to allege an alliance of Islamists and leftist antisemites.[75] While both Hamas and Hezbollah have been characterized as terrorist groups, for some on the left, along with militants such as Che Guevara (1928–1967), they are freedom fighters against oppression, hence Corbyn's support; for his supporters, it mirrors his siding with Nelson Mandela (1918–2013) back in the days when the British Prime Minister Margaret Thatcher (1925–2013) declared Mandela to be a 'terrorist'. But, critics note, Hamas is virulently antisemitic (see Chapter 8), so Corbyn's 'friends' reflect his sympathies. However, arguably, there is a failure here to understand the way that some socialist theory can support even unsavoury militant and revolutionary groups. First off, as noted before, socialism has, on the whole, envisaged itself as progressive. Karl Marx (1818–1883) decried antisemitism, while a variously ascribed saying is that antisemitism is the 'socialism of fools', though Marx's work 'On the Jewish Question' ('Zur Judenfrage', 1843) contained antisemitic phrases. As such, despite Stalinist antisemitism and tendencies in some anti-capitalist movements to demonize Jews, or certain Jews, opposing antisemitism has been part of the left's anti-racism agenda. Indeed, aligning with Marx's idea of the progressive march of the proletariat towards emancipation and the eventual overthrow of capitalism, the progress from prejudice towards the rejection of prejudice is seen to be inherent in socialist movements. This is often aligned with anti-imperialist agendas. As such, with groups such as Hamas, who are seen as anti-imperialist and also anti-capitalist (as anti-Western), it is assumed that any outpouring of racism is only an immature stage on their way towards becoming truly progressive. It is, almost, to be expected as part of those not yet fully 'developed', but is seen as not being part of the essence of who they are and what they will become. While certainly condescending (if not outright neo-colonial), in that it is assumed that Western socialism has a deeper insight into their reality than the people themselves, it is easy for progressive, Western, socialist thinkers to dismiss the virulent antisemitism of groups such as Hamas as merely a temporary aberration as they move towards becoming truly progressive movements. Corbyn's alignment, therefore, with such groups is not indicative of an acceptance of antisemitism but a socialist vision of progress. Arguably, a patronizing and colonial viewpoint – despite being part of a claimed wider anti-colonial and anti-racist worldview – but one fully consistent with being ideologically opposed to antisemitism, though it may support structural antisemitism. As such, problematic notions of left-wing ideology need to be addressed for they are not (as supposed) actually anti-racist (or decolonial[76]).

This returns us to a quandary: Corbyn and others may not be personally antisemitic, but their position allows antisemitic discourse to flourish. As Hirsh imagines (if Corbyn had ever come to power), antisemitic 'bullies will [may?] say they're only repeating what the Prime Minister himself thinks; the teachers will check their union policy and may have trouble making the Jewish kids feel safe [if BDS and Anti-Zionist discourse borders on accepting criticism of Jews as a whole, especially if those Jews say they are Zionist]'.[77] This is the issue that we face with the new antisemitism, for without due nuance of what criticism of Israel is acceptable, and without a clear sense of the distinctions of how Zionism is employed in its many permutations, and without understanding why Jews (and non-Jews) may legitimately be Zionist given a history of antisemitism, it is easy to permit discourse that is structurally antisemitic.

This new antisemitism is distinct in various ways. First, it is manifest as a form of anti-racism, which can hide its antisemitism as seemingly impossible. Second, it is related to an anti-Zionist agenda, with Zionism being read monolithically. Third, it is seemingly possible alongside a personal disavowal of antisemitism, but can support structural antisemitism. Fourth, it may be subtle and garbed in ways that make it difficult to spot, partly for the reasons noted above but also because it is often espoused by Jews – the notion of the self-hating Jew is not new per se, but in previous times it involved a disavowal of one's own Jewishness. Here, Jewishness may be kept, and the antisemitism may seemingly be unknown, while various anti-semitic tropes are expounded. In this sense it is deeply pernicious for it can hide openly and float beneath recognition.

How to be anti-antisemitic today?

The death of 6 million Jews was not enough to rid the West of antisemitism. While less acceptable today, it is back. Moreover, while we can spot it when swathed in swastikas and right-wing paraphernalia, it hides these days behind masks of acceptability: the clean-cut protestors of the alt-right; the discourse of militant evangelical support for Israel; as an alternative viewpoint in pseudo-scholarly Holocaust denial; or as 'anti-racist' anti-Zionism on the left. We have spent the majority of this chapter discussing the new antisemitism of the left, and while many Jews are rightly upset about their treatment and sidelining in left-wing movements, with a danger of antisemitic tropes and attitudes becoming established in discourse and regimes of power, we must not exaggerate it. Real physical threats to Jews exist, but in Western political terms this threat still predominantly comes from the far-right (evidence suggests that antisemitism is more prevalent in the mainstream right), and in its enablers such as Holocaust deniers. (It also comes in the modern manifestation of Islamic antisemitism which has drawn from Western thought.) This is not to dismiss leftist antisemitism. Genocide may end with acts of violence, but it begins with language, an attitude of contempt, and a dismissal of another group. Indeed, we may end by noting a paradox: many on the right are pro-Zionist but personally antisemitic, while many on the left are anti-Zionist but personally not anti-semitic. The former, arguably, constitutes the greatest global threat – both to Jews and non-Jews – but the situation still requires some soul-searching for progressives about how they position themselves in these debates.

CHAPTER SEVEN

'Why do they hate us?' and 'Why do we hate them?': Contemporary Western Islamophobias

Introduction

The Western world, especially Europe, has long regarded 'the Islamic world'[1] as a threatening presence on its borders. Partly, this represents the meeting of empires and the clashes of militarist expansion rather than the meeting of Islamic and Christian worldviews. Nevertheless, both in Christendom and Islamic caliphates, military expansion has been tied to religio-political ideologies. These pressures underlie the growth of Islamophobia in the West. As discussed earlier, the term 'Islamophobia' stands here as a marker for prejudice and discrimination against Muslims. It is not some special form of phobia or prejudice in and of itself.

One approach to getting to grips with Islamophobia is to list examples to which the term applies, and Salman Sayyid gives five categories for this: (1) physical attacks on those perceived as Muslims; (2) attacks on property; (3) acts of intimidation; (4) 'institutional' behaviour from harassment to bullying, to jokes and less favourable treatment; and (5) 'systemic' public disparagement.[2] Another is to give a description, and here we employ Todd Green's definition that Islamophobia is 'the fear of and hostility toward Muslims and Islam that is rooted in racism and that results in individual and systemic discrimination, exclusion, and violence targeting Muslims and those perceived as Muslim'.[3] We will revisit aspects of both of these as we proceed, but we can note several key points. We are talking about fear and hostility, which unsurprisingly come together. Green specifically associates it with racism. This may seem odd because Islam is a religious category; however, like antisemitism, it is racialized; this explains why it also affects 'those perceived as Muslims', with racial profiling being central. Also, it is often 'institutional' in nature such that from having an 'Islamic-sounding' name, to fitting an imagined racial profile (often skin colour based), to other cultural markers, Muslims are on the receiving end of the kind of discrimination in Sayyid's fourth category. This may even come from people who may not regard themselves as prejudiced.

The term 'Islamophobia' is generally seen to come from a 1997 report published by a British anti-racist organization, the Runnymede Trust, which listed eight features of the prejudice.[4] While some argue the Runnymede definition can stifle criticism of Islam, the report makes clear that it is possible to criticize Islam without being Islamophobic (see related discussions on using antisemitism to stifle criticism of Israel).[5] However, Christopher Allen criticizes the Runnymede report for creating a binary of the 'good-Muslim-bad-Muslim'. This seems to make demands on Muslims which exceed those made on other citizens to show they are good citizens, else they risk appearing to be 'bad-Muslims', hence the Runnymede report itself is open to accusations of Islamophobia.[6] Notably, some scholars suggest the problem is not prejudice or fear of Islam, but of Muslims, and suggest we use Anti-Muslimism or Muslimophobia.[7] However, as discussed earlier, we will employ the now standard term.

We start by asking whether fear of Muslims makes sense in the contemporary Western context, then observe how characterizations of Muslims today hark back to older stereotypes. We next address how Islamophobia is generated and sustained by the 'Islamophobia Industry', the media, and politicians, before discussing Islam as a racialized category. Then, we address Islam as a 'securitised faith', including issues of surveillance and social profiling, and how this has affected Muslim communities. Finally, we discuss 'subtle' Islamophobia.

Islamo-phobia or Islamo-realism?

We may have heard the phrase: 'Not all Muslims are terrorists, but all terrorists are Muslims.' The media and politicians certainly keep us alert to a perceived imminent and present danger of 'Islamic terrorism' as we will see below. Since 9/11, boarding an aircraft is a very different experience, while our societies have become securitized and monitored in unprecedented ways with police and security services in many countries especially profiling those who may be perceived as Muslims. From 9/11, through the Bali bombing of 2002, the Madrid Train bombings of 2004, the 2005 7/7 London attacks, the Bataclan theatre attacks in Paris in 2015, the televised ISIS beheadings, to the beheading of a French schoolteacher in 2020 for showing his students cartoons of Muhammad, and many more examples besides, have we not seen the evidence that we should fear Islam and the terror that it brings? This is the claim of many who think the phrase 'Islamophobia' is problematic – fearing Islam and Muslims is not a 'phobia' but a realistic proposition. But: bad news sells; simple narratives about the bad guys get you votes; and, we will readily fear the unknown. Fearing Islam and Muslims may, therefore, seem to reflect the evidence we are presented with, but wider evidence paints a very different story.

For a start, statistics show a very different story. Between 2009 and 2013, less than 2 per cent of terrorist attacks in Europe were religiously motivated.[8] In 2019, more white than Asian people were arrested for terrorism in the UK.[9] While the 2019 Global Terrorism Index noted that while Islamist attacks had been a more serious threat in the West, during 2018 'far-right terrorist attacks accounted for 17.2 while attacks by Islamist groups accounted for 6.8 per cent of attacks', with 62.8 per cent not classified as either, with far-right terrorism seen as the currently rising trend (but not having reached unprecedented levels).[10] Our perception of a 'typical terrorist' depends on how atrocities are presented in our societies and media. For instance, when the 1995 Oklahoma City bombing destroyed a federal building and many surrounding buildings, at the time the deadliest terrorist attack on American soil (killing 168 people and injuring 680), the media went into overdrive linking it to Middle Eastern-inspired 'Islamist terrorism'. However, the killer was Timothy McVeigh (1968–2001), a white American and military veteran. His motivation was political and driven in part by white supremacy. Yet, even after this was known a CNN reporter, Wolf Blitzer, argued there might be a Middle Eastern link.[11] Compare this to the Madrid bombings, when, for several days afterwards, Spanish government officials and the media suggested that the most likely perpetrator was ETA, a Basque separatist organization that has long carried out terrorist attacks in Spain. Only when it became clear who the perpetrators were, was Islamist terrorism discussed.

For much of recent European history, terrorism was primarily associated with separatist movements or left-wing radicals, and in the 1970s and 1980s, Europe experienced far higher levels of deaths from terror attacks than in the last couple of decades from militant neo-Islamic jihadi terrorism. Indeed, the United States has faced far more terrorism from white, right-wing, extremists than it has from those with a Muslim background, both before and after 9/11.[12] Possibly some recent incidents are awakening people to the dangers of the right, with events such as Charlottesville's 2017 'Unite the Right' rally and the 2019 New Zealand Christchurch mosque attack.[13] Moreover, violence and terror come from many religions (and worldviews). Christian responses to the Monty Python film *The Life of Brian* and Martin Scorsese's *The Last Temptation of Christ* included bomb threats and setting fire to a cinema during a screening of the latter in Paris.[14]

Terrorism scholarship traces the origins of the phenomenon to the nineteenth century, particularly to anarchist groups who were the first non-state actors to use 'terror' as a weapon to change the world, gain public attention, or spread their message. Anarchists would bomb cafes arguing that there were no innocent bourgeoisie. The rationale and ideology of terrorism spread from this anarchist wave, into left-wing and anti-colonial waves in the twentieth century, before the current wave of religiously linked terror.[15] Right-wing terrorism is not seen to constitute its own wave but to be a persistent undercurrent. In such areas as the justification to target civilians, tactics, and ideology, today's militant neo-Islamic jihadis[16] (what are commonly termed 'Muslim terrorists') are linked to previous terrorist waves, not Islamic tradition.[17] Even suicide bombing, which some assert is the ultimate irrational and depraved act based in Islamic martyrdom, is rooted in secular terrorist ideologies especially as a tactic of the Liberation Tigers of Tamil Eelam who fought for Tamil Independence in Sri Lanka between 1983 and 2009. Some military scholars even argue that suicide bombing is a tool of asymmetrical warfare as much as a terrorist tactic, while Robert Pape's (disputable) study of suicide attacks between 1980 and 2003 argued that 95 per cent of suicide attacks were linked to foreign occupation.[18] This is not to justify suicide bombings on civilians, but it is often discussed in ways that are deeply Islamophobic without any understanding of the history and practice.

Discussions of Islam often owe more to misunderstandings and misrepresentations, or take cherry-picked facts and unrepresentative examples to castigate the whole tradition, such that we need to talk about the Western imagination of Muslims.[19] For instance, Saudi Arabia and the rule of the Taliban in Afghanistan are often used to suggest that Islam is: inherently oppressive of women; opposed to democracy and human rights; backwards, immoral, and anti-Western. But, the Muslim-majority world is vast and diverse. So, contrary to representations of Islam denying women education, in many Gulf States, such as Bahrain, Kuwait, or Qatar, women have a higher proportion of postsecondary degrees than men. Again, ahead of certain Western countries, female prime ministers or presidents have been found in Turkey, Mauritius, Bangladesh, Pakistan, Singapore, and Indonesia.[20] Green argues that focusing on specific issues in specific countries ignores the fact that in the United States around 321,500 people over the age of 12 are raped each year, mostly women, and that it was ranked in 2018 by the Thomas Reuters Foundation as one of the ten most dangerous countries for women.[21] Meanwhile, high-profile critics of Islam such as Ayaan Hirsi Ali or Irshad Manji give 'simplistic, unnuanced' views of Islam when they call for it to be reformed, rarely mentioning the many Muslim reformers, including women, who have been doing this work, often for decades.[22]

So, are we talking about Islamorealism or Islamophobia? Clearly the threat is not from Islam or Muslims. If Islam really did lead to terrorism, as figures such as Sam Harris argue, given that there are 1.8 billion Muslims, we would be in trouble. Harris' seemingly frankly ignorant and nonsensical argument that only the terrorists are getting Islam right ignores around 1400 years of Islamic tradition, embedded in *shariah* law codes, which is very clear that killing civilians is forbidden, and that suicide attacks are immoral. As noted, we see direct links from today's militant neo-Islamic jihadists to terrorist ideology, but not to Islamic tradition. Ignorance of Islam, and not careful study of it, may lead to Islamophobia. Millions of Muslims worldwide lead peaceful lives as teachers, doctors, lawyers, fashion designers, and human rights activists, living peacefully as citizens based on centuries of Islamic tradition.

Images of Islam: Yesterday and today

Modern fear of Muslims does not come from nowhere. There have been centuries of animosity between Christians and Muslims where empires have collided (see Chapter 4).[23] It would also be wrong, as some apologists for Islam do – Islamophilia is as misguided as Islamophobia – to suggest that Islam is only a religion of peace and has no connection to violence and warfare. Warfare and violence are sanctioned in Islamic tradition, though much scholarship argues that it is hard to justify calling any warfare 'holy' or 'sacred' in Islamic perspective. 'Jihad' does not mean 'holy war', but 'striving' or 'struggle'. One normative meaning is seeking moral perfection, though Islamic tradition uses it for military struggles too. Notably, the Qur'an uses specific Arabic words for battle and warfare, so anybody who says the Qur'an speaks about jihad as 'holy war' is simply ignorant.[24] The fact that warfare has existed between Muslims and Christians does not, however, explain how we have come to think about Islam. For this, we need to consider orientalism.

Just as a largely false representation of Judaism has flourished in the Western world, the same has happened with Islam. Negative tropes abound, and Edward Said (1935–2003) spoke about this as orientalism. The term orientalism previously denoted the study of the Middle East and Asia, but Said rejected the positive connotation and used the term pejoratively to talk about the political aspects of study and false representations of the Orient. So successful has Said's argument been that, these days, to be termed an orientalist is generally an insult. This is related to the way that 'a Christian Europe' was imagined in contradistinction to 'an Islamic Orient' (see Chapter 4). While Said's orientalist thesis can overstate its case, and is not as some assert a unique aspect of Western representations of the world, it helps point us to the way we have constructed a problematic image of Islam.[25]

Europe is an arbitrary construction. For instance, the centuries of common culture and trade links around the Mediterranean Sea made it a central bond with Asia and Africa rather than a barrier.[26] Islamic influences in art, poetry, science, and philosophy underpinned modern Western notions of romantic love and enabled the Renaissance, but orientalist scholarship demarcated a binary opposition of 'us' and 'them', meaning we now envisage Islam as exemplifying a worldview and culture in sharp contrast to the West. This was stated by Ernest Renan (1823–1892): 'To be a Muslim is by definition to reject the "European spirit"' and all that makes this spirit superior: reason, science, and the drive for knowledge.'[27] In the orientalist imagination, Europe is: gender-equal, democratic, progressive, modern, liberal, reasonable, civilized, and white. While, by way of contrast, Islam is: gender-oppressive, authoritarian, backward-looking, traditional, fundamentalist, fanatical, uncivilized, and not-white. These paired binaries valorize Europe and demonize Muslims. As with in-group and out-group formation in general, these binaries tell us next to nothing about the groups so named, and more about the imagination of the definers. Historically, we cannot find the Western worldview and cultural forms which are distinct from an Islamic worldview and cultural forms. An appeal to a supposedly superior 'Christian Europe' suits some people's purposes, but fanaticism, gender-oppression, and resistance to democracy and human rights are as readily found among white supremacists, Christian fundamentalists, or various other 'Westerners', as much as any groups in the Muslim-majority world.

However, of absolute significance for Islamophobia is the perception of centuries of conflict, which in Orientalist formation posits Islam as inherently violent and the Muslim as crazed fanatic in pursuit of 'jihad' (understood as warfare). As indicated above, this is a very problematic trope. The crusader slaughter on first taking Jerusalem was an act of violence which had no precedence in any Islamic conquest before that point. The excesses of the West's own violence, however, became its image of its neighbour. The spread of Islam, given the times, was very often remarkably peaceable, and current evidence suggests that no mass forced conversions, certainly of Christians or Jews, took place in the earliest period. If we contrast this with the situation when Christian rule was enforced over Spain in 1492, the expulsion or forced conversion of both Jews and Muslims that followed speaks of an intolerance and inability to cope with diversity. Moreover, in the seventeenth century, it was the Islamic Ottoman Empire that was held up to Europe as the paradigm of tolerance, with it being noted that 'the Turks put none to death for Religion'.[28] Indeed, many in the Muslim world portray Westerners as fanatics bent on Christian crusades to destroy the Muslim world, something which in their view has continued through colonialism, with Napoleon's invasion of Egypt being a symbolic incursion and one described then as a 'crusade', till the present day, especially as, following 9/11, the American President George W. Bush Jr invoked the term 'crusade' for his 'war on terror'.

The Islamophobia industry

In a context where these background cultural stereotypes of Muslims abound, the flames of mistrust are further stoked by what has been called the Islamophobia industry, or 'Professional Islamophobes'.[29] These terms refer to people who have become famous primarily by using fear of Islam to enhance their reputation. We see crossover, more or less distinctly, with media figures and politicians. We can divide those involved into three camps: 'native informants', which includes such people as Hirsi Ali and Manji; atheist Islamophobes, for instance Harris and Richard Dawkins; and politico-media personalities, including Bill Maher and Geert Wilders.

The term 'native informants' refers to Muslims, and former Muslims, who have used this 'insider status' to claim expertise based on first-hand knowledge of the religion. One argument they may raise is that they cannot be Islamophobic because they actually are Muslims or come from that background. However, in antisemitic terms a long-standing category is what is often termed the 'self-hating' Jew who buys into the negative stereotyping of their people and tradition. This may be to gain acceptance in society, to gain a platform as a native informant speaker, or simply arises from some form of self-loathing. What accounts for it in the figures mentioned here is hard to say, but being a Muslim, or former Muslim, is no defence against being Islamophobic. Again, the claims to insider knowledge are themselves suspicious: an 'insider' speaks from only one place, not for the whole tradition, and former members, like new converts, are often far from impartial. So, when Hirsi Ali uses her experience as a Somali (former) Muslim woman to make claims about Islam as a whole, this at best applies only to her own family, community, and practice of Islam in one localized place at one chronological period. She particularly rails against Islam's bias against women, but, as was noted above, Muslim women are often better educated than men, or have had leadership roles as prime ministers or presidents in Muslim-majority societies and as leaders in Islamic communities. In the traditions of Mohammed and in much Islamic tradition, it has been stressed that women should be educated because they are the ones who will bring up the children; this, while limiting women to a particular domestic role, does not support the arguments that keeping women ignorant is inherent in Islam. Indeed, Mohammed's first wife was a successful businesswoman in her own right and his boss, while one of his wives led an army into battle. Saying 'I had a bad experience and therefore Islam as a whole is bad' is not a credible scholarly argument. We may agree that Islam needs reform, but both men and women in Islam have been saying this long before Hirsi Ali started her campaign.

Harris's misrepresentation of jihad has been noted; indeed, Mohammad Hassan Khalil has argued that Harris presents Islam as inherently more violent than even Osama Bin Laden did.[30] The general New Atheist criticism of religion is particularly levelled towards Islam. This has been influential, though Dawkins received considerable pushback from one tweet (2018) in which he rhetorically asked whether it was his cultural background or whether the bells of Winchester Cathedral were not preferable to the 'aggressive' Allahu Akbar of the Muslim call to prayer.[31] The Twittersphere let him know that it was his cultural background. Indeed, a constant criticism of New Atheists has been their ignorance of the traditions they criticize, and which Dawkins has even said he has no need to know about to be able to criticize. As such, rather than being insightful they often recycle the orientalist tropes of 'folk knowledge' (or common prejudices). Harris, who often portrays himself as an expert on Islam, appears to have a very shaky grasp of the tradition, and in line with confirmation bias seems to interpret the little he does know in line with pre-existing biases.[32]

Much the same can be said about those politico-media personalities who know that Islamophobic rhetoric will get applause. The American television host Bill Maher is a good example and shows that left-leaning figures can be Islamophobic.[33] He regularly offers unsubstantiated, scathing attacks on Islam, with his position as a media personality seemingly offering a trusted opinion when he opines that, for instance, the Qur'an is 'Islam's hate-filled holy book'.[34] Likewise, in Europe and beyond, minor political figures such as Wilders have propelled themselves to centre stage by taking a populist Islamophobic stance that combines fear of Islam, concerns about migrants, and racism into a potent electoral package. We saw something similar with Nigel Farage in the UK who at the end of the UK's Brexit referendum proudly released a poster that brought all these together in one image and which was compared to 1930s fascist propaganda.[35] It appears that Farage also referred to Muslims as 'fifth columnists' in the UK who want to kill British people.[36] Again, in the United States, the campaign of Donald Trump and his proposed 'Muslim ban' played into these fears. This is a good time to move directly into the role of the media and politicians. However, before we do, some may feel that we are talking about just a few individuals not an 'industry', but this is belied by the money which funds it. Between 2008 and 2013, the thirty-three key organizations promoting Islamophobia in the United States received 206,000,000 USD in sponsorship.[37]

The media, politicians, and Muslims

Khaled Beydoun discusses 'structural Islamophobia'[38] to refer to it being built into systems of governance, social norms, and as a powerful impetus in its own right, likening it to structural racism. We will explore a thread that runs through structural forms of Islamophobia which will 'exhibit the Islamophobic base narrative that holds all Muslims guilty of every terror attack'.[39] We will also tie it to the 'good-Muslim-bad-Muslim' trope.[40]

In the aftermath of 9/11, President Bush was often careful to note that the 'war on terror' was not a war on Islam, and he said to Muslims:

We respect your faith. It's practiced freely by many millions of Americans. … Its teachings are good and peaceful, and those who commit evil in the name of Allah blaspheme the name of Allah. The terrorists are traitors to their own faith. … The enemy of America is not our many Muslim friends; it is not our many Arab friends.[41]

However, his language was not always so clear, such as his use of 'crusade'. Moreover, especially after 9/11, while more responsible elements in the media sought to separate Islam from terrorism, other media outlets did not make careful distinctions. Indeed, who were our Muslim friends, the 'good-Muslims', and who were the 'bad-Muslims'? Certainly, one former British prime minister, David Cameron, helped build what has been termed 'guilt-by-association', arguing that if Muslims do not tackle and condemn terrorism then there should be no public funding for them.[42] In other words, the default position was suspicion of Muslims: unless you can prove that you are a 'good-Muslim', you are a 'bad-Muslim'. The orientalist trope of Islam as inherently violent and dangerous made any Muslim potentially suspect. Moreover, studies of the media demonstrate a torrent of stories and images showing Islam in a bad light, with terms such as 'terrorist', 'violence' or 'oppression' often tied to Muslims.[43] Even before 9/11, a study of Swedish media, which is not untypical, showed that '85% of all news reports related to Islam and Muslims are wholly or partly related to violence', while such images and concepts as 'fundamentalisms, the Koran, jihad, minarets, men who are on their knees praying, women in headscarves and Ayatollah Khomeini with bushy eyebrows' typified reporting.[44] Indeed, media reporting would often show Muslims praying before cutting to scenes of violence, suggesting through the imagery a direct connection of Islamic devotion to terror. Again, it is often asserted that Muslims need to condemn these attacks, but this ignores two things: first, Muslims do regularly condemn them but it is not often reported by the media and is thus easily ignored by both the Islamophobia industry and the mainstream media;[45] second, the same demands are not made of Christians when a Christian commits a violent attack, nor of white people after white supremacist terror attacks. A double standard is at play, Muslims are presumed guilty till proven innocent. Moreover, this often means that Muslims are expected to endorse and support Western military and foreign policies despite many valid criticisms that can be made (including by non-Muslims).[46]

In short, we live in a world where Muslims are framed as the bad guys and where such allegations can readily go unchallenged. Indeed, many false charges are made, with Jan Jambon, Belgian's then interior minister, claiming that a 'significant part of the Muslim community danced' after the Brussels attack on 22 March 2016. This phenomenon has many levels from the media framing to populist politics, with Trump failing to call out a supporter who stated, 'We have a problem in this country; it's called Muslims,' and when the same person asked, 'When can we get rid of them?,' Trump's reply was 'I'll look into it.'[47] Again, Wilders has suggested that 'Islam and freedom are not compatible',[48] arguing that Muslims are an inherent problem. Indeed, contrary to claims of supporting Western freedoms and tolerance, such politicians seem to want to restrict freedom, at least for one demographic. Such extreme views on Islam influence the mainstream discourse.

Before moving on, we can briefly note one issue. To distinguish between 'good' and 'bad' Muslims, a distinction between 'Islam' and 'Islamism' (or 'Islamist') is often used. The former is seen to refer to the acceptable parts of the tradition, and the latter to its unacceptable interpretations, either in militant neo-Islamic jihadism or when it becomes illegitimately politicized. This distinction is used by journalists, politicians, and many scholars. However, this distinction is at best unstable and potentially Islamophobic. Islam, like almost every religion, has been linked to political regimes, and its legal systems blur the normative (modern, Western) boundary between religion and secular realms. This is not to deny that there are forms of practice that claim a base in Islam that are politically problematic, especially those enacting terrorism in the name of Islam in ways which clearly deviate from the mainstream tradition. However, Christianity is equally implicated in politics, with evangelical support for Trump being one example in recent times. While there may be good reasons to keep religion out of politics, it is not a legitimate or useful critique of Islam to insist that only the Islam that steers clear of politics is the 'good-Islam' when we do not make this distinction in other religions (e.g. 'Christianity' versus 'Christianism'). Indeed, most people probably would agree that there are some legitimate ways in which religion can be tied to political issues, with few criticizing religious people whose practice inspires them to work for social justice, feed the poor, or fight against inequality and oppression. Critics claiming that Islam must play no role in politics also typically ignore that the United States is framed as 'one nation under God', and that the UK's monarch is head of both church and state, to give just two examples of how Christianity and politics are linked (see Interlude 1).[49] It is an orientalist trope to claim that Islam is incompatible with secular democracy while ignoring how Christianity infringes on it. Muslims are held to different standards.

Islamophobia as racism

Only days after 9/11, Balbir Singh Sodhi, a Sikh, was shot five times and killed while planting flowers outside his petrol station by the white American Frank Roque who stated that he wanted to 'kill the ragheads'.[50] Sodhi is not the only Sikh to have been targeted because they were assumed to be Muslim. Many male Khalsa Sikhs who mandatorily wear a turban have suffered prejudice, if not physical violence, while numerous Gurdwaras have been attacked in Islamophobic incidents.[51] The significance of these attacks on Sikhs is that Islamophobia is not just targeted at Muslims but also 'those perceived as Muslim'. In other words: it is about 'looking like a Muslim'. This is partly to do with culture and ethnicity, and so the Sikh turban is assumed to be Muslim headwear, but also skin colour and racial profiling.[52] Given its ethno-cultural aspects, sociologist Tariq Modood has termed Islamophobia a form of 'cultural racism'.[53]

A number of critics have argued that Islamophobia cannot be racist as it targets a religion and not a race.[54] However, this totally fails to understand the dynamics behind the prejudice. People do not get attacked in the street after it has been ascertained whether they are Muslim or not; if they were, Sodhi would still be alive. Moreover, the right-wing slur of 'race traitor' is applied to white converts (especially women) who convert to Islam as well as those who marry Muslims. What exactly does 'race traitor' mean if Islam is not understood in a racialized way? Here, we need to understand racialization (see Chapter 5), because 'race' does not exist in and of itself, but is socially constructed and changing.

Historically, one clear instance of the racialization of Islam is seen between 1790 and 1952 when being 'white' was a legal requirement for becoming a US citizen, and as Khaled Beydoun demonstrates 'whiteness' was connected with Christianity and 'non-whiteness' with Islam.[55] George Shishim filed a citizenship application case in 1909, which went to court with a report suggesting that, as an Arab, the request should be refused. But to close his petition, Shishim recited the Hail Mary, and so while appearing 'non-white' in the sense of being Middle Eastern, the judge decided that as a Christian he was white by law. However, when Faras Shahid, another Middle Eastern Christian of the Maronite tradition, inspired by Shishim's case, brought his application in 1913, the judge decided that 'Shahid's dark skin signalled that he was either Muslim or the product of racial miscegenation with Muslims that diluted his Christianity': this equated Islam with race by using blood-lineage ideology and 'the language of the "one-drop rule" to hold that any modicum of Muslim blood made Shahid, before the eyes of the court, a Muslim'.[56]

Despite many not recognizing Islamophobia as racism,[57] in day-to-day instances of Islamophobia, its racialization is clear: 'These realities would not disappear even if self-identified Muslims chose to identify with another religious community or dropped a religious identity altogether.'[58] Another point worth noting is that, within the United States, as being Muslim is popularly associated with being Arab, this means that being Black and Muslim may be seen as impossible or gets discounted, despite the long history of many Muslims of Black African ancestry. ('Black' Ethiopian Jews may likewise be subject to intra-Jewish colourism prejudice.)

A securitized faith

According to Green, 'Muslims have emerged as the most overtly targeted besieged minority religious community in the post-9/11 West.'[59] In the United States, it has been suggested that they are the 'new Blacks', while Black Muslims face a double jeopardy, which is intensified for Black female Muslims – the female body, often the hijab, has often been the battlefield of cultural difference.[60] Perceived ethnicity also plays into this, with some ethnicities also seen as threats, resulting in what Tania Saeed has termed a 'hyper-securitization' where people are targeted on account of both ethnicity and religion.[61] However, the securitization of Islam has wider implications seen in the effects of the 'war on terror' which has been used to push back on civil liberties, while the surveillance of mosques is undertaken because it is assumed all Muslims are potentially, if not inherently, guilty.

This securitization falls back upon orientalist motifs of the violent Muslim. However, post-9/11, it has particularly drawn from two American scholars: Bernard Lewis (1916–2018) and Samuel Huntington (1927–2008). Lewis' scholarly works on Islam are seen by many to be imbued with an Islamophobic sprit, and his work is heavily contested by figures such as John Esposito. Huntington popularized the phrase the 'clash of civilisations'[62] to speak about the way that the Western (Christian) world was seen to be, post-Cold War, in a new era of civilizational conflict between eight major blocks which would include the Sinitic (Confucian) world, but most particularly the Islamic world. For Huntington, the values of these civilizations are diametrically opposed and liable to violent confrontation. This worldview was adopted almost wholesale by the Bush administration in the febrile post-9/11 environment with Lewis and Huntington being key advisors to government.[63] Moreover, proliferation of often self-proclaimed 'Islamic experts' (and self-appointed 'terrorism experts') post-9/11 saw Islamophobic 'scholarship', which often repeats nineteenth-century colonial stereotypes, cross over with the Islamophobia industry, the 'Terrorism Industry' and structural Islamophobia. Given scholarly contestation and the clashes of many so-called experts it can be hard for non-experts to not sometimes be under the impression that Islam is anti-Western and prone to violence. Here, we will address two sets of issues to help us understand this. First, some key evidence about Islam and the monolithic and stereotyped view that endorses a clash of civilizations thesis. Second, the evidence about the securitization that Muslims, and others, have faced.

As discussed above, the claim that the Qur'an endorses jihad as 'holy war' is factually inaccurate. Huntington's claim that 'Islam has bloody borders' ignores that the vast majority of these borders emerged during encounters with Western Christians with violence going two ways. Elsewhere, such as in Southeast Asia, including Indonesia which has the world's largest Muslim population, Islam spread peacefully through trade and itinerant missionaries. Muslims have also extolled women's educational rights and promoted tolerance of religious diversity in their polities. While, today, only one in four Muslim-majority countries is democratic,[64] the location and context of these countries is often far more significant an indicator of whether democracy exists. During the twentieth century, places such as Iran experienced Western-backed coups which replaced their democracy with authoritarian dictatorships. More recently, in the 2011 Arab Spring, the United States initially supported its long-time ally the dictator Hosni Mubarak in Egypt against a popular democratic mandate.[65] These examples are only indicative, but point to the fact that any claims about the monolithic nature of an anti-democratic, anti-human rights, pro-violence Islam is based upon cherry-picked and often unrepresentative cases chosen to highlight certain things. For instance, Saudi Arabia, often taken as somehow representing Islamic government, is run in accord with an eighteenth-century reactionary reform movement, and seeing it as normative would be a bit like suggesting that the Amish are representative of Christianity.[66]

Approximately three and a half million Muslims live in the United States and have lived there peaceably for many years, but on 25 October 2001, the US Attorney General John Ashcroft was ready to say that Islamic terrorists 'live in our communities – plotting, planning and waiting to kill Americans again'.[67] Such statements helped blur the line between ordinary Muslims and militant extremists. Indeed, a young child who brought a homemade science project to school was made into a terror suspect. This was the case of 14-year-old Ahmed Mohamed who brought a homemade clock to school and found himself arrested for making a suspected bomb, having been profiled and found dangerous because of his skin colour and religion, in ways that would not have happened to a white Christian.[68]

In the United States, the UK, and elsewhere, programmes against violent extremism have often disproportionally targeted Muslims. This has been true of both the Prevent programme in the UK, though overhauled to more clearly also focus on such things as the dangers of violence from white supremacists and the far-right, and CVE (Countering Violent Extremism) policing in the United States.[69] In the United States, in reaction to 9/11, 1,200 Arab and Muslim men were arrested without charge and with no access to lawyers by the Department of Justice, and their treatment included physical and verbal abuse, leg chains, solitary confinement, and repeated strip searches.[70] The US Patriot Act of October 2001 expanded government power to conduct surveillance and detain immigrants suspected of supporting terrorism, and under the Trump presidency there has been a clear signal that surveillance and suspicion fall directly on Muslims, though he has also targeted the LGBTQI community and the Black Lives Matter movement.[71] The practice of extraordinary rendition also saw Muslims being subject to illegal torture and violations of their human rights – the very rights the West claimed to defend are exactly those it denied to Muslims.[72] Again, the notion of radicalization, while ostensibly about all forms of potentially violent extremism, has been particularly focused on Islam. Following the problematic original usage by the NYPD, the term 'radicalization' has been seen by some as defining a clear pathway to terrorism which may involve acts of Muslim piety, so growing a beard or praying more frequently could lead to detainment or harassment.[73]

Legally enforced structural Islamophobia, based on orientalist stereotypes and outright prejudice, have seen many thousands of innocent Muslims, the vast majority of whom are appalled by the actions of Al-Qaeda or ISIS, surveilled, harassed, or arrested. There is good reason to believe that such policies play into the hands of militant neo-Islamic jihadis who can tell Muslims in the West: 'look, they do not trust you, you do not belong there, you will only face violence and discrimination from your enemies' (i.e. Western Christians). While the number of young Western Muslims who went to fight for ISIS in places such as Syria and Iraq, or who have enacted terrorism against their own fellow citizens, is shocking, that the numbers are so low proportionally is testament to the fact that Muslims do not see violence as inherently stemming from their tradition. Indeed, lives of petty crime, jail, and gang membership are far more likely indicators of radicalization than mosque attendance or signs of Islamic piety, with a vast majority of cases linked to the former. Muslims have been securitized for their religion, when almost the exact opposite should have been the case. Moreover, the foreign policy of many Western nations, which can legitimately be seen as targeting certain Muslim-majority countries, and the social reality of discrimination, have played a large role in leading Muslims into violent militancy.[74]

Subtle Islamophobia

We should note that not all Islamophobia is overt or direct. Indeed, often it may go unnoticed. It can exist in people who see themselves opposed to racism or not prejudiced against Muslims. In this sense, it has similarities with what is sometimes called the new antisemitism. Leon Moosavi has argued that it can manifest in discreet ways that make it harder to perceive or recognize as direct prejudice, but it contributes to structural Islamophobia as a form of racism in society.[75]

A good example of such subtle behaviour is the fact that studies have shown that employers are less likely to ask candidates with 'Muslim sounding' names to interviews. In experiments where two identical CVs were submitted, one under a 'Western/English name' and the other a 'Muslim name', the person with a 'Western/English name' was chosen for interview and the identical candidate with a 'Muslim name' was not called. The statistical significance of this, even among employers who do not regard themselves as being prejudiced, shows that it is a problem within society.[76] Unconscious bias may be a significant factor based on culturally ingrained expectations of particular 'types' of people. Again, there are unspoken rules about who is invited to certain events or who you encourage your children to play with at school.

Forms of prejudice also vary, and we noted above how women's bodies often become the battlefield. Indeed, prejudice may be more or less explicit. In France, for instance, it has been determined by the government that Muslim girls cannot wear the hijab in school as this is seen to violate their vision of a secular society. Yet, in the United States, which is in many ways no less Islamophobic, there is no problem with students wearing the hijab in schools, and indeed when a school did seek to institute a ban on this, the US government even intervened to support a girl's right to wear it.[77] Yet, as we have seen, growing beards, praying frequently, or simply appearing to look Muslim have all been factors in people being given extra screening at airports, killed for their (supposed) Muslim identity, or simply facing day-to-day suspicion or even subtle and discreet displays of prejudice or discrimination. Unfavourable views of Muslims and Islam are common.[78]

Books, cartoons, and stereotypes

We could have noted further incidents that make people suspicious of Muslims, but other evidence undermines such suspicions as we could show. For instance, the Salman Rushdie Affair in which his book *The Satanic Verses* (1988) was burnt and the Iranian leader Ayatollah Khomeini issued a fatwa calling for the author's death,[79] the murder of the film-maker Theo Van Gogh (1957–2004) for his film with Hirsi Ali mocking Mohammed, or the so-called Danish Cartoons incident (2005–6), which saw marches in the streets calling for the deaths of those responsible. However, after the marches against the Danish cartoons, much larger marches by Muslims repudiating the violent and murderous intentions expressed took place but were largely ignored by the media.[80] Again, attacks by a few extremists have seen violence against Muslims in response. After the 2015 Paris attacks, London hate crimes against Muslims tripled, especially targeting females, while a fivefold increase occurred after the 2017 London bridge attacks.[81] This is not to suggest any moral equivalency, but it represents the way that Muslims as a whole are condemned for the actions of a few, and actions which most Muslims equally repudiate. Muslims are often stigmatized. Some argue Muslims are taking over parts of the countries they migrate to, simply because we see cultural changes (an old argument against Jews, Chinatowns, Italian quarters, etc.).[82] Such changes may be resented by some 'locals' or 'indigenous people', but welcomed by others. However, in the case of Muslims it often plays into deeply problematic Islamophobic narratives that paint monolithic and stereotyped images of Muslims. As such, when we turn to the question in our title, the well-known response to the 9/11 attacks of 'why do they hate us?', we can also ask in response: 'why do we hate them?' Islamophobia is rife in Western societies and highlights much about contemporary forms of religious hatred in the West.

INTERLUDE 3

Are antisemitism and Islamophobia connected?

Introduction

When we ask if antisemitism and Islamophobia are connected, an immediate question comes to mind, which is for what purpose(s) are we asking this question? This may seem counter-intuitive, for either they are connected or they are not. But this misses the issue of agency in determining questions and answers, or facts and interpretations. For instance, do we mean are they conceptually linked? Or, are there common origins? Or, do those combatting both forms of prejudice face a common enemy? With these three questions alone, we raise the way that the manner of our enquiry will determine what kind of answer we give. For the purposes of this book, we can certainly say that they are linked. Both are forms of prejudice and discrimination based, historically, in religious discourses, and, in the contemporary context, in racialized perceptions. Like all forms of prejudice, we can say that there are common conceptual bases. We may also explore some other aspects of how they may, or may not, be seen as linked.

There is a growing literature that is looking at the linkages, crossovers, and commonalities.[1] However, this work also shows that there are massive differences in terminology and ideas, while much of the structure of similarity and difference is also geographically, culturally, and chronologically diverse and changeable. Whenever we highlight commonalities, we must also point out the divergences between how antisemitism and Islamophobia manifest in specific contexts. Often, though, especially in Western contexts, whoever hates the Jew, hates the Muslim, and probably quite a few other folks besides. As we noted before, Frantz Fanon (1925–1961) reports being told by his philosophy teacher in Martinique: 'Whenever you hear anyone abuse the Jews, pay attention, because he is talking about you.'[2] Of course, not every antisemite is an Islamophobe, and vice versa; however, studies show that a disproportionate number are both.[3] Also, at least in many countries, while antisemitism is on the rise, it is arguably Islamophobia that is more threatening, with Matti Bunzl suggesting a replacement of the 'Jewish Question' with the 'Muslim Question'.[4]

Terminology, technicalities, theology

While 'the original anti-Semites were proud to mobilise publicly and name themselves', Islamophobia was 'named by their opponents as a badge of shame' and is a term that is commonly rejected by those it applies to.[5] How much we should read into this, especially today, is unclear. A veneer of respectability, justice and reason is sought by many who hold such prejudices and who would vehemently deny any association with the more militant and unsavoury connotations; there has certainly been socially acceptable and 'polite' antisemitism, while, 'today,' Islamophobia has been described as passing 'the dinner-table test'.[6]

Sander Gilman shows that current criticisms of Islam match previous criticisms of Judaism. While some speak of the 'eight hundred pound gorilla' confronting Western Europe in the form of the 'huge presence of an "unassimilable" minority' in its midst, that is, 'the reproductive capacity of a permanent and unassimilable underclass of "Muslim immigrants"', he reminds us that 'exactly the same things have been said … about Jews for two hundred years'.[7] Gilman also offers a case study to show that today's German anti-Muslim circumcision laws repeat previous anti-Jewish discourse and might have a greater effect on Jews as 'Jewish life in Germany might ultimately no longer be possible'.[8] Discrimination against one may affect the other. Europe's unassimilable minority par excellence is interchangeable.

In this context, Gil Anidjar has raised the issue of whether we are not dealing so much with a 'Jewish' or 'Muslim Question' as a 'Christian Question'.[9] He argues that the 'racialised, blood identity of Christendom – of Europe – from the time of the crusades onwards' is central to imagining others.[10] Whether one accepts Anidjar's controversial thesis, there is certainly an underlying Christian framing. Our notions of religion have been shaped by a Christian heritage, which is seen as normative, and criticism of Islam and Judaism has stemmed from this cultural frame. For Christians, law (legalism) has been a key framing concept of both Judaism and Islam. Christian freedom, *pace* Paul, has been contrasted with perceived Jewish legalism and has also been applied to criticize *shariah*. Likewise, because Western secularism grew up in relation to a Protestant Christianity that stressed 'religion' as part of the private, personal, moral sphere, both Jewish law and Islamic law – but today especially the latter – are criticized for illegitimately crossing into secular, civic, societal, familial, and even political realms. Religion, it is believed, should not be involved in politics (though this is readily transgressed for Christianity), and so from the Iranian Revolution to the acts of religiously motivated settlers in the West Bank we see fanaticism and a failure to be secular (see Interlude 1).[11] (This is not to deny the existence of fanaticism, but there is a failure to see other dynamics at play.) That Judaism can be a nation, an ethnicity, a belief system, and a code of family and group behaviour offended European sensibilities, leading to criticisms of Judaism in relation to nationalism in the nineteenth century (see Chapter 5). But, today, this criticism is deployed in reaction to the Islamic notion of the *ummah* (Muslim group feeling), with Muslims facing similar charges of disloyalty. However, Bunzl notes a difference, for today, when attacked by Muslims or by the left, Jews are portrayed as European and colonial, therefore as oppressors deserving of rebuke, which feeds into particular forms of antisemitism.[12] How antisemitism and Islamophobia manifest, while sharing many tropes across time, is always contextual, and the modern dynamics are different for each. Antisemitism and Islamophobia are the same yet different.

The Semite and the European (biblical) imaginary

Although Edward Said (1935–2003) saw the treatment of Islam as a special case, the category of the Semite in early European orientalist scholarship often placed the Muslim and the Jew together, a factor he did not entirely discount. The desert environment, and reference to a more primitive form of religiosity suited to that environment, formed part and parcel of a racialized understanding of both peoples.[13] While, by the late nineteenth century, Jews and Muslims were typically identified by a common racial type, the idea fell quickly into disfavour in the twentieth century. Not, however, for analytical reasons, but for political ones, as the promises made to both Jews and Arabs by British and other colonial powers could not be reconciled, leading to the nationalisms of each becoming competing forces (see Chapter 8).[14] Ivan Kalmar argues that orientalism's medieval origins placed Jews and Muslims together.[15] Certainly, medieval ecclesiastical law typically treated Jews and Muslims in one monolithic category, seen first in the Third Lateran Council (1179), the decrees of which became 'a stock item in canon law collections' by 1190.[16] In the modern period, the tracing of racial groups was often tied into seeking to understand the biblical view of the world, and just as the notions of the races of Ham, Shem, and Japheth were used to justify slavery, so too the tracing of the Semitic people was ideological. The categories and origins were more often than not based in biblical exegesis, with these texts taken as historical documents.[17] This was particularly seen in the work of Ernest Renan (1823–1892) who saw the Aryan and the Semite being the fountain of civilization and the global source of religion and morality. Importantly, for him, they were both 'white races', an idea which conflicts with other interpretations, but racialized categories are fluid and contextual. That these biblical and theological ideas haunt notions of the Semite, the Arab, and the Jew, in what passes for modern secular discourse and the orientalist imagery, must be borne in mind. The easy distinction of the secular and the religious is certainly unstable.[18]

The ongoing legacy of these religious roots can be seen in various ways. Back in 1915, when the British Prime Minister Lloyd George and his ministers were considering what Palestine should look like, they consulted works on biblical geography.[19] Again, when the British and French representatives, Mark Sykes (1879–1919) and François Georges Picot (1870–1951), devised the controversial Sykes–Picot line (1916) they did so based on orientalist agendas. Though, by this time, a difference between Jew and Arab was assumed, the same lineage of thinking persisted.[20] These early twentieth-century decisions still shape world events today. An early video released by the still, then, relatively unknown militant neo-Islamic jihadi group often known as ISIS (the Islamic State in Iraq and Syria) saw them bulldozing a sand bank in the desert. Seemingly mundane, this symbolic destruction of the Sykes–Picot line gained them much popular support as a strike against the oppressive legacy of previous colonial rulers, and helped build them into a power that controlled large parts of current-day Iraq and Syria. We also continue to see the outworking of biblical interpretation in current events, especially in some Israeli claims on the land of Israel–Palestine. The Bible (and it must be said also the Qur'an and Talmud) still plays a real part in thinking through the categories of antisemitism and Islamophobia today.

Fighting racism and prejudice: On being anti-racist, anti-antisemitic, and anti-Islamophobic

While this book seeks to study antisemitism and Islamophobia rather than to advocate for any position on them, it is hoped – even expected(?) – that the reader will themselves be opposed to prejudice and discrimination. The author, as the Introduction states, has written this book because of a perceived need to address this issue. But, why raise this here? The answer, in part, relates to the interconnections of prejudice. Do we see antisemitism or Islamophobia as a greater and more live threat in today's society? Is prejudice, or suspicion, against either Muslims or Jews more justified, or natural, in today's social and political context? Especially in the light of debates around Israel–Palestine, tensions grow high and certain forms of prejudice or discrimination may become ingrained or reinforced. While Bunzl argued that today while antisemitism only exists on the Far Right and Islamophobia is far more widespread, even being reflected within main-stream media, things have shifted in the more than a decade since he wrote. Yet this is not to dismiss Bunzl's words for, as Didier Fassin noted in the wake of the *Charlie Hebdo* attacks of January 2015, that satirical magazine had itself dismissed a staff member for antisemitism but seemed happy to promote Islamophobia, highlighting the differing way these two prejudices sit in relation to perceptions of freedom of speech and socially acceptable prejudice.[21] Certainly, many Muslims perceive themselves, in Europe at least, in a differential equation in relation to Jews, though some Muslims recognize that what they experience now is what Jews experienced in the past – leading to worries by a number of Muslims that murmurings in the press and social sentiments could, in a wartime situation, lead to them being the next victims of an attempted genocide.[22]

What we have discussed above gives rise to a perception of a potential fracture in responses to these two prejudices, exemplified by events in 2004, which saw a serious falling out occurring in public between France's four major anti-prejudice/anti-racism organizations.[23] The reasons can be identified, even if somewhat simplistically, as based on where they stood between two poles: either seeing postcolonial forms of racism, especially Islamophobia, as most central today or seeing antisemitism as the main focus. These two poles also tend to, in general terms, gravitate politically to either a pro-Palestinian or a pro-Israeli camp (see Chapters 6 and 8). The way that those mobilized against prejudice can, themselves, vent energy on others engaged in the same battle for failing to identify the same essential enemies and primary issues is notable; we may agree on 95 per cent of things, but the other 5 per cent is what we will dispute over – what Sigmund Freud termed 'the narcissism of tiny differences'. This is worth dwelling on.

As we have discussed above, there are clear differences and similarities between antisemitism and Islamophobia. But, today, both at heart rest upon racialized differentiations of religious groupings, which within a Western context at least sees previously theological distinctions spilling over into supposedly secular discourses. Both fit standard patterns of prejudice and discrimination, and, indeed, Europeans' previous perceptions of a malaise around the 'Jewish Question' has become a more generalized Western disquiet about its 'Muslim Question'. Both, moreover, rest in many ways upon a wider 'Christian Question' – which is not to say that both Jewish and Islamic traditions do not have their own internal problems haunting their traditions as sources of prejudice. (Though I would resist those who see prejudice formation, and even genocidal tendencies, as being implicit in some aspect of monotheism or the Abrahamic trajectory for, as we will see in Chapters 9 and 10, hatreds, prejudice, and discrimination can manifest with ease in traditions often orientally fetishized by Western discourse as essentially peaceful, even pacifist.) Yet, we return to the central question of human prejudice and how we respond to it. It is natural and normal, and in this sense neither antisemitism nor Islamophobia is some unnatural or pathological facet of Europe, Christianity, or history. The very connection of these hatreds to all other forms of hatred, prejudice, and discrimination is therefore raised. Do Islamophobia and antisemitism have a connection? The answer here is clear: yes. But, at the same time: no. Every hatred is always distinct in how it manifests (geographically, culturally, individually, etc.). Indeed, as we have untheorized antisemitism and Islamophobia we can see that neither names a distinct, discrete, and unchanging phenomenon. As such the varying forms of antisemitisms and Islamophobias are both similar and different; indeed, some forms of antisemitism may have more in common with some forms of Islamophobia than they do with other forms of antisemitism, and vice versa. This is to be expected. If this point is laboured it is for a reason. Opposition to prejudice, to be anti-racist, must, we may contend, be intersectional in the sense of seeing the way that all forms of prejudice are connected. If one is prey to one, then it is possible to be prey to another. Moreover, being opposed to one does not make somebody anti-racist. Indeed, to be truly anti-antisemitic may require that one is also anti-Islamophobic; very often the two prejudices are entwined and interconnected. To invoke both Fanon and Elie Wiesel, it may start with one prejudice but does not end with one prejudice; what they are saying about *them* should make us prick up our ears as they are almost certainly saying it about *us* too.

SECTION IV

Prejudice beyond the West

CHAPTER EIGHT

From People of the Book to enemies of Islam: Islamic antisemitism and Palestine–Israel

Introduction

Today, virulent and dangerous hatred of Jews comes from certain Muslims. Antisemitism is widespread and systematic, taught and embedded in many of the most influential Islamic organizations of the Middle East and North Africa (MENA) and beyond. The roots of this rage against Jews have been traced, variously, to three sources, none of which adequately explains it. Some argue that the Israel–Palestine nexus and the oppression of Palestinians have clouded a largely harmonious historical relationship between Jews and Muslims. However, Islamic antisemitism existed prior to the foundation of the State of Israel, and this argument ignores the massacres of Jews that have occurred at various periods of history (for instance, in 1066 in Granada and 1465 in Fez). Others trace it to the origins of Islam, noting Muhammad's (571–632) violence against Jews in Medina (who broke a treaty with him) and antisemitic sentiments in the Qur'an and *hadith*. This is also inadequate because of the political context of any violence against Jews, while both the Qur'an and *hadith* include injunctions permitting Muslims to live alongside Jews, and historically we know that Jews preferred to live under Islamic rule than Christian rule. Finally, Islamic antisemitism is seen to come from Western sources, in particular colonial and Nazi influences. This, arguably, comes closest to the truth, for modern Islamic antisemitism draws from modern and racialized narratives; however, it negates Islamic agency in developing indigenous forms of antisemitism which draw from the tradition and local context. But, nevertheless, there is clear borrowing.

We will address the question of Islamic antisemitism starting from the modern period because, as we will see, there is a distinctive modern Islamic antisemitism which develops in the early to mid-twentieth century. This is distinct from antisemitism as previously found in the Islamic tradition, and we will assess how far modern Islamic antisemitism builds upon, or departs from, Qur'anic and traditional foundations. We then turn to see how perceptions of the Israel–Palestine situation contribute to an already potent and toxic mix. Finally, we address broader currents of Islamic antisemitism looking to South and South East Asia.

At the outset, though, we must address terminology. This rests on three counts. First, should we speak about 'Islamist antisemitism' rather than 'Islamic antisemitism'? The reason some would advocate for this is because the kind of anti-Jewish sentiment and ideology we see today comes from various forms of modern, generally militant, political organizations which some scholars term 'Islamist', indicating Islam as a political ideology rather than being based in the 'Islamic religion'. Second, would it be better to say 'Muslim antisemitism' rather than 'Islamic antisemitism', to note that it comes from specific Muslims rather than from within Islam per se. Third, should we only ascribe antisemitism to modern forms of Islamic antipathy against Jews, and not speak of antisemitism in the pre-modern tradition? We resist these usages for a number of reasons. In relation to the third point, throughout this book, antisemitism is used to refer broadly to human social prejudice towards Jews, not to define some specific ideology as properly 'antisemitism'. Hence, antisemitism is any form of prejudice, and prejudice has existed throughout the Islamic tradition. On the second, this would be credible, Islamic antisemitism is not as embedded in texts and traditions as Christian antisemitism is within that tradition. However, it is now something which is part of some forms of the Islamic tradition, and is not used to indicate that all Muslims will be antisemitic; Islam, like any religious tradition, is diverse. As for 'Islamist', while it is a politically useful (though not always effective) tool to refer to the misuse of Islam for certain political ends, it also problematically suggests that Islam, as a 'religion', is different from the political sphere. This has been noted previously (see Interlude 1 and Chapter 7), but we can extrapolate here. This suggestion is bound up with modern differentiations between the political and religious as distinct spheres. But it is not how many religions have operated: European monarchs claimed the divine right of kings based in Christian ideology, Chinese emperors had the Mandate of Heaven as a Confucian principle, Israelite kings saw themselves as mandated by God.[1] In linking the political, social, and religious spheres, Islam is neither unique nor aberrant. This is not to say that particularly militant, even terrorist, manifestations of Islamic political and social theory are legitimate, nor that they accord with anything approaching mainstream conceptions through Islamic history. But the terminology 'Islamism' is problematic. As a final response to all three points, while many Muslims base their more tolerant views of Jews on Islamic history, modern Islamic antisemitism has become, for many Muslims, a mainstream expression of their thought and practice. (That it is based in sources coming from outside of Islam, including Nazi-inspired ones, is not pertinent to a sociological statement that it is Islamic; we are not making Islamic juridical-theological claims about the, admittedly, problematic nature of these views.) Therefore, while potentially controversial, we will speak about Islamic antisemitism, noting – as with Christian or Western antisemitism – that it is not uniformly present and comes in many different forms and degrees. Indeed, there has not been a scripturally informed Islamic antisemitism in the same way that there has been a Christian antisemitism, because Islamic attitudes to Jewish people are tied to notions of *ahl al-kitab* ('People of the Book') and *ahl al-dhimma* ('Protected People', often *dhimmis*) which also apply to Christians and others, with discrimination and prejudice against Jews per se having been exceptional rather than normalized. As such, in the historical tradition, it arguably makes sense to speak about Islamic 'dhimmiphobia' rather than either antisemitism or Christianophobia.

Caveat: Islamophobic narratives of Islamic antisemitism

For both Bassam Tibi and Reuven Firestone, antisemitism is not found in traditional Islam but is a modern phenomenon. Tibi argues that it was propagated primarily by figures such as Syed Qutb (1906–1966) and groups such as the Muslim Brotherhood. Tibi argues that antisemitism is a genocidal hatred of Jews and so only found in Nazi and 'Islamist' discourse. But, as noted above, I resist normative accounts of antisemitism. Drawing from figures such as Bernard Lewis (1916–2018), often considered an orientalist critic of Islam, Tibi argues that an 'amity' between Jews and Muslims has been more typical, while long-standing coexistence is shown by Firestone.[2] Therefore, Tibi takes issue with figures such as Andrew Bostom who he believes misconstrues and distorts the Islamic tradition such that modern antisemitism is seen as a natural outgrowth rather than a major rupture.[3] Importantly, an Islamophobic interpretation of Islamic antisemitism is found in much populist writing, and even enters scholarly discourse. For instance, in exploring how Nazi ideology influenced Islamic antisemitism, David Patterson moves from his seemingly correct claim that what 'Islamic Jihadists' do and proclaim 'amounts to a rebellion against God, against Allah', into problematic claims that 'Jew hatred would appear to be a fundamental tenet of Islam'.[4] In Patterson's work, besides scholarly literature, he draws from Bostom, and other populist writers who would seemingly meet the definition of Islamophobia discussed in Chapter 7, such as Bat Ye'or and Yisrael Neeman. Such figures share a misreading of Islamic sources and traditions, especially in relation to antisemitism as well as such concepts as jihad, which is read through the lens of militant neo-Islamic jihadism. Indeed, although Patterson quotes Ronald Nettler's words that Qutb made 'judicious use of ancient sources applied imaginatively' he does not appear to realize the import of Nettler's conclusion that Qutb created a new reading of Islamic tradition.[5] That writers often noted for a harsh criticism of Islam, such as Lewis and Tibi, are keen to distinguish the traditional Islamic stances on Jews from modern Islamic antisemitism is clear evidence that those who seek to erase these differences adopt either a misunderstanding or a direct Islamophobic distortion. This is not to deny that potentially antisemitic sources exist in Islam, and we discuss these in due course. While Esther Webman suggests that she can find 'no definite conclusion' to the debate over whether Islam was traditionally virulently antisemitic or more often merely mildly so, we can be more emphatic.[6] While most of the Islamic tradition has seen Jews, like all others, as belonging to a lesser tradition and has treated Jews as second-class citizens within Muslim-majority polities (like Christians, Zoroastrians, etc.) there has never been a dominant strain of virulent anti-semitic practice or discourse in the mainstream tradition. Hatred of Jews was more muted, sporadic, and part of a general attitude towards *dhimmis*. Webman's own work demonstrates this.

European colonial formations of Islamic antisemitism

In seeking the origins of modern Islamic antisemitism, it will be useful to see what is drawn from outside Islamic tradition. We will discuss the Qur'an and early Islamic tradition later but begin with the modern period. The breakdown of the Ottoman Empire (1299–1922) saw the *millet* system, by which it had regulated its many minorities, become increasingly unstable. Indeed, ill treatment of Jews, like all *dhimmis*, generally occurred in periods of decline or turmoil, rather than being typical of Islamic rule.[7] Persecution, even massacres, occurred in the final years of the empire, but they were sporadic and often officially opposed rather than sanctioned. Arguably the worst, the Armenian genocide (1915–16), targeted Christians rather than Jews. The position of Jews, like Christians, became increasingly tenuous, and this was common across the Islamic world as European colonial incursions put pressure on, or undermined, local Islamic polities.

The first incursions of modern forms of antisemitism did not come into the Arabic world from Muslims, but from Christians.[8] In the nineteenth century, a number of Arab Christians were influenced by primarily French sources; however, such narratives did not resonate widely because of their 'unintelligibility ... to an Arab and Muslim world whose local cultures were not yet familiar with this pattern of Anti-Semitism'.[9] Nevertheless, the narratives of the blood libel and a number of other antisemitic tropes did in due course pass into the Arab Islamic world in the twentieth century, but this came initially almost entirely in the form of Christian Arab antisemitism. Arab antisemitism did not grow up within an Islamic milieu at first, but was nurtured very much by European (especially French) educated Arab Christians under the impact of colonialism. It took a long time for antisemitic tropes to enter Arab Muslim consciousness. Indeed, secular Arab nationalism (involving both Christians and Muslims) became the root through which it would take hold. A key text was Naguib Azouri's *The Revival of the Arab Nation* (1905) which asserted that this revival would only be achieved by killing Jews, with his notion of Jews as enemies relying on European antisemitic ethno-nationalist discourse. Azouri was not a Muslim but a Maronite Christian.

By the 1930s, though, after around a hundred years of direct European colonial influence, antisemitism had become relatively mainstream across the Arab world. Partly this was because Jews were often seen as the middlemen and profiteers between Europeans and Muslims, and became seen as the bearers of secularism, modernity, and liberalizing trends that some Muslims often saw as threats to their way of life and dominance. There was also resentment at perceived Jewish success in benefitting from colonial trade, while middle-class Jews became increasingly Westernized and therefore culturally isolated from their fellow Muslim countrymen. Ironically, it was also the acceptance of Western influences, from nationalism to other concepts, that allowed European antisemitism to make inroads, and Arabic translations of works such as the *Protocols* became widespread from the early twentieth century.

Tibi argues that only in the 1930s did modern Islamic antisemitism arise, coming in alongside Arab nationalism. One key ideologue was Qutb who blended Nazism with a militant neo-Islamic jihadism.[10] He was not the only antisemitic ideologue, but because he has been widely read and continues to be influential we will discuss him here. Before turning to look at Qutb, it will be useful to see why the Arab world was so ready to absorb the German influence of Nazism. Before the breakup of the Ottoman Empire, Muslim nationalisms had arisen. One strand was Turkish nationalism, which was duly established in Mustafa Kemal Atatürk's (1881–1938) new secular Turkey. But many Arabs envisaged a Pan-Arab nationalism. British and French promises to establish an Arab homeland saw many Arabs join the Allied cause in the First World War against the Germans, Ottomans, and other Central Powers. However, British commitments to Jewish Zionists in the Balfour Agreement (1919), to set up a Jewish state in Palestine, and the Anglo-French Sykes-Picot line, which divided Syria and Iraq, betrayed these promises. (Notably, a series of betrayals of Arabs, Kurds, and others in the region by British, French, Americans, and others gives fuel to narratives of conflict or hostility between a Christian West and the Islamic world.) Furthermore, the British and French essentially took over from the Ottomans as the new colonial masters. Two key dynamics arose from this. First, against what were seen as bad, colonial Europeans, especially the British and French, the Germans were seen as good, non-colonial Europeans with a Germanophilia spreading across the Arab world. Second, the conflicting British promises meant that 'when the Great War was over, the Jews and Arabs found themselves in conflict with one another – something that was far from the intentions of either'.[11] This further entrenched the perception of Jews, across the whole region, as both foreign nationals and agents of European colonial powers, despite centuries, over a millennia, of mostly peaceful coexistence.

Qutb and the Nazi connection

In the 1930s, Arab nationalists were quick to reach out to the Nazis to advance their plans for self-determination, not because both were already antisemitic but because it was a way to fight the existing colonial powers, primarily France and the UK.[12] As an anti-colonial movement, antipathy to Jews within Arab nationalism was partly predicated upon how far Jews were seen as agents of the Western colonial powers. Indeed, as mentioned, by the 1930s, the colonial importation of antisemitism (both racist and religious in basis) had laid the ground for Arab antisemitism, which meant greater receptiveness to Nazi ideology. At this point, it may be useful to return to one incident that helped to infuse such sentiments into Arab consciousness, the infamous Damascus Affair.[13]

In 1840, a French priest made the medieval allegation of the blood libel against a Jewish man in Damascus, asserting that he had killed a Christian to make into the matzah bread for Passover. This blood libel, which had no traction or history in the Islamic tradition, was supported by the French Consul and the Jewish man was condemned and killed. Stirred up by Europeans, an outbreak of violence arose against the Jewish community, but the blood libel concept seemingly made little impact among the local Muslims. However, by the early twentieth century, via Christian Arab adoption, these allegations made their way into Muslim thinking about Jews. This was an influence on, and later abetted by, figures such as Qutb who imaginatively transformed European antisemitism into an Islamic form by portraying Jews as an insidious enemy, often taking over alien and un-Islamic ideas, such as the blood libel. As such, around a hundred years later, antipathy to Jews from colonialism was becoming part of Arab discourse given shape by imported European antisemitism.

To solidify modern Islamic antisemitism a narrative was needed, and Qutb's pamphlet *Our Struggle with the Jews* (*Ma'rakutna ma'a al-Yahud*,

1950) is central to this. He takes the conflict between Jews and Muslims back to 622, the start of the Medinan period, and portrays it as a metaphysical struggle between two competing systems and peoples locked in a war for world domination.[14] But the war described is not primarily an encounter with Jewish armies (the State of Israel was still young when he wrote, and he speaks only of 'recent complications in the Holy Land'[15]) but a war of intrigues which has occurred ever since 'the Jews' were first subjugated.[16] *Our Struggle with the Jews* combines quotes from the Qur'an, events in Islamic tradition, and traditional Western antisemitic tropes into a vivid and virulent tract. For instance, Qutb asserts that Jews are behind a vast global conspiracy reminiscent of the *Protocols*, so he asserts that Jews from the earliest times have been seeking to destroy Islam through such groups as polytheists in Arabia, and in more recent times by 'being behind atheistic materialism'.[17] Indeed, Jews are blamed for anything seen as harmful from the beginnings of Islam up until the present day, including an accusation that they plotted 'Ataturk's ending of the caliphate'.[18] Qutb even accuses Jews of influencing the interpretation of the Qur'an to deceive Muslims and talks about the need to expose them.[19] It is seen as a battle of life and death, with enmity beginning from the very start of Islam with Jews seen as denying the truths Muhammad brought, that will only end when one side has destroyed the other. Notably, mirroring Christian antisemitism, Qutb sees the 'crime' of denying Muhammad's prophethood as most culpable for Jews (more so than Christians it seems), because they are seen to have known and yet still denied this (for Christians, the claim is that Jews knew yet denied Jesus as Messiah).[20]

Modern Islamic antisemitism drew heavily from the Nazis, as did Arab nationalism. As noted, the Nazis were seen as 'good Europeans', ones who did not want an empire for themselves but would help free the Arabs from the tyranny of the 'bad Europeans', which laid a groundwork for receptivity to Nazi antisemitism. It did not, as some Islamophobes argue, find ready soil in Islamic tradition, but the imbibed traditions of Christian and racialized antisemitism – often accepted uncritically, with the blood libel and *Protocols* often taken as historical – made the views of the Nazis credible. Prominent in this reception was Hajji Amin Al-Husseini (1895–1974) who became mufti of Jerusalem but spent much of the 1930s in Nazi Germany. He seems to have absorbed antisemitism even before this and became arguably the first influential spokesperson for modern Islamic antisemitism. The influence of Nazism and German thought on modern Islamic antisemitism helped racialize his interpretation of this, so that claimed inherited character traits of 'the Jew' become part of it. With Al-Husseini, an explicit Islamic religious basis was laid for antisemitism and, from the mid-1930s onwards, he gave it religious legitimacy and credibility (as mufti and a respected Islamic scholar). Qutb later codified and systematized Islamic antisemitism in the format of a distributable pamphlet. This religious foundation arguably makes it more toxic and potentially deadly for reasons that align strongly with Mark Juergensmeyer's notions of the cosmic war.

Antisemitism, and Judeophilia, in Islamic tradition

In the early stages of his prophethood, Muhammad seemingly believed himself to be declaring the same message as the Israelite tradition of prophets. At first, his community prayed facing towards Jerusalem and he seemed to assume that the Jewish tribes of Medina would see him as a prophet.[21] Their refusal, which Firestone suggests is natural in the contestation between scriptural monotheisms,[22] possibly factored into the later disputes. But politics was more significant, with some of the Medinan Jewish tribes conspiring with the Meccans against the Medina commonwealth – Muhammad's polity was not first and foremost only a Muslim one. The relevant Jewish tribes were expelled from the city, and some extremely harsh words in the Qur'an date from this period:

> O you who believe! do not take the Jews and the Christians for friends; they are friends of each other; and whoever amongst you takes them for a friend, then surely he is one of them; surely Allah does not guide the unjust people (Q 5.51).

> And the Jews say: 'The hand of Allah is tied up!' Their hands shall be shackled and they shall be cursed for what they say. ... We have put enmity and hatred among them till the day of resurrection; whenever they kindle a fire for war Allah puts it out, and they strive to make mischief in the land; and Allah does not love the mischief-makers. (Q 5.64)

Another verse seems to suggest that Allah made Jews into apes and pigs (Q 5.60). Furthermore, Muhammad allegedly executed an entire Jewish tribe during war, killing, perhaps, four to seven hundred Jewish men, and selling the women and children into slavery. However, this enmity should not be overstated. First, many of these are specific events, that is, the tribe executed, the Banu Qurayzah, was a specific group. The Banu Qurayzah, after signing a non-aggression pact, sided with Muhammad's enemies in an attack on the Medinan commonwealth, and their treatment does not denote behaviour to Jews in general.[23] Often specific groups of Jews (and Christians) are singled out for criticism. In the Qur'an, neither Jews nor Christians are treated as single groups, with differentiation between those who are believing, good, and so on (e.g. Q 2.62, 3.113, 3.119, 4.54, 4.155, 5.69, 22.17, 28.52-55) and those who are not. Further, in both Qur'an and *hadith*, Jews, alongside Christians and others (see Q 22.17), are placed into the category of the 'People of the Book' and positive comments abound:

O children of Israel! call to mind My favour which I bestowed on you
and be faithful to (your) covenant with Me, I will fulfil (My) covenant
with you; and of Me, Me alone, should you be afraid. (Q 2.40)

Both positive and negative comments can be drawn from traditional Islamic
resources in relation to Jews.[24] Jews alone are not picked out for invective as
there is condemnation of Christians and others. Traditional Islamic exegesis
suggests that seemingly hostile passages in the Qur'an or *hadith* are contextual and refer to specific tribes.

Many *hadith* contain antisemitic material and have been used by those
such as Qutb. However, *hadith* are of greater or lesser authenticity, and the
early Islamic collectors of this material sought to gauge for themselves their
reliability. While many antisemitic *hadith* rest on spurious legacies, among
the most problematic is one included in the most authoritative *hadith* collections: the *Hadith* of the Rock. It recounts the final apocalyptic battle
when, it suggests, Jews and Muslims will fight, and Jews will hide behind
trees and rocks and those objects will call out to the Muslims: 'Oh Muslim,
a Jew is hiding behind me, come and kill him!' Jonathan Brown grapples
with this *hadith* at some length given its pedigree.[25] He suggests that as
a *hadith* on apocalyptic themes it may have been less rigorously tested in
terms of its genealogy from Muhammad compared to those dealing with
such areas as family law, which were key to the early *ulama* (Islamic jurists).
Again, as it tackles apocalyptic issues, he suggests that perhaps it should
be read metaphorically (though many metaphorical readings are equally
problematic). But, most significantly, it contravenes mainstream discourse
on Jews. It is not a text that has dominated Islamic understanding of Jews
as *dhimmis*, and its modern usage is untypical. Indeed, 'politics, past and
present, is important in understanding Muslim attitudes at different points
in history and how some figures justified their views based on particular
readings of the texts/tradition, etc'.[26] The *hadith* also seems out of character
and should also be read alongside a range of others which would give us different perspectives. For instance, in stating that whoever takes a single life,
it is as if they killed all of humanity, and whoever saves a single life it is as
if they rescued all of humanity, Muhammad is often seen within the Islamic
tradition as promulgating a path of peace; something often lost on those
who see Islam as inherently stoking militarism and aggression. Nevertheless,
Muhammad was certainly not a quasi-pacifist, and in many ways acted as a
local tribal warlord who sometimes enacted harsh retribution against traitors, but was at other times merciful to the vanquished. Certainly, in another
well-attested *hadith*, we are told that the 'greater jihad' is personal moral
and spiritual improvement, and the 'lesser jihad' is warfare. Understanding
how Muslims have viewed Jews requires a holistic assessment, not achieved
by cherry-picking irenic or aggressive quotes. Of key importance is that the
Qur'an does not treat Jews as a racialized group. It is specific Jews who are

spoken of, and there are good (believing) and bad (unbelieving) Jews, rather than there being any general trait of 'the Jew'.

The tradition of Judaism is also understood as the heritage on which Islam builds, with Adam, Abraham, Noah, Moses, David, Jesus, and others from that lineage being recognized as prophets within the Islamic dispensation. However, as with Christianity's supersessionist relationship to Judaism, so too does Islam see Jews as having failed to live up to the divine message, and at times to have lost or distorted it. But this is equally true of Christians, and so traditionally there is no pervasive hatred of Jews separate from Christians or others. Therefore, as noted, we may better speak of 'dhimmiphobia' rather than antisemitism or Christianophobia within traditional Islam. Indeed, critiques of Christians and expressions of violence against Christians far outweigh expressions of violence or prejudice towards Jews.

Dhimmis and discrimination

If we see Muhammad's attitude as reflected by early precedent, then particularly under Caliph Abu Bakr (573–634, Muhammad's successor) we see a very harmonious context where both churches and synagogues were protected. Arguably, for the earliest Muslims, no major distinction was made between Jews, Christians, and Muslims. But as territories expanded, and civil strife within the Islamic community began, even under Caliph Uthman (577–656, Muhammad's third successor), but certainly under the first dynasty (the Umayyads, 661–750 CE), Christians and Jews were caught in the crossfire and became increasingly stigmatized.

We may pause to note that sometimes it is hard to distinguish early traditions and later developments. Critical scholarship argues that in the first Muslim century (if not after) the Qur'an was not yet fixed, while the *hadith* collections were still very fluid. Indeed, what became confirmed as the Pact of Umar[27] – a text probably from the ninth century that purports to be from Caliph Umar (584–644, Muhammad's second successor) – was influential in determining the prejudicial status of *dhimmis* that seemingly developed in the centuries after Muhammad's life, but is often read as representing seventh-century practice.[28]

While the potential for quite virulent antisemitism exists within Islam, as Firestone perceptively points out, it exists as 'a latent anti-Judaism or antisemitism' and is in both the Qur'an and New Testament.[29] Indeed, it is often discrimination at the social and legal level, rather than an ideological prejudice, that has been strongest within Islam, unlike Christianity which had both. Richard Kimball sums up current scholarship in this regard:

> Once the military campaigns concluded, Christians and Jews of all denominations, as People of the Book, benefitted by a certain *dhimmi*

status that guaranteed protection. ... It is now accepted that the spread of Islam did not require forced conversion of Christians, or Jews. ... As evidence Donner examines the coinage from the period that inscribes the first half of the *shahādah* [testimony of faith], without mention of Muhammad.[30]

This balanced assessment of scholarship contrasts with Islamophobic literature that argues *dhimmis* lived in a state of absolute submission, even serfdom, with forced conversion as the norm (polemically termed '*dhimmitude*').[31] Certainly, *dhimmis* were second-class citizens, but their situation was not generally dire and varied considerably.[32] The right to self-determination and the election of their own leaders, the right to worship and run their own legal system, and the complete protection of the caliph with no need to fight in wars were all granted to those recognized as *dhimmis*, subject to the payment of a tax (*jizya*). Jews, like various unorthodox Christians, often welcomed and even fought alongside Muslims during transitions from mainstream Christian (Catholic or Orthodox) rule to Islamic rule. For instance, the original coming of the Umayyad Dynasty to the Iberian Peninsula was at the invitation of, or at least in cooperation with, Jews and non-Chalcedonian Christians who believed that Islamic rule offered protections against their persecution under Catholic Christian Visigoths.

It would be wrong, though, as some advocates of the period of *convivencia* in the Iberian Peninsula sometimes do, to present the period of Islamic rule and the *dhimmi* system as an interfaith utopia with unqualified tolerance. There was a logic of conquest built into the early Islamic worldview, which saw Muslims move out from their original tribal areas in Arabia across the Levant, North Africa and beyond within a mere few decades of Muhammad's prophetic period.[33] Warfare is always brutal, and many suffered. The way that the *dhimmi* status was understood and enacted varied; after the Almohad Dynasty (mid-twelfth to thirteenth century) took over Iberia, Jews and Christians found themselves in a much less favourable position than under the earlier Iberian Umayyad Dynasty (711–1031). But, even under the harshest Islamic rule, the choice was never the forced conversion, death, or exile enacted by Catholic Christian rulers after 1492.

The position of 'the Jews of Islam', as Lewis termed them, was in almost all cases far preferable to their position under Christian rule, at least until the Jewish emancipation of the nineteenth century, and even then, violence, social exclusion, and prejudice remained the norm well into the twentieth century in Christian-majority societies. Fred Donner suggests that in early Islam, the almost overwhelming emphasis was upon the acceptance of monotheism, meaning that Jews and Christians were quite readily welcomed and embraced within the expanding Islamic polity as fellow People of the Book, which would certainly mitigate against excessive and virulent antisemitism.[34] Nevertheless, structural antisemitism existed, and in some places this would became more marked over time (though it would be wrong to see things simply becoming harsher since the time of Muhammad and Abu Bakr, notwithstanding that the covenants of the earliest Islamic years do seem to grant a good degree of religious tolerance).[35] While there was a logic of expansion built into the Umayyad conquests which were justified under what has been termed a '*jihad* ethic' to expand the Islamic polity, it was also pragmatically necessary that subjugated peoples accept the rule. Ideologically, they were included within the Muslim polity under what Anver Emon calls a universalist outlook but balanced against the empire's logic,[36] and for several centuries non-Muslims far outnumbered the relatively few Muslims in the burgeoning Islamic empire and, indeed, many of the soldiers of the early dynasties were probably not actually Muslims.[37] As such, the situation of *dhimmis* was not always too harsh.

As examples of the way *dhimmi* status became enacted as discrimination, the wearing of distinctive clothes was begun under Umar II (717–720) to demarcate *dhimmis* from Muslims, which probably reflected Sassanian class distinctions in dress.[38] Later, Christian *dhimmis* were marked by blue badges and Jewish *dhimmis* by yellow badges, though these colour schemes were not fixed. For instance, in the Ottoman system, turban colours became the markers, with only Muslims allowed to wear white turbans and others wearing other colours. This colour coding made it easier to identify *dhimmis* who were expected to demur to Muslims in public, and also only Muslims could ride horses with other communities placed upon donkeys, mules, or other lesser beasts. Nevertheless, these structures were not always obeyed and at times *dhimmi*s, though marked out by colour coding in theory, would wear colours reserved for Muslims or else were bedecked with refined and resplendent garments that signified a high social status. Historical testimony to this suggests that, at many times and in many places, the relegation of *dhimmis* to situations of public humiliation was the exception rather than the rule. Moreover, Jews flourished for centuries in such places as Baghdad, Cairo, Damascus, and Cordoba, with the poets, scientists, philosophers, and scholars of the Jewish medieval 'golden period' being products of Muslim-majority societies. Despite very occasional pogroms, Jews lived with a confidence and security not available in Christian-majority societies where they had no legal status and relied upon the largesse and protection of monarchs and nobles. Till at least the end of the nineteenth century, the historical memories that existed were of Jews being welcomed into Muslim empires.[39]

Palestine–Israel and contemporary contestations

The ideology of modern Islamic antisemitism, while becoming known and exemplified in figures such as Al-Husseini, did not become a central feature of Arab Islamic thought till after the founding of the State of Israel. Indeed,

Qutb's key diatribe, *Our Struggle with the Jews*, was not written until 1950. There had arguably been no precedent in previous Islamic history for the demonization of Jews that was to come with the great impetus of events in 1948, though from at least the end of the First World War a resentment between Jews and Muslims was growing regionally over competing nationalist claims.[40] The latent antisemitism of the Qur'an and *hadith* – fuelled and primed by colonial and Nazi discourse – was ignited with the founding of the State of Israel, and what became seen as its battles with the Arab Muslim world. The seeds for this tension, as seen, were laid by the British and French, and to some extent by the first Zionist settlers in the 1880s. The Balfour Declaration helped change political Zionism from mere ideology to something with potential, while the founding of a Jewish state in the historical region of Palestine was at odds with Pan-Arab nationalism.

On 14 May 1948, with the declaration of the State of Israel – which negated the 1947 UN resolution 181 stating that two states, one Jewish, one Palestinian, should be founded – the de facto existence of Israel as a Jewish state was established.[41] Its Arab neighbours immediately launched wars in which – from the Israeli perspective – it stood as a David against the Goliaths trying, unsuccessfully, to crush its first breath. The failure of these, and subsequent wars against Israel, seriously dented the credibility of secular Arab nationalism. The key event was the six-day war of 1967. The crushing and humiliating defeat of the secular Arab governments and their militaries caused a sea change in thinking in the Arab world. A rising tide of Islamic ideologies, often tied to militant neo-Islamic jihadism, rose increasingly from the backstreets and margins to centre stage. This meant that just as Arab nationalist narratives lost their popular influence to Islamic-based narratives, so did secular Arab antisemitism lose ground to modern Islamic antisemitism which was rife in the groups that filled the public space. The 1979 Iranian Revolution was the key marker that rule by Islam was not just desirable but also possible, and by this time the influence of modern Islamic antisemitism had spread outside Sunni Islamic discourse into Shia discourse. This was partly through the representation of Israel as the enemy of all Muslims, and also as the representative of the 'Great Satan', that is, the United States. Hatred of Jews continued to be built upon an anti-colonial narrative. Israel was the symbolic focus of this, and with a racialized reading of Jews via Qutb and his Western interlocutors the stage was set for the widespread adoption of modern Islamic antisemitism.

The rationale and practice of the founders of the State of Israel helped feed into this sense of conflict. In what Palestinians term the *Nakba* ('Catastrophe', 1948) seven hundred thousand Palestinian refugees were dispossessed from their homes and ancestral lands.[42] With the new state and its military victories, what had been the inter-communal warfare of Palestinians and Jewish settlers became, in effect, an all-out, one-sided Jewish offensive, something which Palestinians see as continuing. Both then and today, centuries-old olive groves, which are not only key to economic survival but also tie the people to the land, are torn up by Jewish settlers seeking to force Palestinians from their land.[43] Indeed, in the most extreme militant Jewish narratives, no Palestinians should be left in the State of Israel, the borders of which should be extended to the most exaggerated of biblical proportions.[44] Not all Israelis accept these actions or narratives, and many see today's militant settlers to be extremists or an embarrassment, but under the right-wing Likud government of recent years the settlers have often been able to harass and, in some cases, even murder Palestinians with virtual legal impunity (though political violence based in religious narratives goes both ways). But, from an Arab perspective, such Israeli military and militant settler incursions justify virulent antisemitism, that through racialized narratives particularly as encapsulated by Qutb (though he is not the only ideologue) mean many Muslims see Jews as almost demonic adversaries in eternal conflict with Islam. Indeed, for many Muslims, Israel is often seen as a frontline in the ongoing Western imperial crusade, with many Arab Muslims, and Arab Christians, seeing Israel as a settler colonial state. However, portraying Israel as either colonial or anti-colonial misses many of the specific dynamics behind its founding.

We should not imagine, though, that there is an absolute desire among all Arab Muslims to kill all Jews, nor even has it always been the aim of every surrounding country to destroy Israel. While a *fatwa* (2000) stipulating jihad as warfare emanated from Sheikh Tantawi (1928–2010) of Al Azhar University stating that attacks on Israelis in Palestine were legitimate, he stated that it was only 'as long as the Jews attack us, violate our rights and shed our blood'.[45] Moreover, at least in the 1948 war, the Jordanians only wanted to occupy the West Bank and take over East Jerusalem, which is what the UN defined as Palestinian territory.[46] Indeed, while antisemitism is rife, Webman notes that particularly in recent years a good number of prominent intellectuals and public figures have pushed back against it. Recognizing the fictitious nature of the *Protocols* and the blood libel, Arab intellectuals have lambasted their acceptance. Moreover, they feel that there is a need to recognize that the failures of Arab countries lie very much at their own doors and cannot simply, but conveniently, be laid at the feet of Israel and an alleged global Jewish conspiracy against Islam.[47]

Modern Islamic antisemitism has a very distinct heritage and lineage. The Salafi tradition, today linked to a modern conservative Muslim lineage emanating from Muhammad Ibn Abd al-Wahhab (1703–1792) (this branch is often called Wahhabism) in Saudi Arabia, originally paid no particular heed to antisemitic discourses, referring back to tradition on *dhimmis*.[48] Indeed, many Salafis continue to reject modern Islamic antisemitism. But Muslim Brotherhood infiltration was strong in Saudi Arabia from the 1950s to the 1990s and modern antisemitism was imbibed by Wahhabism; both mainstream Wahhabism and militants such as Al-Qaeda (though for Osama bin Laden (1957–2011), the focus on the 'Great Satan' of the United States was more important than Jews, who played something of a second fiddle).

Since the breakdown of the Israel–Palestine peace agreement in the 1990s, and growing militancy from both the Israeli right, and in parts of the Palestinian community, there has been a tendency to even more polarized attitudes. This is reflected in the 2020 so-called peace plan of US President Donald Trump which effectively grants a wish list of the demands of the Israeli right-wing.[49] Influenced through Al-Husseini and the Muslim Brotherhood, Hamas has long been virulently antisemitic in its discourse and rationale. The destruction of Israel is part of its charter, and antisemitism permeates its ideology. Of course, how far Hamas speaks for all Palestinians is debatable. While Western, often left-wing, supporters minimize or downplay the significance of Hamas' antisemitism (see Chapter 6), it seems core to their ideology. Yet, as noted, there is also Arab resistance to this, and many Palestinians reject such a hard-line antisemitism.

Antisemitism in South and South East Asia

It is worth looking at South and South East Asia to see how patterns of Islamic antisemitism manifest beyond MENA. Antisemitic sentiments can be found in key teachers here such as Shah Wali Allah of Delhi (1703–1762) who, drawing upon tradition, accused Jews of distorting the revelation given to them, though such an accusation was also made of Christians. More virulent was Mawlana Mawdudi (1903–1979), who many see as being as significant a figure as Qutb in the development of Islam's modern antisemitic discourses. He suggested that, after the Medinan truce between Muslims and Jews ended, there was a need to fight them. But this was also his attitude to Christians.[50] Mawdudi's views were a break with Islamic tradition and were drawn upon by Al-Qaeda and others to legitimate their militant attitudes. This we can link to a typical aspect of racism or prejudice, which is that it is often not directed towards a single target but is part of an intersectional set of prejudices. Violence targeted at Jews in India is a recent phenomenon related to the Israel–Palestine nexus, erupting in 1948, 1956, and 1967.[51] Moreover, here, as in much of the world, Saudi oil money has spread antisemitism as part of its promotion of Wahhabism, including as part of militant neo-Islamic jihadism.[52]

A similar dynamic is found in South East Asia which has its own Malay language antisemitic literature.[53] In Malaysia, in 2003, the party of then Prime Minister Mohamad Mahathir handed out copies of the virulently antisemitic *International Jew* by Henry Ford at a campaign rally.[54] Under Mahathir, a politicized and radical Islamic discourse developed in Malay politics. Antisemitic sentiments have been present in the country from the Second World War, when the Japanese handed out antisemitic propaganda during their occupation period. Given the sparsity of Jews in the region – they had been found before the Second World War primarily in Singapore but not in huge numbers and are now demographically insignificant – such an antisemitism without Jews has been seen as an anomaly.[55] However, the Malaysian example shows the way that Islamic identities have become increasingly influenced by patterns in the militant and antisemitic discourse that originally flowed from the Muslim Brotherhood and later through Wahhabi sources, also heightened by perceptions of the Palestine–Israel nexus.[56] This is not to say that local dynamics do not also flow into it, and it has been argued that, in places such as Malaysia, rhetoric on Jews often targets the local Chinese (portrayed as a predatory mercantile ethnicity which undermines local interests).[57]

Tradition versus modernity

Possibly today's greatest threat to Jews globally is coming from those Muslims steeped in modern Islamic antisemitism. Their worldview belies more than a millennia of history in which Jews and Muslims have, in general, lived amicably side by side, often seeing Christians as a threat against them both. The virulent antisemitism, with genocidal intent, found across much of MENA and elsewhere today was learnt and justified through colonial European, often Christian, and also Nazi sources, a learning which has included Holocaust denial.[58] This is not to say that antisemitism is alien to Islam, and certainly resources exist within it that could justify vitriolic repudiation of Jews, but it was always tempered by the notions of the 'People of the Book' with *dhimmis* being protected. Modern Islamic antisemitism is very different from the traditional antisemitism, which was only ever part of a wider dhimmiphobia. Only with the colonial impetus in Arab nationalism, Qutb and other ideologues, and the Muslim Brotherhood, did an antagonistic and targeted antisemitism develop, which learnt from the Nazis both murderous intent and a racialized notion of 'the Jew'. Meanwhile, a continuing anti-colonial sentiment has been fostered by the Israel–Palestine situation which has made Jewish–Muslim enmity seem a major global theme. This may be combined with critiques of Western colonialism and orientalism that mix Christian aggression or proselytization with Zionism as part of an anti-Islamic conspiracy theory.[59] Nevertheless, there are many places where traditional, more irenic arrangements exist. In Morocco, antisemitism is illegal, and it is a place where Muslims were the traditional guardians of the graves of Jews.[60] This is not to say that relationships have always been good there, but a peaceable – if normally one-sided – coexistence has more often than not been the lot of Jews living in Muslim-majority states. It is to be hoped that memories of *convivencia* will win out over the animosity stoked today by militants on both the Jewish and Muslim side of the conversation, including those Islamophobes who demonize Muslims in a distorted retelling of historical Muslim–Jewish relations.

CHAPTER NINE

Killing for the Buddha: Islamophobia in the Buddhist world

Introduction

We may associate Buddhism with meditation and serene statues. Violence, we often imagine, is a facet of the 'Abrahamic' religions (Judaism, Christianity, and Islam) with their absolute monotheism and belief in an exclusive covenant with that deity. However, the dynamics of prejudice and hatred are traits of human beings and their societies, and not the sole preserve of certain ideological formations. For most Buddhists, through most of Buddhist history, and in mainstream normalcy, it was accepted that the tradition justified violence, such that we may be even tempted to say that Buddhism justifies violence.[1] Nevertheless, given the perceived irenic nature of Buddhism we will begin by setting out ways in which Buddhist traditions justify killing and violence. Next we will explore 'modern Buddhist rage' in what journalists sometimes call 'ultranationalist' or 'fundamentalist' Buddhism.[2] We will then explore some of the historical connections of Buddhism and Islam, before looking at modern instances of Islamophobia in Sri Lanka and Myanmar.

Before we begin the chapter, however, we may usefully draw a picture of how such religious hatred against Islam manifests in Buddhism today:

> In Sri Lanka, a saffron robed monk stands before a crowd of people telling them that the teachings (*dharma*) and tradition (*sasana*) of Buddhism are under threat. He asserts that for 2,300 years only in this one nation has pure Theravada Buddhism been preserved, but today the language of

Sinhala (that of the majority, mainly Buddhist, population) and its traditions are fragile and at risk. The threat is aggression – if not violence, then at least proselytisation – from Islam and Christianity. While Buddhism advocates non-harm (*ahimsa*), there is a need to defend Buddhism. The following day, a mob of Sinhalese Buddhists storm into a Muslim part of town, abuse and insult Muslims, and set fire to shophouses. This is later justified as a defensive assault by the Buddhists to forestall attacks by those who seek to destroy Buddhism.[3]

Buddhist violence: Justifications in text and tradition

In contrast to the Hebrew Bible, there are no injunctions in Buddhism's foundational texts (*tripitaka*) to anything that might be termed a holy war, and certainly no omnipotent deity offering injunctions to kill. Buddhism's texts tell us that a person who intentionally kills another human being will be expelled from the community. Some scholars, in analysing the Buddhist doctrinal and ritual systems, have found them utterly devoid of any form of violence.[4] A central principle of the tradition is *ahimsa*, often translated as 'non-violence' though many scholars prefer 'non-harm'.[5] This entails not just an injunction not to kill humans but also not to cause harm to any sentient creature, and the Buddhist tradition includes examples of monks and laypeople protecting animals and birds, even discouraging hunters and fishers from their activities. Yet, to focus only upon this is to miss a very large part of the tradition, because within various texts and teachings of Buddhism there are rationales for supporting the use of violence and even justifying killing humans.[6] Indeed, the expulsion for killing noted above is from the *sangha*, the monastic community, with Buddhism's earliest texts being written primarily for monks and nuns.

In early South Asian thought, the use of violence and even torture by kings was often conceived of as not being a form of harm (*himsa*). Rather, it was seen as a necessary, even beneficial, part of society. While texts suggest that monks should avoid soldiers, and decree that soldiers in service to the state cannot become monks, this is not necessarily because such violent occupations were antithetical to monasticism. Rather, arguably, it was to show that Buddhism was not seeking to subvert the rule of law by inducing soldiers to enter monasteries; for early Buddhists, seeking patronage from rulers was pragmatic to gain protection for the *sangha* (monastic community).[7] Throughout history, Buddhism has made special provision for soldiers and monarchs, suggesting that intention is central to causing harm. While killing in anger will result in rebirths in hell or as an animal, it is said to be possible to kill and commit violence for compassionate reasons, detached from murderous thoughts. While promoting an ideal of *ahimsa*, Buddhism has nevertheless created a set of exceptions, or justifications, for certain acts of violence and killing. This is particularly associated with the man credited with creating the largest empire in South Asia before the British, a symbol of Indian nationalism and Buddhist kingship: King Ashoka (*c*.304–232 BCE). In Buddhist tradition, Ashoka is seen as a *chakravartin*, an ideal monarch who promotes Buddhism. Because of this, his rule represents the ideal of *ahimsa*, nevertheless it inevitably entailed violence. But, envisaged as being for a greater good, such violence could exemplify *ahimsa*. While the figure is possibly exaggerated, Ashoka's virtuous rule is extolled despite stories of him slaughtering 18,000 Jains, because he is seen to defend righteousness. Throughout history, rulers have often claimed Buddhist legitimacy for their wars, claims frequently endorsed by monks.[8] Today, there is considerable debate over whether such violence is 'Buddhism betrayed' or whether a legitimate 'just war' tradition may exist in Buddhism.[9]

The roots of modern Buddhist rage and the Buddhist just war

To understand modern Buddhist manifestations of Islamophobia we need to look at the effects of European colonialism on Buddhism. The experience of colonialism was different in varying countries, and here we pick out three Theravada Buddhist majority countries. First, Thailand, which experienced no colonial conquest, but especially from the nineteenth century felt pressures to modernize, had a very particular trajectory. Second, Myanmar was conquered by the British – who fought three Anglo-Burmese wars between 1823 and 1885 (with insurgencies ongoing till 1889) – with the Burmese empire eventually integrated into British India, being known for a while as 'further India', but eventually as 'Burma' in recognition of the largest ethnic group, the Bamar. Renamed Myanmar in 1989, it regained independence in 1948. However, it was the third country, Sri Lanka, that sojourned under colonial domination for the longest period, and where we see a particular dynamic occurring that has come to be part of the discourse of Buddhist ethno-nationalist sentiment in a range of different countries, including both Myanmar and Thailand, as well as in militant antagonism towards Islam. It was in twentieth-century Sri Lanka that Buddhist 'just war' theory became most notably established.

To provide some background for the colonial encounter, some notes on Buddhism in Sri Lanka are useful, particularly as understood by the largest ethnicity, the Sinhalese. From a Sinhala perspective, Sri Lanka is the source of the original and pure form of Theravada Buddhism, giving them a 'sacred' duty to preserve it.[10] This Buddhist heritage goes back, historically, to around 250 BCE when two of Ashoka's children, Mahinda and

Sanghamitta, a monk and a nun, were believed to have come as Buddhist missionaries and transmitted the oral teaching of Buddhism (Buddhists did not use written texts till several centuries later). However, according to a fifth century CE historical and mythical chronicle of Sri Lanka's early history, the *Mahavamsa*, the Buddha (*c.* sixth century BCE) had miraculously flown from North India to Sri Lanka to give the island, and its guardian spirits, the role of protecting his teachings.

The *Mahavamsa* is key to later developments, telling the story of Sri Lankan kings from around the fourth century BCE till about the fifth century CE. It links from the Buddha to Mahinda who is seen to have founded the Mahavihara ('Great Monastery') which later united all the island's Buddhist lineages, allegedly under King Parakkama Bahu I (1153–86), but they were probably only consolidated in the thirteenth century. Another link in this chain is the most important systematizer of Theravada Buddhism, Buddhaghosa, who around the fifth century CE wrote his key texts at the Mahavihara. In this way, Sinhala Buddhism sees itself as having a pure and unbroken chain from the early councils that codified Buddhism after the Buddha's death up till today, and which in part accounts for the term 'Theravada' which means the 'Tradition of the Elders'. Notably, despite later British and Sinhalese readings, the *Mahavamsa* does not advocate Sinhalese supremacy over the island, and a Tamil king is extolled as a righteous king by the monk author, though its equation of Lanka as a Buddhist island is clear.

The colonial period began in 1505 when the Portuguese arrived. However, they controlled only the coastal areas, and full European imperial dominance over the entire island began in 1815 after the British supplanted the Dutch in 1796 (who had ousted the Portuguese in 1658). Two key facets of this are worth noting, the first of which had some continuity throughout the whole colonial period, and this was an exclusivist religious attitude fostered by European Christians. But the second, nationalist sentiments arose only in the nineteenth century under British rule. When Christian missionaries first arrived in Sri Lanka, the Buddhists took an inclusive stance, attending churches and listening to preaching, but they found this was not reciprocated. Christians were exclusive in that they would not attend the religious rites of another religion, and even preached that Buddhist teachings were false, if not demonic. Over time, the exclusive intolerance of the Christians became mirrored by the Buddhists, with monks forbidding lay Buddhists from attending rival religious places of worship and taking up harshly polemical rhetoric.[11] Aggressive arguments which pitted a Buddhist against a Christian took place across the island in the 1860s and 1870s until Mohottivante Gunananda, a skilled Buddhist preacher, took to the stage and bested his Christian opponents, in the general view, at Panadura in 1873,[12] leading to a cessation of such debates. Notably, at first, Buddhists engaged religious diversity very differently,[13] but later took on attitudes that mirrored Christian exclusivism (though harsh polemic against rivals had long been part of Buddhist practice).

Nationalism, likewise, was learnt from the colonisers. The concept of a nation state as the homeland of a particular racialized ethno-linguistic cultural grouping (see Chapter 5) was imported by the British and imbibed by an emerging Sinhalese nationalist movement, which asserted itself both against the British as invaders and also against Sri Lanka's minorities. This was especially developed by Anagarika Dharmapala (1864–1933), a Buddhist lay preacher (later a monk), who connected Sinhalese race, Theravada Buddhism, and Sinhala nationalism. This is often tied to contemporary justifications for violence to protect Buddhism as an ethno-religio-national identity.[14] A significant figure, Dharmapala had been a speaker at the 1893 Parliament of the World's Religions and helped popularize Buddhism in the West, as well as helping found the Mahabodhi Society that would look after what was believed to be the site where the Buddha attained nirvana at the then newly excavated Bodh Gaya temple complex. Dharmapala, and others, linked Sinhalese nationalism to a reading of the *Mahavamsa* that expounded a glorious Sinhala Buddhist heritage and enthroned the sense of Sri Lanka being the homeland of Theravada Buddhism which needed to be defended. However, this relied upon the British unitary structure enforced on Ceylon, which had previously been multiple kingdoms, and so the Sinhalese nationalist imagined community was reliant on colonial imposition in at least two ways. It further imported a racialized distinction of the two main ethnicities, the Sinhalese, understood as superior Aryan stock, and the Tamils envisaged as inferior Dravidian stock (indigenous southern Indian, often associated with darker skin tones).[15]

Walpola Rahula (1907–1997) would most fully codify what has become called a Buddhist just war theory. Rahula was a famous scholar of Buddhism as well as a monk and wrote an influential textbook on Buddhism, *What the Buddha Taught* (1959), used by generations of students across the world; as an undergraduate, it was one of the main texts recommended to the author. Like others, Rahula went back to the *Mahavamsa* and argued that during the reign of King Dutthagamani (101–77 BCE), monks had accompanied the king to war and some of them had disrobed to fight in a just cause, while others, he stated, gave the war their moral blessing by their presence. In other words, fighting to defend Buddhism, which is how Rahula interpreted this text, was justified, and he argued that 'both bhikkhus and laymen considered that even killing people in order to liberate the religion and the country was not a heinous crime'.[16] Linking this to nationalism, he expounded:

Working for the freedom and uplift of the religion and the country was recognized as so important and noble that the Sinhalese in the 5th century A.C. [after the Buddha], both laity and Sangha, seemed to have believed that arahants themselves had accepted the idea that even the destruction of human beings for that purpose was not a very grave crime. What is evident from this is that the bhikkhus at that time considered it their sacred duty to engage themselves in the service of their country as much as the service of their religion.[17]

This reading of the Mahavamsa as indicating a Sinhalese nationalism combined with a defence of Buddhism was something Rahula learnt from British readings of the text inspired by the work of Dharmapala and others. The kingdoms spoken of in the text had been multireligious, multi-ethnic, and regionalized ones as no unified Sri Lankan entity existed before the British. Nevertheless, this reading inspired a potent brew that would come to the boil in due course. When the British left Ceylon in 1948, it became a secular state respecting all the island's ethnic groups, linked to an inclusive Ceylonese nationalism. However, dissatisfaction with the secular regime grew, and in 1956, the Sinhala language was declared to be the sole official language, and in 1972, when the country was renamed Sri Lanka, Buddhism was protected in the constitution, and has come to be regarded by many as, in effect, the state religion. A key player in these moves, who became prime minister at the 1956 general election, was S. W. R. D. Bandaranaike who introduced the Sinhala Only Act that year. There was strong reaction and he rescinded some of the more ethno-centric policies, but militant Sinhalese counter-reactions led to his assassination in 1959 by a monk who felt he had betrayed Buddhism by conceding too much ground to the Tamil minority. After his death, his wife Sirimavo Bandaranaike took on the role of an ardent Sinhalese Buddhist nationalist in the public sphere pushing back against any concessions to Tamils.[18]

Sinhalese chauvinism, as noted, was particularly directed against the Tamils who felt increasingly oppressed and marginalized. We need not concern ourselves with the details of a brutal civil war that wracked the island from 1983 until 2009, between the Liberation Tigers of Tamil Eelam formed in 1976 and state forces, but it helped reinforce the militant interpretation of Buddhism. This is displayed in a poem of this period that was noted by scholars John Esposito, Darrell Fasching, and Todd Lewis, which states that soldiers defending the 'motherland' will attain nirvana in a future rebirth and extols as the 'triple gems' country, religion, and race.[19] In such poetry we can see how militant Sinhalese Buddhist island-homeland nationalism eclipses traditional Buddhist thought. We can draw out two points further. First, normally becoming a monk would set one on the path to nirvana in a future life, but this poem includes also becoming a soldier who will die to defend the 'motherland' as a route to nirvana. Second, the Buddhist tradition's 'triple gems' (*triratna*) are: the Buddha (trust in his attainment of nirvana); *dharma* (his teachings); and the *sangha* (the community, especially monastic, which preserves the teachings as the route to nirvana). But here they have become: country first; then Buddhism subsumed into a new triple gem set; and, finally, race (the Sinhalese).[20]

Buddhism and Islam in history

Early Islamic dynasties soon encountered Buddhists in Central Asia. Through the Silk Roads, Central Asia was, at the time, the crossroads of the world and many of the greatest cities and empires emerged there. As Muslim generals advanced they met, for them, previously unknown cultural traditions and had to make sense of the religions they met, including Hinduism and Buddhism. This related to two key concepts in Islamic thought, 'People of the Book' (*ahl-al-kitab*) and *dhimmis* ('protected people'). The Qur'an (Q 22.17) mentioned Jews, Christians, Sabians, and Zoroastrians as 'People of the Book' (followers of traditions with a prophet and a revealed text). Meeting others, the question arose as to whether they were likewise 'People of the Book' or polytheists. If the former, they could live as *dhimmis* within the Islamic-dominated empire under the protection of the caliph, and even if living as second-class citizens nevertheless enjoyed freedom of religion and the right to run their own community affairs (see Chapter 8). But, if the latter, they were given a choice of conversion or death in a conflict situation (nonviolent polytheists who were not in a conflict situation were, probably, protected, but their status was certainly below that of *dhimmis*).

Sending information back to Baghdad, then the imperial capital, Muslim generals awaited an answer, and we have *fatwas* (legal opinions) determining that both Buddhists and Hindus were 'People of the Book' and so had the socio-legal status of *dhimmis*. Indeed, archaeological evidence shows that for many centuries mosques, synagogues, Zoroastrian fire temples, and Buddhist viharas existed side-by-side in the Muslim-dominated empires of this region. However, this irenic history, like much of Central Asian history, is lost to our contemporary memories. Rather, at least from the Buddhist side, the memory of later and more militant Islamic empires ravishing Northern India remains prominent, and condemnation of Buddhists as idolaters was also part of the Islamic tradition,[21] though John Elverskog argues that Islam was influenced by Buddhism's rich pictorial traditions leading to images of Muhammad first appearing to appeal to potential converts.[22] In folklore at least, the peaceful Buddhist monks refused to fight back as hordes of Muslim invaders ransacked their monasteries and slaughtered the monks. Most traumatic in the collective memory is the loss of Nalanda, founded in the second century BCE. Arguably the world's first university, it was the intellectual centre of Buddhism. Its library was famed far and wide, and even monks from China made perilous journeys there to learn, the most famous of these being Xuanzang (602–664), whose story is mythologically immortalized in *Journey to the West*. Nalanda's curriculum was not simply about Buddhism but also included architecture, medicine, and various other sciences. It is said that the first Muslim general who reached Nalanda (in 1202), upon hearing that the library did not contain the Qur'an, proceeded to have it burnt down, and the fire allegedly lasted for three days, so great was the stock of manuscripts. However, evidence exists that Nalanda continued to function, though in a depleted form, until at least the seventeenth century. A variety of factors are probably responsible for Buddhism's decline and eventual demise in India, until its nineteenth-century revival. Nevertheless, the shock of Islam has stayed in Buddhist thought with the Mahayana text the Kalachakra Tantra portraying Muslims as *mlecchas* ('barbarians'), with Islam termed *mleccha-dharma* ('barbarian teachings/tradition') and being seen as the worship of a merciless demon, and prophesying that eventually a bodhisattva emperor (*chakravartin*) will return and defeat the Muslims and restore the Buddhist *dharma*.[23]

In South East Asia, waves of missionaries and immigrants saw Buddhism, Hinduism, and Islam all being, at differing times, the predominant religious tradition, often with the conversion of particular rulers. While Islam came with traders and itinerant missionaries, often Sufis, rather than alongside empires, it became the majority tradition after the thirteenth century, with various sultanates including the important Sultanate of Melaka being founded around 1400 when a local prince converted to Islam.[24] Before then, Mahayana Buddhist dynasties had dominated from around the ninth to thirteenth centuries. However, South East Asia, a concept first codified by nineteenth-century colonial writers (and later with Cold War imperatives), is diverse with different dynamics operating in various countries. Theravada Buddhists make up majorities in Thailand, Myanmar, Cambodia, and Laos, and the Muslim-majority countries are Indonesia, Brunei, and Malaysia, which account for the majority population of the region. The only Christian majority country is the Philippines, influenced by a final wave of religious influx that came with European colonialism, while Singapore has a Chinese Buddhist-Daoist majority.

Across South Asia, Central Asia, and South East Asia where Buddhists, while not always dominant, were at least strongly represented, they have seen themselves die out or be replaced as dominant by Muslims, which feeds into traditional Buddhist fears about the eventual potential decline of their tradition.[25] Hence, an existential threat is felt by some Buddhists today, who see their old heartlands lost to Muslims, while scholarship currently argues that Buddhist hatred of Muslims and Islam has reached unprecedented levels.[26] While not true of all, a sense of animosity prevails, on both sides, in some places. The tension was perhaps most dramatically seen in 2001, when the Taliban regime in Afghanistan blew up the world's tallest standing Buddha statues, one reaching 55 metres, at Bamiyan which were probably constructed in the sixth century. Xuanzang visited the site in 629 and recorded it as a bustling monastic centre. Though Buddhists had long since disappeared, the statues had survived many vicissitudes of fate over the centuries. The Taliban regarded statues as idolatrous and decided to destroy them, despite their existence in Islamic-controlled territory for almost fifteen hundred years, which suggested that previous Muslims had not found them offensive, or at least not enough to desecrate them.[27] The early *fatwas* recognizing Buddhists as 'People of the Book' are, for most Muslims, lost to history. Indeed, according to the increasingly dominant Wahhabi–Salafi interpretations of Islam (see Chapter 8), such medieval *fatwas* enjoy no authority. Hostility is often a two-way street, though in certain times and places one side may be the predominant actor, or perceived aggressor.

Yet Muslims and Buddhists have lived for centuries, and still do today, in situations of harmonious coexistence, while interchange has existed between the traditions. The influence of Buddhist art was noted above, while, in places such as Nalanda, Buddhist philosophy developed sophisticated forms of argumentation including the recursive method. As Christopher Beckwith has shown, this was passed to Muslims, who integrated it into the Madrasa educational system and Islamic philosophical reasoning before, around the time of the early crusades, it came to Europe where it underpinned medieval scholasticism and evolved into modern reasoning alongside the Islamic reformulations of Greek philosophy, especially that of Aristotle.[28] The details of this are beyond our scope, but it shows evidence of considerable cultural interchange. Another borrowing is found in the medieval Christian story of Saint Josaphat, who became canonized as a saint by the Roman Catholic Church in the sixteenth century with a feast day on 27 November. Historical records show a lineage of a story of a holy man who was the son of a king yet renounced his wealth to lead an ascetic and holy life being passed to Europe during the crusades from Islamic Sufi traditions wherein he was likewise revered. But the story itself appears to be originally a reformulation of the early life story of the Buddha and his renunciation of the material world. Fascinating though such cultural exchanges are – and showing perceived connections between Buddhist, Islamic, and Christian ideas of the holy life – for our purposes they show the admiration which at least some Muslims had for the Buddha and Buddhist traditions. An admiration that meant Buddhism's founder could become taken up and valorized as a saintly figure of devotion, and indeed one whose story had resonances and could travel such vast distances across diverse parts of the Muslim-majority world.[29]

Other examples of a more irenic and appreciative history of encounter could also be drawn. Not expanded on above, but as 'People of the Book', the corollary was that the Buddha himself was a prophet (of Islam), which some have even linked to evidence in the Qur'an.[30] This, as noted above, meant that reverence for the Buddha led to the spread of his story as a holy person, while Reza Shah-Kazemi has argued for various affinities.[31] We should not, therefore, portray the relationship between Buddhism and Islam as inherently hostile. At both the elite orthodox Islamic jurisprudential level and in popular devotion, there has been a history of affinity and sharing.

Two cases: Islamophobia in Sri Lanka and Myanmar

Even before the ending of the Sri Lankan civil war against the Tamil Tigers in 2009, a new enemy was found by militant Buddhist nationalists: Christians. There had been some religious tinge to the civil war, for although the Tamil Tigers were secular there was some framing about fighting the Hindu Tamils, seen as invaders by the Sinhalese, though the Tamils were by no means solely Hindu (Tamils were, and are, Buddhists, Hindus, Christians, and Muslims), just as the Sinhalese were by no means solely Buddhist. The equation of the Sinhalese with Buddhism is part of the recreation of the memory and re-reading of the *Mahavamsa* which was mostly a result of the British colonial practice. This ideological reading of history is also shared by Sinhala Christians against the Tamils, despite the fact that there are tensions between Buddhists and Christians surrounding proselytization.

The shift of attention to Christianity was not wholly unexpected, though relations had for some time been amicable. The heritage of colonialism, and the drawing of exclusivist boundaries, made ideological borders spatial ones, with Buddhist and Christian zones being constructed in contradistinction to each other.[32] Fear of aggressive missionary proselytization lay behind this, with concerns that Christians would induce Buddhists away from their religious tradition.[33] However, after the civil war, tensions also arose with the Muslim community, and this has become the dominating animosity.[34]

The modern-day tension with Muslims belies various points of contact with the Sinhalese. Muslims had, in 1505, joined forces with a Sinhala Buddhist king to resist the Portuguese invasion of the island, while, during the civil war, Muslim political parties supported the Sinhala nationalists against the Tamils. They even organized large demonstrations opposing the United Nations Human Rights Council-led resolution on Sri Lanka that sought to establish mechanisms of accountability regarding the human rights violations in the last phase of the war.[35] Some demographic and historical background will be useful to understand the vectors at work. The Sinhalese make up 74.9 per cent of the population, Sri Lankan Tamils are 11.2 per cent, Sri Lankan Moors are 9.2 per cent, Indian Tamils are 4.2 per cent, and others are 0.5 per cent. Meanwhile, religiously, the figures are: Buddhist 70.2 per cent, Hindu 12.6 per cent, Muslim 9.7 per cent, Roman Catholic 6.1 per cent, other Christian 1.3 per cent, other 0.05 per cent. Most Sinhalese are Buddhist, most Tamils are Hindu, while some of both are Muslim and Christian. The Muslims are often seen to be composed of groups termed the Sri Lankan Moors, Indian Moors, and Malays.[36] However, these demographic figures are subjective, with ethnicity being a fluid and unstable signifier. The 'Sri Lankan Moors' have been on the island for around 1,200 years and there has been considerable intermarriage over the centuries, as such the phrase operates more as a religious marker than anything else, with some British officials in the nineteenth century identifying the 'Moors' as Sinhalese who practice Islam. Nevertheless, they regard themselves, following the official British colonial classification, as a distinct ethnicity, different from both Sinhalese and Tamils. Regardless of how this is framed, Muslims were also caught up with the civil war, with around a third of all Muslims living in the northern areas where the final and brutal stages of the civil war were fought, and were also targets for the Tamil Tigers.[37] Nevertheless, the relations of the Muslims with other occupants of the island were largely peaceful historically, but pre-colonial contestation existed, while they played a part in the resistance to colonialism.

Distinct hostility to Muslims can be seen first emerging in an attack on the Moors in 1915. While some see this as an aberration among an otherwise irenic relationship, Muslims as much as Christians and Tamils have been perceived as 'foreigners' or outsiders ever since the rise of a distinct Sinhalese Buddhist nationalist sentiment in the 1880s to 1890s.[38] Notably, it was Dharmapala who led these anti-Muslim riots. The 1915 riots, while utilizing religious rhetoric, were seen to be focused upon issues of trade and commerce, an area popularly associated with Islam. These riots centred on relatively late arrivals from Malabar in South India (Indian Moors) and seemed aimed at business rivals whose success was feared and seen as dangerous to indigenous Sinhalese traders.[39] In this, we can note that Dharmapala drew upon European imaginaries of antisemitism by describing Muslims through the lens of 'Shylock' so drawing from Shakespeare and colonial inspiration to develop his Islamophobia, which takes us back to notions about the intersectionality of hatreds, but also points to the strong Western lineage of such modern hatreds, especially as racialized hatreds.[40]

It has been argued that the emphasis upon Muslims as enemies in Sri Lanka today is in some senses a continuation of the violence of the civil war, which arguably has normalized violence in society, justified in the defence of Sri Lanka as a Buddhist nation,[41] one in which the invocation of fear of Muslim businessmen and their success as a local Islamophobic trope can readily be deployed to help fuel anxieties and fears.[42] However, this needs some organizational structure, and just as Dharmapala led the 1915 riots, more recent sentiment and attacks against Muslims have been coordinated by groups such as Bodu Bala Sena ('Buddhist Brigade', or more literally 'Buddhist Army Force'), which has stoked resentments towards Muslims in particular.[43] Militant Buddhist nationalists even sought unsuccessfully to make an alliance with the Tamils against the Muslims, showing shifting in-group and out-group dynamics.

Sinhalese Buddhist nationalists have therefore found a new vehicle for their rhetoric and militancy with the Tamil threat now defeated. This draws from the desire to exclude foreigners, purify Sri Lanka, and protect Buddhism. Arguably, that Muslims are seen as an economic threat makes them an easier target than Christians, as the material self-interest of the Sinhalese can be drawn upon rather than simply ethno-religious sentiments.

Also, wider global Islamophobic sentiment means that, at least in the international media and in the reaction of many countries, targeting Muslims
is probably seen as less problematic than targeting Christians. The 'war on
terror' was certainly evoked in some responses to the Easter Sunday attacks
in 2019 (21 April), when militant neo-Islamic jihadi terrorists targeted a
cathedral and hotels in coordinated suicide attacks which resulted in 259
deaths.[44] In the wake of this, framing local Muslims as potentially dangerous terrorists has played into the hands of militant Buddhist nationalists,
though the threat seems to arise from the infiltration of ISIS which is not
native to the indigenous Muslim community and is vehemently rejected by
most Muslims in Sri Lanka. The attack seems to have been an attempt to
divide Muslims and Christians who had not previously had tensions and
often found common ground against Buddhist militants.[45] After the Easter
Sunday attack, even many Tamils turned against Muslims, and Jude Lal
Fernando has noted that 'A new alliance between Buddhists and Christians,
and Tamils and Sinhalese, has been forged against the Muslims.'[46]

Three further aspects of the offensive against Islam can be picked up
here. One of these is the rejection of halal food. While partly a new phenomenon, it also goes back to Dharmapala who insisted on cow protection
alongside more widespread Buddhist insistence on protection of all sentient creatures (humans and animals) from harm, in terms of the Buddhist
principle of *ahimsa*. While defence of cows is a specifically Hindu rather
than Buddhist issue (see Chapter 10), it was adopted by Dharmapala in
his reformulation of Buddhism, and is invoked today as part of Buddhist
attacks against halal food as being immoral and indefensible on other
grounds.[47] Another is the utilization of online platforms, especially social
media, to expedite the spread of extremist messages and to help coordinate
attacks on Muslim businesses. We will say more about this with the discussion on Myanmar. Finally, there is the growth of a transnational Buddhist
anti-Muslim sentiment, discussed further below, which involves primarily Theravada-majority countries in South East Asia alongside Sri Lanka
which has been something of an ideological bedrock through its development of justifications for Buddhist militancy in the modern period; though
as we will note we should attend very much to the specific dynamics of
each and not see them as simply regional variations of a general Buddhist
militant antipathy to Islam.[48]

On 1 July 2013, *Time Magazine* featured the picture of a man in the
robes of a Buddhist monk on its front cover with the headline: 'The Face
of Buddhist Terror'. The man is Ashin Wirathu, and his status as a monk
has been contested; it is common for males in Myanmar to temporarily
enter monasteries for a few weeks, months, or even years without ordination. However, Wirathu has full ordination, and so his status as monk gives
weight, in the eyes of his dedicated followers, to his speeches – of virulent
anti-Muslim rhetoric – framed as 'Buddhist sermons' (*dharma* talks). Indeed,
part of the power of figures such as Wirathu is that their discourse is framed

in the religious sphere, hence justifying prejudice or bigotry, or sometimes even physical violence, in terms of defence of *dharma* and *sasana*.[49]

Antagonism towards Muslims, however, is not the main framing of the key anti-Muslim organizations such as the 969 movement and MaBaTha. Rather, they are known for community work, social action, and as *dharma* defence organizations.[50] Therefore, when people in Myanmar see outside attacks on MaBaTha, 969, and so on they perceive them as attacks on Buddhists providing social services, education for the poor, and so on. Nevertheless, from such activities, an anti-Muslim sentiment is often engendered with people encouraged to frequent only Buddhist-run shops (they will carry the logo of one of these, or other, organizations in their window) and so steer clear of Muslim businesses. This is often on the assumption of a growing Muslim threat, both demographically as well as in business terms, with allegations (partially true) that Muslims will only frequent Muslim businesses (required to obtain things such as halal meat) rather than Buddhist ones.[51] Demographic threats are often not very credible, with the Bamar ethnicity being the majority one (at around 68 per cent), and also religiously the country remains staunchly Buddhist (2020 statistics): Buddhist 87.9 per cent, Christian 6.2 per cent, Muslim 4.3 per cent, Animist 0.8 per cent, Hindu 0.5 per cent, other 0.2 per cent, and none 0.1 per cent.[52] Nevertheless, within South East Asia, the notion of a long-term Muslim takeover is part of the wider discourse, with a perceived need to defend Buddhism lest other countries also fall, which is also related to allegations of a 'love jihad' in which Muslims are seen as being demographically ascendant, with Buddhist women seen to be at risk from predatory Muslim men.[53] Notably, monks have often been involved in politics in Myanmar and so their involvement in such issues is not surprising.[54]

Another specific dynamic within Myanmar is the Rohingya conflict in the west of the country. A wide public distrust, even hatred, of the Rohingya permeates the national consciousness. The Rohingya are perceived as a distinct ethnicity and are almost entirely Muslim. Muslims have been in the region of the modern Rakhine state for centuries, but as the term Rohingya is fairly recent (primarily consolidated as a term post-Second World War), although there are earlier mentions of the term, the Myanmar authorities argue that they are recent Bangladeshi migrants and not Myanmar citizens. While, with their long history in Myanmar, the Bangladeshis do not recognize them as their citizens. It may be noted that, for many centuries, the borders have been somewhat fluid and ill defined, and while the British brought some Bangladeshi workers, and others have crossed more recently as economic migrants, this does not affect a long-established Rohingya presence.[55] The Rohingya are not the only oppressed minority group in Myanmar, with military violence against a number of other ethnic minorities (there are 135 recognized ethnic groups in the country, but if every cultural-linguistic sub-group were recognized as an ethnicity it has been estimated that the number would be over four hundred). But, by being denied citizenship, the

Rohingya have a peculiar place. The background to this, and other, conflicts is complex and contextual, but rather than being only a religio-ethnic dispute in origins, economics is also responsible.[56] The Rohingya, like many other oppressed groups, live on land that the military sees as having economic value. Although Myanmar transitioned from being a military dictatorship into a partial democracy with elections (2011–15), the military remains outside the control of the civilian government and large swathes of the country are under direct military control, including the territories in which the Rohingya are found.[57] Antipathy towards the Rohingya is widespread in Myanmar, especially as they are seen as foreign interlopers and, since 2013, have been involved in a fairly one-sided insurgency against the military. This has allowed the Myanmar military to frame their offensive against the Rohingya as part of the war on terror, though many analysts are suspicious of claimed links between the main insurgency group, the Arakan Rohingya Salvation Army, and outside militant neo-Islamic jihadi organizations.[58] Notably, other Muslim groups in Myanmar have been keen to distance themselves from the Rohingya.

For Myanmar's Buddhist militants, this conflict is framed within a wider context of violence between Muslims and Buddhists, both historically and in the contemporary context. The negative aspects of history, as noted above, are remembered, while Myanmar Buddhist militants have been forging links with compatriots in Sri Lanka and Thailand. In the latter, an insurgency in the southern Pattani region aiming for political self-determination, without a specifically religious animus, has been linked by some to the alleged wider Buddhist–Muslim antagonism,[59] though there are particular contextual aspects of the history of violence in Thai Buddhism.[60] Ironically, perhaps, these Buddhist militants see militant neo-Islamic jihadis as a model, both in terms of creating a pan-Buddhist ideology of hatred and in developing networks on a transnational basis.[61] Many other Buddhists within these countries oppose them, though, a matter we discuss further below.

Within Myanmar, outbreaks of violence against Muslims have often been linked to rumours and false news spread on social media. This has been particularly associated with Facebook which for many in Myanmar represents their primary interaction with the Internet; indeed for many Myanmar citizens the two are more or less interchangeable. Following United Nations investigations in 2018, Facebook removed eighteen accounts, fifty-two pages, and one Instagram account, with a combined following of almost 12 million people, showing the impact of a few hate-based accounts.[62] A UN official stated that 'Facebook played the "determining role" in accelerating the violence and had "substantively contributed to the level of acrimony" toward the Rohingya'.[63] While Facebook predominates in such markets (through deals to make it accessible on low-end mobile phones), social media more widely is a factor in the spread of prejudice and allows rumours and false news to spread quickly and accessibly, thus potentially fomenting widespread acts of violence in hotbed settings.

Before leaving our two case studies, we must address one issue, raised above, which is how far such sentiments may be said to be widespread within the Buddhist worldview and the values of these countries. As noted, the kind of Buddhist just war ideology promoted by figures such as Rahula are seen as a 'betrayal of Buddhism' by others. Certainly, within Myanmar, the Great Buddhist Council (the Sangha Maha Nayaka) has forbidden Wirathu from preaching as a monk as well as censuring him,[64] and has also closed down some of the militant groups operating as Buddhist organizations. Nevertheless, with immense popularity and an online presence, the Council and the government have found it hard to silence Wirathu, while monastic organizations which are shut down simply reopen in civil society forms. We can therefore see, in Myanmar, something of a top-down Buddhist elite resistance to the kind of aggressive rhetoric and demonization of Muslims found in figures such as Wirathu. Nevertheless, negative sentiment towards the Rohingya is widespread in society, and given the relatively closed nature of Myanmar society it is hard to assess how much of this is shared by monks or Buddhists as a whole. In Sri Lanka, meanwhile, the more militant advocacy of violence is probably a minority stance among monastics, though many support the notion, based in readings of the *Mahavamsa*, that Sri Lanka should be a pure Buddhist island. The Easter Sunday terror attacks of 2019 means prejudice against Muslims is on the rise there, however, it is doubtful that this is primarily framed as a cause for Buddhist antipathy as opposed to a general nationalist or security concern, but these play into each other (or, are indistinguishable) for many Sinhalese.

Prejudice, history, and contemporary conflicts

As a form of prejudice, distinct animosity of Buddhists towards Muslims goes back centuries; indeed, in some medieval Tibetan Buddhist texts Muslims appear as demons. Nevertheless, while some aspects of the historical encounters play into the perceptions that Buddhists have towards Muslims today, we can also see some very specific and contextual modern dynamics at play. In Sri Lanka, for militant Buddhist nationalists, Muslims have come to take the key role of the outsider as threat to the integrity of an imagined pure insider identity. This is posited very much upon a modern reconceptualization of Buddhism in response to Western colonialism. Indeed, the type of Buddhism reformulated by Dharmapala has even been called a 'Protestant Buddhism'.[65] It is also based around a racialized ethnonationalism in which religion plays a key legitimizing part. Muslims are simply one group perceived as outsiders, or foreigners, within this matrix, but have become the fixation. In Myanmar, aspects of the Rohingya situation have led to perceptions of the (Rohingya) Muslims as militant foreign outsiders who are aggressive in attacking the country's integrity and Buddhist traditions. It plays out upon wider perceptions of a global 'war on terror', while an unrelated conflict in Thailand is used to help frame a pan-Asian Muslim–Buddhist conflict which has been ongoing for centuries with perceptions of a Muslim demographic takeover posited historically and imagined in the contemporary context. It also plays into what Iselin Frydenlund sees as a conspiracy theory in which local Muslims are framed as actors in a global Muslim plot for domination.[66] A largely peaceful history between the communities in both countries is therefore eclipsed, to at least some degree, by a modern prejudice which sees itself enacted in militant violence against minority Muslim groups.

CHAPTER TEN

Hindutva as hatred: Hindus, Muslims, and the fatherland

Introduction

These are not the words I originally intended to use to start this chapter:

> A mosque in Ashok Nagar was set on fire late on Tuesday afternoon. A mob shouting 'Jai Shri Ram' [Victory to Lord Rama] and 'Hinduon ka Hindustan' [India for Hindus] paraded around the burning mosque and a Hanuman flag was placed on the minaret'.[1]

This is not the first version of this introduction I have written. This may not seem surprising, authors do draft and redraft their work many times. However, in this case, something changed. I had planned to start off talking about the Babri Masjid in Ayodhya, destroyed by Hindu militants in 1992 and the site of continued dispute. I will still talk about that, but, as I am writing, the US President Donald Trump is in India meeting the Indian Prime Minister Narendra Modi and riots are happening on the streets: mosques are being torched, Muslims are being beaten up, even killed, while often the police stand by. What is going on? During such a vital state visit, why is basic law and order not enforced (according to some reports, the police have even joined in the violence), and what has led to this huge eruption, one that does not seem to hinder the rapport between these two politicians? Though, after several days, as the violence grabs headlines, Modi has turned belatedly to address it. This may seem a puzzle, and, in a sense, it is. That is, until you see the pieces, when a clear picture falls into place, a bit like a jigsaw. Instead of just taking the theme of the Babri Masjid as a central motif to run through this chapter as a linking point, I will also take this contemporary violence (in February 2020), which this chapter will seek to explain. Each puzzle is in many ways similar, and we will see many of the same pieces whichever way I write this chapter, but this new emphasis helps us see the global picture into which Hindu Islamophobia fits, and will assist in bringing various aspects of religious hatred together as this book nears its conclusion.

It is not usual for authors to reveal the process of writing, books often seem to drop as a finalized and polished product onto the shelves, so why have I started with this? I will address, here, a question raised in the introduction: why this book? Prejudice, Islamophobia, and antisemitism are, regrettably, factors that persist in our world today. I felt an urgency to write this book, and so while I may affect the stance of a detached observer, of academic neutrality, the fact is that my life and experience build into this book. In his book on Hindu–Muslim violence in India, psychoanalyst Sudhir Kakar starts with the way that the image of a disfigured 2-year-old girl has haunted his imagination, and often returned unbidden to his mind. Against any sense of academic neutrality, he notes that 'quantum physicists realized the importance of the interaction of subject and object in the comprehension of reality – "We cannot describe the world if we do not belong to it," was the credo of the pioneers'.[2] The need to recognize authorial positionality, and a deep reflexivity in understanding this, is key in many disciplines, while the pathways of life affect which books we write, which books we read, and how we react to them.[3] Prejudice and violence happen to people. While studied here as interesting social phenomena, they occur in the world we belong to, no matter how distant the events in India and between religious groups we may or may not understand, or even know members of, may seem. These are, after all, not just objects of study, but the daily experience of Hindus and Muslims, among others, in India. I have friends, students, and colleagues – both Muslim and Hindu – who are either directly affected by the dynamics described, or whose family is affected.

Muslims and Hindus in South Asian history

South Asia, in the modern period, has been dramatically affected by the arrival of two colonizing empires associated with distinct religions: the Moghuls (Islam) and the British (Christianity). By the eighth century, Islamic empires had spread to the edges of South Asia, while Muslim traders had settled along the West coast. The major incursion into Sind (modern-day Gujarat) by the Turkic sultan Mahmud of Ghazni (971–1030) was well documented by a courtier, the polymath Al-Biruni (973–1050), who gave the most thorough external accounts of Hinduism[4] until the nineteenth century.[5] He attests to considerable animosity arising from Muslim raids, and it was at this time that an iconic temple to Shiva at Somnath was first destroyed. Indeed, from at least the twelfth century, Muslims were portrayed as *rakshasas* or *asuras* ('demons') in Hindu thought,[6] though this referred to those Muslims who were raiding and therefore a direct threat. In a situation of more fluid religious identity boundaries than found today, Hindus never represented 'all Muslims' as 'demons' (itself an inadequate translation of *asuras*).[7]

While earlier Muslim dynasties existed, of paradigmatic significance in subsequent representations and historical memory is the Moghul Empire which was established in the sixteenth century and which finally ended in 1858 when the British Raj was established, though some client rulers remained until the twentieth century. The first Moghul emperor Babur (1483–1530) built the contested Babri Masjid in 1528, and if modern Hindu antagonism to Islam has a symbol, then that symbol is this mosque, destroyed on 6 December 1992 when Hindu militants breached police lines. According to Hindu nationalists today, the site is the birthplace of the revered Hindu deity Rama. As with many conquering rulers, the Moghuls destroyed existing buildings and replaced them with their own, and a policy of destroying, or sometimes repurposing, Hindu temples to replace them with mosques was practiced. This is a common aspect of imperial rule, or the control of space by any hegemonic power, in which the architectural environment is shaped and formed to show ownership and dominance, though Muslim rulers also endowed Hindu temples at other times.[8] Nevertheless, there were many aspects of the historical encounter that gave rise to animosity, and Aurangzeb's (reigned 1658–1707) legacy is particularly remembered. Perhaps most famous for imprisoning and allegedly gouging out the eyes of his father, Shah Jahan, the builder of the Taj Mahal, some see Aurangzeb as an austere fanatic. He is said to have destroyed all remaining Hindu temples in Ayodhya and had them replaced with mosques in 1697, something he had earlier done in Mathura in 1688, a city sacred to Krishna. He also re-imposed the *jizya* ('poll tax') on *dhimmis*, which had been abolished by the emperor Akbar (1542–1605). Aurangzeb's reign is remembered as having ruptured communal bonds built since the time of Akbar. Like other Moghul emperors, Aurangzeb was often pragmatic, and on occasions endowed Hindu temples, but his reign seemingly ignited tensions, especially around the *jizya*.[9]

Akbar, arguably the greatest Moghul emperor, had earlier expanded the empire including by taking the Chittorgarh fortress of the renowned Rajput warriors, while art and poetry flourished under his patronage. He also sought a rapprochement between the religions of India, announcing in 1582 his own creedal statement in the *Din-i-ilahi* ('the Divine Faith') which combined Sunni Islam, Sufism, Hinduism, and Zoroastrianism, leading to allegations of apostasy by some Muslims.[10] While some have dismissed Akbar as a singular aberration, he arguably represents a mainstream, street-level dynamic between Hindus and Muslims, with syncretism being a norm. This is seen in the Sant tradition out of which Sikhism appeared. Across much of

North India, Sant tradition fused Sufi and Hindu *bhakti* (devotional) currents in shrines, poetry and devotional songs, holy people, and festivals. The
mystical poet and holy man Kabir, revered by Hindus, Muslims, and Sikhs,
is the most notable representative, but he is only one of many. Such sharing of practices between Hindus and Muslims still occurs in the villages of
South Asia.[11]

Even a site posited as holy to Rama such as Ayodhya has been for over
two thousand years religiously shared, with not just Vaishnavite Hindu but
also Jain, Buddhist, Shaivite Hindu, Muslim, and other groups present. In
the contemporary situation, at the level of lived religion in the countryside,
but also sometimes in the cities, coexistence and mutual exchange is part
of the ongoing practice of everyday life, though such dialogical exchange
is often ignored by elites.[12] Certainly, more intolerant and partisan narratives exist as another mainstream option, and Hindu nationalists who see
themselves responding to a threat from Muslims can appeal to a legacy that
makes their stories existentially credible, but other stories can also be told.

Hindu nationalism: A British legacy

Hindu nationalism was created around the period 1870 to 1920, though
its early development continued till the 1950s.[13] It was largely a response
to British colonialism and was an attempt to hang onto a cultural identity
in the face of social change. Its development was coterminous with a secular Indian nationalism, both being responses to the modern, Western conception of the nation state. Under the Mughals or Emperor Ashoka (*c.*250
BCE), the Indian subcontinent had never been politically united, and regional
identities predominated. India, as we now understand the idea, is a British
creation. The British arrived in the sixteenth century, with the British East
India Company becoming the dominant trading and political force by the
nineteenth century. After the Indian Mutiny, or First War of Independence,
of 1857, the British government took up direct rule in 1858, establishing the
British Raj which was to last until 1947 and has a contested legacy.[14] This
is what led to the importation of the modern, Western notion of the nation
state, with British India creating both the notion of a united India and a
nationalist aspiration among the Indian people.

Indian nationalism envisaged a united India (Akhand Bharat or Akhand
Hindustan) inclusive of all religions and ethnicities and is associated with
the Indian National Congress (INC, founded 1885), and its successor the
Congress Party which came to power at independence. Leading figures
included Jawaharlal Nehru (1847–1964), India's first prime minister, and
Mohandas 'Mahatma' Gandhi (1869–1948). Indeed, early on, most Hindu
nationalists remained within the INC. The leading movement of Hindu
nationalism, the Hindu Mahasabha (Hindu Great Council) (1915), was an

interest group in the INC, while the influential Hindu nationalist Pandit Mohan Malaviya (1861–1946) was twice president of the INC. As a distinct trend against secular Indian nationalism, Hindu nationalism grew in the 1920s with concerns about Muslims who, in opposition to the British, were talking about establishing a new caliphate, with the First World War having ended the Turkish Sultan's claim to be a global caliph.[15] However, Hindu nationalism only became electorally significant under the BJP (Bharatiya Janata Party) in the 1980s and 1990s, and dominant only in the early twenty-first century under Modi. As such, in 1948, India was founded as a secular multicultural democracy but saw religion as an important component of the identity of the country.[16] While Congress officially kept religion and politics separate, it did manipulate religious sentiments, including orchestrating the 1984 anti-Sikh riots, while Muslims and Christians fitted less comfortably into national narratives, which contributed to communal tensions that Hindu nationalists could exploit.[17]

The British also influenced Indian representations of the Muslim. Despite real tensions and differences, there were previously fluid and nuanced differentiations between those we would term Hindus and Muslims, with local caste identities often being a more significant marker of difference. But, for the British, distinct communal identities were key to governance and, taking on board Foucault's (1926–1984) insights on power and knowledge, we can see that there were implications for the Indian nation state.[18] In the aftermath of the 1857 rebellion (or, war of independence), which British rulers attributed to 'Muslim intrigue and Muslim leadership ... aimed at the extinction of the Raj', Muslims became conceived 'as one unique and monolithic entity', who were seen as (repeating old tropes) 'violent, legalistic, and unwilling to be governed by non-Muslims'.[19] Texts such as William Wilson Hunter's (1840–1900) *The Indian Musalmans: Are They Bound in Conscience to Rebel against the Queen* (1871) have had an ongoing legacy.[20] Influential British representations of the 'jihadi' Muslim no doubt fed into earlier Hindu perceptions lighting flames of suspicion between the communities, and so we can link contemporary outbreaks of orchestrated mob violence against Hindus back to the colonial period.

Hindutva as Islamophobic ideology and its organization

After 1813, in response to increased incursions of Christian missionaries (prior to 1813, the British East India Company had banned missionaries for creating tensions unconducive for trade), what is termed the Hindu Renaissance sought to adapt Hinduism to Western social, intellectual, and ethical norms. But, by the late nineteenth century, groups such as the Arya Samaj, founded by Swami Dayananda Saraswati (1824–83), offered a robust defence of Hindu tradition. He stressed an advanced Vedic Golden Age, arguing, in a nineteenth-century context, that steamships and telegrams were found in the Vedas. While Saraswati was not a Hindu nationalist, his ideas have provided fuel for today's Hindu nationalists. They assert that Hindu culture has always been the greatest and most advanced on the planet, and any decline today is therefore blamed on the invaders (Muslims then Christians). So, today, everything from airplanes to transplant surgery, and microscopes to nuclear weapons are claimed as being found in ancient India. Such views, associated with Purushottam Nagesh Oak (1917–2007), lead to a reading of the Vedas that Julius Lipner argues could be seen as fundamentalist.[21] While seemingly benign, such views undergird Hindu nationalist assertions of primacy and superiority on the spiritual, ethical, and scientific level for an ancient Hindu culture, and can legitimate a violent defence of this. Moreover, as with many 'fundamentalisms' (despite its manifold problems as a concept), Hindu nationalism is essentially a product of the modern world, its claims to ancient origins being selective imaginings of these in a contemporary idiom.[22] Hindu nationalists also seek validation from more inclusive strands. This includes appropriating Swami Vivekananda (1863–1902), of the Ramakrishna movement, whose assertions of Hinduism's religious superiority are read as triumphalist nationalist claims, seemingly against Vivekananda's own intentions.[23]

The exclusivist tenor of Hindu nationalism's worldview, though, came from an atheist, V. D. Savarkar (1883–1966), whose writings laid the foundation for contemporary militant *Hindutva* ideology; it should be stressed that older, inclusive notions of *Hindutva* (roughly 'Hinduness') exist.[24] As a 15-year-old, Savarkar made a pledge to the fierce goddess Durga to drive the British from India. This led him to jail in 1911 for his involvement in an armed revolt in 1909. However, before his release in 1937, he was busy writing and meeting people, including Nathuram Godse, a Rashtriya Swayamsevak Sangh (RSS) member who would later assassinate Gandhi; Savarkar stood trial as an accomplice but was acquitted. The most influential of his writings is *Hindutva: Who Is a Hindu?*[25]

For Savarkar, several important facets are built into the notion of *Hindutva*, the first of which is to be an inhabitant of Hindustan (i.e. India). For him, Hindustan runs from the Indus to the sea. This is Akhand Bharat, generally seen as encompassing the Himalayas in the north to the tip of the landmass in the south, and from the Arabian Sea to the Bay of Bengal, though some even extend a 'Greater India' to Southeast Asia. This 'undivided India', invoked from Gandhi to the BJP, is key to the politics of division, as discussed below. One's identity and belonging should be linked to this area. This leads to the other pillars of Savarkar's *Hindutva*, that the Hindus are a people with a 'bond of common blood' who regard India as their 'holyland' or 'fatherland'. It is not, for Savarkar, a racialized identity, and he states that those who come to India and embrace Hindu ways and traditions can become Hindus, while the intermixing of indigenous peoples and Aryans is presupposed by him.[26] Nevertheless, there will be hierarchies, for Savarkar's term 'race' translates the Sanskritic term *jati* (literally, a group with something in common) which he glosses as 'brotherhood', but normally refers to subdivisions within castes. That this is his meaning is spelt out by a hierarchy with the brahmin or priestly class at the top and others descending within a system of inherent differences.[27] Also, of interest, is that Savarkar who, like many Hindu nationalist leaders was influenced by European fascism (see further below), drew a direct parallel with Nazi attitudes to Jews in developing his own *Hindutva* ideology, stating that: 'the Indian Muslims are on the whole more inclined to identify themselves and their interests with Muslims outside India than Hindus who live next door, like Jews in Germany', while he had also praised the Nazi project as a 'national regime' against the 'communal one' of 'the Jews'.[28] That Savarkar's *Hindutva* drew from European Nazi antisemitism rather than indigenous Indian tropes which are, arguably, what we see in the earlier more inclusive forms of *Hindutva* is telling.

It should be noted here that Hindu identity is not natural to 'Hindus'. Hinduism as a term is a foreign imposition, though it is an orientalist assertion that this was not, or could not have been, indigenously characterized.[29] Identity as regional, caste-based (*jati* was often given to British census takers seeking 'religious' identifications), or devotional (as Rama, Durga, Shiva, etc. devotees, though many Hindus wear sectarian identities lightly) was, and remains, common. Just as no Indian national identity preceded the British, a unifying Hindu identity was rare. Differentiation of 'orthodox' and 'unorthodox' (*astika/nastika*) traditions existed (primarily, what we today call Hinduism versus Jainism and Buddhism), but the encounter with Western colonialism changed Hindu identity. This is not particularly remarkable because we always recreate in-group identities in relation to different outgroups.[30] However, the end result of Moghul incursions, British categorization, and certain modern indigenous narratives gave a stark choice: you are Hindu or Muslim, not both, with no middle ground. Hindu nationalists, who have most benefited from such narratives, depending on the perspective, either created it, or else, on a longue durée, are merely products of this historical process.[31]

Such ideas, however, needed an institutional form and this is found in various interrelated organizations.[32] The BJP is the political wing of the Sangh Parivar, or 'family of right-wing organisations', which includes the RSS and the Vishva (or Vishwa) Hindu Parishad (VHP). All come, indirectly, from the Hindu Mahasabha, with the RSS being the link. The RSS was founded in 1925 by K. B. Hedgewar (1889–1940), and both he and his successor M. S. Golwalkar (1906–1973) were inspired by Savarkar. Hedgewar was also inspired by European fascist movements, both in terms of ideology, but most especially in organizational structures, and direct influence from Italy's example saw the RSS set up as an activist organization that would train a militant group of young volunteers with a distinctive uniform, fitness training, and a military-style discipline.[33] This is based in local chapters, the *shakha*, where fitness and ideology are taught, while a strong group bond is built among the male members – an aggressive masculinity, seen as necessary to defend 'Mother India' and 'the Hindu woman' is found across Hindu nationalist movements.[34] They have been the 'shock troops' of Hindu nationalism, often associated with riots and violence, especially against Muslims. Indeed, a number of those arrested in the wake of the Delhi 2020 violence were RSS members.[35] The RSS claims to be based in a revival of Indian traditions, and its military training has been likened to the wrestling traditions of the north. The core members called *pracharaks* ('preachers' or 'missionaries') adopt a celibate, ascetic lifestyle and see themselves as *karma yoginis* (practitioners of the yoga of action).

The BJP was founded in 1951 by Syama Prasad Mookerjee (1901–1953) as the Bharatiya Jana Sangh, changing its name to the BJP in 1971, to fight the cause of Hindu Bengalis in what was then East Pakistan (now Bangladesh). But, after seeking an alliance with other parties to take on Congress under Prime Minister Indira Gandhi in 1977, it became a force in its own right from around 1980 when it started to forge its contemporary identity.[36] This trajectory came from links with the RSS built in the 1950s. Notably, a number of parties associated with Hindu nationalism were initially regional and not originally Hindu nationalist, such as the Shiv Sena movement in Maharashtra.[37]

Golwalkar, leader of the RSS, envisaged a broad Indic religion alliance, which after a 1964 conference with the Dalai Lama, Sikh and Jain leaders, and the five Shankaracharyas (leaders of the five lineages claiming descent from the sage Shankara, and the closest that exists to a pan-Hindu leadership), founded the VHP in 1966. Following Savarkar, Hindu nationalists see all these traditions as 'Hindu'. However, despite such ecumenical overtures, the VHP has been a vehicle of Hindu nationalism, used for 'the staging of huge religious processions designed to arouse popular fervour for "Hindu causes" and to intimidate Muslims and other "outsiders"'.[38] The VHP also reaches out to all Hindu devotional strands, and Dalits and other scheduled castes and tribes. This contrasts with a focus on high caste, especially brahmanical, traditions in Hindu nationalism overall.[39] This is partly political pragmatism, because electoral success requires the support of these groups. But it also relates to the fear of Islam. During Moghul rule there had been some forced conversions, but many Dalits and low caste Hindus had converted to Islam voluntarily to improve their situation. Likewise, under the British, many low caste people converted to Christianity as there were benefits in being Christian. There were also mass conversions to Buddhism during the twentieth century. Therefore, the VHP functions to counter all of these perceived risks, but mass conversions to Islam, something which has picked up again from 1981, has been a main concern. The RSS has also been involved in working with scheduled castes, including recent *ghar wapsi* ('reconversion') projects, whereby Indian Muslims and Christians are persuaded to return to Hinduism. This required ritual innovation as the Hindu tradition had previously had no rites for, nor any conception of, a reconversion. Meanwhile, recently, the BJP and its partners have enacted state-level laws forbidding conversion by force or fraud, but which are typically seen as targeting Muslims and Christians by creating 'a hostile, and on occasion violent, environment for religious minority communities because they do not require any evidence to support accusations of wrongdoing'.[40]

Savarkar's *Hindutva* picks out both Christianity and Islam (and potentially Judaism) as not properly belonging to the imagined Indian nation. Christians have been responsible for mass conversions, and they are associated with colonial invasion and the desecration of Hindu property and sentiments. While Christianity is picked out as an enemy, the Muslim is the Hindu nationalist's bête noire. One reason is that they are a much larger demographic in South Asia, and a deep-seated historical (potential for) animosity exists, which has been fed by British colonial and contemporary global Islamophobia, including the 'war on terror'. Indeed, Kakar hypothesized that Muslim rather than Western beef-eating has been more offensive because it is seen up close: your neighbour slaughtering a cow or the village Muslim butcher with his blood-splattered apron, as opposed to the British within their colonial villas isolated from the general population. Again, he notes that 'The most hated out-group will be the one used most as a bad example in child training.'[41] Another issue is the historical events that led to the separation of modern-day India and Pakistan and the ongoing tension between those two countries perceived as, respectively, a 'Hindu' and a 'Muslim' nation and people. The narratives of partition are still rehearsed in antagonistic ways.[42]

Politics and power

The relationship between India and Pakistan remains key in maintaining antagonism between Hindus and Muslims. This concerns the notion of Akhand Bharat and Mother India (Bharat Mata). The partition of India in 1948 between India, Pakistan, and Bangladesh (then East Pakistan) was traumatic for many who envisaged a 'united India' comprising the whole area. The role of Muhammad Ali Jinnah (1876–1948), of the Muslim League, in vehemently insisting upon a separate state for Muslims (the role of the British is invoked less often) has been seen as causing Mother India, in Hindu nationalist rhetoric, to have her arms torn off. Mother India is not simply a symbol, but a potent part of the social imaginary of many Hindus, and images of her under attack are emotionally stirring. Conflict along the border has been ongoing with various disputed territories including Kashmir.[43]

The growing Muslim demographic in India is also invested with meaning. The 2011 census data was delayed as it showed that Hindus had fallen below the symbolic 80 per cent mark to 79.8 per cent while Muslims had grown to 14.2 per cent of the population, with Christians on 2.3 per cent. In the first census after independence (1951), Christians were 2.3 per cent, but then Hindus were 84.1 per cent and Muslims 9.8 per cent. In the Hindu nationalist imagination, this is part of a progressive takeover, sometimes termed 'population jihad'.[44] Moreover, despite there being a small change, *Hindutva* ideologues predict that within decades Muslims will become a majority in India, or at least reach the symbolic 33 per cent target – the proportion of Muslims just prior to Independence – when they will further dismember Mother India.[45] Hence, every Muslim is perceived as a danger to Hinduism/India.

Political scientists often discuss the nuclear threat between India and Pakistan as a source of tension, though it is perhaps also a deterrence preventing border skirmishes becoming wars. However, a more potent image, related to the demographic threat, is of the imagined hypersexualized Muslim seducing or raping Hindu girls. Kakar found that the prospect of a Hindu girl going to the cinema with a Muslim boy was a potent preoccupation, with Muslims portrayed in Hindu nationalist propaganda as lewd, promiscuous, and dangerous to Hindu women. This reflects a fear among Hindus of being replaced in their own homeland, with allegations made of a 'love jihad' (i.e. Muslim men seducing Hindu women as part of a repopulation plan).[46] This relates to perceived threats to the masculinity of the Hindu man and the cultivation of an underlying sense of vulnerability in the face of a global Islamic presence.

Ironically, Hindu nationalism can also be bred from more inclusive roots. The rise of the RSS, BJP, and VHP among other groups has not simply been through spreading fear and speaking about the enemy. Community activism and perceived support for Hindu virtues, such as tolerance and inclusion, are part of their appeal. Meera Nanda argues that a Hindu nationalist journalistic organization, the Voice of India, draws from ideas such as those of Vivekananda, as noted above, valorizing Hindu religiosity as tolerant and inclusive. However, this vaunting of in-group tolerance relies upon its contrast to a posited less tolerant out-group in this proclamation of cultural chauvinism. Therefore, we see Islam and Christianity dismissed as *tamasika-rajasika* (dark-passionate) religions with an inadequate conception of deity (exclusive monotheism) appealing to the '"lower" kinds of minds'.[47] The posited inclusive identity is weaponized against the created other, especially the Muslim, as the opposite of one's own virtue and inclusivity.[48]

These dynamics have helped the BJP attain power. First, as part of a coalition for a short time in the 1990s, but most notably with Modi's victory in the 2014 general election, in which he won 286 of the 543 seats, making the BJP the first party since 1984 to have an overall majority. The majority increased in the 2019 general election. To understand this rise, it is necessary to revisit the violence of the Babri Masjid event and look at how the ensuing riots and communal clashes have shaped the relationship of Hindus and Muslims in India. This dispute is only one of many, but given its iconic significance, and that it caused waves of violence around India, both in the run up to it, and subsequently, it is worth looking at in some detail.

The disputes around the Babri Masjid date back to 1853, when British authorities demarcated Hindu and Muslim sections of the site,[49] but a major impetus was in 1949 when Hindu activists placed a statue of Rama in the Muslim section, leading to the Indian government closing the site and declaring it disputed, but resentments simmered. The BJP and VHP took up the case in the 1980s, when, as noted above, there was growing concern over conversions to Islam. Quite why this Ayodhya temple took on such iconic dimensions is unclear. The temple is not the most important among those which Hindu nationalists have pledged to rebuild, with the rebuilding of the Somnath temple also promised. Neither had Rama previously been a key figure of Hindu nationalism, being seen as too gentle. But, over time, the compassionate and ideal king of traditional iconography was transformed into a warrior God, bow and arrow in hand. In the film *Slumdog Millionaire* (2008), the image of a young child painted blue and holding a bow and arrow in the early riot scene is not simply for visual effect, for it depicts the warrior Rama; this scene led some militant Hindu organizations to demand a ban on the film for upsetting Hindu sensibilities. The priority of Ayodhya combines a memory of Islamic oppression with Rama as militant defender of Hinduism, at what is his claimed birthplace.[50]

In 1989, members of the BJP and VHP laid the foundation stone of a Rama temple just outside the Babri Masjid, and after the BJP took power in Uttar Pradesh (1991), where the temple is located, they instigated a year-long pilgrimage, asking followers to collect bricks and make donations to build a Rama temple. Notably, this was enabled by Congress under the then Prime Minister Rajiv Gandhi who was trying to placate and forestall Hindu nationalist sentiments, but it seems a miscalculation that emboldened such sentiments and the Sangh Parivar mobilized to take advantage of this. Likewise, Gyanendra Pandey suggests that liberal commentators who used the term *Ram Janmabhumi*, denoting that this was the land (*bhumi*) of Rama's birth, conceded the contested history to the militant Hindu nationalists.[51] This culminated with the mosque's destruction in 1992, and in ensuing riots over two thousand died; indeed, these riots and others – as we will discuss below – may well have been orchestrated by parts of the Sangh Parivar including influential leaders, and the periodic outbursts of violence may well be managed for political gain. Since then, until 2019, the matter was passed through the courts, with the Indian Supreme Court in 2017 ruling that there was no current ownership of the site. But, in November 2019, it ruled again, arguing that archaeological evidence showed it was originally a temple site. The archaeological evidence is far from clear; a temple may lie beneath it, but, even if so, was it a Rama temple or intended to mark Rama's birthplace?[52] The ruling gave permission for a Hindu temple to be built there. As a concession to Muslims, a 'prominent place' in the city would be set aside for a mosque.[53]

Some recent trends

Here, two key issues will be addressed. First, the effects on India of BJP rule, especially in what is now Modi's second term, with *Hindutva* ideology being increasingly reflected in government policy and legislation. Second, some global connections where Hindu nationalist Islamophobia intersects with Islamophobia elsewhere.

Modi's victory in 2014 has been termed not only a populist one with 'many parallels with other populist strongmen' but also a situation that is 'historically complex and in large measure unique to India'.[54] Modi had been chief minister of Gujarat during 2002 when some of the worst inter-communal violence of recent times took place. It is alleged that, at best, he acted too slowly to protect Muslims, who were the primary targets. At worst, he and the BJP were complicit in the violence and responsible for the fact that police often did not intervene;[55] indeed, the events in Gujarat, like some others, have even been termed 'organized political massacres',[56] something which may equally apply to the 2020 Delhi violence. While Modi did not stress his *Hindutva* credentials in the 2014 election, it has been stated that the 'Gujarat … pogrom against Muslims … had already earned him … the status of a *"Hindu Hriday Samrat"* (Emperor of the Hindu Heart)'.[57] There are certainly allegations that, under his premiership, India is becoming more illiberal, less friendly to its minorities, and more biased in favour of the upper castes.[58] Although Modi seeks to vaunt himself as an economic mastermind bringing prosperity to India, his economic record has been ambivalent, at best, while his appeals to economic reform and prosperity often employ images of India's past status as envisaged by Hindu nationalists.[59] Again, although Modi is seen by some as promoting benign Hindu values, for instance in having International Yoga Day recognized by the United Nations, celebrated internationally as showcasing India's spirituality and open-minded religiosity, at home BJP ministers have said that if Muslims do not join in then they should be thrown into the sea.[60]

Another manifestation of what appears to be violence directed against Muslims, and to which the governing powers often seem to turn a blind eye, are the killings associated with cow vigilante groups, framed as *Gau Raksha Dals* (GRDs, 'cow protection committees'). Cow protection as a feature of Hindu nationalism dates back to at least 1966 (with roots in the nineteenth century), but cow vigilantism is a contemporary phenomenon and it is estimated (as no official figures are kept) that 97 per cent of all attacks between 2010 and 2017 have occurred since the BJP ascended to power in 2014.[61] Cow protection is a key facet of what has become Hindu self-perception (cow sacrifice appears in the early Vedas, and its rejection probably came through developing notions of *ahimsa* shared with, and driven by, Buddhist and Jain concerns).[62] This is especially evident in the distinction between the beef-eating Muslim and Christian and the cow-venerating Hindu, for whom the maternal instincts of this animal are valorized, making its slaughter deeply repugnant. As noted, Muslims have been especially stigmatized for beef consumption and are the main targets of vigilante violence. However, the slaughter of cows has been a common occupation for Dalits, who are also hit badly by new laws and the violence of cow protection.[63] Cow husbandry and consumption has occurred across South Asia for millennia, and it is important economically for India as a whole, as one of the world's major beef exporters, and for some Dalit and Muslim communities it is their main income. Today, many states have banned cow slaughter, and while the vigilantes are prosecuted and no explicit BJP or RSS support is given, these groups and 'the state' have given 'tacit support' while 'Hindutva ideology' has been 'the fuel' for cow vigilantism 'to smoulder'.[64]

As the prime minister of India, Modi pragmatically needs to appeal to Muslim voters and cannot appear overtly prejudiced towards a key demographic.[65] Though, in the 2014 election campaign, this was often more symbolic than substantive, and Prashant Waikar argues that Modi's appeal to Muslims as 'loyal and patriotic citizens' is reliant upon representing an Indian Islam, specifically Sufism, as 'the Hinduization of Islam', tempered by the virtues of Hinduism.[66] In other words, it is another version of the good-Muslim-bad-Muslim dichotomy. Moreover, it seems that Modi is emboldened in his second term, with two recent developments pointing towards this. One is the direct rule taken over the State of Kashmir which has caused a major humanitarian disaster.[67] The other is new citizenship laws: the 2019 Citizenship Amendment Act (CAA) and the proposed all-India National Register of Citizens (NRC). The latter requires citizens to register using specified documents, often unavailable to poorer, especially low caste, people, meaning that citizenship and voting rights may be denied. The former offers a path to citizenship for immigrants as long as they are not Muslims.[68] Largely peaceful protests over several months, often led by women,[69] were met on Sunday 23 February 2020 with an inflammatory speech by the BJP minister Kapil Mishra who threatened that if the police did not act within three days then his activists would put an end to the protests. However, it did not take three days, with the first violence breaking out that evening – discussed at the beginning of this chapter – and which continued throughout the week, with hundreds injured, at least forty-eight killed, and mosques, Muslim-owned shops and homes being burned down in Delhi. It has been compared to the 2002 Gujarat riots, also described as a 'Muslim pogrom' where, with government complicity alleged, the police often stood by or even helped rioters, as Muslims were explicitly targeted.[70]

To address the global context, it may seem remarkable that as Trump was visiting India, 'hardline government supporters were rampaging through

New Delhi hunting Muslims'.[71] But Hindu nationalism has had a long and strong foothold outside India, especially in the United States, where a connection to a valorized homeland arguably gives diaspora Hindus a sense of worth and identity when faced with discrimination.[72] But, recently, centred around a common antipathy to Muslims, there are growing connections between the alt-right and Hindu nationalists.[73] Some *Hindutva* ideologues have even found common ground with racist European neo-pagan groups.[74] The well-documented case of 'Hindus for Trump' reveals that a shared Islamophobic discourse exists between them and the alt-right, with violence instigated against Muslims being alleged to be primarily caused by Muslims themselves.[75] Trump's visit to India saw a 'Namaste Trump' event to match the 'Howdy Modi' event previously held in which these two leaders, seen by some as populist and Islamophobic, sought to bolster themselves in the eyes of their own supporters with shows of statesmanship while enacting seemingly Islamophobic laws and measures, engaging in what has been seen as hate-filled rhetoric, and potentially endangering the rule of law.[76] The constructed common enemy, 'the Muslim', provides a global connection between what may otherwise be opposed and disparate groups, and is part of a wider global alliance growing between what may be termed ethno-nationalist, populist, Islamophobic demagogues often utilizing religious narratives as foundations for their views.[77]

Hindu prejudice against Muslims

Hindu nationalist Islamophobia is a phenomenon inscribed with a particular and unique background given the history of that region. However, as a modern occurrence, it is shaped by colonial and Western thought where 'Hindu' and 'the Muslim' have been created as binary polar identities. Nevertheless, Hinduism's nascent sense of internal coherence vis-à-vis its others (indigenous and non-indigenous to South Asia) was present before either Moghul or British rule began. Furthermore, Hindu antipathy and in-group and out-group identification against Muslims dates back to at least the eleventh century. This has become built upon by modern militant *Hindutva* ideology that has moved from the margins to the mainstream of Indian thought, and from being more about generating an ethos into something that determines policy.[78] However, despite its specificity, it links into patterns of prejudice and identity creation that are common in human societies and social structures, while it exemplifies a global Islamophobia linked to a religiously affiliated populist ethno-nationalism in many countries. What we see in India could, therefore, be said to potentially have wider lessons and implications for understanding the development of Islamophobic (and, by analogy, anti-semitic) narratives in such movements globally.

INTERLUDE 4

Can we regulate religious hatred?

Introduction

We have seen that genocide begins with words, and even if matters do not reach such extremes, lesser acts of violence and discrimination are all based in language which ferments religious hatred. Given this, the question inevitably arises: what can be done to eliminate or at least to mitigate such harm? In the first instance, victims of Islamophobia and antisemitism typically look to the law to protect their rights and guard against prejudice.

A fundamental point is worth stating upfront: unlike in the dystopia of George Orwell's (1903–1950) *1984* (1949), there is no such thing as 'thoughtcrime'. Modern legal regimes do not generally regulate the sentiments of a population. Therefore, legal regulation cannot prevent religious hatred, or any other prejudice. But it can proscribe actions arising from religious hatred, whether that be discrimination or violence. According to one perspective, this is perfectly adequate because, after all, only words or behaviours can harm another. Another point of view holds that this is deeply unsatisfactory because holding hate-filled opinions about Muslims or Jews, say, even without giving voice to them, is bound to result in fractured societies. But we should be clear about the inherent limits of the legal approach.

Here, we will note some important aspects of the global and regional human rights regimes, including the United Nations (UN) Universal Declaration on Human Rights (UDHR), the UN International Covenant on Civil and Political Rights (ICCPR), and the European Convention on Human Rights (ECHR). We will then discuss some national case studies, including India, Singapore, and the UK. We will stress how global, regional, and national legal regimes relate to antisemitism and Islamophobia, examine the protections that they provide but will also note some common problems in the application of legal regulations. Finally, we address the controversy surrounding a specific statement, the International Holocaust Remembrance Alliance (IHRA) definition of antisemitism, and its quasi-legal status.

International frameworks

The UDHR was adopted by the UN General Assembly (UNGA) on 10 December 1948.[1] Post-Second World War, and with the Holocaust in recent memory, the UDHR can be seen as an attempt to establish a common standard of respect for the dignity of the individual and protection of the fundamental rights and freedoms of all people, particularly vulnerable minorities. Article 2 establishes the universal scope of the UDHR: all people are entitled to the rights described, regardless of their race, religion, or location. Article 3 of the UDHR provides that everyone has the right to life, liberty, and the security of the person. Article 7 provides that all people are entitled to equal protection against any discrimination that would violate their rights under the UDHR and against any incitement to such discrimination. Of particular relevance to religious prejudice and discrimination is the following:

> Everyone has the right to freedom of thought, conscience and religion; this right includes freedom to change his [sic] religion or belief, and freedom, either alone or in community with others and in public or private, to manifest his religion or belief in teaching, practice, worship and observance.[2]

While this is not specific to religious hatred, it is part of the bedrock of international law and means that Muslims, Jews, and others have a right to practice their religions, or to have no religion, protected from discrimination and violence which would interrupt their ability to do so freely. The final provision of the UDHR is also significant:

> In the exercise of his [sic] rights and freedoms, everyone shall be subject only to such limitations as are determined by law solely for the purpose of securing ... the rights and freedoms of others and of meeting the just requirements of morality, public order and the general welfare in a democratic society.[3]

Article 29 means that in certain cases rights may be curtailed. A pertinent one is freedom of expression: when my speech infringes upon another's rights, especially in the form of hate speech, it is no longer covered by free speech protections. Mr X's right to freedom of expression (UDHR Article 19) may be legally limited as he has no right to speech that incites violence against Mrs Y and potentially violates her right to life, liberty, and security (UDHR Article 3). However, as we will see, the limits on what speech is allowed vary from one jurisdiction to another. We are also reminded of Jacques Derrida's (1930–2004) argument that law, justice, and ethics will ultimately be incompatible because our particular duty of justice to every individual's uniqueness will conflict with the general principles of any law.[4]

The ICCPR contains similar but more specific provisions to the UDHR and Article 20(2) states that 'any advocacy of national, racial or religious hatred that constitutes incitement to discrimination, hostility or violence shall be prohibited by law', which is a clear limitation on the freedom of expression provision in ICCPR Article 19.[5] However, Nazila Ghanea and others have emphasized the high threshold required for ICCPR 20 to apply, noting that it will seldom be reached 'in the absence of a pattern, if not long history, of gross human rights violations against a particular minority group'.[6]

We have seen that Muslims and Jews have become racialized groups and thus the regulation of racial hatred is as relevant as the regulation of religious hatred. The International Convention on the Elimination of All Forms of Racial Discrimination (ICERD) requires signatory states to inter alia outlaw all dissemination of ideas based on racial superiority or hatred and incitement to racial discrimination.[7]

Despite the existence of human rights instruments, the Pew Research Centre has noted, over the decade 2007–17, a marked increase in legislation targeting religion,[8] and a 2011 UNGA resolution noted 'with deep concern the overall rise in instances of intolerance and violence ... directed against members of many religious and other communities in various parts of the world, including cases motivated by Islamophobia, anti-Semitism [sic.] and Christianophobia'.[9] Interestingly, the same resolution, like many before it, emphasized that 'no religion should be equated with terrorism, as this may have adverse consequences on the enjoyment of the right to freedom of religion ... of the religious communities concerned'.[10]

While the UDHR, the ICCPR, and other UNGA resolutions set more or less powerful international norms and expectations for the behaviour of states, not all are legally binding and even for those that are, perceived domestic political pressures or the realpolitik of international relations means that states will nevertheless often prioritize other national interests over human rights.[11] Further, as discussed in Chapter 10, certain international norms are weakening. By focusing on the ICCPR, we can illustrate some weaknesses in the international regime. The ICCPR purports to bind signatory states to provide the rights it contains to people in its territory. But the first issue is that not all states are signatories. Singapore, for example, is not. Even for signatory states, the ICCPR needs to be implemented into national legal regimes to protect citizens. As such, its effectiveness depends on the adequacy and enforcement of the relevant national legislation. The ICCPR in fact envisages this problem and provides, in an Optional

Protocol,[12] a mechanism for individuals in signatory states to appeal directly to the UN Human Rights Committee. But a second issue is that not all ICCPR signatory states, with the UK being one example, have opted to sign up to the Optional Protocol. Further, while there is provision for periodical oversight by a Human Rights Committee, the Committee has no real power.

As well as global human rights regimes, there are regional rights regimes which purport to provide protection against religiously motivated violence and discrimination. For example, forty-seven states are signatories to the ECHR,[13] which protects freedom of religion (Article 9) and prohibits discrimination on the basis of religion (Article 14). But regional regimes have similar weaknesses to the global regimes surveyed above, in that they rely on effective implementation at the national level. By way of illustration, the passing of the UK Human Rights Act in 1998 brought the ECHR directly into UK law and since then it has been possible for individuals in the UK to enforce their ECHR rights in the domestic courts, but these rights may now be under threat. While the UK's exit from the European Union (EU) need not affect the ECHR rights of individuals in the UK because the UK is a signatory to the ECHR in its own right, the UK Conservative Party's (successful) 2019 election manifesto stated that it would 'update the Human Rights Act' after Brexit and there is much uncertainty about the rights that people in the UK will retain in relation to the ECHR.[14]

The ECHR right to freedom of expression (Article 10) may be raised in opposition to accusations of antisemitism and Islamophobia. In the report of its investigation into antisemitism in the UK Labour Party mentioned in Chapter 6, the UK Equality and Human Rights Commission noted that it is obliged to act in a way that is compatible with the ECHR and should not label as harassment and sanction conduct where that would breach the Article 10 or 11 (freedom of assembly/association) rights of the individual whose conduct is under investigation. But the Commission also noted that:

> the ECHR does not protect racist speech that negates its fundamental values. The European Court of Human Rights has held that speech that is incompatible with the values guaranteed by the ECHR, notably tolerance, social peace and non-discrimination, is removed from the protection of Article 10 because of Article 17. This may include antisemitic speech and Holocaust denial.[15]

In terms of the implementation of human rights at the EU level, given modern European history, it is perhaps unsurprising that in cases of Holocaust denial, the European Commission and EU courts have often given greater weight to prohibitions on incitement of hatred than the right to freedom of expression. For example, the European Commission upheld a German court order prohibiting an applicant from displaying pamphlets which described the Holocaust as a 'Zionist swindle or lie'.[16] Again, this reminds us of the post-Second World War context out of which the international and regional legal frameworks arose.

National case studies

As we have seen, international protections, while functioning as important statements, do not, in and of themselves, provide effective legal protections against religious hatred and require implementing legislation at the national level and effectively functioning judiciaries. Alternatively, states that are not among the signatories to certain human rights conventions may seek to regulate religious hatred independently of international legal regimes, while other signatory states may supplement legal protections deriving from international law with additional domestic legislation. In some jurisdictions, the cost or time required for an individual to enforce their rights in the national courts makes it almost impossible to enforce these rights. Elsewhere, corruption or lack of judicial independence can be key issues. In Chapter 10, the controversy surrounding the November 2019 ruling of the Indian Supreme Court that the Ayodhya site should be used for the construction of a Hindu temple was discussed. We do not take a position on this difficult issue here, but among many Indian Muslims there is at least a perception that they cannot rely on the Indian courts to protect them against religious prejudice, notwithstanding the principle of non-discrimination on the basis of religion which is enshrined in the Indian constitution.

Singapore, one of the world's most multicultural and religiously diverse societies, has a highly interventionist model for regulating religious hatred. That is not to say that every incident is met with the full force of the law but the legal powers that do exist are significant. In early 2017, when leading Friday prayers at a Singaporean mosque, Imam Nalla Mohamed Abdul Jameel, an Indian citizen working in Singapore, recited an old Arabic text which read 'God help us against Jews and Christians'.[17] The District Court found Imam Nalla guilty of promoting enmity between different groups under section 298A of the Penal Code.[18] He was fined $4,000 SGD and, notwithstanding that he appeared genuinely remorseful and had won the support of much of the interfaith community in Singapore, the government later deported him. The District Judge had said that remarks such as Imam Nalla's 'can create friction and conflict between different religious groups and Singapore … can't allow anyone to sow discord or promote enmity when we've worked so hard to promote harmony'. In addition to the Penal Code, which explicitly outlaws the uttering of words with the deliberate intent to wound the religious feelings of any person, Singapore has the Maintenance of Religious Harmony Act 1990 (amended 2019) (MRHA).[19] The MRHA provides the government with the power to grant a restraining order against those attempting to cause 'enmity, hatred, ill-will or hostility between different religious groups'.

In the UK, there have been several instances of the criminal law being used against Christian street preachers who have been accused of disturbing the peace and, in particular, of making Islamophobic statements. In July 2016, Michael Overd and Michael Stockwell delivered a street sermon at a shopping centre in the city of Bristol. The pair allegedly shouted 'Mohammad is a liar' but denied aiming hostility at another faith, saying that they were only quoting from the King James Bible, motivated by 'love' and a desire to spread the 'good news about Jesus Christ'.[20] A Magistrates' Court found the men guilty of a hate crime for using 'threatening or abusive words or behaviour or disorderly behaviour within the hearing or sight of a person likely to be caused harassment, alarm or distress, thereby, and the offence was religiously aggravated'.[21] But the preachers' lawyer called it a 'modern day heresy trial'[22] and, on appeal, the judges decided that the men had only expressed their religious beliefs and had not showed hostility to Muslims. It is likely that Singapore's legal framework would have seen a different outcome.

In another UK case, Oluwole Ilesanmi preached outside a north London tube station in February 2019, reading from the Bible but also calling Islam an 'aberration' and Allah an 'idol'. There has been a strong suggestion that Mr Ilesanmi, like Mr Overd, was on the receiving end of aggressive behaviour from a person or people who were upset by his words. But the London Metropolitan police used section 35 of the Anti-social Behaviour, Crime and Policing Act 2014 to handcuff Mr Ilesanmi and remove him from the area, before de-arresting him. Mr Ilesanmi was later compensated for wrongful arrest and humiliating treatment. As he was being handcuffed, the police confiscated his Bible and he has since complained that 'They couldn't do that to the Koran. They dare not do that to the Koran. The policeman wanted to even throw the Bible on the floor.'[23] This plays into a narrative proposed by Christian rights advocates that Christians are not free to challenge Islam and that there is unfair treatment between different religions.

Relevant UK laws can be usefully split into two offences: hate crime and hate speech, though the two can overlap.[24] A hate crime is any crime that is aggravated by a designated type of hostility and, since 2001, this includes hostility towards religion. Hate speech requires some 'stirring up' of hatred (including, since the Race and Religious Hatred Act 2006, religious hatred).[25] Furthermore, the relevant words or conduct must be threatening – not just abusive or insulting – and must be *intended* to stir up religious hatred, rather than uttered or performed with a mere recklessness as to that possibility (which differentiates it from hate speech involving 'race'). Interestingly, section 29J of the Public Order Act 1986, 'Protection of freedom of expression', states that the prohibition of hate speech in that Act does not prohibit or restrict discussion, criticism, expressions of antipathy towards, ridicule or abuse of religious beliefs, nor does it prohibit proselytization.

The IHRA working definition of antisemitism

The IHRA's non-legally binding definition of antisemitism is controversial largely because one of the illustrative examples of antisemitism that it lists is 'Denying the Jewish people their right to self-determination, e.g., by claiming that the existence of the state of Israel is a racist endeavour'.[26] As we saw in Chapter 6, some on the political left claim that a reasonable expression of anti-Zionism could describe Israel as an illegitimate state given the circumstances of its creation and its treatment of certain minorities; many have struggled to accept the working definition. Indeed, while it is not legally binding, the way it has often been adopted by groups from political parties to governments means that a 'self-described "non-legally binding working definition" is given quasi-legal status through its indeterminate relationship to the law'.[27] The definition (along with the illustrative examples) has been increasingly adopted by organizations around the world, including the White House through an Executive Order of Donald Trump.[28] Many Jews in the United States actually objected to the Executive Order on the basis that it emphasizes a perceived inherent national characteristic of Jewish people that 'hinted at dividing "Jewish" from "American"' in a form of 'Trumpist anti-Semitism'.[29] Though, ironically, it is as members of a minority racial or national group, rather than a religious group, that minorities in the United States are provided with important protections under Title VI of the US Civil Rights Act.[30]

Protections and pitfalls: A balancing act

The international legal framework which seeks to regulate religious hatred is of limited effectiveness. Indeed, the division between the international and national frameworks, while helpful in getting to grips with the issues, is somewhat illusory because human rights conventions are only effective when signatory states implement their provisions into national law. In the national case studies, we have seen differing issues and approaches in the UK, Singapore, and India. While each of these is more of a cameo than a fully developed survey, they have helped highlight some issues for us. One of the main dangers of over-regulating religiously insensitive language would appear to be the problem identified by Deborah Lipstadt when she noted that legal restraints transform Holocaust deniers into martyrs on the altar of freedom of speech, which is, of course, not to equate Imam Nalla or the Christian street preachers with Holocaust deniers.[31] A major danger of under-regulation is that it allows hateful rhetoric too much opportunity to take hold in society. In this context, and in diverse jurisdictions, there remain many difficult questions about what forms of speech are potentially illegal and where and when limiting free speech is justified to protect minority groups or secure public order.

Epilogue: The good news: Dialogue, civil rights, and peacebuilding

The Other or othering

At the end of Chapter 1, we discussed the notion of the Other in the work of Emmanuel Levinas (1906–1995). For Levinas, the term signified that, as we stand before the Face of the Other, we should see other human beings as holding absolute value and recognize that we owe a duty to their life, integrity, and dignity. We can see Levinas' Other as linked to the work of an earlier Jewish philosopher,[1] Martin Buber (1878–1965), who has become famous for the phrase 'I and Thou', in which he likewise speaks about the need to make the Thou–Other (to combine these terms) present to us in direct and authentic encounters with them.[2] Buber wrote in the context of the First World War with *I and Thou* first published in 1923, and Levinas after the Holocaust. Both of these events had seen enormous human suffering and the brutal inhumanity of one person to another person, of one group to another group. Their work, the notion of the Thou–Other, may be said to be a solution to the problem of othering and deindividuation, to see each individual person as valuable and inherently precious in their own right. While they have systematized these ideas in philosophical forms, Albert Bandura has noted that the pathways to violence and dehumanization we identified were matched by a natural human tendency to humanization, and as discussed in Chapter 2, depending upon our social and cultural context, as human beings we can become predisposed to violence towards others or towards an irenic encounter with the Other. These both come naturally to us, but the path towards one or the other needs structures, organizations, leaders, role models, and narratives to put them in place. This was noted by Eboo Patel who, as an angry young Muslim in the United States, noted that while he took the path towards being an interfaith youth leader, with his anger channelled into social activism, he could equally have ended up on the path towards militant neo-Islamic jihadism.[3]

While not neglecting some 'good news', that is, positive encounters across religious, racial, ethnic, and cultural divides (howsoever we define those), we have in this book mainly focused on the 'bad news', the pathways into the prejudices of antisemitism and Islamophobia, and also towards violence and even genocide. Of course, understanding such vectors is already a guide to an alternative pathway that may overcome them. But, here, we directly discuss the pathways which have gone the other way, towards dialogue, understanding, and reconciliation across these divides. Again, this raises questions we have raised before in this book concerning our position in these debates, questions highlighted by the subject matter, for as John Roth has noted: 'Remembering the holocaust confers obligations in the present and for the future.'[4] Is the idea that we can study just for academic interest, or as neutral observers, based in an epistemology grounded in a sense of elite (i.e. primarily today white, male) privilege? For those not oppressed by the system, it may be something to study. But for scholars such as Levinas, William DuBois (1868–1963), Jacques Derrida (1930–2003), Gayatri Chakravorty Spivak, Patricia Hill Collins, or Khaled Beydoun, to study systems of oppression, prejudice, and discrimination is to be engaged in the struggle against them. Derrida's concern for the deconstruction of notions was not simply a means to see how they worked and how we could dismantle the conceptions, but a concern for justice and to make a better world. However, alongside the intentions with which we began this study, our aim is not to advocate, in the sense of telling people how to respond, but to raise this question and to be aware that no study is simply neutral, above the fray, or not involved in systems which may themselves entail structural inequality.[5]

A further key issue that we can add on to this point, and is central in this study, is a recognition that prejudice arises, in some senses, naturally from how we make sense of the world. As such, a key strategic point to consider is how we approach those who exhibit prejudice. We do not live in a binary world of prejudiced people and non-prejudiced people – or those who are racist/anti-racist (antisemitic/anti-antisemitic, Islamophobic/anti-Islamophobic, etc.) – but we will all exhibit some form of prejudice, or have the potential inherent in us. Therefore, we must consider a constant personal vigilance about our own attitudes to the Other as imperative, and with this – while vehemently opposing all forms of prejudice – a non-judgemental stance to those who hold them, and to seek to understand their pathways into prejudice, because we must make bridges to overcome stereotypes and bias. The solution does not arise in condemnation and building walls in weaponized positions, but in reaching out to those who hold prejudices which we may abhor, but whose lifepath has taken them in different ways.[6]

Interreligious networks and ethics

A good start for getting to grips with religious hatred is religious literacy, but we might amend this to interreligious literacy (including those without religion and atheists in the conversation). While there is much virtue in digging down deeply into each religious tradition and understanding its specificities on a one-by-one basis, these traditions have always existed in relation to each other. They have competed and interacted, and often bumped up against each other in terms of their differences. Each one is very different, as Stephen Prothero has famously put it: *God Is Not One.*[7] However, Prothero's book misses, we may argue, a few steps along the way. First, to make clear how distinct each religious tradition is he sets them out in terms of four issues: a problem, a solution, a technique, and an exemplar. Broken down like this he sets out how every religion has a very different problem and solution, for example, Christianity's problem is 'sin' and its solution is 'salvation'; Buddhism's problem is 'suffering' and its solution is 'nirvana'; while Islam's problem is 'pride' and its solution is 'submission'.[8] However, this makes each tradition into a monolithic block, which they are not. It also sums up each one in a single (normally English) word, which ignores that both over time and in different cultural–linguistic contexts these words, even assuming they are universally agreed on, mean very many differing things. Again, religions exist both in terms of what we may term an 'elite' fixation, often about certain transcendent goals, and what is often termed 'lived religion', which is what the ordinary rank-and-file members do and believe.[9] Indeed, the way people act may also belie what they say they believe. Now, Prothero knows that what he has set out is very simplified, even over-simplified,[10] so our reason for picking this out is not to score points over him in understanding 'religion' better. Rather, we need to point to two common assumptions, which he helps us see: on the one hand, some people believe that all religions are basically the same and say the same things, which is especially asserted at the ethical level, because we all know that some talk about deities and others do not and so on; on the other hand, all religions are different, and this means that they are somehow incompatible, have completely different systems of thought and behaviour, and so will be ethically incompatible. In some ways, this revisits the discussion in Chapter 1 between universalists and relativists, where we noted the words of Bonaventura de Sousa Santos: 'All cultures are relative, but cultural relativism, as a philosophical posture, is wrong. All cultures aspire to ultimate concerns and values, but cultural universalism, as a philosophical posture, is wrong.'[11] Bringing this back to our interests here, we want to discuss interreligious literacy and ethics for a specific reason. Clearly, not every religious tradition says the same thing about ethical issues; indeed, no religious tradition even agrees within itself about these questions, and debates on what is right and wrong have wracked thinkers and societies for millennia. However, it does not mean that everything about them is incompatible. We have already noted in the preceding chapters areas where religions have borrowed from each other, learnt from another religion, and cross-fertilized each other. But, here, we can show a very particular lineage of interreligious engagement between some major twentieth-century peace advocates and civil rights activists. Indeed, working alongside those with other worldviews and commitments for a common purpose is a key way to break down barriers.[12]

This lineage concerns three particular figures, among some others. These key players are: the 'Black' Christian Martin Luther King, Jr. (1929–1968), the 'white' Jewish Abraham Joshua Heschel (1907–1972), and the 'East Asian' Buddhist Thich Nhat Hanh. Among the others are the 'South Asian' Hindu Mohandas Karamchand Gandhi (1869–1948) and the 'white' Christian Leo Tolstoy (1828–1910). We will quote at length, as the narrative is mostly well and succinctly summed up here:

> In April of 1968, Martin Luther King, Jr., often referred to as 'the American Gandhi' went to Memphis to help black workers settle a garbage strike. At this time, this Baptist minister from the black church tradition was looking forward to spending the approaching Passover with Rabbi Abraham Joshua Heschel. Heschel, who had marched with him in a civil rights protest at Selma, Alabama three years earlier, had become a close friend and supporter. Unfortunately, King was not able to keep the engagement. Like Gandhi before him, on April 4, 1968, Martin Luther King, Jr., a man of non-violence, was violently assassinated. Another of King's friends, the Buddhist monk and anti-Vietnam war activist, Thich Nhat Hanh, whom King had nominated for the Nobel Peace Prize, received the news of his death while at an interreligious conference in New York City. Only the previous spring, King had officially come out against the Vietnam War, partly at the urging of Thich Nhat Hanh and Abraham Joshua Heschel. ... Now, the man who had called for an end to hatred, violence and war was dead. But the spiritual and ethical vision he shared with his friends, across religions and cultures, was not. It was alive and well.[13]

We share this story not so much because it shows that certain ideas are transferable across religious boundaries, we already know that. Indeed, it was the Christian Tolstoy, based on his reading of Jesus, who inspired Gandhi's interest in non-violence, which the latter understood in relation to the *ahimsa* traditions of South Asia, and whose ideas on which were, when heard by King, 'electrifying' and is a principle King shared with Heschel, and was further strengthened in King by Nhat Hanh who also drew from *ahimsa* traditions in his understanding of what he would term *Being Peace*.[14] Rather it shows that interreligious learning and alliances are possible across boundaries of race, ethnicity, and religion which are not just built on same-ness but on a dynamic learning and exchange. These people drew from dif-ferent scriptural texts, varying religious and metaphysical epistemologies and cosmologies, yet managed to find a working commonality and cross-fertilizing inspiration in relation to notions that we can gloss as 'non-vio-lence'.[15] We also share this story because personal narratives are often seen as important in inspiring people into action. Principles and shared ideas are good, but real-life stories of those who have walked the walk are often what will be meaningful to people.[16]

Two further points are worth drawing out from this story. First, it men-tions that Heschel marched alongside King at the Selma to Montgomery voting rights march (1965). We have noted previously that Black–Jewish relations have often been strained, and indeed in the film *Selma* (2014) this was explicit when Heschel's character was removed from the film despite marching in the front row arm-in-arm with King.[17] Second, and going fur-ther forwards in time, this tradition of non-violent direct action has been picked up by both Christian and Muslim peace activists in Israel–Palestine:

> including Naim Ateek, Mubarak Awad, and Sari Nusseibeh ... [who] have worked to promote nonviolent resistance to the occupying Israeli power structure in the West Bank and Gaza. As Ateek has described it, the Israelis 'know we are working for peace, and that we are a greater threat to them than Hamas, [because] Hamas allows them a pretext to continue the occupation – we do not'.[18]

It should be noted to end this discussion that we certainly do not want to suggest that non-violence or its various equivalents, euphemisms, or forms, that is, Gandhi's *satyagraha*, Indic *ahimsa*, and so on,[19] are some universal forms across religious traditions. As we have seen, while *ahimsa* is found in both Hindu and Buddhist traditions this does not mean that it either prevents physical violence or is always even seen as incompatible with quite brutal activities.[20] Meanwhile, Christians, Jews, Muslims, atheists, and oth-ers have always found ample justification for murder within their traditions (much as they *all* have found justifications for non-violence and pacifism in their respective traditions). To defend their 'sacreds', religious, and non-religious, actors will often justify violence in many forms.[21] As such, it is important that legitimating worldviews exist. As mentioned in Chapter 1, Allport's contact theory needs supporting structures from leaders and the tradition. Therefore, it is important that public discourse must include rea-sons and rationales (drawing from, as needed, such things as scriptural injunctions and real-world stories of respected figures) exemplifying the case for irenic coexistence, and that militant discourses are opposed, mean-ing that we do not simply just tolerate those different from us for pragmatic reasons.[22]

Understanding and engagement

The above discussion raises questions about how we may live together, although we have noted some strategies for this already. One much-discussed notion is cosmopolitanism, raised by such figures as Kwame Anthony Appiah and Ulrich Beck, which concerns a respect for 'legitimate difference'.[23] This involves learning to live graciously alongside differences, and, as an important addition to what has been noted above, we should add that it cannot simply be inter-religious but must be inter-worldview to include atheists, agnostics, and many others who may not identify with any specific religious tradition. Certainly, it has been suggested that what is traditionally termed interreligious dialogue needs to open up to become an inter-worldview dialogue.[24]

Interreligious dialogue may be seen by some as a rather abstract discussion among leaders and scholars, but in scholarly terms, and as exemplified in numerous practitioner activities, it includes much more than simply the dialogue of theological exchange. It also includes what is termed the dialogue of life which involves everyday encounters; the dialogue of action, where social activism – noted above as a key strategy – is engaged in across religious (and beyond religious) borders; and interior dialogue or exchanges in meditation and prayer.[25] However, in the post-Holocaust context, dialogue between Christian theologians and their Jewish counterparts has often proved fruitful in increasing understanding and, importantly, in overcoming misunderstandings. While much of this, as discussed in Chapter 6, has not trickled down through to the communities, it is partly a problem of institutions and messaging rather than dialogue per se.[26]

Beyond institutional dialogue, a cosmopolitan attitude may lay the basis for understanding within the dialogue of life, or the day-to-day encounters of living alongside Others. Certainly, an attitude of acceptance towards 'commonplace diversity' will allow a civil day-to-day exchange where the reality of diversity is accepted, which is seen in various contexts of 'super-diversity' in today's multicultural cities.[27] However, such living alongside each other is no guarantee of acceptance or understanding with prejudices still lingering among those who live and work together on a day-to-day convivial basis.[28] Indeed, even in areas where a generally positive coexistence has occurred for centuries, the possibility of life being torn apart and violence ensuing, even with genocidal intent, has been seen. Two particular cases may be noted: the South East European Balkans civil wars of the 1990s; and the Indonesian Moluccas Island conflict centring on Ambon from 1999 to 2002. In both places, arguably, an amicable living alongside each other did not go deep, or rested on structures easily torn apart by extremist rhetoric and prejudice. Living together does not lead to tolerance, and contact in society is not enough to build solidarity and resilience. Nevertheless, seeing the Other as humanized rather than dehumanized remains a possibility even in times of war and ethnic violence.

Max Bergholz recounts how, during the Second World War, within a very close distance, one group of Bosniak Muslims were slaughtered by groups of Serbian Orthodox Christian militias, while nearby other Serbian Orthodox Christians faced down a militia of their fellow Orthodox Serbs to defend their Bosniak Muslim neighbours.[29] The question of human agency, which we have discussed previously, comes to the fore again. But, as discussed in Chapter 2, the possibility for generative violence having its own dynamic raises the issue that a complex set of social and psychological factors will be at play, and so combatting prejudice will be a constant work and can readily be undermined by activity on the ground. Hence, words alone are not enough and a performative display against prejudice will be needed.

We must therefore not discount a variety of factors as important. One is individual psychology, of which we have discussed various aspects. But to add here that studies show that a lack of acceptance of ambiguity correlates with stereotyping and ethnocentrism, while those more tolerant of ambiguity have a more open attitude.[30] Another aspect is the social frames in which we live, and certainly from the example of 1930s Germany among others we can see what a social order which refuses tolerance and builds enmity and prejudice looks like. Unfortunately, it is not always so clear what the positive examples look like, but they need to be worked on. While far from the modern notions of acceptance of diversity and social equality, Muslim-majority empires showed that multireligious and multi-ethnic coexistence was possible over sustained periods of time. Moreover, in small-scale groups we have good examples showing how those who were previously intolerant of each other and bore strong prejudices and stereotypes of the other can be brought together to live with difference.[31] How to upscale this to wider societies remains an issue, and as we have seen both Jews and Muslims face, if anything, growing prejudice in today's world. The need to consider legal frameworks is part of this (see Interlude 4).[32] Education will also be key in this, meaning not just at schools and universities but across society, building an understanding of the value of diversity and the extent to which we live in an interconnected world where many traditions form part of who we are.[33] A further important issue is organizations, and various groups promoting hatred from the (Christian/Western) far-right to militant Buddhists, Hindus, and Muslims have harnessed group membership that gives a sense of belonging and purpose, combined often with an easy to ingest narrative of good and evil, right and wrong, where the need to fight to defend one's world is foregrounded. Those standing for anti-racism, anti-prejudice, and against antisemitism and Islamophobia need to foster their own narratives and organizations, meaning that good leadership from the political level to the grassroots is needed.[34] To stand for ambiguity and acceptance is not such a simple narrative to sell, but the work needs to be done. We may hope that, together, we can overcome antisemitism and Islamophobia and other forms of religious hatred and prejudice.

NOTES

Introduction

1 See Pew, 'A Closer Look at How Religious Restrictions Have Risen around the World', *Pew* (25 July 2019), available at https://www.pewforum. org/2019/07/15/a-closer-look-at-how-religious-restrictions-have-risen-around-the-world/.

2 See Paul Hedges, *Towards Better Disagreement: Religion and Atheism in Dialogue* (London: Jessica Kingsley, 2017), 96–113.

3 We discuss 'religion' further in Interlude 1, but for a wider discussion on how we can understand this 'essentially contested concept' and ways it is commonly misunderstood or misrepresented, see Paul Hedges, *Understanding Religion: Theories and Methods for Studying Religiously Diverse Societies* (Berkeley: University of California Press, 2021), 29–30, but more generally 19–35.

4 ISGAP is the Institute for the Global Study of Antisemitism and Policy, https://isgap.org/wp-content/uploads/2019/08/ISGAP-Oxford-Summer-Institute-2019-Program.pdf, accessed 15 October 2020.

5 https://www.rsis.edu.sg/research/srp/, accessed 15 October 2020.

6 At least in some quarters, though in others it involved violence by Britain's Jews to quell the still rampant fascists on that nation's streets, see Daniel Sonabend, *We Fight Fascists: The 43 Group and Their Forgotten Battle for Post-War Britain* (London: Verso, 2019); and Harriet Sherwood, 'The British Jews Who Fought Postwar Fascism on London's Streets', *The Guardian* (24 May 2020), available at https://www.theguardian.com/news/2020/may/24/the-british-jews-who-fought-postwar-fascism-on-londons-streets, accessed 15 October 2020.

7 On how the author assesses these questions, especially in relation to being reflexive in our own position in the world, see Hedges, *Understanding Religion*, 52–6, and for more on the autobiographical aspect of scholarship, see Paul Hedges, 'Encounters with Ultimacy? Autobiographical and Critical Perspectives in the Academic Study of Religion', *Open Theology* 4 (2018): 355–72.

8 Paulo Freire, *Pedagogy of the Oppressed* (London: Penguin, 1972).

9 Salman Sayyid argues that Islamophobia is more than prejudice as it is governmental. This is certainly not neglected here nor ruled out by the usage of prejudice employed herein. See S. Sayyid, 'Out of the Devil's Dictionary', in *Thinking through Islamophobia*, ed. S. Sayyid and Abdoolkarim Vakil (New York: Columbia University Press, 2010), 5–18 (15–17).

10 Walter Laquer, *The Changing Face of Antisemitism: From Ancient Times to the Present Day* (Oxford: Oxford University Press, 2008).

11 Partha Chatterjee, *The Nation and Its Fragments: Colonial and Postcolonial Histories* (Princeton, NJ: Princeton University Press, 1993). For a wider discussion on this issue, see Hedges, *Understanding Religion*, especially chapters 7 and 18.

12 See Deborah Lipstadt, *Antisemitism: Here and Now* (London: Scribe, 2019).

13 See S. Sayyid, 'A Measure of Islamophobia', *Islamophobia Studies Journal* 2.1 (2014): 10–25; and Todd Green, *The Fear of Islam: An Introduction to Islamophobia in the West*, 2nd edn (Minneapolis, MN: Fortress Press, 2019), 20–35.

CHAPTER ONE

1 John Dovidio, Samuel Gaertner and Adam Pearson, 'On the Nature of Prejudice: The Psychological Foundations of Hate', in *The Psychology of Hate*, ed. R. J. Sternberg (Washington, DC: American Psychological Association, 2005), 211–34 (212), italics in original.

2 It may also be noted that prejudice is also used as a technical term outside of this context. One interesting usage is that of hermeneutical philosopher Hans Georg Gadamer (1900–2002), who argues that we should see prejudice as positive. In his usage, prejudice refers to our existing knowledge and concepts; as such we always come to the world with pre-understanding (prejudices) based upon our prior experience, learning, and socialization. Prejudices are necessary for learning anything at all, because, as humans, we can only integrate new knowledge by placing it alongside, and thereby also modifying, our existing knowledge. This allows us to expand our awareness in an 'opening of horizons' of our world view. Gadamer, however, suggests that we can have both positive prejudices, which allow us to expand our knowledge, and negative prejudices which hinder new learning (when, for instance, we think we already know everything about a topic, or are closed off to learning in some situations, etc.). On the usage of 'opening of horizons' (which modifies Gadamer's own phrase of 'fusion of horizons') and on Gadamer's notion of prejudice, see Paul Hedges, 'Gadamer, Play, and Interreligious Dialogue as the Opening of Horizons', *Journal of Dialogue Studies* 4 (2016): 5–26.

3 Bernard Whitley and Mary Kite, *The Psychology of Prejudice and Discrimination*, 2nd edn (Belmont, CA: Wadsworth, 2010), 9.

4 One may say that one's neighbour, colleague, and so on (as Chinese, Jewish, Muslim, Black, etc.) is a 'good one' of that type but still hold prejudice against others.

5 Whitley and Kite, *The Psychology of Prejudice and Discrimination*, 19, see also Geoffrey Beattie, *Our Racist Heart? An Exploration of Unconscious Prejudice in Everyday Life* (Hove: Routledge, 2013).

6 See Irwin Katz, 'Gordon Allport's "The Nature of Prejudice"', *Political Psychology* 12.1 (1991): 125–57.

7 Gordon Allport, *The Nature of Prejudice* (New York: Doubleday, [1954] 1958).

8 Henri Tajfel, *Social Identity and Intergroup Relations* (Cambridge: Cambridge University Press, 1981). For an overview, see Angela Coco and Paul Hedges, 'Belonging, Behaving, Believing, Becoming: Religion and Identity', in *Controversies in Contemporary Religion*, vol. I, ed. Paul Hedges (Santa Barbara, CA: Praeger, 2014), 163–90.

9 See Kristin Anderson, *Benign Bigotry: The Psychology of Subtle Prejudice* (Cambridge: Cambridge University Press, 2010).

10 See Frantz Fanon, *Black Skin, White Masks*, trans. Charles Markmann (London: Pluto Press, [1952] 1986); and Paula Ioanide, '"Why Did the White Woman Cross the Street?": Cultural Countermeasures against Affective Forms of Racism', *Souls: A Critical Journal of Black Politics, Culture, and Society* 20.2 (2018): 198–221.

11 See Judith Butler, 'Gender Performativity' (video) *Open Culture* (2018), available at http://www.openculture.com/2018/02/judith-butler-on-gender-performativity.html; and Stephen Young, 'Judith Butler: Performativity', *Critical Legal Thinking* (2016), available at http://criticallegalthinking. com/2016/11/14/judith-butlers-performativity/#fnref-22068-7. For a recent example of a performative act in relation to the global BLM (Black Lives Matter) protests, see the discussion in Paul Hedges, 'The Global BLM Movement: Public Memorials and Neo-Decolonisation?', *RSIS Commentary* CO20127 (2020), available at https://www.rsis.edu.sg/wp-content/uploads/2020/06/CO20127.pdf.

12 Allport, *The Nature of Prejudice*, 14.

13 Allport, *The Nature of Prejudice*, 14–15.

14 Allport, *The Nature of Prejudice*, 15. See Interlude 2 where we discuss the Nazi programme.

15 See, for example, Sudhir Kakar, *The Colors of Violence: Cultural Identities, Religion, and Conflict* (Chicago, IL: University of Chicago Press, 1996), 153–66.

16 On the concept of intersectionality, the classic work is by Kimberlé Crenshaw, 'Demarginalizing the Intersection of Race and Sex: A Black Feminist Critique of Antidiscrimination Doctrine, Feminist Theory and Antiracist Politics', *University of Chicago Legal Forum* 1.8 (1989): 139–67, available at https:// chicagounbound.uchicago.edu/cgi/viewcontent.cgi?article=1052&context =uclf. See also Patricia Hill Collins, *Black Feminist Thought: Knowledge, Consciousness, and the Politics of Empowerment* (Boston, MA: Unwin Hyman, 1990); Francis Beale, *Double Jeopardy: To Be Black and Female* (Detroit, MI: Radical Education Project, 1969); and Biko Agozino, 'Theorizing Otherness, the War on Drugs and Incarceration', *Theoretical Criminology* 4.3 (2000): 359–76 (363). For an overview of these ideas as related to religion and gender in particular, see Paul Hedges, *Understanding Religion: Theories and*

Methods for Studying Religiously Diverse Societies (Berkeley: University of California Press, 2021), 242–45.

17 Whitley and Kite, *The Psychology of Prejudice and Discrimination*, 7, italics in original. More widely on privilege as a concept, see ibid., 6–8. See also Anderson, *Benign Bigotry*.

18 Robert Sternberg, 'A Duplex Theory of Hate: Development and Application to Terrorism, Massacres, and Genocide', *Review of General Psychology* 7 (2003): 299–328 (306).

19 Robert Sternberg and Karin Sternberg, *The Nature of Hate* (Cambridge: Cambridge University Press, 2008), 51–2.

20 Sternberg and Sternberg, *The Nature of Hate*, 52.

21 See Mark Schaller, Lucian Gideon Conway III and K. Michelle Peavy, 'Evolutionary Processes', in *The Sage Handbook of Prejudice, Stereotyping and Discrimination*, ed. John Dovidio, Miles Hewstone, Peter Glick and Victoria Esses (London: Sage, 2010), 81–96. More widely on cognitive science, including in relation to religion, see Jason Sloane and William McCorkle, eds, *The Cognitive Science of Religion: A Methodological Introduction to Key Empirical Studies* (London: Bloomsbury, 2019).

22 Whitley and Kite, *The Psychology of Prejudice and Discrimination*, 171, italics in original.

23 Sternberg and Sternberg, *The Nature of Hate*, 73–6.

24 Sternberg and Sternberg, *The Nature of Hate*, 77.

25 Sternberg and Sternberg, *The Nature of Hate*, 59.

26 Sternberg and Sternberg, *The Nature of Hate*, 59–60.

27 See Eliot Smith and Diane Mackie, 'Affective Processes', in *The Sage Handbook of Prejudice*, 131–45 (137–41).

28 Sternberg and Sternberg, *The Nature of Hate*, 60.

29 Bonaventura de Sousa Santos, 'Towards a Multicultural Conception of Human Rights', in *Spaces of Culture: City, Nation, World*, ed. Mike Featherstone and Scott Lash (London: Sage, 1999): 214–29 (221).

30 Vincent Lloyd, *Religion of the Field Negro: On Black Secularism and Black Theology* (New York: Fordham University Press, 2017), 63.

31 On such debates, see Terry Eagleton, *The Illusions of Postmodernity* (Oxford: Blackwell, 1996); Sumner Twiss, 'A Constructive Framework for Discussing Confucianism and Human Rights', in *Confucianism and Human Rights*, ed. Tu Weiming and William Theodore de Bary (New York: Columbia University Press, 1998), 27–53; and Santos, 'Towards a Multicultural Conception'. This is not to say that Western theory (often embedded in a white, male, and elitist tradition) should remain a norm (it is where most of our theory comes from). Rather, we need to recognize that we can meaningfully translate and communicate between cultures, for, as Souleymane Bachir Diagne notes, 'the language of the universal is translation', Souleymane Bachir Diagne, 'On the Postcolonial and the Universal?' *Rue Descartes* 78.2 (2013): 7–18 (15). For some examples of developing theory from non-Western

sources, see: Paul Hedges, 'Theorising a Decolonising Asian Hermeneutic for Comparative Theology: Some Perspectives from Global and Singaporean Eyes', *International Journal of Asian Christianity* 3.2 (2020), 152–68; Syed Farid Alatas, *Applying Ibn Khaldūn: The Recovery of a Lost Tradition in Sociology* (New York: Routledge, 2015); James Spickard, *Alternative Sociologies of Religion: Through Non-Western Eyes* (New York: State University of New York Press, 2017); Syed Farid Alatas and Vineeta Sinha, *Sociological Theory beyond the Canon* (London: Palgrave Macmillan, 2017).

32 Coco and Hedges, 'Belonging, Behaving, Believing, Becoming'.

33 Adapted from Hedges, *Understanding Religion*. On how those posited as 'religious' or 'non-religious' may relate, and problems with this as a stark distinction, see Paul Hedges, *Towards Better Disagreement: Religion and Atheism in Dialogue* (London: Jessica Kingsley, 2017).

34 See Sean Harvey, 'Ideas of Race in Early America', *Oxford Research Encyclopaedias: American History* (2016), available at http://oxfordre. com/americanhistory/view/10.1093/acrefore/9780199329175.001.0001/ acrefore-9780199329175-e-262.

35 See Benedict Anderson, *Imagined Communities: Reflections on the Origin and Spread of Nationalism* (London: Verso, 1983); and Hedges, *Understanding Religion*. See also the discussion of Rogers Brubaker's notion of groupism below and in Chapter 5.

36 See Hedges, *Understanding Religion*, 150–1.

37 Rogers Brubaker, 'Ethnicity without Groups', *Archives Européenes de Sociologie* 43.2 (2002): 163–89 (171–3).

38 Whitley and Kite, *Psychology of Prejudice and Discrimination*, 122, 127–34.

39 See Jay Bavel, Jenny Xiao and Leor Hackel, 'Social Identity Shapes Social Perception and Evaluation: Using Neuroimaging to Look Inside the Social Brain', in *Neuroscience of Prejudice and Intergroup Relations*, ed. Belle Derks, Daan Scheepers and Naomi Ellemers (New York: Psychology Press, 2013), 110–29 (113).

40 Stuart Hall, 'Ethnicity: Identity and Difference', *Radical America* 23 (1989): 9–20. On difference, see also Stuart Hall, *Stuart Hall: Critical Dialogues in Cultural Studies*, ed. Dave Morley and Kuan-Hsing Chen (London: Routledge, 1996), 444–9.

41 See Tania Saeed, *Islamophobia and Securitization: Religion, Ethnicity and the Female Voice* (Cham: Palgrave Macmillan, 2016). This is discussed further in relation to Islam in Chapter 7.

42 Miroslav Mareš Tore Bjøgo, 'Vigilantism against Migrants and Minorities', in *Vigilantism against Migrants and Minorities*, ed. Tore Bjørgo and Miroslav Mareš (Abingdon: Routledge, 2019), 1–30.

43 Chris Allen, '"People Hate You Because of the Way You Dress": Understanding the Invisible Experiences of Veiled British Muslim Women Victims of Islamophobia', *International Review of Victimology* 21.3 (2015): 287–301 (300). On dehumanization, see John Rector, *The Objectification*

Spectrum: Understanding and Transcending Our Diminishment and Dehumanization of Others (Oxford: Oxford University Press, 2014).

44 Sometimes an individual may be isolated and othered, but the dynamics remain the same, while the individual, typically, represents some 'type' rather than being stigmatized for who they are per se.

45 Jennifer Crocker and Julie Garcia, 'Internalized Devaluation and Situational Threat', in *The Sage Handbook of Prejudice*, 395–409.

46 Rector, *The Objectification Spectrum*, 21–37 and 14–20.

47 See Mary Douglas, *Purity and Danger: An Analysis of the Concepts of Pollution and Taboo* (London: Routledge and Kegan Paul, 1966).

48 Mariña Fernández-Reino, 'Migrants and Discrimination in the UK', *Migration Observatory* (20 January 2020), available at https://migrationobservatory. ox.ac.uk/resources/briefings/migrants-and-discrimination-in-the-uk/.

49 Anderson, *Benign Bigotry*, 3.

50 See Whitley and Kite, *The Psychology of Prejudice and Discrimination*, 12–18, 370–4.

51 Allport, *The Nature of Prejudice*, 236.

52 Allport, *The Nature of Prejudice*, 238.

53 Allport, *The Nature of Prejudice*, 244.

54 René Girard, *To Double Business Bound: Essays on Literature, Mimesis, and Anthropology* (Baltimore, MD: Johns Hopkins University Press, 1978).

55 Whitley and Kite, *Psychology of Prejudice and Discrimination*, 346–9. Ideological theory draws on Peter Glick, 'Sacrificial Lambs Dressed in Wolves' Clothing: Envious Prejudice, Ideology, and the Scapegoating of Jews', in *Understanding Genocide: The Social Psychology of the Holocaust*, ed. L. S. Newman and Ralph Erber (Oxford: Oxford University Press, 2002), 113–42.

56 Edward Herman and Noam Chomsky, *Manufacturing Consent: The Political Economy of the Mass Media*, rev. edn (New York: Pantheon Books, 2002).

57 Allport, *The Nature of Prejudice*, 453–58. See Buhle Zuma, 'Contact Theory and the Concept of Prejudice: Metaphysical and Moral Explorations and an Epistemological Question', *Theory and Psychology* 24.1 (2014): 40–57.

58 See Whitley and Kite, *Psychology of Prejudice and Discrimination*, 551–6. On the practical, and successful, engagement of bringing diverse groups together, see Adam Seligman, Rahel Wasserfall and David Montgomery, *Living with Difference: How to Build Community in a Divided World* (Berkeley: University of California Press, 2015).

59 Whitley and Kite, *Psychology of Prejudice and Discrimination*, 556–9. Though, see Seligman, Wasserfall and Montgomery, *Living with Difference*.

60 See Andrew Wilshere, 'Emmanuel Levinas', in *Dialogue Theories II*, ed. Omer Sener, Frances Sleap and Paul Weller (London: Dialogue Society, 2016), 189–203.

CHAPTER TWO

1 See Tania Saeed, *Islamophobia and Securitization: Religion, Ethnicity and the Female Voice* (Cham: Palgrave Macmillan, 2016), 122–4.

2 Though important recent literature refocuses on physical violence, for example, Stathis Kalyas, *The Logic of Violence in Civil War* (Cambridge: Cambridge University Press, 2006), and Manuel Eisner, 'The Uses of Violence: An Examination of Some Cross-Cutting Issues', *International Journal of Conflict and Violence* 3.1 (2009): 40–59.

3 Gyanendra Pandey, *Routine Violence: Nations, Fragments, Histories* (Stanford, CA: Stanford University Press, 2006), 12.

4 Johan Galtung, 'Violence, Peace, and Peace Research', *Journal of Peace Research* 6.3 (1969): 167–91 (170–1).

5 See, for instance, Frederick Douglass, *Narrative of the Life of Frederick Douglass, an American Slave* (Boston: Anti-Slavery Office, 1845), available at https://docsouth.unc.edu/neh/douglass/douglass.html.

6 The London borough of Kensington and Chelsea, which contains some of the city's most expensive properties, has child poverty of almost 50 per cent (figures for July–September 2017) in some wards, see https://infogram.com/annex-1-north-kensington-area-profile-1hxj48rkjykq6vg. The area is notorious for the Grenfell Tower fire of 2017, see Gordon MacLeod, 'The Grenfell Tower Atrocity', *City* 22.4 (2018): 460–89.

7 Notwithstanding that in some contexts, for example. S&M or MMA, violence may be perceived as part of self-actualization. Culturally some forms of perceived bodily harm may be part of self-actualization but would not be seen this way in other cultural settings, for example, scarification rituals or tattoos. The social acceptance of certain forms of violence, or bodily harm and alteration, is no guarantee that self-actualization is, or is not, attained through them. FGM (female genital mutilation) may be one example of a practice socially accepted in many places but which would not be conducive to self-actualization, whereas the other practices noted here may be more contextual (culturally and personally) in terms of whether they promote self-actualization.

8 N. Scheper-Hughes and P. Bourgois, *Violence in War and Peace: An Anthology* (London: Blackwell, 2004), 1.

9 Siniša Malešević, *The Rise of Organised Brutality: A Historical Sociology of Violence* (Cambridge: Cambridge University Press, 2017), 69–70.

10 See Malešević, *The Rise*, 71; and Frans de Waal, *Mama's Last Hug: Animal Emotions and What They Tell Us about Ourselves* (New York: W. W. Norton, 2019). Though violence levels are culturally variable in chimpanzee and bonobo tribes.

11 Gordy Slack, 'Why We Are Good: Mirror Neurons and the Roots of Empathy', in *The Edge of Reason?: Science and Religion in Modern Society*, ed. Gordon Bentley (London: Continuum, 2008), 65–72. Mirror neurons are common in social species.

12 See Elaina Zachos, 'Another Heart-Warming Way Apes Beat Us at Being
Human', *National Geographic* (10 November 2017), https://www.
nationalgeographic.com/news/2017/11/bonobo-help-stranger-behavior-
animals-speed/; and Jingzhi Tan, Dan Ariely and Brian Hare, 'Bonobos
Respond Prosocially toward Members of Other Groups', *Scientific Reports* 7,
14733 (2017), https://doi.org/10.1038/s41598-017-15320-w.

13 Malešević, *The Rise*, 67–98.

14 Malešević, *The Rise*, 77 and 85.

15 See Herbet Maschner and Katherine Reedy-Maschner, 'The Evolution of
Warfare', in *The Edge of Reason?*, 57–64.

16 See Malešević, *The Rise*, 107 n.5.

17 See especially Malešević, *The Rise*, 99–141.

18 For discussions, see Nina Tannenwald, 'The Nuclear Taboo: The United States
and the Normative Basis of Nuclear Non-Use', *International Organization*
53.3 (1999): 433–46; Scott Sagan and Kenneth Waltz, *The Spread of Nuclear
Weapons: A Debate Renewed* 2nd edn (New York: W. W. Norton, 2002);
and Scott Sagan and Kenneth Waltz, 'Nuclear Zero the Best Option?',
National Interest 109 (2010): 88–96. Notably, in the Sagan–Waltz debate,
Sagan's argument is not primarily that nuclear deterrence did not work in
situations such as the Cold War (between the West/United States and the
Soviet Bloc/USSR) but that in today's context nuclear proliferation may be
a terrorist opportunity, especially in unstable states. The thesis that the long
period of post-Second World War peace across much of Europe and between
superpowers has been based on the fear of MAD remains viable regardless of
current contexts or such disagreements.

19 See James Tyner, *Violence in Capitalism* (Lincoln: University of Nebraska
Press, 2016); Ashley Nellis, 'The Color of Justice: Racial and Ethnic Disparity
in State Prisons', *Sentencing Project* (14 June 2016), available at https://www.
sentencingproject.org/publications/color-of-justice-racial-and-ethnic-disparity-
in-state-prisons/; Dan Berger, 'How Prisons Serve Capitalism', *Public Books* (17
August 2018), available at https://www.publicbooks.org/how-prisons-serve-
capitalism/; and David Greenberg, ed., *Crime and Capitalism: Readings in
Marxist Criminology* (Philadelphia, PA: Temple University Press, 1993). On the
notion of intersectionality in law, see Kimberlé Crenshaw, 'Demarginalizing the
Intersection of Race and Sex: A Black Feminist Critique of Antidiscrimination
Doctrine, Feminist Theory and Antiracist Politics', *University of Chicago Legal
Forum* 1.8 (1989): 139–67, available at https://chicagounbound.uchicago.edu/
cgi/viewcontent.cgi?article=1052&context=uclf. Note that, in this book, we
include class alongside race and gender.

20 See Michel Foucault, 'The Subject and Power', *Critical Inquiry* 8.4 (1982)
777–95; Johanna Oksala, *Foucault, Politics, and Violence* (Boston, MA:
Northwestern University Press, 2012); and Malešević, *The Rise*, 33–9.

21 See Irm Haleem, 'How Violence Is Normalized: On the Process of Violence',
in *Normalization of Violence: Conceptual Analysis and Reflections from Asia*,
ed. Irm Haleem (London: Routledge, 2020), 12–32; and Malešević, *The Rise*,

243–4. To quote Pandey at more length, who is specifically referring to India but with wider implications:

> The routine ordinary practice of violence – for instance, the beating, rape, and indeed burning of women, in homes, in village squares and barely secluded parking lots, and their general humiliation on the streets, in public buses, in films, and so on – gives rise to a considerable tolerance (not to say celebration) of such violence, even when carried out on a frightening scale in mass campaigns of ethnic cleansing and the destruction of people who were formerly neighbors. ... [This] will underline the need for closer investigation of the pervasiveness of the spirit of violence.

Pandey, *Routine Violence*, 12.

22 See Paul Hedges, 'Radicalisation: Examining a Concept, Its Use, and Abuse', *Counter Terrorist Trends and Analysis* 9.10 (2017): 12–18. Issues of spectacle and video games have also been raised in relation to ISIS' graphic physical violence.

23 See Kalyvas, *The Logic*, 9.

24 Kalyvas, *The Logic*, 20–1.

25 See Kalyvas, *The Logic*, 26–30, 32–5; and Malešević, *The Rise*.

26 Kalyvas, *The Logic*, 20

27 Gayatri Chakravorty Spivak, *The Post-colonial Critic*, ed. Sarah Harasym (London: Routledge, 1990).

28 Albert Bandura, *Social Foundations of Thought and Action: A Social Cognitive Theory* (Englewood Cliffs, NJ: Prentice-Hall, 1986).

29 Albert Bandura, 'Selective Moral Disengagement in the Exercise of Moral Agency', *Journal of Moral Education* 31.2 (2002): 101–19 (103).

30 Bandura's systematic and multi-faceted categorization is a more adequate analysis than, for instance, the one-dimensional 'imaginary screen' of Slavoj Žižek, *The Plague of Fantasies* (London: Verso, 1997).

31 In Max Bergholz's important study *Violence as a Generative Force: Identity, Nationalism, and Memory in a Balkan Community* (Ithaca, NY: Cornell University Press, 2016), he shows that 'many Communist Party figures were amongst those urging restraint against inter-ethnic violence [on the basis of pan-ethnic working-class solidarity]. Others [who urged restraint] built friendships across purported ethnic borders even in the context of inter-ethnic violence, sometimes even because of that violence' (ibid., 137).

32 See Kalyvas, *The Logic*, 25.

33 See Hedges, 'Radicalisation'.

34 Hannah Arendt, *Eichmann in Jerusalem: A Report on the Banality of Evil* (London: Penguin, 1994). Arendt's account is inadequate in painting Eichmann as simply unimaginative and doing a mundane, bureaucratic job, which fails to realize his deep antisemitism (see Deborah Lipstadt, *The Eichmann Trial*, New York: Nextbook, 2011). Žižek's argument that Arendt ignores the

possible jouissance, or transgressive pleasure, of those inflicting pain is also pertinent (*The Plague of Fantasies*).

35 Richard Zimbardo, *The Lucifer Effect: Understanding How Good People Turn Evil* (New York: Random House, 2008). For Zimbardo's response to some recent criticism of the experiment, see https://www.prisonexp.org/response.

36 See Stanley Milgram, *Obedience to Authority* (New York: Harper Perrenial, 2009).

37 See Magnus Lindén, Fredrik Björklund, Martin Bäckström, Deanna Messervey and David Whetham, 'A Latent Core of Dark Traits Explains Individual Differences in Peacekeepers' Unethical Attitudes and Conduct', *Military Psychology* 31.6 (2019): 499–509. Importantly, these are tendencies and we all exhibit them along a continuum.

38 See Ruth Seifort, 'The Second Front: The Logic of Sexual Violence in Wars', *Women's Studies International Forum* 19.1/2 (1996): 35–42; Franziska Karpinski and Elysia Ruvinsky, 'Sexual Violence in the Nazi Genocide', in *Genocide: New Perspectives on Its Causes, Courses, and Consequences*, ed. Ugür Ümit Üngör (Amsterdam: Amsterdam University Press, 2016), 149–73; and Maria Eriksson Baaz and Maria Stern, *Sexual Violence as a Weapon of War? Perceptions, Prescriptions, Problems in the Congo and Beyond* (London: Zed Books, 2013).

39 See Kalyvas, *The Logic*, 330–63. For graphic accounts of how neighbours may turn on each other see: Bergholz, *Violence as a Generative Force* on the Balkans; and Michael Vatikiotis, *The Spice Garden* (Jakarta: Equinox, 2004) on Indonesia, which, while a fictionalized account, is based on a solid knowledge of the events.

40 UN, 'Convention on the Prevention and Punishment of the Crime of Genocide' (1948), Article 2.

41 Defined by the 1998 Rome Statute, which established the International Criminal Court, as including: murder, extermination, enslavement, deportation or forcible transfer of population, imprisonment, torture, grave sexual violence, persecution, enforced disappearance, apartheid, and other inhumane acts.

42 See Malešević, *The Rise*, 214–19.

43 Daniel Chirot and Clark McCauley, *Why Not Kill Them All?: The Logic and Prevention of Mass Political Murder* (Princeton, NJ: Princeton University Press, 2006), 13.

44 Some forms of killing may not seem to be covered, for instance, a cat's play with a mouse when it is not hungry (practice hunting?). Again, is letting someone die a form of killing? But these are not significant for our usage of these terms, or could potentially be included as sub-items.

45 See Mike Sosteric, 'How to Be Human? Abraham Maslow and His Hierarchies of Need (Hierarchy of Needs)', *SocJourn* (2017), available at https://www.sociology.org/how-to-be-human/.

46 de Waal, *Mama's Last Hug*, 181–9, see also Jonathan Webb, 'Murder "Comes Naturally" to Chimpanzees', *BBC* (18 September 2014), available at https://www.bbc.com/news/science-environment-29237276.

47 See, for example, Uwe Steinhoff, *On the Ethics of War and Terrorism* (Oxford: Oxford University Press, 2007); and Andreas Anter, *Max Weber's Theory of the Modern State: Origins, Structure and Significance*, trans. Keith Tribe (Basingstoke: Palgrave Macmillan, 2014), 34–7.

48 See Nadja Heym, 'Five Things You Didn't Know about Psychopaths', *The Conversation* (3 October 2018), available at https://theconversation.com/five-things-you-didnt-know-about-psychopaths-103865.

49 While intelligence and sociality in animals are generally seen as linked, octopi have the former but not normally the latter, which perhaps highlights their very distinct, even unique, evolutionary pathway.

50 See, for instance, Rutger Bregman, *Humankind: A Hopeful History* (London: Bloomsbury, 2020).

51 See, for instance, Kalyas, *The Logic*; and Bergholz, *Violence as a Generative Force*, 81, *passim*.

52 See Malešević, *The Rise*, 223–34, 227–31, 236; and Zygmunt Baumann, *The Holocaust and Modernity* (Cambridge: Polity Press, 1989). Baumann nevertheless usefully moves towards demystifying genocide in his early chapters.

53 See Roger Petersen, *Understanding Ethnic Violence: Fear, Hatred, and Resentment in Twentieth-Century Eastern Europe* (Cambridge: Cambridge University Press, 2002).

54 Ugür Ümit Üngör, 'Introduction: Genocide an Enduring Problem of Our Age', in *Genocide: New Perspectives*, 11–23 (15).

55 Qn iconography, see Haleem, 'How Violence Is Normalized', 24–7.

56 Reports on the sterilization of Uighur women in China would fit many definitions of genocide, but seems to be without a particularly fraught social situation, although the Uighur people have been heavily othered, securitized, and managed as a socially problematic minority, subject to structural and cultural violence, for many years. See Adrian Zenz, 'China's Own Documents Show Potentially Genocidal Sterilization Plans in Xinjiang', *Foreign Policy* (1 July 2020), available at https://foreignpolicy.com/2020/07/01/china-documents-uighur-genocidal-sterilization-xinjiang/. On the wider Uighur situation, see Dana Carver Boehm, 'China's Failed War on Terror: Fanning the Flames of Uighur Separatist Violence', *Berkeley Journal of Middle Eastern and Islamic Law* 2.1 (2009): 61–124; Dru Gladney, 'Constructing a Contemporary Uighur National Identity: Transnationalism, Islamicization, and State Representation', *CEMOTI, Cahiers d'Études sur la Méditerranée Orientale et le monde Turco-Iranien Année* 13 (1992): 165–184.

57 See Mark Levene, 'Genocide', in *The Cambridge World History*, vol. 7, ed. J. McNeill and K. Pomeranz (Cambridge: Cambridge University Press, 2015), 420–41 (439–40).

58 See Bergholz, *Violence as a Generative Force*, 111, 178, 280–1, 296, and *passim*.

59 See M. Mann, *The Dark Side of Democracy: Explaining Ethnic Cleansing* (Cambridge: Cambridge University Press, 2005).

60 While definitionally different from genocide (but genocidal in nature), the African slave trade has been termed 'the most thoroughly destructive act ever to be perpetrated by one group of people upon another', Marimba Ani, *Let the Circle Be Unbroken: The Implications of African Spirituality in the Diaspora* (New York: Nkonimfo, 1997), 12. It relied upon the logic of racism tied to prejudice and genocide (see Chapter 5) and a willingness to murder those deemed lesser and seemingly had genocidal aspects. See also Joseph-Achille Mbembé, trans. Libby Meintjes, 'Necropolitics', *Public Culture* 15.1 (2003): 11–40. However, slavery, while in its particularly racialized form in relation to Black African slaves and the route through the Middle Passage is tied to modern European colonialism, is not simply a feature of Western modernity but has been common throughout history and across cultures. Nevertheless, both the scale and the ongoing social, economic, legal, and political consequences of Western racialized slavery mean that it needs highlighting as distinctive and fundamental to the contemporary global context (see Chapter 5).

61 See Nelson Maldonado Torres, 'Outline of Ten Theses on Coloniality and Decoloniality', (2018), available at https://fondation-frantzfanon.com/wp-content/uploads/2018/10/maldonado-torres_outline_of_ten_theses-10.23.16.pdf.

62 Interestingly, Bergholz shows how mass ethnic killings during the Second World War in what is now Bosnia-Herzegovina, while based upon an ideology imposed by the elite, were not necessarily started because of this. The elite narrative advocated the removal of certain ethnic groups, but the killings were a 'ground-up' result of the legitimized banditry and looting of local militia units, which the elite organization wished to stop. This shows the importance of microscale studies of the specificities of particular cases, see Bergholz, *Violence as a Generative Force*, 291.

63 See Bergholz, *Violence as a Generative Force*, who notes that much of the violence in his case study was not built on a background of intercommunal conflict but was done by small groups who saw 'unprecedented opportunity to profit and settle local conflicts once and for all by employing violence on an ethnic axis' (6). He also notes the opinion of one military officer of those in the militia groups who became involved in much of the violence that could be seen as ethnic cleansing: 'a bunch of good-for-nothing troublemakers, who for years have walked the streets ... without work, and now are making use of today's circumstances for their personal gain' (81). As such, many acted for economic gain. While, in relation to his notion of violence as a 'generative force', Bergholz noted how these acts created grounds for vengeance and retaliation which had not existed before: 'The sudden violence had a deeply polarizing effect on intercommunal relations, leading to a rapid transformation of neighbors into collective categories of enemies, and calls for retaliation along such lines. ... [While] [m]any of the survivors ... suddenly viewed all "Muslims" and "Croats" as guilty' (111 and 112). He notes that such dynamics were also seen in South Asia and Greece, referencing Kalyvas, *The Logic*; and Das, 'Collective Violence and the Shifting Categories of Communal Riots, Ethnic Cleansing and Genocide', in *The Historiography of Genocide*, ed. Dan Stone (New York: Palgrave Macmillan, 2008), 93–127; and more

generally to Bowman, 'The Violence in Identity', in *Anthropology of Violence and Conflict*, eds Bettina Schmidt and Ingo Schröder (London: Routledge, 2001), 25–46. See also the previous note.

64 See Haleem, 'How Violence Is Normalized'; and Pandey, *Routine Violence*.

65 Levene, 'Genocide', 420–2.

66 See, for example, Mark Levene, *Genocide in the Age of the Nation State*, vol. 1 (London: I.B. Tauris, 2008).

67 Hannah Arendt, *The Origins of Totalitarianism*, rev. edn (New York: HarperCollins, 1986). Moreover, defining antisemitism as genocidal is an example of what we need to untheorize with regard to that term, for it posits a single transhistorical imperative as being behind diverse (socially contextual and psychologically driven) acts and notions directed against Jews across time and space.

68 See Kate Temoney, 'Religion and Genocide Nexuses: Bosnia as a Case Study', *Religions* 8.6 (2017), doi:10.3390/rel806112.

69 See Shawn Kelly, *Genocide, the Bible, and Biblical Scholarship* (Leiden: Brill, 2016).

70 See Naim Stifan Ateek, *Justice and Only Justice: A Palestinian Theology of Liberation* (Maryknoll, NY: Orbis, 1989), 84–5, citing Mose Segal in Robert I. Friedman, 'No Land, No Peace for Palestinians', *Nation* (23 April 1988): 563.

71 See Benny Morris, 'A New Look at the 1948 War', Lecture, ISGAP Critical Antisemitism Summer Institute, St John's College Oxford, 9 July 2019; and Francisco Bethencourt, *Racisms: From the Crusades to the Twentieth Century* (Princeton, NJ: Princeton University Press, 2013), 316–20.

72 See Malešević, *The Rise*, 233–4.

73 Daniel Chirot and Clark McCauley, *Why Not Kill Them All? The Logic and Prevention of Mass Political Murder* (Princeton, NJ: Princeton University Press, 2006), 27.

74 See Levene, 'Genocide', 429–31; and Malešević, *The Rise*, 234–5.

75 On the connection of civilization and religion in colonial projects, see Paul Hedges, *Understanding Religion: Theories and Methods for Studying Religiously Diverse Societies* (Berkeley: University of California Press, 2021), 164–5.

76 Torres, 'Outline of Ten Theses on Coloniality', italics in original.

77 Mbembé, 'Necropolitics', 40.

78 See Levine, 'Genocide'; and Chirot and McCauley, *Why Not Kill Them All?*

79 See Malešević, *The Rise*, 18–40.

80 See Bethencourt, *Racisms*, 352; Levene, 'Genocide', 436–8; and Malešević, *The Rise*, 215, 236. See also Breann Fallon, 'The Fetishization Effect: The Manipulation Power of the Machete in the Rwandan Genocide', *Implicit Religion* 20.4 (2017): 319–33.

81 Malešević, *The Rise*, 30, and see 124–5.

82   Certainly, for many, that it was the Germans – the people of the land of Bach, Beethoven, Goethe, Humboldt, Kant, Schelling, and others – who committed the Holocaust seemed incomprehensible. How could such civilization and such inhumanity be linked? However, we must untheorize any connection of violence and genocide to a lack of civilization or to the savagery of certain peoples ('tribes'). While a direct link of civilization to genocide is untenable, the development of what we see as 'civilization' and 'culture' is certainly not a hindrance to human urges to murder and genocide. Indeed, historically, the rise of what we often seen as 'civilizations' has been directly related to the ability to organize and orchestrate violence against various populations made subject to those 'civilizations'. This includes in such ways as the 'pacification' of the 'natives' or 'tribal people' of the border lands, often including slavery (to build the structures of 'civilization'), as well as in enforcing universalizing codes or rules. In this sense, civilization may simply denote the ability to control power with great effect. See Malešević, *The Rise*. This is not to suggest (à la Rousseau) that previously humans lived only in peaceable systems as 'noble savages', but civilization is, in part at least, organized brutality. As a final note, some editing is occurring as we lead into what many see as a vital US election (November 2020) that may restore 'civility' in domestic political life; however, the paragon of this civility is a man who was vice-president in a regime that massively increased the use of drone strikes around the world with the inevitable 'collateral damage' (deaths to children, infants, civilians) that would come with it. American 'civilization' is not always viewed as benign around the world, see Mohammed Hanif, 'The rest of the world has had it with US presidents, Trump or otherwise' *The Guardian* (3 November 2020), available at: https://www.theguardian.com/commentisfree/2020/nov/03/donald-trump-us-presidents-joe-biden.

83   See Frank Chalk and Kurt Jonassohn, *The History and Sociology of Genocide: Analyses and Case Studies* (New Haven, CT: Yale University Press, 1990), 33–7; and Wm. Plouffe, Jr., 'Genocide', in *Encyclopedia of Transnational Crime and Justice*, ed. Margaret Beare (Thousand Oaks, CA: Sage, 2012), 163–4. However, Malešević (*The Rise*) convincingly disputes many early exaggerated death rates and refutes authors who claim that most ancient wars were genocidal in nature (33), arguing, among other points, that the destruction of Carthage fails to meet our typical definition of genocide (41–99).

84   See Hedges, *Understanding Religion*. Mbembe also links sovereignty to the power over death from a more conceptual angle (see 'Necropolitics') though it is somewhat reductionist to link or equate politics to death as he seems to do following some aspects of continental philosophy. It seems to envisage the polis, the people as social animal (though not necessarily in a city), within the human as chimp paradigm, envisaged as aggressive and murderous, ignoring the human as bonobo paradigm, as nurturing and empathetic. Our politics may encapsulate many aspects or take various forms. With this in mind, how we envisage 'civilization' may be in need of rethinking given that the rise of 'civilizations' (so-called) has often been about the organization and control of violence. See note 82 above.

85 On the historical context, see Charles Tilly, 'Some Problems in the History of the Vendée', *American Historical Review* 67.1 (1961): 19–33; and see Levine, 'Genocide', 432.

86 See Bergholz, *Violence as a Generative Force*, 235–42, where he narrates the way in which choices were made, within the same time frame and same location by neighbours, to either massacre or save those who came to be perceived by some as ethnic enemies.

Interlude 1

1 See Paul Hedges, *Understanding Religion: Theories and Methods for Studying Religiously Diverse Societies* (Berkeley: University of California Press, 2021).

2 See Timothy Fitzgerald, *The Ideology of Religious Studies* (Oxford: Oxford University Press, 2000); and Russell McCutcheon, *Manufacturing Religion: The Discourse on Sui Generis Religion and the Politics of Nostalgia* (Oxford: Oxford University Press, 1997). While such critics correctly identity conceptual issues with 'religion' as a category, their claims for abandoning the term are conceptually and philosophically unsubstantiated. See Paul Hedges, 'Deconstructing Religion: Where We Go from Here – a Hermeneutical Proposal', *Exchange* 47.1 (2018): 5–24; and Kevin Schilbrack, 'A Realist Social Ontology of Religion', *Religion* 47.2 (2017): 161–78. For an overview see Hedges, *Understanding Religion*, 19–35; and Paul Hedges and Anna King, 'What Is Religion? Or What Is It We're Talking about?', in *Controversies in Contemporary Religion*, ed. Paul Hedges, vol. I (Santa Barbara, CA: Praeger, 2014), 1–30.

3 See Hedges, *Understanding Religion*, 28–9.

4 See Paul Hedges, 'Discourse on Discourses: Why We still Need the Terminology of "Religion" and "Religions"', *Journal of Religious History* 38.1 (2014): 132–48.

5 See Hedges, *Understanding Religion*; and Timothy Fitzgerald, *Discourse on Civility and Barbarity: A Critical History of Religion and Related Categories* (Oxford: Oxford University Press, 2007).

6 See Hedges, *Understanding Religion*, chapters 1, 3, and 11.

7 See Paul Hedges, 'Multiple Religious Belonging after Religion: Theorising Strategic Religious Participation in a Shared Religious Landscape as a Chinese Model', *Open Theology* 3.1 (2017): 48–72.

8 Mark Juergensmeyer, *Terror in the Mind of God: The Global Rise of Religious Violence*, 4th edn (Berkeley: University of California Press, 2017), 182–203.

9 Notably, no language has a word for 'nonviolence' except as a negative, that is, it is not violence. See Mark Kurlansky, *Nonviolence: Twenty-Five Lessons from the History of a Dangerous Idea* (New York: Modern Library, 2006).

10 Scott Appleby, *The Ambivalence of the Sacred: Religion, Violence, and Reconciliation* (Lanham, MD: Rowman and Littlefield, 2000); and Perry Schmidt-Leukel, 'Interreligious Relations: From Conflict to Transformation',

in *Interreligious Engagement and Theological Reflection: Ecumenical Explorations*, ed. Douglas Pratt (Bern: Stämplfi AG, 2014), 6–19 (7).

11　Frederic Raphael, *Anti-Semitism* (London: Biteback, 2015), 109, *passim*.

12　See Hedges, *Understanding Religion*, 260 textbox 11.3, and Jonathan Brown, *Misquoting Muhammad: The Challenge and Choices of Interpreting the Prophet's Legacy* (Oxford: Oneworld, 2014), especially 17–18.

13　See Gordon Lynch, *The Sacred in the Modern World: A Cultural Sociological Approach* (Oxford: Oxford University Press, 2012); and Hedges, *Understanding Religion*, 432–5.

14　On this term, see Paul Hedges, 'Radicalisation: Examining a Concept, Its Use, and Abuse', *Counter Terrorist Trends and Analysis* 9.10 (2017): 12–18.

15　Aida Arosoaie, 'In the Name of Honour and Freedom: The Sacred as a Justifying Tool for ISIS' and Secular Violence', *Culture and Religion* 18.3 (2017): 278–95.

16　See Benjamin Weber, 'The Journey of the Word Crusade – from Holy to Oppressive … and Back again', *The Conversation* (5 March 2020), available at https://theconversation.com/the-journey-of-the-word-crusade-from-holy-to-oppressive-and-back-again-132124.

17　See Paul Hedges, *Towards Better Disagreement: Religion and Atheism in Dialogue* (London: Jessica Kingsley, 2017), 96–113.

18　See Hedges, *Towards Better Disagreement*, 138–60.

19　For one example of religion's reassertion in what has been termed a post-secular age, see Paul Hedges, 'Hagia Sophia as Mosque or Museum: Religion in a Post-Secular World', *RSIS Commentary* CO20142 (2020), available at https://www.rsis.edu.sg/wp-content/uploads/2020/07/CO20142.pdf.

20　On trends around secularism, fundamentalism, religion, and their relationships, see Hedges, *Understanding Religion*; and Hedges, *Towards Better Disagreement*.

CHAPTER THREE

1　Crucifixion was only used for those considered traitors to Rome, hence we know that Jesus was killed under Roman jurisdiction. If the charge was blasphemy under Jewish law, as the Gospels claim, Jesus would have been stoned. Under Roman rule, many communities retained such rights, and in the Acts of the Apostles Stephen is stoned under Jewish law. Jesus was killed as a traitor to Rome, and scholars hypothesize that the so-called cleansing of the temple incident may have been the cause for Jesus' arrest and death. See Geza Vermes, *The Passion: The True Story of an Event That Changed Human History* (London: Penguin, 2006).

2　Reuven Firestone, personal correspondence with author (13 March 2020).

3　On such problematic portrayals of religion as monolithic entities bound by common beliefs, see Paul Hedges, *Understanding Religion: Theories and*

Methods for Studying Religiously Diverse Societies (Berkeley: University of California Press, 2021), especially chapters 1 and 3. Notably, such a conception of 'religion' is based in part upon a modern, Western, and Protestant Christian perspective from an elite, textual lens.

4 Greek: Gehenna.

5 On Jesus as a prophet of the poor and countryfolk, see Amy-Jill Levine, Dale Allison and John Crossnan, eds, *The Historical Jesus in Context* (Princeton, NJ: Princeton University Press, 2006).

6 See Pamela Eisenbaum, *Paul Was Not a Christian: The Original Message of a Misunderstood Apostle* (New York: HarperOne, 2010).

7 Critical scholarship dates Mark to *c.*65–75 CE, Matthew and Luke to *c.*75–85 CE, and John to *c.*85–100 CE. A minority of scholars argue John came first, but arguments for the priority of John are deeply problematic, with the internal textual evidence (it is seemingly written by John's own disciples after his death) and Christian tradition (we are told John lived to a very old age) pointing to a late date for it. Its highly developed Christology is also indicative of this. Christian apologist scholarship, and some specific arguments, may give dates *c.*10–20 years earlier for each text; however, the dates here follow the majority of critical scholarship.

8 Jaroslav Pelikan, *Jesus through the Centuries: His Place in the History of Culture* (New Haven, CT: Yale University Press, 1985).

9 See Hedges, *Understanding Religion*, 106–10.

10 See Judith Lieu, *Neither Jew Nor Greek? Constructing Early Christianity* (London: Bloomsbury, 2016), 31–49. It is generally held that a clear split between Christianity and Judaism did not occur until the fourth century, after Constantine (*c.*272–337 CE) adopted Christianity as a tool of imperial rule. We have texts up till this period which we cannot, based on their internal evidence alone, place as either clearly Christian or Jewish, while the identity of Christians by a strict definition of orthodoxy delineated via a distinct theological set of claims is a product of the age of the church councils which start under Constantine. See also Paula Fredriksen, *When Christians Were Jews: The First Generation* (New Haven and London: Yale University Press, 2018). However, we see a distinction arising from the second century.

11 See Rosemary Ruether, *Faith and Fratricide: The Theological Roots of Anti-Semitism* (New York: Seabury Press, 1974), 117–23.

12 Cited from Thomas Falls, ed., *The Fathers of the Church*, vol. 6 (Washington, DC: Catholic University of America Press, 1977), 164.

13 On these debates the literature is voluminous. A survey of arguments can be found in Anna King and Paul Hedges, 'What Is Religion? Or What Is It We're Talking about?', in *Controversies in Contemporary Religion*, ed. Paul Hedges, vol. I (Santa Barbara, CA: Praeger, 2014), 1–30. See also Interlude 1.

14 These three covenants were seen as made with, chronologically, Noah, Abraham, and Moses. For Orthodox Jews, a covenantal relationship with Christians may be framed through the Noahide covenant rather than the Abrahamic one (the latter containing circumcision as a requirement, which Christians reject, though they claim to retain the monotheistic fidelity to

Abraham's God). The Noahide covenant, in Jewish thought, is made with all people and requires adherence to basic ethical tenets: no idolatry; no cursing God; courts with fair laws; no murder; no sexual immorality; no stealing; and no eating flesh from a live animal. This they see as their shared basis with Christians. We may note that Justin's quote above refers to the Mosaic covenant made at Horeb which, for Jews, is their specific relationship with their deity and concerns the laws, which as we have noted – and will see further in later chapters – is contrasted by Christians with 'Christian freedom (from the law)'. As such, for Christians to speak of only one covenant before Jesus is a discursive rethinking of Jewish tradition to position themselves in relation to the one distinctive Jewish covenant (as the Noahide is generic) that they see themselves in line with. Indeed, arguably, Muslims retain a greater covenantal link with Judaism by adherence to both the Noahide and Abrahamic covenants (morality, circumcision, and monotheism). See Alana Vincent, 'Convergence and Asymmetry: Some Brief Observations on the Current State of Jewish-Christian Dialogue', *Interreligious Studies and Intercultural Theology* 4.2 (2020), 201–23.

15 John Chrysostom, *Adversus Judaeos*, Oratio 2 (lost section) (2010), Fordham University Sourcebooks, available at https://sourcebooks.fordham.edu/source/chrysostom-jews6-homily2LOST.asp.

16 See Walter Laqueur, *The Changing Face of Antisemitism* (Oxford: Oxford University Press, 2006), 47–8.

17 Augustine's legacy is disputed in the literature, see James Carroll, *Constantine's Sword: The Church and the Jews* (Boston, MA: Houghton Mifflin, 2001), 215–19; Robert Chazan, *From Anti-Semitism to Anti-Judaism: Ancient and Medieval Christian Constructions of Jewish History* (Cambridge: Cambridge University Press, 2016); and Paula Fredriksen, *Augustine and the Jews: A Christian Defense of Jews and Judaism* (New York: Doubleday, 2008).

18 Ronald Miller, 'Judaism: Siblings in Strife', in *Christian Approaches to Other Religions*, ed. Paul Hedges and Alan Race, SCM Core Text (London: SCM, 2008), 176–90, 181–2, italics in original.

19 See Joshua Trachtenberg, *The Devil and the Jews: The Medieval Conception of the Jew and Its Relation to Modern Anti-Semitism* (Philadelphia, PA: Jewish Publication Society of America, [1943] 1983), 140–55.

20 Trachtenberg, *The Devil and the Jews*, 126–7.

21 For a discussion of various incidents, see Carroll, *Constantine's Sword*, 272–7; and Trachtenberg, *The Devil and the Jews*, 124–55.

22 See Susan Sontag, *Illness as Metaphor and AIDS and Its Metaphors* (New York: Picador, 2001); and Farish Noor, 'The Virus Scare as a Mirror to Ourselves and Our Society', *Straits Times* (10 February 2020), available at https://www.straitstimes.com/opinion/cartoons/the-virus-scare-as-a-mirror-to-ourselves-and-our-society.

23 Carroll, *Constantine's Sword*, 273.

24 Laqueur, *The Changing Face*, 57.

25 See David Nirenberg, *Neighboring Faiths: Christianity, Islam, and Judaism in the Middle Ages and Today* (Chicago, IL: University of Chicago Press, 2014).

26 See David Nirenberg, *Communities of Violence: Persecution of Minorities in the Middle Ages*, updated edn (Princeton, NJ: Princeton University Press, 2015).

27 Carroll, *Constantine's Sword*, 257.

28 See Laqueur, *The Changing Face*, 52–3.

29 Ruether, *Faith and Fratricide*, 206–7.

30 See Nirenberg, *Communities of Violence*.

31 Nirenberg, *Communities of Violence*, 229.

32 On the theological debates of the Reformations (there were, properly speaking, several rather than one), see Alister McGrath, *Historical Theology: An Introduction to the Christian Tradition* (Oxford: Blackwell, 1998). On the significance of Protestant-Catholic polemic on later thinking around religion, see Hedges, *Understanding-Religion*, 212–16.

33 For a fuller account of Luther's times and attitudes, see Thomas Kaufmann, *Luther's Jews: A Journey into Anti-Semitism* (Oxford: Oxford University Press, 2017).

34 These draw from Dan Cohn-Sherbok, *The Crucified Jew: Twenty Centuries of Christian Anti-Semitism* (Grand Rapids, MI: Eerdmans, 1997), 71.

35 Laqueur, *The Changing Face*, 63.

36 Martin Luther, *The Jews and Their Lies*, translator unnamed (York, SC: Liberty Bell, [1543] 2004), 14, 21.

37 Luther, *The Jews and Their Lies*, 29–30.

38 Luther, *The Jews and Their Lies*, 31–2.

39 Luther, *The Jews and Their Lies*, 31.

40 Luther, *The Jews and Their Lies*, this translation cited from Cohn-Sherbok, *The Crucified Jew*, 73.

41 Cohn-Sherbok, *The Crucified Jew*, 63.

42 See Daniel Schwartz, *Ghetto: The History of a Word* (Cambridge, MA: Harvard University Press, 2019), 7, 163–94.

43 Schwartz, *Ghetto*, 199–200. This, naturally, is often deeply resented by some Jews, though others understand and empathize with the usage.

44 See Schwartz, *Ghetto*, 26–31.

45 Schwartz, *Ghetto*, 31–2, citing *Cum nimis absurdum* from Kenneth Stow, *Catholic Thought and Papal Jewish Policy, 1555–1593* (New York: Jewish Theological Seminary, 1977), 294–5.

46 Schwartz, *Ghetto*, 46–51.

47 See, for example, Laqueur, *The Changing Face*, 71.

48 Schwartz, *Ghetto*, 81.

49 Schwartz, *Ghetto*, 52.

50 Schwartz, *Ghetto*, 35.

51 Miller, 'Judaism'.

CHAPTER FOUR

1 Deepa Kumar, *Islamophobia and the Politics of Empire: The Cultural Logic of Empire* (Chicago, IL: Haymarket Books, 2012). Kumar's argument that 'the history of "Islam and the West" … is a story not of religious conflict but rather conflict born of *political* rivalries and competing imperial agendas' (9, italics in original) accords with the evidence presented herein.

2 Samuel Huntington, 'The Clash of Civilizations', *Foreign Affairs* 72.3 (1993): 22–49 (35).

3 Franco Cardini, *Europe and Islam*, trans. Caroline Beamish (Oxford: Blackwell, 2001), 62.

4 See Peter Frankopan, *The Silk Roads: A New History of the World* (London: Bloomsbury, 2016), 79–85. For differing perspectives on the dynamics, see Perry Schmidt-Leukel and Lloyd Ridgeon, eds, *Islam and Inter-Faith Relations* (London: SCM, 2007). Certainly, the Qur'an contains elements both positive and negative towards Christians and Jews, see Abdullah Saeed, *The Qur'an: An Introduction* (London: Routledge, 2008), 69–70.

5 See Cardini, *Europe and Islam*, 45–8.

6 See Paul Hedges, *Understanding Religion: Theories and Methods for Studying Religiously Diverse Societies* (Berkeley: University of California Press, 2021), 202. For a wider discussion on the possibility of a 'just war' in Islam and usages of *jihad* as striving, see John Kelsay, *Arguing the Just War in Islam* (Cambridge, MA: Harvard University Press, 2007). See also Reuven Firestone, *Jihad: The Origin of Holy War in Islam* (Oxford: Oxford University Press, 2002).

7 See Cardini, *Europe and Islam*, 32, 39–41, and 58. See also Heather Selma Gregg, *The Path to Salvation: Religious Violence from the Crusades to Jihad* (Lincoln, NE: Potomac Books, 2014), 37.

8 The term refers to those who are held to have had a revelation (as a book/scripture) from God delivered by a prophet and who followed, although inaccurately, these teachings.

9 David Thomas, 'Dialogue before Dialogue', in *Contemporary Muslim-Christian Encounters: Developments, Diversity and Dialogues*, ed. Paul Hedges (London: Bloomsbury, 2015), 1–15 (5–7).

10 For an overview of these debates, see Paul Hedges, 'The Contemporary Context of Muslim-Christian Dialogue', in *Contemporary Muslim-Christian Encounters*, 17–31 (24–6). For an extended treatment see Clinton Bennett, *Understanding Christian-Muslim Relations: Past and Present* (London: Continuum, 2008).

11 For an overview of recent debates, see Bennett, *Understanding Christian-Muslim*, 216–18, and the overview in David Kerr, 'The Prophet Mohammad in Christian Theological Perspective', in *Islam in a World of Diverse Faiths*, ed. Dan Cohn-Sherbok (New York: St Martin's Press, 1997), 119–33. The best known Christian argument for accepting Muhammad's

prophethood is probably Hans Küng, *Christianity and the World Religions*
(London: HarperCollins, 1986), 24–8, but for a more recent discussion,
see Paul Hedges, 'Hospitality, Power and the Theology of Religions',
in *Interreligious Engagement and Theological Reflection: Ecumenical
Explorations*, ed. Douglas Pratt (Bern: Stämpfli AG, 2014), 156–75. On
Muslim views of Jesus, see Oddbjørn Leirvik, *Images of Jesus in Islam*, 2nd
edn (London: Bloomsbury, 2010).

12 On Muslim thought through the centuries on this question, see Todd Lawson,
    The Crucifixion and the Qur'an: A Study in the History of Muslim Thought
    (Oxford: Oneworld, 2009).

13 For recent debates, see Bennett, *Understanding Christian-Muslim*, 219–21,
    for a contemporary Islamic view, see Mahmoud Ayoub, *A Muslim View
    of Christianity: Essays on Dialogue by Mahmoud Ayoub*, ed. Irfan Omar
    (Maryknoll, NY: Orbis, 2007), 159–70.

14 See Abdullah Saeed, 'The Charge of Distortion of Jewish and Christian
    Scriptures', *Muslim World* 92 (2002): 419–36.

15 See Paul Hedges, *Preparation and Fulfilment: A History and Study of
    Fulfilment Theology in Modern British Thought in the Indian Context*
    (Bern: Peter Lang, 2001).

16 See David Waines, *An Introduction to Islam* (Cambridge: Cambridge
    University Press), 20, 30, 105–8 and 126–8; and Jonathan Brown, *Misquoting
    Muhammad: The Challenge and Choices of Interpreting the Prophet's Legacy*
    (Oxford: Oneworld, 2014), 82, 207–8.

17 See Nicholas Rescher, 'Nicholas of Cusa on the Qur'an: A Fifteenth-Century
    Encounter with Islam', in *The Routledge Reader in Christian-Muslim
    Relations*, ed. Mona Siddiqui (London: Routledge, 2013), 122–8. On Aquinas's
    attitude, see James Waltz, 'Muhammad and the Muslims in St. Thomas
    Aquinas', in *The Routledge Reader in Christian-Muslim Relations*, 112–21.
    This is notwithstanding Aquinas' indebtedness to Ibn Sina and the way that
    medieval Christian thought borrowed heavily from the world of Islam, see
    Bryan van Norden, *Taking Back Philosophy: A Multicultural Manifesto*
    (New York: Columbia University Press, 2017), 18.

18 See Cardini, *Europe and Islam*, 58 and 67. The term 'Holy Pilgrimage' was
    employed by Pope Urban II (*c*.1035–1099).

19 See Cardini, *Europe and Islam*, 58–63.

20 Bernard of Clairvaux, 'Why Another Crusade?' (*c*.1145), available at https://
    www.bartleby.com/268/7/4.html.

21 See James Kroemer, 'Vanquish the Haughty and Spare the Subjected: A Study
    of Bernard of Clairvaux's Position on Muslims and Jews', *Medieval Encounters*
    18.1 (2012): 55–92. It may seem ironic, therefore, that Bernard was given
    the exalted theological title of Doctor of Love by the Catholic Church for his
    devotional mysticism as loving union to Jesus.

22 Cardini, *Europe and Islam*, 56–7.

23 Frankopan, *The Silk Roads*, 135.

24 Cardini, *Europe and Islam*, 58–9.

25 See Jacques Waardenburg, 'Encounters between European Civilisation and Islam in History', in *The Christian-Muslim Frontier: Chaos, Clash or Dialogue?*, ed. Jørgen Nielsen (London: I.B. Tauris, 1998), 5–22 (9–12).

26 See Cardini, *Europe and Islam*, 36–44.

27 On representations of this event, see John Tolan, 'The Friar and the Sultan: Francis of Assisi's Mission to Egypt', *European Review* 16.1 (2008): 115–26.

28 See Waardenburg, 'Encounters between European', 11, but most particularly Sidney Griffith, *The Church in the Shadow of the Mosque: Christians and Muslims in the World of Islam* (Princeton, NJ: Princeton University Press, 2008).

29 See Cardini, *Europe and Islam*, 61–2.

30 See Griffith, *The Church in the Shadow*.

31 Griffith, *The Church in the Shadow*, 97.

32 Griffith, *The Church in the Shadow*, 104.

33 See Griffith, *The Church in the Shadow*, 17–20 and 147–9.

34 Maria Rosa Menocal, *The Ornament of the World: How Muslims, Jews and Christians Created a Culture of Tolerance in Medieval Spain* (New York: Bayback, 2002); and see Fernández-Morera, Darío, *The Myth of the Andalusian Paradise: Muslims, Christians, and Jews under Islamic Rule in Medieval Spain* (Wilmington, DE: Intercollegiate Studies Institute, 2014).

35 See Hedges, *Understanding Religion*, 316–19; Sarah Pearce, 'Paradise Lost' [Review of Darío Fernández-Morera, *The Myth of the Andalusian Paradise: Muslims, Christians, and Jews under Islamic Rule in Medieval Spain*] (2017), available at https://wp.nyu.edu/sjpearce/2017/03/17/paradise-lost/; and Jocelyn Hendrickson, 'Andalusia', in *Oxford Islamic Studies Online* (n.d.), available at http://www.oxfordislamicstudies.com/print/opr/t236/e1129.

36 Cardini, *Europe and Islam*, 42.

37 Hendrickson, 'Andalusia'.

38 On some of the global links behind the rise of Western science and related fields, see Paul Hedges, *Towards Better Disagreement: Religion and Atheism in Dialogue* (London: Jessica Kingsley, 2017), 138–41; and John Hobson, *The Eastern Origins of Western Civilization* (Cambridge: Cambridge University Press, 2004), 173–83.

39 See Cardini, *Europe and Islam*, 33–4.

40 See Aaron Hollander, 'Blazing Light and Perfect Death: The Martyrs of Cordoba and the Growth of Polemical Holiness', in *Contested Spaces, Common Ground: Space and Power Structures in Contemporary Multireligious Societies*, ed. Ulrich Winkler, Lidia Fernández and Oddbjørn Leirvik (Leiden: Brill, 2017), 203–24; and Jessica Coope, *The Martyrs of Córdoba* (Lincoln: University of Nebraska Press, 1995).

41 Frankopan, *The Silk Roads*, 244–9.

42 On some of this history, see Ian Almond, *Two Faiths, One Banner: When Muslims Marched with Christians across Europe's Battlegrounds* (Cambridge, MA: Harvard University Press, 2011).

43 The notion of a startling historical resistance stopping an implacable advance is still found in the literature, see Frankopan, *The Silk Roads*, 90, but it does not accurately represent the context, see Cardini, *Europe and Islam*, 4–9.

44 Cardini, *Europe and Islam*, 27, but see also, 27–8, 31, 43 and 56–7.

45 Today, some Muslims see this as inevitable, claiming that a *hadith* prophesied the fall of Constantinople (Caesar's city) to Islam (for a discussion, see https://www.islamweb.net/en/fatwa/290122/the-commander-referred-to-in-the-hadeeth-you-will-conquer-constantinople-). This is the *hadith* about Costantiniyya (Constantinople), which reads: 'Verily you shall conquer Constantinople. What a wonderful leader will he be, and what a wonderful army will that army be!' Some narrations add: 'The first army that goes on expedition to Constantinople will be forgiven.' However, contemporary biographers of Mehmed II who conquered the city do not draw a parallel to this hadith, which most traditional Muslim commentators on the *hadith* collections considered to be apocalyptic and speak about the end times when the 'Romans' (Europeans) were believed to join the Muslims in the fight against the anti-Christ, but the former would in the end betray the Muslims, who would then take Constantinople in overcoming their former allies. Apocalyptic interpretation follows a *hadith* in the Salah Muslim *hadith* collection (available at https://sunnah.com/muslim/54/44) which explicitly makes the conquest apocalyptic and conducted by an army which has just left from Medina (of which one third enacts the conquest after one third has died in the battle with the Romans, and one third ran away), as such Mehmed's conquest does not fit the alleged prophesy (for various other hadith on Constantinople's conquest, which typically refer to an apocalyptic period, see https://sunnah. com/search?q=constantinople). If this hadith was associated with anyone by traditional interpreters, the connection was to the Umayyad caliph Yazid Ibn Mua'wiyah (646–83) who was the first to attempt a conquest of the city. The apocalyptic interpretation remained the main one until the nineteenth century. Further, the *hadith* prophesying the fall of Constantinople is not in the *hadith* collections considered to be the six most authentic or reliable ones, though it is widely accepted. However, other *hadith* do refer to this conquest, including one *hadith* in the important al-Bukhari collection, known as 'The Fighting against Ar-Rum' (the Romans or Byzantines), available at https:// sunnah.com/bukhari/56/137. My thanks to Mohamed Gamal Abdelnour, 'Personal Correspondence' (7 July 2020) for some of this information. For a discussion of some contemporary resonances, see Paul Hedges and Mohamed Gamal Abdelnour, 'Hagia Sophia: The Meaning of Ottoman Symbolism', *RSIS Commentary* CO210159, available at: https://www.rsis.edu.sg/rsis-publication/rsis/hagia-sophia-the-meaning-of-ottoman-symbolism/#.X4lMydMzZhE. See also Paul Hedges, 'Hagia Sophia as Mosque or Museum: Religion in a Post-Secular World', *RSIS Commentary* CO20142, available at: https://www.rsis.edu.sg/wp-content/uploads/2020/07/CO20142.pdf, and Hedges, *Understanding Religion*, 406–07.

46 For an accessible overview, linking to contemporary Islamophobic accounts that inaccurately paint the 1683 Battle of Vienna as a Christian–Muslim battle, see Dag Herbjørnsrud, 'The Real Battle of Vienna', *Aoen*, 24 July 2018,

available at https://aeon.co/essays/the-battle-of-vienna-was-not-a-fight-between-cross-and-crescent.

47 Adam Francisco, 'Luther's Knowledge of and Attitude towards Islam', in *The Routledge Reader in Christian-Muslim Relations*, 129–53 (129).

48 Francisco, 'Luther's Knowledge', 133.

49 Francisco, 'Luther's Knowledge', 134.

50 Francisco, 'Luther's Knowledge', 142.

51 Francisco, 'Luther's Knowledge', 132.

52 The perceptions of Sunni, Shia, and other Islamic traditions were different, so this represents a Sunni perception. While the Mongols had sacked the great cultural centre of Baghdad in 1258 and taken many Muslim lands, both the Turkic and Mongol conquerors of Islam had, in time, converted, with their descendants founding significant Islamic dynasties (Ottomans and Moghuls, respectively). As such, barring the loss of Al-Andalusia, territories conquered by Islam's first three dynasties had been held, and Muslim-majority lands extended further.

53 See Hedges, *Preparation and Fulfilment*.

54 See Abdullah Saeed, 'Secularism, State Neutrality, and Islam', in *The Oxford Handbook of Secularism*, ed. Phil Zuckerman and John Shook (Oxford: Oxford University Press, 2017), 188–200.

55 Mona Siddiqui, *Christians, Muslims, and Jesus* (New Haven, CT: Yale University Press, 2013).

56 See Hedges, 'The Contemporary Context', 27–9; and Hedges, *Understanding Religion*, 313 textbox 13.8.

CHAPTER FIVE

1 In Black studies, and more widely, it is argued that 'Blacks' should be treated the same way we treat other racialized groups and so capitalized, see Lori Tharps, 'The Case for Black With a Capital B', *New York Times* (18 November 2014), https://www.nytimes.com/2014/11/19/opinion/the-case-for-black-with-a-capital-b.html. Some may ask why 'white' is not also given an uppercase, as it is also a racialized category. The answer is partly that 'white' is racialized in a different way, with 'whites' not typically being treated as a monolithic racial group (like Blacks, Chinese, Semites, etc.) (notwithstanding white supremacist ideologues). Of course, there is no 'Black', 'white', yellow', 'brown', 'red', or other race, and so there will be some arbitrary sense in how groupism operates to denote racial categories and how our discourse of anti-racism responds to this. Our use of 'Black', but 'white', may be said to be because BLM, see German Lopez, 'Why You Should Stop Saying "All Lives Matter," Explained in 9 Different Ways', *Vox* (11 July 2016), available at https://www.vox.com/2016/7/11/12136140/black-all-lives-matter.

2 See Nasar Meer, 'Racialization and Religion: Race, Culture and Difference in the Study of Antisemitism and Islamophobia', *Ethnic and Racial Studies* 36.3 (2013): 385–98.

3 Herein, Enlightenment refers to primarily late seventeenth- and eighteenth-century intellectual, social, and political developments. Many use it more widely as an intellectual movement developing from even the late sixteenth century. Our usage is not intended to define precisely what the Enlightenment is, nor when it took place, but to delineate aspects of interest in this text. For a description and references, see Paul Hedges, *Understanding Religion: Theories and Methods for Studying Religiously Diverse Societies* (Berkeley: University of California Press, 2021), 375–76 textbox 16.1.

4 Some argue it can be traced to the Middle Ages or antiquity, but the discourse on race then is different from the modern form. See Geraldine Heng, *The Invention of Race in the European Middle Ages* (Cambridge: Cambridge University Press, 2018).

5 Steve Garner, *Racisms: An Introduction*, 2nd edn (London: Sage, 2017).

6 Kwame Antony Appiah, 'Reconstructing Racial Identities', *Research in African Literatures* 27.3 (1996): 68–72.

7 Adam Hochman, 'Racialization: A Defense of the Concept', *Ethnic and Racial Studies* 42.8 (2019): 1245–62 (1249).

8 National Human Genome Research Institute, 'Genetics vs. Genomics Fact Sheet' (2018), available at https://www.genome.gov/about-genomics/fact-sheets/Genetics-vs-Genomics (accessed 18 November 2019).

9 See Wilson Jeremiah Moses, *Afrotopia: The Roots of African American Popular History* (New York: Cambridge University Press, 1998), 20; and Anita Kalunta-Crumpton, 'The Inclusion of the Term "Color" in Any Racial Label Is Racist. Is It Not?', *Ethnicities* 20.1 (2020): 115–35.

10 Gordon Allport, *The Nature of Prejudice* (Reading, MA: Addison-Wesley, [1954] 1979), 110.

11 Allport, *The Nature of Prejudice*, 125.

12 Ibram Kendi, *How to Be an Antiracist* (London: Bodley Head, 2019), 37.

13 Allport, *The Nature*, 192.

14 Kendi, *How to Be an Antiracist*, 238.

15 Joe Feagin and Debra Van Ausdale, *The First R: How Children Learn Race and Racism* (2001), have shown that children as young as 3 may exhibit learnt racism, and cite evidence that white children have preferred their own racial group, while low levels of cross-race friendship (in certain Western contexts) may be suggestive that such prejudice is readily adopted (11). Nevertheless, in other cultural contexts, it is normal to see cross-cultural and cross-racial friendships.

16 Francisco Bethencourt, *Racisms: From the Crusades to the Twentieth Century* (Princeton, NJ: Princeton University Press, 2013), 372–3.

17 Xiaomei Chen, *Occidentalism: A Theory of Counter-Discourse in Post-Mao China* (New York: Oxford University Press, 1995). See also Hedges, *Understanding Religion*, 167 textbox 7.4.

18 See Steve Fenton, *Ethnicity*, 2nd edn (Cambridge: Polity Press, 2010).

19 Rohit Barot and John Bird, 'Racialization: The Genealogy and Critique of a Concept', *Ethnic and Racial Studies* 24.4 (2001): 601–18.

20 Hochman, 'Racialization: A Defense', 1250.

21 See Rogers Brubaker, 'Ethnicity without groups', *Archives Européenes de Sociologie* 43.2 (2002): 163–89; Ien Ang, 'Beyond Chinese Groupism: Chinese Australians between Assimilation, Multiculturalism and Diaspora', *Ethnic and Racial Studies* 37.7 (2014): 1184–96; and Andreas Wimmer, 'Elementary Strategies of Ethnic Boundary Making', *Ethnic and Racial Studies* 31.6 (2008): 1025–55.

22 Economist, 'Who Is a Jew?', *The Economist* (11 January 2014), available at https://www.economist.com/international/2014/01/11/who-is-a-jew.

23 Kendi, *How to Be an Antiracist*.

24 In terms of understanding prejudice, we are all aware of stereotypes but our buy-in to these may be more or less committed. It may be an explicit prejudice we hold, or a trigger in certain circumstances may incline us to accept some stereotypes at particular times. Hence prejudice is more of a scale than a simple in–out, pro–anti, situation. Again, as our discussion of violence noted, it is rarely so simple that people are either perpetrators or victims. As people learn more about racism, or antisemitism and Islamophobia, they may be on a journey from being prejudiced to being anti-racist. Potential allies may be alienated if they feel that they are castigated as pro-prejudice for not being deemed sufficiently anti-racist. This is not to deny that it is necessary to be anti-racist because systemic racism exists in institutions and world views (cultural and structural violence *pace* Johan Galtung) and simply seeing oneself as non-racist while this persists is not enough; rather, racism and prejudice need to be fought against. Yet, surely, given the many forms and types of racism and prejudice, we are all on a path towards anti-racializing (ourselves and our societies), rather than there being fixed and static boxes that we can clearly demarcate that are either racist or anti-racist (prejudicial or anti-prejudicial). See Smithsonian, 'Talking about Race', *National Museum of African American History and Culture* (n.d.), https://nmaahc.si.edu/learn/talking-about-race/topics/being-antiracist.

25 Biko Agozino, *Black Women and the Criminal Justice System: Towards the Decolonisation of Victimisation* (London: Ashgate, 1997).

26 Indeed, the academic study of religion has been argued to be embedded in structural racism, with whiteness as a norm, see Christopher Driscoll and Monica Miller, *Method as Identity: Manufacturing Distance in the Academic Study of Religion* (Lanham, MD: Lexington, 2019). This applies to academia more widely, including some parts that may see themselves as 'critical', see Hedges, *Understanding Religion*, chapter 7, but also chapters 5 and 18. On Eurocentrism, see Syed Farid Alatas, 'Academic Dependency and the Global Division of Labour in the Social Sciences', *Current Sociology* 5.1 (2003): 599–613.

27 Bethencourt, *Racisms*.

28 Allport, *The Nature*, 109.

29 See David Nirenberg, *Neighbouring Faiths: Christianity, Islam and Judaism in the Middle Ages and Today* (Chicago, IL: University of Chicago Press, 2016), 176–7. Notably, this is a reversal of traditional Christian baptismal theology

which is seen to make people anew, following especially Paul's claim that in Christ other identities are erased (Gal. 3.28).

30 See Bethencourt, *Racisms*, 252.

31 Immanuel Kant, *Lectures on Anthropology* (Cambridge: Cambridge University Press, [1781–2] 2013), 301–3. See Katrin Flikschuh and Lea Ypi, eds, *Kant and Colonialism: Historical and Critical Perspectives* (Oxford: Oxford University Press, 2014).

32 See Ellis Monk, 'The Color of Punishment: African Americans, Skin Tone, and the Criminal Justice System', *Ethnic and Racial Studies* 42.10 (2019): 1593–612.

33 See, for one case study, Syed Hussein Alatas, *The Myth of the Lazy Native: A Study of the Image of the Malays, Filipinos and Javanese from the 16th to the 20th Century and Its Function in the Ideology of Colonial Capitalism* (New York: Routledge, [1977] 2010).

34 See Isabelle Winder, 'Botswana Is Humanity's Ancestral Home, Claims Major Study – Well, Actually …', *The Conversation* (31 October 2019), available at https://theconversation.com/botswana-is-humanitys-ancestral-home-claims-major-study-well-actually-126130.

35 See Felipe Fernandez-Armesto, *So You Think You're Human?: A Brief History of Humankind* (Oxford: Oxford University Press, 2005).

36 See Hedges, *Understanding Religion*, 433.

37 See Angela Saini, *Superior: The Return of Race Science* (Boston: Beacon Press, 2019), 159–60. There have been recent discussions on differences of racial intelligence in some circles, often under the guise of showing that no questions are off limits. However, while this needs to be discussed – to show that no evidential basis exists for claims of race-based IQ differentials – such discussions can be a somewhat covert way to promote racist ideologies while pretending to simply be having open discussion of all questions. The discursive framing of such discussions is therefore very important. Indeed, even opening up the discussion may be a way to suggest that different human races exist.

38 Ham, Shem, and Japheth were sons of Noah, but Ham was cursed by their father to be a servant of the others (Gen. 9.18-27). Ham was early on associated with Canaan, but the three sons have become, in modern times, associated with three distinct racialized groups: Ham with Black Africans, Shem with the Semitic peoples, and Japheth with Eurasians. Importantly, the etymology of the Hebrew term for Ham is not innately linked to Africa or the colour black (though it may have associations with something being burnt, but ash can be white in colouration), and certainly not with a racialized understanding of the latter.

39 See, e.g. David Goldenberg, *The Curse of Ham: Race and Slavery in Early Judaism, Christianity, and Islam* (Princeton, NJ: Princeton University Press, 2003).

40 William David Hart, 'Theorizing Race and Religion: Du Boi, Cox, and Fanon', in *Religion, Theory, Critique: Classic and Contemporary Approaches and Methodologies*, ed. Richard King (New York: Columbia University Press,

2017), 563–71 (564). See also Theodore Vial, *Modern Religion, Modern Race* (Oxford: Oxford University Press, 2016).

41 See Michael Hanchard, *The Spectre of Race: How Discrimination Haunts Western Democracy* (Princeton, NJ: Princeton University Press, 2017).

42 See Tomoko Masuzawa, *The Invention of World Religions* (Chicago, IL: University of Chicago Press, 2005), 238–9. More widely on connections of race, civilization, and religion, see Hedges, *Understanding Religion*, 174–77.

43 Bethencourt, *Racisms*, 47.

44 See Jennifer Guglielmo and Salvatore Salerno, eds, *Are Italians White?: How Race Is Made in America* (New York: Routledge, 2012).

45 David Hume, *Essays, Moral, Political, and Literary* (Indianapolis: Liberty Fund, [1777] 1987), 208 n.10.

46 Peter Park, *Africa, Asia and the History of Philosophy: Racism in the Formation of the Philosophical Canon, 1780–1830* (Albany: State University of New York Press, 2013).

47 See Park, *Africa, Asia and the History*, xii–xiii, 92–5; and Bryan Van Norden, *Taking Back Philosophy: A Multicultural Manifesto* (New York: Columbia University Press, 2017).

48 See, e.g. John Hobsbawm, *The Eastern Origins of Western Civilisation* (Cambridge: Cambridge University Press, 2004); Jürgen Osterhammel, *Unfabling the East* (Princeton: Princeton University Press, 2018); and Heiner Roetz, 'The Influence of Foreign Knowledge on Eighteenth Century European Secularism', in *Religion and Secularity: Transformations and Transfers of Religious Discourses in Europe and Asia*, eds Marion Eggert and Lucian Hölscher (Leiden: Brill, 2013), 9–33.

49 Hallam Stevens, 'Retracing the Spice Road: How Southeast Asia Shaped Europe's Tastes', lecture at the National Museum of Singapore (22 April 2017), available at https://www.roots.sg/-/media/Roots/Images/resources/videos/ historia-sg/historiasg-lecture-4-summary-report.pdf?la=en&hash=47BC4365 28C5D13ED0599D6832710FE346819074, video available at https://www. youtube.com/watch?v=BdoSz8V4hfY.

50 See Kenneth Pomeranz, *The Great Divergence: China, Europe, and the Making of the Modern World Economy* (Princeton, NJ: Princeton University Press, 2000); and Prasannan Parthasarathi, *Why Europe Grew Rich and Asia Did Not: Global Economic Divergence, 1600–1850* (New York: Cambridge University Press, 2011).

51 See, variously, https://www.nytimes.com/interactive/2019/08/14/magazine/ slavery-capitalism.html; https://www.taxjustice.net/2020/06/09/slavery- compensation-uk-questions/; https://www.runnymedetrust.org/blog/ why-we-need-to-talk-about-slavery; and https://www.nytimes.com/ interactive/2019/08/14/magazine/racial-wealth-gap.html.

52 See David Nirenberg, *Anti-Judaism: The History of a Way of Thinking* (New York: W. W. Norton, 2013), 325–60.

53 Nirenberg, *Anti-Judaism*, 338.

54 See Hedges, *Understanding Religion*, chapter 16.

55 Erica Benner, 'Nationalism: Intellectual Origins', in *The Oxford Handbook of the History of Nationalism*, ed. John Breuilly (Oxford: Oxford University Press, 2013), 36–55.

56 Nirenberg, *Anti-Judaism*, 364.

57 Nirenberg, *Anti-Judaism*, 382, see 377–80.

58 Davis, Kenneth C., 'God and Country: The Image of the United States as a Bastion of Religious Tolerance Is Reassuring – and Utterly at Odds with the Historical Record', *Smithsonian* 41.6 (October 2010), available at https://link. gale.com/apps/doc/A243456956/ITOF?u=nantecun&sid=ITOF&xid=dae7bca4.

59 See Paul Hedges and Liu Yue, 'Interreligious Studies and Law: Decolonizing Freedom of Religion and Belief', in *Georgetown Companion to Interreligious Studies*, ed. Lucinda Mosher (Washington, DC: Georgetown University Press, 2022).

60 See Hedges, *Understanding Religion*, chapter 7.

61 Not all dissenters were equally accepted, and 2019 marked only the second time a Quaker held the role of Professor of Theology at a British University, though they had not been technically barred from most posts for well over a century. While SDC in theory admitted anyone, the perception of it as a priestly training college meant that, until around the 1950s, it did not start admitting a greater demographic variety, meaning Jews, Catholics, women, and its first Buddhist, the noted activist Sulak Sivaraksa. William Price, 'Personal Correspondence with Author' (26 March 2020).

62 Paul Mendes-Flohr and Jehuda Reinharz, eds, *The Jew in the Modern World: A Documentary History*, 3rd edn (Oxford: Oxford University Press, 2011), 167.

63 Deborah Lipstadt, *Antisemitism Here and Now* (London: Scribe, 2019), 225–6.

64 Frantz Fanon, *Black Skin, White Masks*, trans. Charles Markmann (London: Pluto Press, [1952] 1986), 122.

65 Golash-Boza, *Race and Racism*, 54.

66 Ansel Brown, 'Common Bonds and Experiences of the African and Jewish Diasporas', ISGAP Critical Antisemitism Summer Institute, St John's College, Oxford (17 July 2019). See Michael Lerner and Cornel West, *Jews and Blacks: A Dialogue on Race, Religion, and Culture in America* (New York: Plume, 1996).

67 Lipstadt, *Antisemitism Here and Now*, 69.

68 James Baldwin, 'Negroes Are Anti-Semitic Because They're Anti-White', *New York Times* 9 April 1967, available at https://archive.nytimes.com/www. nytimes.com/books/98/03/29/specials/baldwin-antisem.html?mcubz=0.

69 The film *Fiddler on the Roof* is based on the short stories about the simple farmer Tevye the Dairyman written by Sholem Rabinovitch (1858–1925, pen name Sholem Aleichem) who was born in Ukraine. They are considered, though fictional and comedic, to resonate with the experience of the Shtetl life in the late nineteenth and early twentieth centuries.

70 Bethencourt, *Racisms*, 314.

71 Erin G. Carlston, *Double Agents: Espionage, Literature, and Liminal Citizens* (New York: Columbia University Press, 2013).

72 Christopher E. Forth, 'Intellectuals, Crowds and the Body Politics of the Dreyfus Affair', *Historical Reflections/Réflexions Historiques* 24.1 (Spring 1998): 63–91 (65).

73 Forth, 'Intellectuals, Crowds', 81, quoting Marcel Braunschvig, *L'Antisimitisme* (Cahors: impr. de A. Coueslant, 1902), 5.

74 See Esther Webman, *The Global Impact of the Protocols of the Elders of Zion: A Century-Old Myth* (Abingdon: Routledge, 2011).

75 See Walter Laqueur, *The Changing Face of Anti-Semitism* (Oxford: Oxford University Press, 2008).

76 See Michele Battini, Noor Mazhar and Isabella Vergnano, *Socialism of Fools: Capitalism and Modern Anti-Semitism* (New York: Columbia University Press, 2016).

77 Bethencourt, *Racisms*, 327.

78 Nirenberg, *Anti-Judaism*, 456.

79 See David Patterson, *Anti-Semitism and Its Metaphysical Origins* (Cambridge: Cambridge University Press, 2015).

80 Nirenberg, *Anti-Judaism*, 458.

81 Bethencourt, *Racisms*, 321.

82 See Friedrich Max Müller, *Rig-Veda Sanhita, the Sacred Hymns of the Brahmans*, 6 vols. (London: Trübner, 1849–74).

83 Bethencourt, *Racisms*, 325, 332–3.

84 See Michael Burleigh and Wolfgang Lieppermann, *The Racial State: Germany, 1933–1945* (Cambridge: Cambridge University Press, 1991); and Peter Longerich, *Holocaust: The Nazi Persecution and Murder of the Jews* (Oxford: Oxford University Press, 2010).

85 Bethencourt, *Racisms*, 331–2.

86 Certainly, a perceived decline in terms of the status/power/wealth of perceived 'white' (who gets to decide who is white?) ethnic majorities lays the seeds for right-wing racialized nationalism and populism, see Eric Kauffman, *Whiteshift: Populism, Immigration, and the Future of White Majorities* (New York: Abrams Press, 2019). On Murray's book, see Murtaza Hussain, 'The Far Right Is Obsessed with a Book about Muslims Destroying Europe. Here's What It Gets Wrong', *The Intercept* (25 December 2018), available at https://theintercept.com/2018/12/25/strange-death-of-europe-douglas-murray-review/.

Interlude 2

1 Roger Ballard, 'Islam and the Construction of Europe', in *Muslims in the Margin: Political Responses to the Presence of Islam in Western Europe*, ed. W.

A. R. Sahdid and P. S. van Koningsveld (Kampen: Kok Pharos, 1996), 15–51. See also, Denis Lacorne, *The Limits of Tolerance: Enlightenment Values and Religious Fanaticism* (New York: Columbia University Press, 2019), 187.

2 See Robert Michael, *Holy Hatred: Christianity, Antisemitism, and the Holocaust* (Basingstoke: Palgrave Macmillan, 2006), 153–64.

3 See, for example, Frederic Raphael, *Anti-Semitism* (London: Biteback, 2015), 127–8.

4 David Nirenberg, *Anti-Judaism: The History of a Way of Thinking* (New York: W. W. Norton, 2013), 458–9.

5 Nirenberg, *Anti-Judaism*, 459.

6 Deborah Lipstadt, *The Eichmann Trial* (London: Penguin, 2011), xiv–xv.

7 See Hannah Arendt, *Eichmann in Jerusalem: A Report on the Banality of Evil*, rev. and expanded edn (London: Penguin, 1994), 56–111; Lucy Dawidowicz, ed., *A Holocaust Reader* (West Orange, NJ: Behrman House, 1976), 35–140; and Gordon Horwitz, *In the Shadow of Death: Living Outside the Gates of Mauthausen* (London: I.B. Tauris, 1991), 8–22.

8 Adolf Hitler, 'From Hitler's Reichstag address, January 30, 1939', in *A Holocaust Reader*, 32–3 (33).

9 Herman Göring, 'Göring Commission to Heydrich July 31, 1941', in *A Holocaust Reader*, 72–3 (73).

10 'Minutes of the Wannsee Conference January 20, 1942', in *A Holocaust Reader*, 73–82 (78 and 82).

11 See BBC, 'The Wannsee Conference', *Witness History* (2012), available at https://www.bbc.co.uk/programmes/p00mwzb7.

12 See Lipstadt, *The Eichmann Trial*.

13 See Martin Gilbert, *Auschwitz and the Allies* (London: Rainbird, 1981), 13–20.

14 See Deborah Lipstadt, *Antisemitism: Here and Now* (London: Scribe, 2019); Gideon Hausner, *Justice in Jerusalem* (London: Nelson, 1967), 69–97; Gilbert, *Auschwitz and the Allies*, 231–9; Filip Müller, *Auschwitz Inferno: The Testimony of a Sonderkommando* (London: Routledge and Kegan Paul, 1979); Eugene Davidson, *The Trial of the Germans: An Account of the Twenty-Two Defendants before the International Military Tribunal at Nuremberg* (Columbia: University of Missouri Press, [1966] 1997); Ernest Klee, Willi Dressen and Volker Riess, eds, *'The Good Old Days': The Holocaust as Seen by Its Perpetrators and Bystanders*, trans. Deborah Burnstone (New York: Free Press, 1991); and Elie Wiesel, *Night*, trans. Marion Wiesel (New York: Hill and Wang, [1958 as *La Nuit*] 2006).

15 See Michael, *Holy Hatred*, 166–76.

16 Martin Sasse, *Martin Luther über die Juden. Weg mit ihnen!* (Freiburg: Sturmhut-Verl, 1938), 2, cited in Hans-Martin Kirn, *Hebrew Texts in Jewish, Christian and Muslim Surroundings* (Leiden: Brill, 2018), 188.

17 Marvin Perry and Frederick M. Schweitzer *Antisemitism: Myth and Hate from Antiquity to the Present* (London: Palgrave Macmillan, 2002), 83, citing a

quotation in Dennis Prager and Joseph Telushkin, *Why the Jews? The Reason for Antisemitism* (New York: Simon & Shuster, 1983), 107.

18   Michael, *Holy Hatred*, 159 and 161, citing Dietrich Bonhoeffer, *Gesämmelte Schriften* (Munich: Chr. Kaiser Verlag Munchen, 1965), 2:49–50; and Karl Barth, *Church Dogmatics* (Edinburgh: T&T Clark, 1957), 2:208–9, respectively.

19   Simon Levis Sullam, *The Italian Executioners: The Genocide of the Jews of Italy* (Princeton, NJ: Princeton University Press, 2018), 3. On the traditional view, see Jonathan Steinberg, *All or Nothing: The Axis and the Holocaust 1941–43* (London: Routledge, 1990). Sullam's account does not deny that a stark distinction existed between the situation of Jews under German- and Italian-controlled territories, but many Italians were deeply antisemitic and a purge of Jews occurred in Italy in the latter stages of the war. As such, we need to be aware of the myth-making process of the 'good Italians' (*italiani brava gente*) in this context (Sullam, *The Italian Executioners*, 134–8).

20   Robert Lifton, *The Nazi Doctors: Medical Killing and the Psychology of Genocide* (New York: Basic Books, 2000), 22–3.

21   See Lifton, *The Nazi Doctors*, 193–213.

22   See Horowitz, *In the Shadow of Death*, 11–12, referencing Yehuda Bauer, 'The Death Marches, January-May 1945', *Modern Judaism* 3 (1983): 1–21 (7 and 9).

23   Anon., 'The Righteous Among the Nations', Yad Vashem (The World Holocaust Remembrance Centre) (2020), available at: www.yadvashem.org/righteous.html.

CHAPTER SIX

1   Reckoning with the Holocaust and antisemitism was not, however, always done quickly after the war. In Germany, after the Nuremberg trials were over, it was often not raised as many former Nazis were reintegrated into society. A wider discussion and a working through of history (*vergangenheitsaufarbeitung*) occurred in phases. Some have dated its real beginnings to the questioning of the 1960s when a younger generation asked about their parents' involvement, others suggest that it began in earnest in 1979 in the wake of the showing of the American drama series *Holocaust*, while others note the mid-1990s exhibition on the crimes of the Wehrmacht (general German army, rather than the SS or other groups). Notably, the former Communist East Germany investigated this more readily than the former democratic West Germany. For a study on the importance of this, see Susan Nieman, *Learning from the Germans: Race and the Memory of Evil* (New York: Farrar, Straus and Giroux, 2019).

2   Deborah Lipstadt, *Antisemitism Here and Now* (London: Scribe, 2019).

3   We will use Israel–Palestine to refer to the territory that is today encompassed by the State of Israel and the occupied Palestinian territories. Israel or the State of Israel signifies that nation state. Palestine is used for the areas pre-1948. United Nations resolutions recognize two states: Israel and Palestine. Some

sources employ Palestine–Israel to give priority to the rights of Palestinians as the 'native occupants'. As with other terms, we employ standard usages, which are not intended to indicate any political stance.

4 See Patrick Kingsley, 'Anti-Semitism Is Back, from the Left, Right and Islamist Extremes: Why?', *New York Times* (4 April 2019), available at https://www.nytimes.com/2019/04/04/world/europe/antisemitism-europe-united-states.html.

5 See, for instance, Bernard Harrison, *The Resurgence of Anti-Semitism: Jews, Israel, and Liberal Opinion* (Lanham, MD: Rowman and Littlefield, 2006), 1–25. Though, notably, the term 'new' and antisemitism have been used variously, see Walter Laqueur, *The Changing Face of Antisemitism* (Oxford: Oxford University Press, 2006), 5–7.

6 We will see some examples below, but one movement currently gaining traction with both what might be seen as traditionally more 'right-wing' (populist/nationalist) and 'left-wing' (progressive/socially liberal) people and groups is the QAnon conspiracy theory. QAnon has clear antisemitic tropes, see Ben Sales, 'QAnon an old form of anti-Semitism in a new package, say experts', *The Times of Israel* (20 September 2020), available at https://www.timesofisrael.com/qanon-is-an-old-form-of-anti-semitism-in-a-new-package-say-experts/. On traction with what may be seen as more progressive groups, see Jules Evans, 'Nazi Hippies: When the New Age and Far Right Overlap', *GEN* (4 September 2020), https://gen.medium.com/nazi-hippies-when-the-new-age-and-far-right-overlap-d1a6ddcd7be4.

7 See Bernd Riegert, 'Anti-Semitism on the Rise in the EU', *DW* (14 October 2019), available at https://www.dw.com/en/anti-semitism-on-the-rise-in-the-eu/a-50820057; and Anon., 'France Anti-Semitism: Jewish Graves Desecrated near Strasbourg', *BBC* (19 February 2019), available at https://www.bbc.com/news/world-europe-47289129.

8 In October 2018, a far-right extremist killed eleven worshippers at the Pittsburgh Tree of Life synagogue. In April 2019, a far-right gunman killed one and injured three at the Congregation Chabad synagogue in Poway, California. More attacks occurred at the end of 2019, see Nigel Chiwaya, 'It's Not Just New York: Anti-Jewish Attacks Are Part of a Wave of "More Violent" Hate Crimes' (4 January 2020), available at https://www.nbcnews.com/news/us-news/anti-semitic-attacks-more-violent-hate-crimes-new-york-n1110036.

9 Lipstadt, *Antisemitism Here*, 29, 35.

10 Lipstadt, *Antisemitism Here*, 35–41.

11 See Mark Gardner, 'David Icke's Ages Old New Age Antisemitism', *Community Security Trust* (5 January 2017), available at https://cst.org.uk/news/blog/2017/01/05/david-ickes-ages-old-new-age-antisemitism. Icke himself denies being antisemitic and sometimes claims that ordinary Jews are also affected, but his targets seem to be overwhelmingly Jewish and Jewish/Israeli symbolism abounds in what he demonizes.

12 See note 6 above, also 13 below.

13 See Sasha Polakow-Suransky, 'The Ruthlessly Effective Rebranding of Europe's New Far Right', *The Guardian* (1 November 2016), available at https://www.theguardian.com/world/2016/nov/01/the-ruthlessly-effective-rebranding-of-

europes-new-far-right. On the environment, see Bernhard Forchtner, *The Far Right and the Environment: Politics, Discourse and Communication* (New York: Routledge, 2020); and also Marc Hudson, 'Beware Far-Right Arguments Disguised as Environmentalism', *Conversation* (28 March 2020), available at https://theconversation.com/beware-far-right-arguments-disguised-as-environmentalism-134830.

14 See Laqueur, *The Changing Face*, viii, 131.

15 Lauren Fox, 'The Hatemonger Next Door', *Salon* (29 September 2013), available at https://www.salon.com/2013/09/29/the_hatemonger_next_door/.

16 Lipstadt, *Antisemitism Here*, 29–33.

17 See Commission for Religious Relations with the Jews, 'A Reflection on Theological Questions Pertaining to Catholic-Jewish Relations on the Occasion of the 50th Anniversary of "Nostra Aetate" (No. 4)' (10 December 2015),' available at http://www.vatican.va/roman_curia/pontifical_councils/chrstuni/relations-jews-docs/rc_pc_chrstuni_doc_20151210_ebraismo-nostra-aetate_en.html; and Nostra Aetate 4, available at http://www.vatican.va/archive/hist_councils/ii_vatican_council/documents/vat-ii_decl_19651028_nostra-aetate_en.html. But see Chapter 3, note 14 on Jewish understandings of the covenantal relationship.

18 See Tom Heneghan, 'Retired Pope Benedict Accused of Anti-Semitism after Article on Christians and Jews', *National Catholic Reporter* (6 August 2018), available at https://www.ncronline.org/news/vatican/retired-pope-benedict-accused-anti-semitism-after-article-christians-and-jews.

19 On some problematics of the term fundamentalism, see Paul Hedges, *Understanding Religion: Theories and Methods for Studying Religiously Diverse Societies* (Berkeley: University of California Press, 2021), 349–52, and on literal textual interpretation, *ibid.*, 126. See also Christopher van der Krogt, 'The Rise of Fundamentalisms', in *Controversies in Contemporary Religion*, ed. Paul Hedges (Santa Barbara, CA: Praeger, 2014), vol. 3, 1–38.

20 See Anon., 'Mel Gibson's Great Passion', *Zenit* (6 March 2003), available at https://zenit.org/articles/mel-gibson-s-great-passion/.

21 See Chrissy Stroop, 'Taking Evangelical Support of Israel at Face Value Is a Terrible Idea: A Response', *Religion Dispatches* (23 September 2019), available at https://rewire.news/religion-dispatches/2019/09/23/taking-evangelical-support-of-israel-at-face-value-is-a-terrible-idea-a-response/; and Christina Maza, 'Trump Will Start the End of the World, Claim Evangelicals Who Support Him', *Newsweek* (12 January 2018), available at https://www.newsweek.com/trump-will-bring-about-end-worldevangelicals-end-times-779643.

22 Deborah Lipstadt, *History on Trial: My Day in Court with a Holocaust Denier* (New York: Harper Perennial, 2006), dramatized in the film *Denial* (2016), and https://www.hdot.org/trial-materials/witness-statements-and-documents/.

23 See Deborah Lipstadt, *Denying the Holocaust: The Growing Assault on Truth and Memory* (New York: Plume, 1994).

24 *ICRC Bulletin* 25 (1 February 1978), 11.

25 Lipstadt, *Denying the Holocaust*, 111–12.

26 Lipstadt, *Denying the Holocaust*, 112–14.

27 Lipstadt, *Denying the Holocaust*, 157–82.

28 See Lipstadt, *History on Trial*, 22–3.

29 See https://www.youtube.com/watch?v=yH7ktvUWaYo, accessed 28 October 2020.

30 Dave Rich, *The Left's Jewish Problem: Jeremy Corbyn, Israel and Anti-Semitism*, 2nd edn (London: Biteback, 2018), 270–1.

31 Lipstadt, *Denying the Holocaust*, 3.

32 Lipstadt, *Denying the Holocaust*, 110.

33 More broadly, on early twentieth-century leftist antisemitism, see Laqueur, *The Changing Face*, 171–80.

34 Rich, *The Left's Jewish*, 278–9. The complete group was: Rothschild (Jewish), Rockefeller (Baptist), Morgan (Episcopalian), Carnegie (Presbyterian), Warburg (Jewish), Aleister Crowley (Satanist).

35 Lipstadt, *Antisemitism Here*, 59–61. See also the useful analysis in Ben Gidley, Brendan Mcgeever and David Feldman, 'Labour and Antisemitism: A Crisis Misunderstood', *The Political Quarterly* 91.2 (2020), 413–21 (419).

36 Lipstadt, *Antisemitism Here*, 60. However, being 'demons' seemed to apply equally to the other bankers, and also Crowley.

37 Hirsh, *Contemporary Left*, 95–134, especially 100–1 and 119–24.

38 Lipstadt, *Antisemitism Here*, 177–8.

39 Anthony Julius, *Trials of the Diaspora* (Oxford: Oxford University Press, 2010).

40 Rich, *The Left's Jewish*, 1–3.

41 Rich, *The Left's Jewish*, 23.

42 Julius, *Trials of the Diaspora*, 441.

43 Rich, *The Left's Jewish*, 8.

44 Rich, *The Left's Jewish*, 16.

45 Nora Gold, 'Fighting Antisemitism in the Feminist Community', in *Global Antisemitism: A Crisis of Modernity*, ed. Charles Asher Small, vol. II (New York: ISGAP, 2013), 21–8 (23).

46 Hirsh, *Contemporary Left*, 118–21.

47 See Hirsh, *Contemporary Left*, 184–219. This returns us to a problematic opened up in Chapter 5 (see note 24) about being anti-racist, that either one is racist or anti-racist, with no space to be simply non-racist. While it is correct that seeking the non-racist 'middle ground' may mean at least implicit support (or lack of opposition) to structural racism, it also opens up a dangerous identity politics game of the 'good' and the 'bad' which may alienate people who may be on a journey or learning curve. It also fails to consider motive and context in people's attitudes, enforcing instead fixed, static, battle lines, which may be reminiscent of Juergensmeyer's cosmic war (see Interlude 1), or

a contestation of secular sacreds (see Interlude 1, and Hedges, *Understanding Religion* 432–35).

48 The original data has now been removed, but see https://www.channel4.com/news/factcheck/factcheck-antisemitism-political-parties.

49 It may be noted that, despite strong opposition from members of his own party, British Prime Minister Boris Johnson has felt able to ally himself in Europe with the extreme right, including fascists and even parties with Nazi links, and which has passed with barely a comment in the UK media, see Rob Merrick, 'Boris Johnson condemned for "appalling" Tory alliance with neo-Nazi and anti-Muslim parties across Europe', *The Independent* (24 October 2020), available at: https://www.independent.co.uk/news/uk/politics/boris-johnson-tory-neo-nazi-anti-islam-hitler-conservative-party-b1254794.html.

50 BBC, 'Labour Anti-Semitism: Ruling Body Backs Corbyn Expulsion Plan', https://www.bbc.com/news/uk-politics-49082083.

51 See Daniel Finn, 'Corbyn under Fire', *Jacobin* (4 September 2018), available at https://www.jacobinmag.com/2018/04/jeremy-corbyn-antisemitism-labour-party.

52 Hirsh, *Contemporary Left*, 85.

53 See Gidley et al., 'Labour and Antisemitism', who provide an excellent survey of why we would expect to see antisemitism in Labour party ranks.

54 The EHRC report (EHRC, *Investigation into antisemitism in the Labour Party*, October 2020) can be accessed here, https://www.equalityhumanrights.com/sites/default/files/investigation-into-antisemitism-in-the-labour-party.pdf. Perhaps the most shocking aspect of the publication of the EHRC report was the Labour Party's suspension of Corbyn in response to his statement in the immediate aftermath of its publication. The Party made the decision that Corbyn's suggestion that the report's allegations of antisemitism in the Labour Party had been overstated for political purposes was a disciplinary breach. The full consequences of this are still playing out. Arguably, Corbyn's words reflect, as we argue here, a failure on the left to see systemic aspects of antisemitism for what they are, a point also argued in Gidley et al., 'Labour and Antisemitism'.

55 EHRC, Investigation into antisemitism, 100.

56 Hirsh, *Contemporary Left*, 5.

57 The term refers to a prominent UK Labour politician, and former mayor of London, Ken Livingstone, who was often seen to make this response to any allegations of his being antisemitic. See David Hirsh, 'Accusations of Malicious Intent in Debates about the Palestine-Israel Conflict and about Antisemitism', *Transversal* 1 (2010), available at https://engageonline.wordpress.com/2010/10/05/david-hirsh-the-livingstone-formulation/.

58 Among the most controversial parts of this definition are the way it seems to suggest that the following are inherently antisemitic: saying that the existence of any form of the State of Israel is a racist endeavour; and any application of double standards in terms of requiring behaviour from Israel not expected, or demanded, of any other democratic nation. With the latter, in particular, critics of Israel can be accused of antisemitism if they do not also say similar

things about the behaviour of, for instance, China, the United States, Syria, Iraq, and so on. Certainly, in as far as double standards are applied to Israel it is problematic, that is, offences by the state are seen as exemplifying a special fault of that state and its ideology (which then becomes, typically, a critique of Zionism in all forms – discussed further below); however, that a critic of Israel has not critiqued every other country that may have behaved badly is not, in and of itself, evidence of antisemitism.

59 Lipstadt, *Antisemitism Here*, 207.

60 This is discussed further in Chapter 8, but on the ideology and practice see Moshe Hellinger, Isaac Hershkowitz and Bernard Susser, *Religious Zionism and the Settlement Project: Ideology, Politics, and Civil Disobedience* (Albany: State University of New York Press, 2018).

61 Theodor Herzl, *The Jewish State* (New York: Dover, 1998), 95–6, available at http://www.gutenberg.org/files/25282/25282-h/25282-h.htm.

62 Theodore Herzl, *Complete Diaries*, ed. Patai Raphael, trans. Harry Zohn (New York: Herzl Press, 1960), 88–9, cited in Derek J. Penslar, 'Herzl and the Palestinian Arabs: Myth and Counter-Myth', *Journal of Israeli History* 24.1 (2005): 65–77 (67).

63 See Elliott Horowitz, *Reckless Rites: Purim and the Legacy of Jewish Violence* (Princeton, NJ: Princeton University Press, 2006), 2–3; and Gerald Cromer, 'Amalek as Other, Other as Amalek: Interpreting a Violent Biblical Narrative', *Qualitative Sociology* 24.2 (2001): 196. See 1 Sam 15.1-3:

> And Samuel said to Saul, "The LORD sent me to anoint you king over his people Israel; now therefore hearken to the words of the LORD." Thus says the LORD of hosts, "I will punish what Am'alek did to Israel in opposing them on the way, when they came up out of Egypt. Now go and smite Am'alek, and utterly destroy all that they have; do not spare them, but kill both man and woman, infant and suckling, ox and sheep, camel and ass".

See also Deut 2.34; 3.6; 20.16-18.

64 On the ideology and development of religious Zionism, see Hellinger, Hershkowitz and Susser, *Religious Zionism*.

65 Rich, *The Left's Jewish*, 37.

66 Rich, *The Left's Jewish*, 32.

67 Richard Falk and Virginia Tilley, *Israeli Practices towards the Palestinian People and the Question of Apartheid* (Beirut: United Nations Economic and Social Commission for Western Asia, 2017).

68 See 24 January 2011 letter from the UN Secretary General's office to UN Watch, available at https://unwatch.org/un-chief-condemns-un-palestine-expert-preposterous-denial-911-terror-attacks/.

69 Jessica Elgot, 'PM Condemns UN Adviser's "Antisemitic" Cartoon', *Jewish Chronicle* (12 October 2011), available at https://www.thejc.com/news/uk-news/pm-condemns-un-adviser-s-antisemitic-cartoon-1.28337.

70 This is the view of over two hundred Jewish studies scholars including Susannah Heschel (daughter of Abraham Joshua Heschel) who is a signatory of an open letter, available at https://www.annexation.site/. See also Alon Liel, 'Trump's Plan for Palestine Looks a Lot Like Apartheid', *Foreign Policy* (27 February 2020), available at https://foreignpolicy.com/2020/02/27/trumps-plan-for-palestine-looks-a-lot-like-apartheid/.

71 Across 2019 and 2020 three elections resulted in hung parliaments indicating that not all Israeli Jews support the militancy and oppression. With the Covid-19 pandemic, a bargain saw the Blue and White political alliance led by Benny Gantz agree to share power with Netanyahu's Likud party until November 2021. However, Gantz is seemingly not resisting the settlement or annexation programme which, with US support under Trump, seems to be becoming part of the political mainstream. See Chaim Levinson and Jonathan Lis, 'Netanyahu, Gantz Agree on West Bank Annexation Proposal as Unity Deal Nears', *Haaretz* (4 July 2020), available at https://www.haaretz.com/israel-news/elections/. premium-netanyahu-gantz-agree-on-west-bank-annexation-as-unity-deal-nears-1.8745742.

72 Rich, *The Left's Jewish*, 111.

73 Rich, *The Left's Jewish*, 115–49.

74 Rich, *The Left's Jewish*, 156.

75 Rich, *The Left's Jewish*, 159–93.

76 Certainly, Marx himself saw potential benefits in European colonialism in moving countries from feudalism towards capitalism, and hence towards what he envisaged as the emancipation of the workers through history. Marxist or socialist thinkers cannot, by dint of ideology alone, claim any special anti-imperial, or decolonial, kudos or perspective over capitalism or other systems. (This is not to deny capitalism's complicity with colonialism and racism, only to note this is equally true of strands of Marxist and socialist thought too.)

77 Hirsh, *Contemporary Left*, 280.

CHAPTER SEVEN

1 There is, of course, no single 'Islamic world', see Cemil Aydin's *The Idea of the Muslim World* (Cambridge, MA: Harvard University Press, 2017).

2 S. Sayyid, 'A Measure of Islamophobia', *Islamophobia Studies Journal* 2.1 (2014): 10–25 (15–16).

3 Todd Green, *The Fear of Islam: An Introduction to Islamophobia in the West*, 2nd edn (Minneapolis, MN: Fortress Press, 2019), 9.

4 Runnymede Trust Commission on British Muslims and Islamophobia, *Islamophobia: A Challenge for Us All* (London: Runnymede Trust, 1997). Bassam Tibi argues that the term 'Islamophobia' was first used in Iran in the 1980s, 'The Islamisation of Antisemitism', Lecture, St John's College, Oxford (8 July 2019). On the eight features, see Green, *The Fear*, 12–20.

5 Runnyemede, *Islamophobia*, 4.

6 See Christopher Allen, *Islamophobia* (Aldershot: Ashgate, 2010). Tania Saeed further notes that it failed to understand 'the complexities of Islamophobia', especially its cultural and structural elements, see Tania Saeed, *Islamophobia and Securitization: Religion, Ethnicity and the Female Voice* (Cham: Palgrave Macmillan, 2016), 6.

7 See Fred Halliday, '"Islamophobia" Reconsidered', *Ethnic and Racial Studies* 22 (1999), 892–902; and Burak Erdenir, 'Islamophobia qua Racial Discrimination: Muslimophobia', in *Muslims in 21st Century Europe*, ed. Anna Triandafyllidou (Abingdon: Routledge, 2010), 27–44.

8 Green, *The Fear*, 136.

9 Lizzie Dearborn, 'More White People Arrested over Terrorism Than Any Other Ethnic Group for Second Year in a Row', *The Independent* (6 March 2020), available at https://www.independent.co.uk/news/uk/crime/white-people-terror-offences-number-ethnic-group-asian-home-office-a9376846.html.

10 GTI 2019, available at http://visionofhumanity.org/app/uploads/2019/11/GTI-2019web.pdf. See also Jenny Gross, 'Far-Right Groups Are Behind Most U.S. Terrorist Attacks, Report Finds', *The New York Times* (24 October 2020), available at: https://www.nytimes.com/2020/10/24/us/domestic-terrorist-groups.html.

11 See Khaled Beydoun, *American Islamophobia: Understanding the Roots and Rise of Fear* (Berkeley: University of California Press, 2018), 70–5.

12 See Dale Watson, 'Testimony before the Senate Select Committee on Intelligence', *FBI* (6 February 2002), available at https://archives.fbi.gov/archives/news/testimony/the-terrorist-threat-confronting-the-united-states; and Seth Jones, 'The Rise of Far-Right Extremism in the United States', *CSIS* (7 November 2018), available at https://www.csis.org/analysis/rise-far-right-extremism-united-states. Some have even seen right-wing terrorists empowered by significant political actors in the United States, see Jesse Jackson, 'Donald Trump was complicit in the plot to kidnap Michigan Gov. Gretchen Whitmer', *Chicago Sun Times* (12 October 2020), available at: https://chicago.suntimes.com/2020/10/12/21513347/michigan-right-wing-militia-kidnap-gretchen-whitmer-proud-boys-jesse-jackson. See also the references in notes 10 and 13.

13 See Art Jipson and Paul Becker, 'White Nationalism, Born in the USA, Is Now a Global Terror Threat', *The Conversation* (20 March 2019), available at https://theconversation.com/white-nationalism-born-in-the-usa-is-now-a-global-terror-threat-113825; Lizzie Dearborn, 'Far Right Poses Fastest Growing Terror Threat to UK, Head of Terror Police Says', *The Independent* (19 September 2019), available at https://www.independent.co.uk/news/uk/home-news/terror-attack-plots-uk-far-right-wing-extremism-threat-met-police-neil-basu-a9112046.html; and Mirren Gidda, 'Most Terrorists in the U.S. Are Right Wing, Not Muslim: Report', *Newsweek* (22 June 2017), available at https://www.newsweek.com/right-wing-extremism-islamist-terrorism-donald-trump-steve-bannon-628381. See also note 12.

14 Green, *The Fear*, 197–8.

15 See David C. Rapoport, 'The Fourth Wave: September 11 in the History of Terrorism', *Current History* 100.650 (2001): 419–24; and Peter Neumann, *Radicalized: New Jihadists and the Threat to the West* (London: I.B. Tauris, 2016), 9–52.

16 On this term, see Paul Hedges, 'Radicalisation: Examining a Concept, Its Use, and Abuse', *Counter Terrorist Trends and Analysis* 9.10 (2017): 12–18.

17 See Neumann, *Radicalized*, and Paul Hedges, *Understanding Religion: Theories and Methods for Studying Religiously Diverse Societies* (Berkeley: University of California Press, 2021), 361–7.

18 Robert Pape, *Dying to Win: The Strategic Logic of Suicide Terrorism* (New York: Random House, 2005). Pape's methodology has been criticized, but the links between suicide bombing and asymmetrical warfare remain, with, for instance, the Japanese Kamikaze suicide attacks in the Second World War. See James Kiras, 'Dying to Prove a Point: The Methodology of Dying to Win', *Journal of Strategic Studies* 30.2 (2007): 227–41.

19 See Sophia Rose Arjuna, *Muslims in the Western Imagination* (Oxford: Oxford University Press, 2015).

20 That Mauritius and Singapore are not Muslim-majority countries still shows the possibility for educated Muslim women to rise to such prominent roles from within their communities.

21 Green, *The Fear*, 232–3.

22 Green, *The Fear*, 231.

23 See Deepa Kumar, *Islamophobia and the Politics of Empire: The Cultural Logic of Empire* (Chicago, IL: Haymarket Books, 2012), 9.

24 See Reuven Firestone, *Jihad: The Origin of Holy War in Islam* (Oxford: Oxford University Press, 1999); and Asma Afsaruddin, *Striving in the Path of God: Jihad and Martyrdom in Islamic Thought* (Oxford: Oxford University Press, 2013). For a shorter discussion, see Hedges, *Understanding Religion*, 362.

25 See for an example Hedges, *Understanding Religion*, 166–9.

26 Roger Ballard, 'Islam and the Construction of Europe', in *Muslims in the Margin: Political Responses to the Presence of Islam in Western Europe*, ed. W. A. R. Shadid and P. S. van Koningsveld (Kampen: Kok Pharos, 1996), 15–51. See, Monique O'Connell and Eric Dursteler, *The Mediterranean World: From the Fall of Rome to the Rise of Napoleon* (Baltimore, MD: John Hopkins University Press, 2016).

27 Green, *The Fear*, 91.

28 Denis Lacorne, *The Limits of Tolerance: Enlightenment Values and Religious Fanaticism* (New York: Columbia University Press, 2019), 100.

29 See Nathan Lean, *Islamophobia Industry* (London: Pluto, 2017); and Green, *The Fear*, 205.

30 See Mohammad Hassan Khalil, *Jihad, Radicalism, and the New Atheism* (Cambridge: Cambridge University Press, 2017).

31 Samuel Osborne, 'Richard Dawkins Accused of Islamophobia after Comparing "Lovely Church Bells" to "Aggressive-Sounding Allahu Akhbar"', *The Independent* (17 July 2018), available at https://www.independent.co.uk/news/uk/home-news/richard-dawkins-allahu-akhbar-church-bells-criticism-religion-a8451141.html.

32 On confirmation bias in relation to religion and atheist debates, see Paul Hedges, *Towards Better Disagreement: Religion and Atheism in Dialogue* (London: Jessica Kingsley, 2017), 167. On Harris, see Khalil, *Jihad*; and Anwar Omeish, 'Sam Harris, Maajid Nawaz, and the Illusion of Knowledge', *Harvard Political Review* (6 October 2015), available at https://harvardpolitics.com/harvard/sam-harris-maajid-nawaz-illusion-knowledge/.

33 See Hamid Dabashi, 'The Liberal Roots of Islamophobia', *Al Jazeera* (3 March 2017), available at https://www.aljazeera.com/indepth/opinion/2017/03/liberal-roots-islamophobia-170302152226572.html; and Evelyn Alsultany, '*Real Time with Bill Maher* and the Good Muslims of Liberal Multiculturalism', in *Muslims and US Politics Today*, ed. Mohammad Hassan Khalil (Cambridge, MA: Harvard University Press, 2019), 83–103.

34 See Beydoun, *American Islamophobia*, 30.

35 Anon, 'Nigel Farage's "Vile" Anti-Immigration Poster Criticised', *Irish Times* (19 June 2016), available at https://www.irishtimes.com/news/world/uk/nigel-farage-s-vile-anti-immigration-poster-criticised-1.2690915.

36 Rowena Mason, 'Nigel Farage: British Muslim "Fifth Column" Fuels Fear of Immigration', *Guardian* (12 March 2015), available at https://www.theguardian.com/politics/2015/mar/12/nigel-farage-british-muslim-fifth-column-fuels-immigration-fear-ukip. Such claims are made by many in the Islamophobia industry, and on one occasion I was in a talk where the speaker (a well-known Islamophobe discussed herein) said that any Muslim who grew a beard or wore a headscarf wanted to chop off the head of every non-Muslim. The absurdity of this, to anyone who has Muslims friends, colleagues, neighbours, and so on, should be apparent, but the often-widespread ignorance and media-stoked fear of Islam apparently means that such claims do nothing to dent the credibility of such figures among their supporters.

37 CAIR, 'Confronting Fear: Islamophobia and Its Impact in the United States', Council on American-Islamic Relations and the Center for Race and Gender at the University of California, Berkeley (2016), available at https://tinyurl.com/ycgglfud.

38 Beydoun, *American Islamophobia*, 36–9.

39 Beydoun, *American Islamophobia*, 41. Beydoun correctly notes that personal Islamophobic actions are legitimated by institutional and social contexts, but we do not employ his 'dialectical Islamophobia' terminology.

40 See Andrew Shylock, 'Islam as an Object of Fear and Affection', in *Islamophobia/Islamophilia*, ed. Andrew Shylock (Bloomington: Indiana University Press, 2010), 1–25; and Mahmood Mamdani, *Good Muslim/Bad Muslim* (New York: Pantheon, 2004).

41 George W. Bush, 'Address to the Joint Session of the 107th Congress, United States Capitol, Washington D.C' (20 September 2001), 68, available at

http://georgewbushwhitehouse.archives.gov/infocus/bushrecord/documents/
Selected_Speeches_George_W_Bush.pdf.

42 Green, *The Fear*, 187.

43 See Edward Said, *Covering Islam* (New York: Pantheon Books, 1981); Evelyn Alsutany, *Arabs and Muslims in the Media* (Albany: New York University Press, 2012); and Kimberley Powell, 'Framing Islam: An Analysis of U.S. Media Coverage of Terrorism since 9/11', *Communication Studies* 62 (2011): 90–112.

44 Dalia Abdelhady and Gina Fristedt Malmberg, 'Swedish Media Representation of the Refugee Crisis', in *Antisemitism, Islamophobia, and Interreligious Hermeneutics: Ways of Seeing the Religious Other*, ed. Emma Polyakov (Leiden: Brill, 2018), 107–36 (109).

45 See Todd Green, *Presumed Guilty: Why We Shouldn't Ask Muslims to Condemn Terrorism* (Minneapolis, MN: Fortress Press, 2018), 49–72.

46 Beydoun, *American Islamophobia*, 123–4.

47 Theodore Schleifer, 'Trump Doesn't Challenge Anti-Muslim Questioner at Event', *CNN* (18 September 2015), available at https://tinyurl.com/yamy4wpt.

48 Kim Hjelmgaard, 'Would-Be Dutch PM: Islam Threatens Our Way of Life', *USA Today* (21 February 2017), available at https://tinyurl.com/y7vhbrjb.

49 See Hedges, *Understanding Religion* 374–8, 384 textbox 16.8, 391–4.

50 Stephan Salisbury, *Mohamed's Ghosts* (New York: Perseus, 2010), 3.

51 See Katy P. Sian, 'Surveillance, Islamophobia, and Sikh Bodies in the War on Terror', *Islamophobia Studies Journal* 4.1 (2017): 37–52.

52 See Erik Love, *Islamophobia and Racism in America* (Albany: New York University Press, 2015).

53 Tariq Modood, 'Islamophobia and Normative Sociology', *Journal of the British Academy* 8 (2020): 29–49 (37–9).

54 See Pascal Bruckner, *An Imaginary Racism: Islamophobia and Guilt* (Cambridge: Polity Press, 2018).

55 Beydoun, *American Islamophobia*, 59–69.

56 Beydoun, *American Islamophobia*, 62 and 63.

57 See Nasar Meer and Tariq Modood, 'Refutations of Racism in the "Muslim Question"', *Patterns of Prejudice* 43.3–4 (2009): 335–54.

58 Green, *The Fear*, 31. See also, Christopher Kyriakides, Satnam Virdee and Prof. Tariq Modood, 'Racism, Muslims and the National Imagination', *Journal of Ethnic and Migration Studies* 35.2 (2009): 289–308. As discussed in Chapter 5, with regard to the experience of Jews and Black people, the perceived racial features of many Muslims ('looking' Middle Eastern, South Asian, etc.) mean that such prejudice becomes a part of their day-to-day experience and cannot simply be switched off, in the way that a 'Caucasian-looking' Jew could, for instance, avoid some antisemitism by not dressing as a Jew. For the person who fits society's profile as 'looking' Muslim or Black this is never an option. Of course, skin colour, dress, or manners is never an indication of somebody's origins, religious affiliation, or so on, but in terms of structural prejudice it

is the 'look' that often matters (alongside, with an intersectional lens, such markers as name, dialect, gender, dress, etc.) in terms of enacted discrimination.

59 Green, *The Fear*, 274.

60 See Paul Hedges, 'Women's Bodies as Ideological Battlefield: Fashion, Feminism and Freedom in France's Burkini Ban', unpublished paper (2016), available at https://www.academia.edu/28167498/Womens_Bodies_as_Ideological_Battlefield_Fashion_Feminism_and_Freedom_in_Frances_Burkini_Ban_1. See also Paul Hedges, 'Fashion, Feminism or Freedom: Dissecting France's Ban on Burkini', *RSIS Commentary* CO16219 (2016), available at www.rsis.edu. sg/wp-content/uploads/2016/08/CO16219.pdf, and Hedges, *Understanding Religion*, 391–4.

61 Saeed, *Islamophobia and Securitization*, 4, 117–19.

62 Samuel Huntington, 'The Clash of Civilizations', *Foreign Affairs* 72.3 (1993): 22–49. See Hedges, *Understanding Religion*, 331–2 for a critique.

63 Green, *The Fear*, 123, 125.

64 Esposito, *Future of Islam*, 65.

65 Green, *The Fear*, 144.

66 On the form of Salafi Islam in Saudi Arabia, often known as Wahhabism, see Natana DeLong-Bas, *Wahhabi Islam: From Revival and Reform to Global Jihad* (Oxford: Oxford University Press, 2008).

67 John Ashcroft, 'Prepared Remarks for the US Mayors Conference', *Yale Law School, Avalon Project* (25 October 2001), available at https://tinyurl.com/y8rqo6wx.

68 Anon, 'Muslim Teen Arrested for Bringing Reassembled Clock to School', *This Day in History* (14 September 2015), available at https://www.history.com/ this-day-in-history/muslim-teen-arrested-for-bringing-homemade-clock-to-school.

69 See Beydoun, *American Islamophobia*; and Arun Kundnani and Ben Hayes, *The Globalisation of Countering Violent Extremism Policies: Undermining Human Rights, Instrumentalising Civil Society* (Amsterdam: Transnational Institute, 2018), available at https://tinyurl.com/ycbshl7r.

70 Green, *The Fear*, 290–1.

71 Green, *The Fear*, 279. Beydoun argues that Trump's policy is not an aberration, simply an extension of previous policy, see *American Islamophobia*, 95–109.

72 Amnesty International, *State of Denial: Europe's Role in Rendition and Secret Detention* (London: Amnesty International, 2008), available at https://www.amnesty.org/download/Documents/52000/eur010032008eng.pdf.

73 See Green, *The Fear*, 283; and Beydoun, *American Islamophobia*, 126–9. On problems with 'radicalization', see Hedges, 'Radicalisation'.

74 In general, the United States has institutionally refused to consider how US foreign policy contributed to 9/11, see John Esposito and Dalia Mogahed, *Who Speaks for Islam? What a Billion Muslims Really Think* (New York: Gallup, 2007), 91–4.

75 Leon Moosavi, 'The Racialization of Muslim Converts in Britain and Their Experiences of Islamophobia', *Critical Sociology* 41.1 (2015): 41–56.

76 BBC, 'Is It Easier to Get a Job If You're Adam or Mohamed?', *BBC News* (6 February 2017), available at https://www.bbc.com/news/uk-england-london-38751307. For a more recent survey, see Anthony Heath and Lindsay Richards, 'How Racist Is Britain Today? What the Evidence Tells Us', *Conversation* (1 July 2020), available at https://theconversation.com/how-racist-is-britain-today-what-the-evidence-tells-us-141657.

77 Lacorne, *The Limits of Tolerance*, 162–71.

78 See Green, *The Fear*, 2.

79 See Paul Weller, *A Mirror for Our Times: The Rushdie Affair and the Future of Multiculturalism* (London: Continuum, 2009); and Shabbir Akhtar, *Be Careful with Muhammad! The Salman Rushdie Affair* (London: Bellow, 1989).

80 Green, *The Fear*, 195.

81 See Oliver Wright, 'Paris Attacks: Women Targeted as Hate Crime against British Muslims Soars Following Terrorist Atrocity', *The Independent* (22 November 2015), available at http://www.independent.co.uk/news/uk/home-news/paris-attacks-british-muslims-face-300-spike-in-racialattacks-in-week-following-terror-a6744376.html; and Sarah Mangla Ismat and Marguerite Ward, 'French Muslim Parents, Terrified of Backlash, Urge Their Children to Stay Indoors, Downplay Religious Identity', *International Business Times* (19 November 2015), available at http://www.ibtimes.com/french-muslim-parents-terrified-backlash-urge-their-children-stay-indoors-downplay-2192505.

82 Melanie Phillips, *Londonistan* (New York: Encounter, 2006).

Interlude 3

1 See, for instance, Matti Bunzl, *Anti-Semitism and Islamophobia: Hatreds Old and New in Europe* (Chicago, IL: Prickly Paradigm Press, 2007); Nasar Meer and Tehsen Noorani, 'A Sociological Comparison of Anti-Semitism and Anti-Muslim Sentiment in Britain', *Sociological Review* 56.2 (2008): 195–219; Nasar Meer, ed., *Racialization and Religion: Race, Culture and Difference in the Study of Antisemitism and Islamophobia* (Abingdon: Routledge, 2014); Gil Anidjar, *Semites: Race, Religion, Literature* (Stanford, CA: Stanford University Press, 2008); Ivan Kalmar, *Early Orientalism: Imagined Islam and the Notion of Sublime Power* (Abingdon: Routledge, 2012); and James Renton and Ben Gidley, eds, *Antisemitism and Islamophobia in Europe: A Shared Story?* (London: Palgrave Macmillan, 2017).

2 Frantz Fanon, *Black Skin, White Masks*, trans. Charles Markmann (London: Pluto, [1952] 1986), 122.

3 PRC, 'Pew Global Attitudes Project: Unfavorable Views of Jews and Muslims on the Increase in Europe', *Pew Research Centre* (2008), 9, available at https://www.pewresearch.org/global/2008/09/17/unfavorable-views-of-jews-and-muslims-on-the-increase-in-europe/.

4 Bunzl, *Anti-Semitism and Islamophobia*.

5 James Renton and Ben Gidley, 'Introduction: The Shared Story of Europe's Ideas of the Muslim and the Jew – A Diachronic Framework', in *Antisemitism and Islamophobia*, 1–21 (7). Though this is not always so, and Filip Dewinter of the Belgian right-wing Flemish Identity movement embraced the term, see Bunzl, *Anti-Semitism and Islamophobia*, 40–1.

6 Deborah Lipstadt, *Antisemitism Here and Now* (London: Scribe, 2019); and David Batty, 'Lady Warsi Claims Islamophobia Is Now Socially Acceptable in Britain', *The Guardian* (20 January 2011), available at https://www.theguardian.com/uk/2011/jan/20/lady-warsi-islamophobia-muslims-prejudice.

7 Sander Gilman, 'The Case of Circumcision: Diaspora Judaism as a Model for Islam?', in *Antisemitism and Islamophobia*, 143–64 (157).

8 *Der Spiegel*, 'The Word from Berlin: Circumcision Ruling Is "a Shameful Farce for Germany"', *Der Spiegel Online* (13 July 2012), available at https://www.spiegel.de/international/germany/german-press-review-on-outlash-against-court-s-circumcision-ruling-a-844271.html, cited in Gilman, 'The Case of Circumcision', 154.

9 See especially, Gil Anidjar, 'Jesus and Monotheism', *Freudian Futures* 51.S1 (2013): 158–83; and Gil Anidjar, *Blood: A Critique of Christianity* (New York: Columbia University Press, 2014).

10 Renton and Gidley, 'Introduction', 11.

11 On the imagination and varieties of the secular, see Paul Hedges, *Understanding Religion: Theories and Methods for Studying Religiously Diverse Societies* (Berkeley: University of California Press, 2021), chapter 16, while on the importance of the Protestant imaginary more widely, see 212–16.

12 See Bunzl, *Anti-Semitism and Islamophobia*.

13 For an overview, see James Renton, 'The End of the Semites', in *Antisemitism and Islamophobia*, 99–140; and Edward Said, *Orientalism* (New York: Pantheon Books, 1978).

14 But Jew and Muslim started to be distinguished on other grounds too, see Renton, 'The End', 99–100, 111–27.

15 See Kalmar, *Early Orientalism*; and Ivan Kalmar and Derek Penslar, eds *Orientalism and the Jews* (Hanover: University of New England Press, 2005).

16 Andrew Jotischky, 'Ethnic and Religious Categories in the Treatment of Jews and Muslims in the Crusader States', in *Antisemitism and Islamophobia*, 25–49 (29).

17 Renton, 'The End', 101–8.

18 See Hedges, *Understanding Religion*, 377, and, relating this to the present discussion, see Renton, 'The End', 100–1.

19 Renton, 'The End', 109.

20 Renton, 'The End', 111–20.

21 Fassin Didier, 'In the Name of the Republic: Untimely Meditations on the Aftermath of the *Charlie Hebdo* Attack', *Anthropology Today* 31.2 (2015): 3–7 (4–5). For a discussion about issues raised in the cartoon debate,

see Paul Hedges, 'In Defence of Free of Speech and Against the Publication of Certain Cartoons', *RSIS Working Papers* no. 294, available at: https://www.rsis.edu.sg/rsis-publication/srp/wp294/?doing_wp_cron=1604542268.2079908 847808837890625#.X6NfPVMzZhE.

22 See Yulia Egrova and Fiaz Ahmed, 'The Impact of Antisemitism and Islamophobia on Jewish-Muslim Relations in the UK: Memory, Experience, Context', in *Antisemitism and Islamophobia*, 283–301.

23 See the discussion in Daniel Gordon, 'Antisemitism, Islamophobia, and the Search for Common Ground in French Antiracist Movements since 1898', in *Antisemitism and Islamophobia*, 217–66.

CHAPTER EIGHT

1 See Paul Hedges, *Understanding Religion: Theories and Methods for Studying Religiously Diverse Societies* (Berkeley: University of California Press, 2021), 376 textbook 16.2.

2 See Reuven Firestone, 'Muslim-Jewish Relations', *Oxford Research Encyclopedia of Religion* (2016), doi:10.1093/acrefore/9780199340378. 013.17.

3 Bassam Tibi, *Islamism and Islam* (New Haven, CT: Yale University Press, 2012), 56. Andrew Boston (MD) is an associate professor at Brown University specializing in family medicine with seemingly no academic training in religion or Islam; a contributor to Jihad Watch (arguably an Islamophobic website), he states a desire to respond to the 'charnel house' of 9/11, see Andrew Bostom, 'Sharia "Thirst", Christian Persecution, & Islamic Antisemitism', *Centre for Security Policy* (1 November 2019), available at https://www.centerforsecuritypolicy.org/2019/11/01/dr-andrew-bostom-briefing-sharia-thirst-christian-persecution-islamic-antisemitism/.

4 David Patterson, *A Genealogy of Evil: Anti-Semitism from Nazism to Islamic Jihad* (Cambridge: Cambridge University Press, 2011), 7 and 50–1.

5 See Tibi, *Islamism and Islam*; and Ronald Nettler, *Past Trials and Present Tribulations: A Muslim Fundamentalist's View of the Jews* (Oxford: Pergamon Press, 1987).

6 Esther Webman, 'From the Damascus Blood Libel to the "Arab Spring": The Evolution of Arab Antisemitism', *Antisemitism Studies* 1.1 (1997): 157–206 (190).

7 See Firestone, 'Muslim-Jewish Relations'.

8 Walter Laqueur, *The Changing Face of Antisemitism: From Ancient Times to the Present Day* (Oxford: Oxford University Press, 2008), 194–5.

9 Tibi, *Islamism and Islam*, 63.

10 See Tibi, *Islamism and Islam*, 63–9; Patterson, *A Genealogy of Evil*, 74–89; and Jeffrey Herf, *Nazi Propaganda for the Arab World* (New Haven, CT: Yale University Press, 2009).

11 Franco Cardini, *Europe and Islam*, trans. Caroline Beamish (Oxford: Blackwell, 1999), 209.

12 Tibi, *Islamism and Islam*, 60–1, here provides a more scholarly corrective to the reading of, for instance, Patterson, *A Genealogy of Evil*, who seems to read all contacts through the lens of antisemitism.

13 See Jonathan Frankel, *The Damascus Affair: 'Ritual Murder', Politics, and the Jews in 1840* (Cambridge: Cambridge University Press, 1997).

14 Sayyed Qutb, 'Our Struggle with the Jews', in *Past Trials and Present Tribulations*, 72–89.

15 Qutb, 'Our Struggle with the Jews', 87.

16 Qutb, 'Our Struggle with the Jews', 84.

17 Qutb, 'Our Struggle with the Jews', 83.

18 Qutb, 'Our Struggle with the Jews', 83.

19 Qutb, 'Our Struggle with the Jews', 75–6, 84.

20 This accusation is foreshadowed in the Qur'an (see Reuven Firestone, 'Qur'anic Anti-Jewish Polemics', in *Intolerance, Polemics, and Debate in Antiquity*, ed. George van Kooten and Jacques van Ruiten (Leiden: Brill, 2019), 443–62) but not in the racialized and conspiratorial frame of Qutb.

21 See Fred Donner, *Muhammad and the Believers* (Cambridge, MA: Belknap Press, 2010).

22 See Firestone, 'Muslim-Jewish Relations'.

23 Meir Kister, 'The Massacre of the Banū Qurayẓa: A Re-Examination of a Tradition', *Jerusalem Studies in Arabic and Islam* 8 (1986): 61–96. Some scholars have suggested that the entire event may never have happened due to inconsistencies in the story.

24 See Firestone, 'Qur'anic Anti-Jewish Polemics'.

25 Jonathan Brown, *Misquoting Muhammad* (Oxford: Oneworld, 2015), 257–9. For the *hadith*, see https://sunnah.com/muslim/54/105.

26 Abdullah Saeed, 'Personal Correspondence with Author' (9 March 2020). See also Firestone, 'Muslim-Jewish Relations'.

27 See Jacob Marcus, *The Jew in the Medieval World: A Sourcebook, 315–1791* (New York: JPS, 1938), 13–15, available at http://www.bu.edu/mzank/Jerusalem/tx/pactofumar.htm.

28 Christopher van de Krogt suggests that the Pact of Umar may have first developed in the eighth century, and sees it as reflecting practices put in place under the Abassid Dynasty (750–1258 CE). It seems that their discriminatory practices, implemented against *dhimmis*, were lifted from Byzantine (and Sassanian) prescriptions against Jews. Hence, an argument could be made that what became standard treatment of those termed *dhimmis* in Islam arose – in part at least – from Christian antisemitism, rather than being an outgrowth of Islamic rationales in relation to Jews and Christians. See Christopher van der Krogt, 'Jews and Christians as Second-Class Citizens in Islamic Egypt', in *The Citizen: Past and Present*, eds Andrew Brown and John Griffiths (Auckland: Massey University Press, 2017), 119–45.

29 Reuven Firestone, 'Contextualizing Antisemitism in Islam: Chosenness and Choosing and the Emergence of New Religion', *International Journal of Applied Psychoanalytic Studies* 4.3 (2007): 235–54 (237).

30 Richard Kimball, *The People of the Book* (Bern: Peter Lang, 2019), 148–9.

31 The term *dhimmitude* is associated with Bat Ye'or.

32 See Youssef Courbage and Philippe Fargues, *Christians and Jews under Islam: From the Arab Conquests to the Lebanese Civil War*, trans. Judy Mabro (London: I.B. Tauris, [1997] 2018), 14–25.

33 See Shabbir Akhtar, *Islam as Political Religion: The Future of an Imperial Faith* (Abingdon: Routledge, 2011).

34 Donner, *Muhammad and the Believers*.

35 See Craig Considine, 'Religious Pluralism and Civic Rights in a "Muslim Nation": An Analysis of Prophet Muhammad's Covenants with Christians', *Religions* 7 (2016). Krogt argues that the Pact of Umar was used to override earlier, more lenient, covenants with *dhimmis*, see Krogt, 'Jews and Christians', 126–27.

36 Anver Emon, *Religious Pluralism in Islamic Law: Dhimmis and Others in the Empire of Law* (Oxford: Oxford University Press, 2012), 64–5.

37 At first, it seems that only Muslims could be regular soldiers in the caliph's armies, but this did not stop irregular troops or mercenaries being employed, and under the Abbasid Dynasty non-Muslims became part of the regular reformed army. This was not to be the default, as *dhimmi* status came to mean that non-Muslims were exempt from military service, but in new conquests or in alliances Muslims regularly fought alongside non-Muslims. Furthermore, rather than paying the *jiyza* taz on *dhimmis* (which guaranteed their protection under the caliph in the Islamic polity with exemption from military service), at times People of the Book could take on military service as an alternative. See Jason Porterfield, *The Islamic Golden Age and the Caliphates* (New York: Rosen Publishing, 2017), 25, and Donner, *Muhammad and the Believers*, chapter 4.

38 See Krogt, 'Jews and Christians', 127, citing Milka Levy-Rubin, *Non-Muslims in the Early Islamic Empire: From Surrender to Coexistence* (Cambridge: Cambridge University Press, 2011), 95, 97–8, 127–9, 136–7, 141–3.

39 See Firestone, 'Muslim-Jewish Relations'; and Denis Lacorne, *The Limits of Tolerance: Enlightenment Values and Religious Fanaticism* (New York: Columbia University Press, 2019), 101–2.

40 See Benny Morris, *1948: A History of the First Arab-Israeli War* (New Haven, CT: Yale University Press, 2008).

41 Sources suggest that just as the Palestinians, who saw themselves, justifiably, as the indigenous inhabitants, would not accept the two-state solution (in line with wider Arab and Muslim sentiment), so neither was it part of the Zionist ideology of the early settlers, or the intentions of the founders of the State of Israel, see Morris, *1948*, especially 1–36.

42 Benny Morris, 'A New Look at the 1948 War', Lecture, ISGAP Critical Antisemitism Summer Institute, St John's College Oxford, 9 July 2019.

43 PNN, 'Israeli Settlers Damage 780 Trees in Three Days', *PNN* (1 March 2020), available at http://english.pnn.ps/2020/03/01/israeli-settlers-damage-780-trees-in-three-days/.

44 See Kati Marton, *A Death in Jerusalem: The Assassination by Jewish Extremists of the First Arab/Israeli* (New York: Pantheon, 1994). On the ideology of the extreme religious settler programme, see Moshe Hellinger, Isaac Hershkowitz and Bernard Susser, *Religious Zionism and the Settlement Project: Ideology, Politics, and Civil Disobedience* (Albany: State University of New York Press, 2018).

45 Cited in Esther Webman, 'The Undiminished Threat of Political Islam', in *Middle East Contemporary Survey*, vol. 24, ed. Bruce Maddy-Weitzman (Tel Aviv: Tel Aviv University, 2002), 91–126 (113). An earlier *fatwa* asking all Arabs and Muslims to come to the aid of Palestinians had emanated from Al Azhar in 1947.

46 Morris, 'A New Look at the 1948 War'.

47 See Webman, 'From the Damascus'.

48 See Elizabeth Sirriyeh, 'Wahhabis, Unbelievers and the Problems of Exclusivism', *British Journal of Middle Eastern Studies* 16.2 (1989): 123–32. See also Trevor Stanley, 'Understanding the Origins of Wahhabism and Salafism', *Terrorism Monitor* 3.14 (2005), available at https://jamestown.org/program/understanding-the-origins-of-wahhabism-and-salafism/.

49 See Rashid Khalidi, 'President Trump's Peace Plan Is the Latest in a Century of Outrageous Deals for the Palestinians', *Time* (31 January 2020), available at https://time.com/5774722/trumps-plan-outrageous-palestinians/.

50 See Navras J. Aafreedi, 'Antisemitism in the Muslim Intellectual Discourse in South Asia', *Religions* 10.7 (2019), available at https://doi.org/10.3390/rel10070442. It may be noted that Mawdudi's wife Maryam Jameelah, a Jewish white convert, was equally virulent in her antisemitism, and wrote books that were also anti-Christian (Mohamed Imran Mohamed Taib, 'Personal Correspondence with Author,' 4 June 2020).

51 Aafreedi, 'Antisemitism in the Muslim'.

52 See Mario Silva, 'Antisemitism and the Global Jihad', in *Terrorism Revisited: Islamism, Political Violence and State-Sponsorship*, ed. Paulo Casaca and Siegfried Wolf (Cham: Springer, 2017), 157–80.

53 This includes a nine hundred-page encyclopaedia on the Jewish threat (Mohamed Imran Mohamed Taib, 'Personal Correspondence with Author,' 4 June 2020).

54 Reuters, 'Malaysian Assembly Hands Out Copies of the "International Jew"', *Haaretz* (21 June 2003), available at https://www.haaretz.com/1.5483613.

55 See Mary Ainslie, *Anti-Semitism in Cotemporary Malaysia: Malay Nationalism, Philosemitism and Pro-Israel Expressions* (Singapore: Palgrave Macmillan, 2019), 4.

56 See Ahmad Fauzi Abdul Hamid, *The Extensive Salafization of Malaysian Islam* (Singapore: ISEAS, 2016).

57 See A. Reid, 'Jewish Conspiracy Theories in Southeast Asia: Are Chinese the Target?', *Indonesia and the Malay World* 38.112 (2010): 373–85.

58 Meir Litvak and Esther Webman, *From Empathy to Denial: Arab Responses to the Holocaust* (Oxford: Oxford University Press, 2011), 155–92.

59 See Mohamed Imran Mohamed Taib, 'On Orientalism and Orientalism-in-Reverse among Muslims: Some Aspects of Edward Said's Contributions and Its Misappropriation' (Personal Blog, 2009), available at https://dialogosphere.wordpress.com/2015/03/11/on-orientalism-and-orientalism-in-reverse-among-muslims-some-aspects-of-edward-saids-contributions-and-its-misappropriation/, citing As'ad Abu Khalil, 'Orientalism in the Arab Context', in *Revising Culture, Reinventing Peace: The Influence of Edward W. Said*, ed. Naseer Aruri and Muhammad A. Shuraydi (New York: Olive Branch Press, 2001), 100ff.

60 See Rebecca Ann Parker and Ibraham Farajajé, 'Out Beyond: Forging Resistance and Hope through Multireligious Friendship', in *My Neighbour's Faith: Stories of Interreligious Encounter, Growth, and Transformation*, ed. Jennifer Howe Peace, Or N. Rose and Gregory Mobley (Maryknoll, NY: Orbis, 2010), 228–33.

CHAPTER NINE

1 Here, we can refer back to our discussion in the Introduction about how we may speak of specific religious traditions, but several points are worth noting here specifically. A tradition is not, in and of itself, a thing with agency, and so cannot, of course, justify violence. Only specific Buddhists can do this. Nevertheless, we need to understand that institutions and traditions do have a life of their own, and so in certain practical ways we may see – in the experience of actors – Buddhism being pitted against, variously, Christianity, Hinduism, or Islam. In this sense, a tradition may seemingly even operate as if it had agency, even if this is not the case. Of course, there is never any singular form of 'Buddhism'/'the Buddhist tradition', or any other religion, but we speak here of what was the overwhelming mainstream expression of those traditions which stemmed from the Buddha, whether known as Buddhadharma, fojiao, Buddhism, or similarly in other languages. On the imagination, or mythologization, of Buddhism as peaceful, see Iselin Frydenlund, '"Buddhism has made Asia Mild" The Modernist Construction of Buddhism as Pacifism', in *Buddhist Modernities: Re-Inventing Tradition in the Globalizing Modern World*, eds Hanna Havnevik, Ute Hüsken, Mark Teeuwen, Vladimir Tikhonov and Koen Wellens (New York: Routledge, 2017), 204–21.

2 Alan Strathern, 'Why Are Buddhist Monks Attacking Muslims?', *BBC News* (2 May 2013), available at https://www.bbc.com/news/magazine-22356306.

3 Paul Hedges, *Understanding Religion: Theories and Methods for Studying Religiously Diverse Societies* (Berkeley: University of California Press, 2021),

367–8; this scene is based around a recorded incident, see Michael Jerryson, *If You Meet the Buddha on the Road: Buddhism, Politics, and Violence* (Oxford: Oxford University Press, 2018), 35.

4 Naoka Kumada, 'Buddhism, Violence, and Extremism', Lecture delivered at SRP Executive Programme (18 November 2015), Singapore.

5 See Cathy Cantwell, *Buddhism: The Basics* (New York: Routledge, 2010), 22–4; and Paul Williams with Anthony Tribe and Alexander Wynne, *Buddhist Thought: A Complete Introduction to the Indian Tradition*, 2nd edn (New York: Routledge, 2012), 1–15.

6 See Jerryson, *If You Meet the Buddha*, 17–48.

7 See Stanley Tambiah, *Buddhism Betrayed? Religion, Politics and Violence in Sri Lanka* (Chicago, IL: University of Chicago Press, 1992); Tessa Bartholomeusz, *In Defence of Dharma: Just-War Ideology in Buddhist Sri Lanka* (Richmond: Curzon, 2002); and Jerryson, *If You Meet the Buddha*. For an overview, see Hedges, *Understanding Religion*, 368–9.

8 See Jerryson, *If You Meet the Buddha*, 30, 55–60. Here, we are discussing Theravada Buddhism, but Ashoka is also invoked in Mahayana Buddhism, see Xue Yu, 'Buddhism and the Justification for War with Focus on Chinese Buddhist History', in *Buddhism and Violence: Militarism and Buddhism in Modern Asia*, ed. Vladimir Tikhonov and Torkel Brekke (London: Routledge, 2013), 194–208.

9 On some of the sources and for a discussion around this, see Hedges, *Understanding Religion*, 367–70, 371–2.

10 Notably, the sense of a continuing Theravada tradition is read back, anachronistically, to this earlier period. Before the modern era, a greater concern seems to have been with *vinaya* lineages (i.e. monastic discipline). Nevertheless, a nascent split occurred between those schools we know as Theravada (the Buddhism of such places as Sri Lanka, Thailand, and Myanmar) and Mahayana (the Buddhism of such places as China, Korea, and Japan), with Mahayana texts and apologetics dismissing what we today term Theravada by the polemical term of Hinayana ('lesser vehicle'; Mahayana means 'greater vehicle'). While scholars dispute whether they are a third major school, for our purposes the Vajrayana traditions of such places as Tibet and Nepal fall within the Mahayana tradition.

11 On the process, see Elizabeth Harris, 'Buddhism and the Religious Other', *Interreligious Studies and Intercultural Theology* 4.1 (2020): 3–20 (3–8, 13–16). On the usage of exclusivist and inclusivist as employed here, see Hedges, *Understanding Religion*, 306–11. For a wider discussion on the specifically Christian basis for their employment, see Paul Hedges, *Controversies in Interreligious Dialogue and the Theology of Religions* (London: SCM, 2010), 17–30, and on their wider usage, see Paul Hedges, 'The Theology of Religions Typology Redefined: Openness and Tendencies', in *Twenty-First Century Theologies of Religions: Retrospection and New Frontiers*, eds Elizabeth Harris, Paul Hedges and Shanthikumar Hettiarachchi (Leiden: E. J. Brill, 2016), 76–92.

12 See Elizabeth Harris, *Theravada Buddhism and the British Encounter: Religious, Missionary and Colonial Experience in Nineteenth Century Sri Lanka* (London: Routledge, 2006), 201–3; and Richard Fox Young and J. Somaratna, *Vain Debates: The Buddhist-Christian Controversies of Nineteenth Century Ceylon* (Vienna: University of Vienna Institute for Indology, 1996).

13 As 'religion' is a modern, Western term, what we call 'religious diversity' was managed under very different nomenclature by Buddhists in pre-modern South Asia. For our purposes, we can merely note this, but see Hedges, *Understanding Religion*, chapter 13 on the general issue. See also John Holt, *The Buddhist Viṣṇu: Religious Transformation, Politics, and Culture* (New York: Columbia University Press, 2004).

14 See Anuruddha Pradeep, 'The Political Dimension of Buddhism in Sri Lanka', in *Buddhism in Asia: Revival and Reinvention*, ed. Nayanjot Lahiri and Upinder Singh (Singapore: Institute of South East Asia Studies, 2016); and Jude Lal Fernando, 'Buddhism, Nationalism, and Violence in Asia', in *Controversies in Contemporary Religion*, vol. 3, ed. Paul Hedges (Santa Barbara, CA: Praeger, 2014), 61–90 (61–76).

15 See Arjun Guneratne, 'What's in a Name?: Aryans and Dravidians in the Making of Sri Lankan Identities', in *Perspectives on Modern South Asia: A Reader in Culture, History, and Representation*, ed. Kamala Visweswaran (Chichester: Wiley-Blackwell, 2011), 78–86.

16 Walpola Rahula, *The Heritage of the Bhikkhu* (New York: Grove Press, [1946] 1974), 21.

17 Rahula, *The Heritage*, 22.

18 Briefly, see Heather Selma Gregg, *The Path to Salvation: Religious Violence from the Crusades to Jihad* (Lincoln, NE: Potomac Books, 2014), 82–6; for a more detailed exposition, see James Manor, *The Expedient Utopian: Bandaranaike and Ceylon* (Cambridge: Cambridge University Press, 2009), 254–318.

19 See the poem cited in John Esposito, Darrell Fasching and Todd Lewis, *World Religions Today* (Oxford: Oxford University Press, 2006), 409.

20 This triple gem formulation is intended for soldiers rather than monks, and so does not replace the former one (Iselund Frydenlund, 'Personal Correspondence with Author', 26 October 2020). However, it shows a new nationalist ideology in the public sphere which is, arguably, directly influenced through a colonial lens via an old British formulation of 'God, King, and Country', with the latter two often seen to take precedence. Readers may be familiar with a scene in the film *Chariots of Fire* (1981), in which when the character Eric Liddell refuses to run on a Sunday (as the Sabbath) he is reprimanded by Lord Cadogan's character with the words: 'In my day it was King first God after.'

21 John Elvserkog, *Buddhism and Islam on the Silk Road* (Philadelphia: University of Pennsylvania Press, 2013), 70–1, 88–9, 117–74.

22 Elverskog, *Buddhism and Islam*, 165–9.

23 See John Newman, 'Islam in the Kālacakra Tantra', *Journal of the International Association of Buddhist Studies* 21.2 (1998): 311–72.

24 Anon., 'Islam in Southeast Asia', *Institute for South Asia Studies, UC Berkeley* (2011–16), available at https://southasia.berkeley.edu/islam-southeast-asia.

25 This relates to alleged prophesies of the Buddha that the lineage he founded would pass away, though hope for the coming of a future Buddha, Maitreya, who would revitalize the lineage also exists. On this, in relation to Buddhist Islamophobia, see Iselin Frydenlund, 'Buddhist Islamophobia: Actors, Tropes, Contexts', in *Handbook of Conspiracy Theory and Contemporary Religion*, eds Asbjørn Dyrendal, David G. Robertson and Egil Asprem (Leiden: Brill, 2018), 279–302, who notes the distinction of the need to protect the *sasana* (lineage of teachings), rather than the perceived eternal *buddhadharma* (or truths and teachings) (285–6). See also Iselin Frydenlund and Michael Jerryson, 'Buddhists, Muslims and the Construction of Difference', in *Buddhist-Muslim Relations in a Theravada World*, eds Iselin Frydenlund and Michael Jerryson (Cham: Palgrave Macmillan, 2020), 263–97 (281, also 281–90).

26 See Frydenlund, 'Buddhist Islamophobia', 280–1. See also Iselund Frydenlund and Michael Jerryson, 'Introduction: Buddhist-Muslim Relations in a Theravada World', in *Buddhist-Muslim Relations*, 1–21 (2–3).

27 Nasir Behzad and Daud Qarizadah, 'The Man Who Helped Blow Up the Bamiyan Buddhas', *BBC News* (12 March 2015), available at https://www.bbc.com/news/world-asia-31813681.

28 Christopher Beckwith, *Warriors of the Cloister: The Central Asian Origins of Science in the Medieval World* (Princeton, NJ: Princeton University Press, 2013).

29 Donald Lopez and Peggy McCracken, *In Search of the Christian Buddha: How an Asian Sage Became a Medieval Saint* (New York: W. W. Norton, 2014).

30 See Imtiyaz Yusuf, 'Islam and Buddhism', in *The Wiley-Blackwell Companion to Inter-Religious Dialogue*, ed. Catherine Cornille (Chichester: Wiley-Blackwell, 2013), 360–75 (363, 364–6, 367–9).

31 Reza Shah-Kazemi, *Common Ground between Islam and Buddhism: Spiritual and Ethical Affinities* (Cambridge: Fons Vitae, 2010).

32 See Elizabeth Harris, 'Exclusivism, Inclusivism and Pluralism: A Spatial Perspective', in *Twenty-First Century Theologies*, 57–75.

33 See Bruce Matthews, 'Christian Evangelical Conversions and the Politics of Sri Lanka', *Pacific Affairs* 80.3 (2007): 455–72.

34 See Athambawa Sarjoon, Mohammad Agus Yusoff and Nordin Hussin, 'Anti-Muslim Sentiments and Violence: A Major Threat to Ethnic Reconciliation and Ethnic Harmony in Post-War Sri Lanka', *Religions* 7 (2016).

35 Jude Lal Fernando, 'Personal Correspondence with Author' (24 March 2020).

36 Ahmad Sunawari Long, Khaidzir Hj. Ismail, Kamarudin Salleh, Saadiah Kumin, Halizah Omar and Ahamed Sarjoon Razick, 'An Analysis of the Post-War Community Relations between Buddhists and Muslims in Sri Lanka: A Muslim's Perspective', *Journal of Politics and Law* 9.6 (2016): 42–54. Further on the historical context and ethnic matrix, see Rohan Bastin and Premakumara de Silva, 'Historical Threads of Buddhist–Muslim Relations in Sri Lanka', in *Buddhist-Muslim Relations in a Theravada World*, 25–62.

37 Anon, 'Sri Lanka's Muslims: Caught in the Crossfire', *International Crisis Group Report 134* (29 May 2007), available at https://www.crisisgroup.org/asia/south-asia/sri-lanka/sri-lanka-s-muslims-caught-crossfire.

38 James Stewart, 'Muslim–Buddhist Conflict in Contemporary Sri Lanka', *South Asia Research* 34.3 (2014): 241–60 (242).

39 On this general consensus in the literature on the economic factor, see K. M. De Silva, *A History of Sri Lanka* (Colombo: Vijitha Yapa, 2005), 474–5; and Kumari Jayawardena, 'Economic and Political Factors in the 1915 Riots', *Journal of Asian Studies* 29.2 (1970): 223–33.

40 See Frydelund, 'Buddhist Islamophobia', 286–87. She quotes Dharmapala on this as follows: 'The Mohammaden, an alien people by Shylockian method, became prosperous like the Jews' (287, quoting Anagarika Dharmapala, *Return to Righteousness: A Collection of Speeches, Essays and Letters of the Anagarika Dharmapala*, ed. A Guruge (Colombo: Anagarika Dharmapala Birth Centenary Committee, Ministry of Education and Cultural Affairs, Ceylon, 1965), 207.

41 See Harris, 'Buddhism and the Religious Other', 8–16.

42 See Stewart, 'Muslim-Buddhist Conflict'.

43 See Rohan Gunaratna, 'Sinhala-Muslim Riots in Sri Lanka: The Need for Restoring Communal History', *Counter Terrorist Trends and Analyses* 10.4 (2018): 1–4.

44 See Michael Safi and Asiri Fernando, 'Sri Lanka: Churches Shut as Worshippers Mourn One Week after Bombings', *The Guardian* (28 April 2019), available at https://www.theguardian.com/world/2019/apr/28/sri-lanka-churches-shut-as-tv-service-replaces-first-mass-since-bombings.

45 See Paul Hedges and Jude Lal Fernando, 'Sri Lankan Attacks and Inter-Communal Relations', *RSIS Commentary* CO19095 (2019), available at https://www.rsis.edu.sg/wp-content/uploads/2019/05/CO19095.pdf.

46 Fernando, 'Personal Correspondence'.

47 See Stewart, 'Muslim-Buddhist Conflict', 252–6. Notably, most Sri Lankans (like most Buddhists) are not vegetarian, even if many recognize an impetus to vegetarianism in Buddhist teachings. Dharmapala became an advocate of vegetarianism, and probably adopted cow protectionism from movements that had arisen first among Sikhs in India in the late nineteenth century, see James Stewart, 'Cow Protectionism in Sinhala Buddhist Sri Lanka', *Journal of the Oriental Society of Australia* 45 (2013): 19–48.

48 See on this especially, Benjamin Schonthal and Matthew J. Walton, 'The (New) Buddhist Nationalisms? Symmetries and Specificities in Sri Lanka and Myanmar', *Contemporary Buddhism* 17.1 (2016): 81–115.

49 See Matthew Walton and Susan Hayward, *Contesting Buddhist Narratives: Democratization, Nationalism, and Communal Violence in Myanmar* (Honolulu, HI: East-West Centre, 2014), 20–3.

50 See, specifically, Frydenlund, 'Buddhist Islamophobia', 282–83, and also Nyi Nyi Kyaw, 'The Role of Myth in Anti-Muslim Buddhist Nationalism in Myanmar', in *Buddhist-Muslim Relations*, 197–226.

51 See Mohamed Nawab Bin Mohamed Osman, 'Understanding Islamophobia in Asia: The Cases of Myanmar and Malaysia', *Islamophobia Studies Journal* 4.1 (2013).

52 http://worldpopulationreview.com/countries/myanmar-population/, accessed 21 October 2020.

53 This has much in common with the 'love jihad' discussed in Chapter 10 in relation to Hinduism, and is not disconnected to European far-right worries about a Muslim demographic takeover. On these dynamics in contemporary Buddhist Islamophobia, see Frydenlund, 'Buddhist Islamophobia', 294–97, who discusses the posited jihads of 'birth', 'rape', and 'love'. On the gender representation of militant Buddhist rhetoric, see Farzana Haniffa, 'Sri Lanka's Anti-Muslim Movement and Muslim Responses: How Were They Gendered?', *Buddhist-Muslim Relations*, 139–67.

54 See Syed Mohammed Ad'ha Aljuneid, 'Politics and Religion in Contemporary Burma: Buddhist Monks as Opposition', *Yonsei Journal of International Studies* 8 (2012): 37–49, available at http://theyonseijournal.com/wp-content/uploads/2012/08/politics-and-religion-in-contemporary-burma.pdf; and Walton and Hayward, *Contesting Buddhist Narratives*.

55 See Matthew Walton, 'Buddhist-Muslim Interactions in Burma/Myanmar', in *Buddhist-Muslim Relations*, 63–99 (69–72).

56 On the ethnic side, see Walton, 'Buddhist-Muslim'; on recent land grabs, see Brian McCartan, 'Myanmar: Land Grabbing as Big Business', *CETRI* (11 March 2013), available at: https://www.cetri.be/Myanmar-Land-grabbing-as-big?lang=fr. Drawing these both together, see Mayesha Alam, '5 things you need to know about the Rohingya crisis – and how it could roil Southeast Asia', *The Washington Post* (14 September 2017), available at: https://www.washingtonpost.com/news/monkey-cage/wp/2017/09/14/5-things-you-need-to-know-about-rohingya-crisis-and-how-it-could-roil-southeast-asia/.

57 As such, international condemnation of Aung San Suu Kyi and her government for the Rohingya crisis is often misplaced as she is unable to influence the military, and direct criticism of it may endanger the partial democracy and civilian rule which exists entirely at the will of the military, which also maintains a majority within the parliament, making any action against it impossible.

58 C. Christine Fair, 'Arakan Rohingya Salvation Army: Not the Jihadis You Might Expect', *Lawfare* (9 December 2018), available at https://www.lawfareblog.com/arakan-rohingya-salvation-army-not-jihadis-you-might-expect.

59 Thanet Aphornsuvan, *Rebellion in Southern Thailand: Contending Histories* (Washington, DC: East-West Centre, 2007).

60 See Suwanna Satha-Anand, 'Question of Violence in Thai Buddhism', in *Buddhism and Violence: Militarism and Buddhism in Modern Asia*, ed. Vladimir Tikhonov and Torkel Brekke (London: Routledge, 2013), 175–93.

61 This was an observation made to the author by a researcher who had done fieldwork with these groups.

62 Makarim Wibisono and Bahtiar Manurung, 'How Facebook Contributes to Myanmar Violence', *Jakarta Post* (27 September 2018), available at

https://www.thejakartapost.com/academia/2018/09/27/how-facebook-contributes-to-myanmar-violence.html.

63 Cited in Brandon Paladino and Hunter Marston, 'Facebook Can't Resolve Conflicts in Myanmar and Sri Lanka on Its Own', *Brookings Institute* (27 June 2018), available at https://www.brookings.edu/blog/order-from-chaos/2018/06/27/facebook-cant-resolve-conflicts-in-myanmar-and-sri-lanka-on-its-own/.

64 See Anon., 'Wanted Myanmar Firebrand Abbot Summoned by Buddhist Council', *Straits Times* (29 May 2019), available at https://www.straitstimes.com/asia/se-asia/firebrand-anti-muslim-buddhist-monk-charged-with-sedition-in-myanmar.

65 See https://www.oxfordreference.com/view/10.1093/oi/authority.2011080 3100350816, accessed 21 October 2020.

66 Frydenlund, 'Buddhist Islamophobia', 288–97. In this, it mirrors older European tropes of Jewish power, a point Frydenlund also notes (292).

CHAPTER TEN

1 Naomi Barton, 'Delhi Riots: Mosque Set on Fire in Ashok Nagar, Hanuman Flag Placed on Minaret', *The Wire* (25 February 2020), available at https://thewire.in/communalism/delhi-violence-mosque-set-on-fire-in-ashok-vihar-hanuman-flag-placed-on-top/amp/.

2 Sudhir Kakar, *The Colors of Violence* (Chicago, IL: University of Chicago Press, 1996), 4, see 205 n.1.

3 See Paul Hedges, 'Encounters with Ultimacy? Autobiographical and Critical Perspectives in the Academic Study of Religion', *Open Theology* 4 (2018): 355–72. On the politics of such study, see Paul Hedges, *Understanding Religion: Theories and Methods for Studying Religiously Diverse Societies* (Berkeley: University of California Press, 2021), 422–24, 435–36.

4 Some scholars argue that 'Hinduism' as a system was only created by European scholars in the nineteenth century, but it existed as a unified system of thought from the medieval period. See Andrew Nicholson, *Unifying Hinduism: Philosophy and Identity in Indian Intellectual History* (New York: Columbia University Press, 2014). For the debates, see Hedges, *Understanding Religion*, 179–82.

5 David Smith, *Hinduism and Modernity* (Oxford: Blackwell, 2003), 51–2.

6 See Sheldon Pollock, 'Ramayana and Political Imagination in India', *Journal of Asian Studies* 52 (1993): 261–97.

7 See Daniel Gold, 'The Sufi Shrines of Gwalior City: Communal Sensibilities and the Accessible Exotic under Hindu Rule', *Journal of Asian Studies* 64.1 (2005): 127–50 (129–30).

8 On the use of architecture to control space, see Lily Kong and Orlando Woods, *Religion and Space* (London: Bloomsbury, 2017); and Hedges, *Understanding Religion*, 408–10. On this in the Indian context, see Romila Thapar, *The Past as Present: Forging Contemporary Identities through History* (New Delhi: Aleph Books, 2014). Notably, around the time that Babur built the Babri Masjid it is recorded he also gave about 300 acres to a Hindu swami, see Gyanendra Pandey, *Routine Violence: Nations, Fragments, Histories* (Stanford, CA: Stanford University Press, 2006), 99.

9 See Audrey Truschke, *Aurangzeb: The Man and the Myth* (London: Penguin, 2018) though her claims of Aurangzeb's tolerance are highly contested, see, for example, Milinda Banerjee, 'Audrey Truschke: Aurangzeb, the Life and Legacy of India's Most Controversial King', *Sehepunkte* 18.5 (2018), available at http://www.sehepunkte.de/2018/05/30625.html. See also Smith, *Hinduism and Modernity*, 60–3; and Lisa Balabanlilar, *Imperial Identity in the Mughal Empire: Memory and Dynastic Politics in Early Modern South and Central Asia* (London: I.B. Tauris, 2012), 41–4, 140–55. Pandey notes one of Aurangzeb's decrees from *c.*1658–1659: 'the ancient temples shall not be overthrown but … no new ones shall be built', Pandey, *Routine Violence*, 100.

10 See Audrey Truschke, *Culture of Encounters: Sanskrit at the Mughal Court* (New York: Columbia University Press, 2016).

11 On the Sants and Hindu–Muslim fusion, meeting, and syncretism, see Karine Schomer and W. H. McLeod, eds, *The Sants: Studies in a Devotional Tradition of India* (Delhi: Motilal Banarsidass, 1987); Soumen Mukherjee, 'Sufis, Yogis, and genealogies of "Islamic yoga": Broaching religio-cultural encounters in premodern eastern India', *Religion Compass* 14:e12368 (2020), doi.10.1111/rec3.12368; Gavin Flood, *An Introduction to Hinduism* (Cambridge: Cambridge University Press, 1996), 144–5; and Anne Bigelow, 'Muslim-Hindu Dialogue', in *The Wiley-Blackwell Companion to Inter-Religious Dialogue*, ed. Catherine Cornille (Chichester: Wiley-Blackwell, 2013), 279–95. On contemporary and village religion, see Haroon Khalid, *In Search of Shiva: A Study of Folk Religious Practices in Pakistan* (New Delhi: Rupa, 2015); Virinder Kalra and Navtej Purewal, *Beyond Religion in India and Pakistan: Gender and Caste, Borders and Boundaries* (London: Bloomsbury, 2020); and Peter Gottschalk, *Beyond Hindu and Muslim: Multiple Identity in Narratives from Village India* (Oxford: Oxford University Press, 2005). Pandey, citing Ashis Nandy, suggests that 'everyday Hinduism' provides a counter to the militant exclusivism of Hindu nationalism, especially at the village level, see Pandey, *Routine Violence*, 175, citing Ashis Nandy, 'The Twilight of Certitudes: Secularism, Hindu Nationalism and Other Masks of Deculturation', in *Tradition, Pluralism, and Identity: In Honour of T. N. Madan*, ed. Veena Das, Dipankar Gupta and Patricia Oberoi (New Delhi: Sage, 1999). On syncretism as normative, see Hedges, *Understanding Religion*, 72–9, especially 72–5.

12 See Muthuraj Swamy, *The Problem with Interreligious Dialogue: Plurality, Conflict and Elitism in Hindu-Christian-Muslim Relations* (London: Bloomsbury, 2016), 145–60.

13 See Christophe Jaffrelot, *The Hindu Nationalist Movement in India* (New York: Columbia University Press, 1996), 11–33.

14 See, for conflicting perceptions, Niall Ferguson, *Empire: How Britain Made the Modern World* (London: Penguin, 2003); and Shashi Tharoor, *Inglorious Empire: What the British Did to India* (London: Penguin, 2018).

15 See Jaffrelot, *The Hindu Nationalist Movement*, 18–20.

16 See, Rajeev Bhargava, ed., *Secularism and Its Critics* (Oxford: Oxford University Press, 2005). Though Tariq Modood and others dispute that India's is entirely a different model, as there are religiously friendly versions of secularism in Western contexts too, see Paul Hedges, *Understanding Religion*, chapter 16, and Paul Hedges, 'The Secular Realm as Interfaith Space: Discourse and Practice in Contemporary Multicultural Nation-States', *Religions* 10.498, doi:10.3390/rel10090498.

17 Pandey notes that 'The Hindu [nationalist] movement benefitted from the open or tacit support of elements of the old Congress Party, including several Congress governments in the 1980s and 1990s, in part motivated by the same kind of electoral calculations', Pandey, *Routine Violence*, 69. See also Julius Lipner, *The Hindus: Their Religious Beliefs and Practices* (London: Routledge, 2010), 18–19; and Mark Juergensmeyer, *Terror in the Mind of God: The Global Rise of Religious Violence*, 4th edn (Berkeley: University of California Press, 2017), 103–27.

18 Partha Chatterjee, *The Nation and Its Fragments: Colonial and Postcolonial Histories* (Princeton, NJ: Princeton University Press, 1993). See also Walter Mignolo, 'Subalterns and Other Agencies', *Postcolonial Studies* 8.4 (2005): 381–407.

19 Ilyse Morgenstein Fuerst, *India Muslim Minorities and the 1857 Rebellion: Religion, Rebels, and Jihad* (London: I.B. Tauris, 2017), 52–3.

20 Fuerst, *Indian Muslim Minorities*, 57–85.

21 Julius Lipner, 'Hindu Fundamentalism', in *Fundamentalisms: Threats and Ideologies in the Modern World*, ed. James Dunn (London: I.B. Tauris, 2016), 93–116 (96–7).

22 See Hedges, *Understanding Religion*, 349–52.

23 See Stephen Gregg, *Swami Vivekananda and Non-Hindu Traditions* (London: Routledge, 2019).

24 The term dates back to at least the 1870s in Bengal where the great poet Rabindranath Tagore (1861–1941) used it to mark a wide Indian cultural identity, while non-Hindu Indians, including the Catholic Christian convert Brahmabandhab Upadhyay (1861–1907), also used it in this way.

25 V. D. Savarkar, *Hindutva: Who Is a Hindu?* 5th edn (Bombay: M/s Bhave, [1923] 1969), available at https://archive.org/stream/hindutva-vinayak-damodar-savarkar-pdf/hindutva-vd-savarkar_djvu.txt.

26 Traditional readings of Indian history see what becomes Hinduism being brought by an invading group from central Asia, the Aryans (linked to what was understood as a common ethno-linguistic group that also moved into Europe, see Chapter 5), who suppressed indigenous groups including the

Indus Valley and Harappan civilizations. This thesis explains archaeological evidence of the destruction of the earlier civilizations of northern India, certain differences of southern and northern Indian languages and practices, and linguistic structures of Sanskrit that come into Greek, Latin, and then modern European languages. See Flood, *An Introduction to Hinduism*, 30–35. For Savarkar and later Hindu nationalists, the Aryan invasion (or immigration) thesis is contested, with claims that the Aryans are indigenous, and that it is an orientalist piece of propaganda to dismiss the Indian origins of Hinduism and thereby extol Western superiority. However, by linking Sanskrit as the oldest part of the language group, and claiming a lineage of descent that links modern Hindus and Europeans, it is not exactly a thesis to show Europe's inherent superiority. On the discursive use of the term Aryan/arya, see Thapar, *The Past*, 17–19, 44–48, 66–68, and 179–91.

27 See Jaffrelot, *The Hindu Nationalist Movement*, 25–33.

28 Marzia Casolari, 'Hindutva's Foreign Tie-Up in the 1930s: Archival Evidence', *Economic and Political Weekly* 35.4 (2000), 218–28 (224 and 223), citing, respectively, V. D. Savarkar, 'Presidential Speech', 21ˢᵗ Session of the Mahasabha (1939) from summary in *Bombay Chronicle* (29 December 1939), and V. D. Savarkar, cited in MSA, Home Special Department, 60D(g) Pt III, 1938, 'A report of the meeting held on December 11, 1938'. While Savarkar's attempts to establish contacts with Nazi Germany were largely unsuccessful, some of his speeches were printed in German newspapers in exchange for Marathi newspapers running favourable articles on Germany's Jewish policy (225). See also Palash Ghosh, 'Hindu Nationalist's Historical Links to Nazism and Fascism', *International Business Times* (3 June 2012), available at: https://www.ibtimes.com/hindu-nationalists-historical-links-nazism-fascism-214222.

29 See note 4. See also notes 26, 30, and 39.

30 Suggestions that modern Indian identities are 'inauthentic' because they combine Western and indigenous categories is both ahistorical (cultures have interacted for millennia, there is no 'pure' Indian/Hindu identity or culture) and implicitly orientalist by promoting the old trope that India's essence is only a timeless past (i.e. any modern form cannot represent the 'real' India).

31 Jeffrey Long, 'Personal Correspondence with Author' (13 March 2020).

32 See Rogers Brubaker, 'Ethnicity without Groups', *Archives Européenes de Sociologie* 43.2 (2002): 163–89 (171–3).

33 See Casolari, 'Hindutva's Foreign Tie-Up', 218–22. Casolari argues convincingly, *contra* Jaffrelot, that the fascism of the RSS and other right-wing Hindu movements is not a distinct form from that of Europe, but directly inspired by direct contacts and purposeful borrowing and imitation (219), concluding that 'the main historical organisations and leaders of Hindu nationalism had a distinctive and sustained interest in fascism and nazism … and … to a certain extent, these influences were channelled through direct contacts' (227).

34 For one case study see Abhik Roy, 'Regenerating Masculinity in the Construction of Hindu Nationalist Identity: A Case Study of Shiv Sena', *Communication Studies* 57.2 (2006): 135–52.

35 See Aishwarya S. Iyer, 'Delhi Riots Exclusive: RSS Members Arrested for Murder, Rioting', *Quint* (3 July 2020), available at https://www.thequint.com/news/india/delhi-riots-rss-vhp-members-accused-murder-rioting-arrested-delhi-police.

36 See Kingshuk Nag, *The Saffron Tide: The Rise of the BJP* (New Delhi: Rupa, 2014).

37 See Roy, 'Regenerating Masculinity', and Hedges, *Understanding Religion*, 154–7.

38 Scott Appleby, *The Ambivalence of the Sacred: Religion, Violence, and Reconciliation* (Lanham, MD: Rowman and Littlefield, 2000), 110.

39 Indeed, considerable evidence suggests that Dalits were not seen as actually being Hindus by upper class Hindus in the early twentieth century, as such their inclusion within the fold is partly a pragmatic decision by Hindu nationalist movements given demographics. Their numbers are required to ensure electoral success. It may be noted that still, in Tamil Nadu, the term Hindu is used to differentiate upper class Hindus from Dalits. See Pandey, *Routine Violence*, 111, where he cites R. V. Russell and Hiralal, *Tribes and Castes of the Central Provinces*, vol. 3 (London: Macmillan, 1916), 315.

40 Law.gov, 'State Anti-Conversion Laws in India', *Law Library of Congress* (updated 11 October 2018), citing *USCIRF Annual Report* (2016), Tier 2 Countries – India, supra note 10.

41 See Kakar, *The Colors of Violence*, 109–12.

42 See Anam Zakaria, *Footsteps of Partition: Narratives of Four Generations of Pakistanis and Indians* (New York: HarperCollins, 2015).

43 Asad Hashim, 'Timeline: India-Pakistan Relations', *Al Jazeera* (1 March 2019), available at https://www.aljazeera.com/indepth/spotlight/kashmirtheforgottenconflict/2011/06/2011615113058224115.html.

44 See Kanchan Srivastava, 'Muslims Pursuing Population and Land Jihad: Pramod Mutalik', *DNA* (29 August 2015), available at https://www.dnaindia.com/mumbai/interview-muslims-pursuing-population-and-land-jihad-pramod-mutalik-2119612.

45 Dibyesh Anand, *Hindu Nationalism in India and the Politics of Fear* (New York: Palgrave Macmillan, 2011), 51–3.

46 See Kakar, *The Colors of Violence*, 139–42; Anand, *Hindu Nationalism in India*, 63–81; Christophe Jaffrelot, 'A *De Facto* Ethnic Democracy? Obliterating and Targeting the Other: Hindu Vigilantes, and the Ethno-State', in *Majoritarian State: How Hindu Nationalism Is Changing India*, ed. Angana Chatterji, Thomas Hansen and Christophe Jaffrelot (London: HarperCollins, 2019), 41–67, 57–9; and Jaffrelot, *The Hindu Nationalist Movement*, 338–45.

47 Meera Nanda, 'Hindu Triumphalism and the Clash of Civilizations', *Economic and Political Weekly* 44.28 (2009): 106–14 (109).

48 See Kakar, *The Colors of Violence*, 152–66.

49 On an earlier intra-Hindu (Rama–Shiva) and interreligious (Rama–Sufi) dispute in Ayodhya, see Smith, *Hinduism and Modernity*, 196.

50 On the significance of Rama and Ayodhya, see Kapur Anuradha, 'Deity to Crusader: The Changing Iconography of Ram', in *Hindus and Others: The Question of Identity in India Today*, ed. Gyanendra Pandey (New Delhi: Viking, 1993), 74–109; more briefly, see Smith, *Hinduism and Modernity*, 190–6. For a detailed discussion on the site's history and contestation, see Pandey, *Routine Violence*, 68–102.

51 Pandey, *Routine Violence*, 89. See also Zoya Hasan, *Congress after Indira: Policy, Power, Political Change (1984–2009)* (Delhi: Oxford University Press, 2014).

52 See Supriya Varma and Jaya Menon, 'Was There a Temple under the Babri Masjid? Reading the Archaeological "Evidence"', *Economic and Political Weekly* 45.50 (11–17 December 2010): 61–72.

53 See Isha Dueby, 'Ayodhya Land Ruling Has Thrust History into the Centre of Indian Politics – What This Means for the Future', *The Conversation* (11 December 2019), available at https://theconversation.com/ayodhya-land-ruling-has-thrust-history-into-the-centre-of-indian-politics-what-this-means-for-the-future-127970; and Anon., 'Chronology of the Ayodhya Case', *The Hindu* (27 September 2018 – updated subsequently), available at https://www.thehindu.com/news/national/chronology-of-ayodhya-case/article25060329.ece.

54 Angana Chatterji, Thomas Hansen and Christophe Jaffrelot, 'Introduction', in *Majoritarian State*, 1–17 (2).

55 Dipankar Gupta, *Justice before Reconciliation: Negotiating a 'New Normal' in Post-Riot Mumbai and Ahmedabad* (Abingdon: Routledge, 2011), 34.

56 Pandey, *Routine Violence*, 188. His wider list includes: Colombo 1983, Delhi 1984, and Bombay and elsewhere 1992–3, 187–8.

57 Chatterji, Hansen and Jaffrelot, 'Introduction', 3.

58 Though making appeals to the lower castes was essential for Modi's electoral victory, see Eswaran Sridharan, 'India's Watershed Vote: Behind Modi's Victory', *Journal of Democracy* 25.4 (2014): 20–33 (24).

59 See Christophe Jaffrelot, 'The Modi-Centric BJP 2014 Election Campaign: New Techniques and Old Tactics', *Contemporary South Asia* 23.2 (2016): 155–66; Prashant Waikar, 'Reading Islamophobia in Hindutva: An Analysis of Narendra Modi's Political Discourse', *Islamophobia Studies Journal* 4.2 (2018): 161–80 (170–1); and Kunai Sen, 'Narendra Modi's Performance on the Indian Economy – Five Key Policies Assessed', *The Conversation* (8 May 2019), available at https://theconversation.com/narendra-modis-performance-on-the-indian-economy-five-key-policies-assessed-116485.

60 See Juhi Ahuja, 'International Yoga Day Controversy: India's Soft Power or Modi's Hindu Agenda?' *RSIS Commentary* CO15155 (2015), available at https://www.rsis.edu.sg/wp-content/uploads/2015/07/CO15155.pdf; and Paul Hedges, 'Yoga and Violence: International Yoga Day and Indian Religious Politics', *RSIS Commentary* CO15154 (2015), available at https://www.rsis.edu.sg/wp-content/uploads/2015/07/CO15154.pdf.

61 Juhi Ahuja, 'Protecting Holy Cows: Hindu Vigilantism against Muslims in India', in *Vigilantism against Migrants and Minorities*, ed. Tore Bjørgo and Miroslav Mareš (Abingdon: Routledge, 2019), 55–68 (57–8).

62 See Kenneth Valpey, *Cow Care in Hindu Animal Ethics* (Cham: Springer, 2020).

63 See Juhi Ahuja and Pravin Prakash, 'Cow Vigilantism in India: Modi's Dilemma or Legacy?' *RSIS Commentary* CO17131 (2017), available at https:// www.rsis.edu.sg/wp-content/uploads/2017/07/CO17131.pdf; and Paul Hedges, 'Religion and Society: Of Hindu Extremists, Cows, and Muslims', *RSIS Commentary* CO15232 (2015), available at https://www.rsis.edu.sg/ wp-content/uploads/2015/10/CO15232.pdf; and Jaffrelot, 'A *De Facto* Ethnic Democracy?', 59–63.

64 Ahuja, 'Protecting Holy Cows', 56 and 65.

65 At least one poll before the 2019 election suggested that more Muslims (26 per cent) than either Christians (20 per cent) or Sikhs (21 per cent) were prepared to give Modi another chance in office, this compared dramatically to Hindus (51 per cent). Opposition to a second Modi term was, respectively: 56 per cent, 62 per cent, 68 per cent, and 31 per cent. See Hilal Ahmed, 'BJP Is Emerging as Second-Most Preferred Political Choice for Muslim Voters in India', *The Print* (24 April 2019), available at https://theprint.in/opinion/muslim-vote/bjp-is-emerging-as-second-most-preferred-political-choice-for-muslim-voters-in-india/225041/.

66 See Jaffrelot, 'The Modi-Centric BJP 2014 Election Campaign', 160; Waikar, 'Reading Islamophobia in Hindutva', 171 and 173; and Ashutosh Varshney, 'India's Watershed Vote: Hindu Nationalism in Power?', *Journal of Democracy* 25.4 (2014): 34–45.

67 Abdullah Yusuf, 'Kashmir: How Modi's Aggressive "Hindutva" Project Has Brought India and Pakistan to the Brink – Again', *The Conversation* (5 September 2019), available at https://theconversation.com/kashmir-how-modis-aggressive-hindutva-project-has-brought-india-and-pakistan-to-the-brink-again-122851.

68 Puja Changoiwala, 'India's Muslim Are Terrified of Being Deported', *Foreign Policy* (21 February 2020), available at https://foreignpolicy.com/2020/02/21/ india-muslims-deported-terrified-citizenship-amendment-act-caa/.

69 Alka Kurian, 'Indian Women Protest New Citizenship Laws, Joining a Global "Fourth Wave" Feminist Movement', *Conversation* (25 February 2020), available at https://theconversation.com/indian-women-protest-new-citizenship-laws-joining-a-global-fourth-wave-feminist-movement-129602.

70 See Barkha Dutt, 'India's Politics of Hate Have Erupted for All the World to Witness', *Washington Post* (26 February 2020), available at www. washingtonpost.com/opinions/2020/02/25/indias-politics-hate-have-erupted-all-world-witness/; Soutik Biswas, 'Why Delhi Violence Has Echoes of the Gujarat Riots', *BBC News* (26 February 2020), available at www.bbc. com/news/world-asia-india-51641516?SThisFB; and Rahul Sambaraju and Suryapratim Roy, 'Indian Citizenship Has Now Been Reduced to "Us" versus "Them"', *The Conversation* (28 February 2020), available at https:// theconversation.com/indian-citizenship-has-now-been-reduced-to-us-versus-them-130422. On semi-official RSS vigilantes, see Jaffrelot, 'A *De Facto* Ethnic Democracy?', 51–7. At the time of writing, protests are impossible under the

conditions of Covid-19, but even this virus has been utilized to incite further Islamophobia, see Nazneen Mohsina and Joseph Franco, 'Rising Islamophobia in India: Exploiting the Pandemic?', *RSIS Commentary* CO20109 (2020), available at https://www.rsis.edu.sg/wp-content/uploads/2020/06/CO20109. pdf.

71 Tim Hume, 'Hindu Nationalist Mobs in India Are Hunting and Beating Muslims', *Vice News* (25 February 2020), available at www.vice.com/en_us/ article/jgeva3/hindu-nationalist-mobs-in-india-are-hunting-and-beating-muslims. Though it has been suggested that the violence was partially held back till Trump left, see Lauren Frayer, 'Delhi Riots Aftermath: "How Do You Explain Such Violence?"', *NPR* (7 March 2020), available at https://www.npr.org/2020/03/07/812193930/ delhi-riots-aftermath-how-do-you-explain-such-violence.

72 See Sangeeta Kamat and Biju Mathew, 'Mapping Political Violence in a Globalized World: The Case of Hindu Nationalism', *Social Justice* 30.3 (2003): 4–16 (11–14).

73 See Sitara Thobani, 'Alt-Right with the Hindu-Right: Long-Distance Nationalism and the Perfection of Hindutva', *Ethnic and Racial Studies* 42.5 (2019): 745–62.

74 See Nanda, 'Hindu Triumphalism', 111–13.

75 Thobani, 'Alt-Right with the Hindu-Right', 746.

76 See Ratna Kapur, '"Belief" in the Rule of Law and the Hindu Nation and the Rule of Law', in *Majoritarian State*, 353–71.

77 See Kenneth Roth, 'The Dangerous Rise of Populism: Global Attacks on Human Rights Values', *Human Rights Watch World Report* (2017), available at https://www.hrw.org/world-report/2017/country-chapters/ dangerous-rise-of-populism; Edward Luce, 'The Global Advance of Ethno-Nationalism', *Financial Times* (24 May 2019), available at https://www.ft.com/ content/0c6e40ec-7dcc-11e9-81d2-f785092ab560; Daniel Steinmetz-Jenkins and Anton Jäger, 'The Populist Right Is Forging an Unholy Alliance with Religion', *The Guardian* (11 June 2019), available at https://www.theguardian. com/commentisfree/2019/jun/11/populists-right-unholy-alliance-religion; and Jaffrelot, 'A *De Facto* Ethnic Democracy?'.

78 See Edward Anderson and Christophe Jaffrelot, 'Hindu Nationalism and the "Saffronisation of the Public Sphere": An Interview with Christophe Jaffrelot', *Contemporary South Asia* 26.4 (2018): 468–82.

Interlude 4

This section is written by Paul Hedges with Luca Farrow.

1 https://www.un.org/en/universal-declaration-human-rights/index.html, accessed 21 October 2020.

2 UDHR Article 18.

3 UDHR Article 29.

4 Jacques Derrida, 'Force of Law: The "Mystical Foundation of Authority",' in *Acts of Religion*, ed. Gil Anidjar (London: Routledge, 2002), 228–98.

5 ICCPR adopted by UNGA resolution (16 December 1966), available at https://www.ohchr.org/en/professionalinterest/pages/ccpr.aspx.

6 Nazila Ghanea, 'Minorities and Hatred: Protections and Implications', *International Journal on Minority and Group Rights* 17.3 (2010): 423–46 (435).

7 ICERD adopted by UNGA resolution (21 December 1965), available at https://www.ohchr.org/en/professionalinterest/pages/cerd.aspx.

8 Pew Research Centre, 'A Closer Look at How Religious Restrictions Have Risen around the World' (15 July 2019), available at https://www.pewforum.org/2019/07/15/a-closer-look-at-how-religious-restrictions-have-risen-around-the-world/.

9 UN, Resolution 66/168 of 2011, Article 5, available at https://undocs.org/en/%20A/RES/66/168.

10 UN, Resolution 66/168, Article 10.

11 Articles 10 and 14 of the UN Charter, available at https://www.un.org/en/sections/un-charter/un-charter-full-text/, describe UNGA resolutions as 'recommendations'. The UDHR defines the 'human rights' and 'fundamental freedoms' that are referred to in the UN Charter. While the UN Charter is generally binding on the UN Member States that have signed up for membership of the bloc, it does not provide individuals who believe their human rights have been infringed with specific, actionable rights. There are more specific UN conventions that expand on the protection of rights referred to in the UDHR and UN Charter, such as the ICCPR, to which not all Member States are signatories.

12 https://www.ohchr.org/en/professionalinterest/pages/opccpr1.aspx, accessed 21 October 2020.

13 https://www.echr.coe.int/Documents/Convention_ENG.pdf, accessed 21 October 2020.

14 See page 48 of the Manifesto, available at https://assets-global.website-files.com/5da42e2cae7ebd3f8bde353c/5dda924905da587992a064ba_Conservative%202019%20Manifesto.pdf. However, it has been argued that whatever the fate of the Human Rights Act 1998, English common law rights, 'more easily than [ECHR] rights, can give effect to the rich vein of rights guarantees which are to be found in the customary international law of human rights.' See Eirik Bjorge, 'Common Law Rights: Balancing Domestic and International Exigencies', *Cambridge Law Journal* 75.2 (July 2016): 220–43. DOI: https://doi.org/10.1017/S0008197316000258.

15 EHRC, *Investigation into antisemitism in the Labour Party* (October 2020), 26, available at https://www.equalityhumanrights.com/sites/default/files/investigation-into-antisemitism-in-the-labour-party.pdf. Article 17 of the ECHR states, 'Nothing in this Convention may be interpreted as implying ... any right to engage in any activity ... aimed at the destruction of any of the rights

and freedoms set forth herein or at their limitation to a greater extent than is provided for in the Convention.'

16 *X v Federal Republic of Germany*, App. No. 9235/81, 29 Eur. Comm'n H.R. 194 (1982), cited in Ghanea, 'Minorities and Hatred', 440.

17 Channel News Asia, 'Imam Who Made Offensive Remarks against Jews, Christians Fined $4,000' (3 April 2017), available at https://www.todayonline. com/imam-who-made-offensive-remarks-against-jews-christians-charged-promoting-enmity.

18 Penal Code available at https://sso.agc.gov.sg/Act/PC1871.

19 MRHA available at https://sso.agc.gov.sg/Act/MRHA1990. For a wider discussion of the context of this legislation, see Paul Hedges and Mohamed Imran Mohamed Taib, 'The Interfaith Movement in Singapore: Precarious Toleration and Embedded Autonomy', in The Interfaith Movement, eds John Fahy and Jan-Jonathan Bock (New York: Routledge, 2019), 139–56.

20 Christian Concern, 'Christian Street Preachers Acquitted of Public Order Offences' (19 June 2017), available at https://christianconcern.com/news/ christian-street-preachers-acquitted-of-public-order-offences/.

21 Section 31 of the Crime and Disorder Act 1998, available at http://www. legislation.gov.uk/ukpga/1998/37/contents.

22 Christian Concern, 'Street Preachers Convicted for Quoting Bible in "Modern Day Heresy Trial"' (28 February 2017), available at https://christianconcern. com/ccpressreleases/street-preachers-convicted-for-quoting-bible-in-modern-day-heresy-trial/.

23 Tom Goodenough, 'Bible Bashers: Why Was a Christian Preacher Carted Off the Streets of London in Handcuffs?', *Spectator* (16 March 2019): 27, available at https://www.spectator.co.uk/article/bible-bashers.

24 See Peter Edge, 'Oppositional Religious Speech: Understanding Hate Preaching', *Ecclesiastical Law Journal* 20 (2018): 278–89.

25 Part 3A of the Public Order Act 1986, available at http://www.legislation.gov. uk/ukpga/1986/64.

26 IHRA Working Definition of Antisemitism, 26 May 2016, available at https:// www.holocaustremembrance.com/working-definition-antisemitism.

27 Rebecca Ruth Gould, 'Legal Form and Legal Legitimacy: The IHRA Definition of Antisemitism as a Case Study in Censored Speech', *Law, Culture and the Humanities* (August 2018), https://doi.org/10.1177/1743872118780660.

28 Executive Order on Combating Anti-Semitism, 11 December 2019, available at https://www.whitehouse.gov/presidential-actions/executive-order-combating-anti-semitism/.

29 David Schraub, 'Why Trump's Executive Order on Anti-Semitism Touched off a Firestorm', *Atlantic* (12 December 2019), available at https://www.theatlantic. com/ideas/archive/2019/12/dilemma-jewish-identity/603493/.

30 Transcript of US Civil Rights Act (1964), available at https://www.ourdocuments. gov/doc.php?flash=true&doc=97&page=transcript.

31 Deborah Lipstadt, *Denying the Holocaust: The Growing Assault on Truth and Memory* (New York: Plume, 1994), 220.

EPILOGUE

1 See Oddbjørn Leirvik, *Interreligious Studies* (London: Bloomsbury, 2014), 17–31.

2 See Martin Buber, *I and Thou* (London: Bloomsbury, [1923] 2013); and Jürgen Habermas, 'A Philosophy of Dialogue', in *Dialogue as a Trans-Disciplinary Concept: Martin Buber's Philosophy of Dialogue and Its Contemporary Reception*, ed. Paul Mendes-Flohr (Berlin: De Gruyter, 2015), 7–20. Notably, the fortuitous phrasing of 'I and Thou' is from the English translation for, in German, Buber used the more familiar 'Ich und Du' which would translate more literally as 'I and You'.

3 Eboo Patel, *Acts of Faith: The Story of an American Muslim, in the Struggle for the Soul of a Generation* (Boston, MA: Beacon Press, 2010).

4 John Roth, *Ethics during and after the Holocaust: In the Shadow of Birkenau* (Basingstoke: Palgrave Macmillan, 2005), 33.

5 The question of academic study as neutral, objective, and non-partisan, and the engagement with justice, activism, and the politics of academia is addressed in Paul Hedges, *Understanding Religion: Theories and Methods in Studying Religiously Diverse Societies* (Berkeley: University of California Press, 2021).

6 See, on the practical process of not judging others in the process of deradicalization, Christian Picciolini, 'Filling the Potholes', in *Faith, Identity, Cohesion: Building a Better Future*, eds Jolene Jerard and Amanda Huan (London, Singapore, and Hackensack, NJ: World Scientific, 2020), 123–26. On how to dialogue, debate, and disagree productively, see Christian Jarrett, 'How to politely and productively disagree', *BBC* (15 October 2020), available at: https://www.bbc.com/worklife/article/20200930-how-to-politely-and-productively-disagree; Devorah Schoenfeld and Jeanine Diller, 'Using Hevrutra to Do and Teach Comparative Theology', in *Teaching Interreligious Encounters*, eds Marc Pugliese and Alexander Hwang (Oxford: Oxford University Press, 2017), 163–77; and Laura Chasin, *Fostering Dialogue across Divides: A Nuts and Bolts Approach* (Watertown, MA: Public Conversations Project, 2006). Meanwhile, on understanding that we also have, within ourselves, the potential for the negative attitudes and way of life that we may see in others, see Thich Nhat Hanh's poem of the sea pirate 'Please Call Me By My True Names', available at: https://www.brookes.ac.uk/poetry-centre/national-poetry-day/thich-nhat-hanh--please-call-me-by-my-true-names/.

7 Stephen Prothero, *God Is Not One: The Eight Rival Religions That Run the World* (New York: HarperCollins, 2010).

8 Prothero, *God Is Not One*, 14.

9 See Meredith McGuire, *Lived Religion* (Oxford: Oxford University Press, 2008); and Hedges, *Understanding Religion*, 68–72.

10 Prothero, *God Is Not One*, 15.

11 Bonaventura de Sousa Santos, 'Towards a Multicultural Conception of Human Rights', in *Spaces of Culture: City, Nation, World*, ed. Mike Featherstone and Scott Lash (London: Sage, 1999): 214–29 (221).

12 See, variously: Jayeel Cornelio and Timothy Andrew E. Salera, 'Youth in Interfaith Dialogue: Intercultural Understanding and Its Implications on Education in the Philippines', in *Interreligious Dialogue*, ed. Christoffer Grundmann (Winona, MN: Anselm Academic, 2015), 155–68; IFYC, 'The Update – 6 Successful Strategies', *IFYC* (13 November 2014), available at: https://www.youtube.com/watch?v=MvRAoKgSQQs; and Paul F Knitter, 'Inter-Religious Dialogue and Social Action', in *The Wiley-Blackwell Companion to Inter-Religious Dialogue*, ed. Catherine Cornille (Chichester: Wiley-Blackwell, 2013), 133–48.

13 Darrell Fasching, Dell Dechant and David Lantingua, *Comparative Religious Ethics: A Narrative Approach to Global Ethics*, 2nd edn (Chichester: Wiley-Blackwell, 2011), 4.

14 See Jeffry Halverson, *Searching for a King: Muslim Nonviolence and the Future of Islam* (Washington, DC: Potomac Books, 2012), 26–36; and Thich Nhat Hanh, *Being Peace* (Berkeley, CA: Parallax Books, 1996).

15 This is not to say that there is a shared morality across religions, for despite the advocacy for a supposed common Global Ethic by figures such as Hans Küng that supplies, at most, a thin set of agreeable terms, we see huge disagreements. For instance, in terms of non-violence, some may advocate for pacifism, others for self-defence, while some may assert it also includes 'just' or 'holy' wars. On such debates, see Paul Hedges, 'Concerns about the Global Ethic: A Sympathetic Critique and Suggestions for a New Direction', *Studies in Interreligious Dialogue* 18.1 (2008): 1–16. For some thoughts on thinking beyond this, see Paul Hedges, *Controversies in Interreligious Dialogue and the Theology of Religions* (London: SCM, 2010), 254–70. It is also worth noting that a discursive framing of one's own tradition as non-violent is very different from the actual practice of non-violence, and one figure noted in these pages as stirring up animosity and violence across ethno-religious lines, Anagarika Dharmapala, was among those who contributed to framing Buddhism as a pacifist tradition in the modern world, see Iselin Frydenlund, ' "Buddhism has made Asia Mild" The Modernist Construction of Buddhism as Pacifism', in *Buddhist Modernities: Re-Inventing Tradition in the Globalizing Modern World*, eds Hanna Havnevik, Ute Hüsken, Mark Teeuwen, Vladimir Tikhonov and Koen Wellens (New York, Routledge, 2017), 204–21 (213–15).

16 See Eboo Patel, April Kunze and Noah Silverman, 'Storytelling as a Key Methodology for Interfaith Youth Work', *Journal of Ecumenical Studies* 43.2 (2008), 35–46.

17 William Bole ' "Selma" Is True to the Story It Needs to Tell', *Tikkun Daily* (19 January 2015), available at https://www.tikkun.org/tikkundaily/2015/01/19/selma-is-true-to-the-story-it-needs-to-tell/.

18 Halverson, *Searching for a King*, 35, citing Naim Ateek, quoted in Matthew Duss, 'A History of Nonviolence', *American Prospect* (15 November 2007),

available at https://prospect.org/article/history-nonviolence/. Halverson's work outlines further examples of Muslims promoting nonviolence, on which see also Mohammed Abu-Nimer, 'A Framework for Nonviolence and Peacebuilding in Islam', *Journal of Law and Religion* 15.1/2 (2000–1): 217–65. For other examples of interreligious peace work in Israel–Palestine see Yafiah Randall, *Sufism and Jewish-Muslim Relations: The Derekh Avraham Order in Israel* (London: Routledge, 2016).

19 On nonviolence, see, variously, Sudhir Chandra, ed., *Violence and Non-Violence across Time: History, Religion and Culture* (London: Routledge, 2018); and Ramin Jahanbegloo, *Introduction to Nonviolence* (Basingstoke: Palgrave Macmillan, 2014). On reasons why some actors may avoid 'nonviolence' as a term, see Sixte Vigny Nimuraba, '"Do It with Them": Community Service as a Tool for Nonviolence Education in Burundi', in *Connecting Contemporary African-Asian Peacemaking and Nonviolence: From Satagraha to Ujamaa*, ed. Vidya Jain and Matt Meyer (Newcastle: Cambridge Scholars' Press, 2018): 26–43 (31).

20 See note 15.

21 See Hedges, *Understanding Religion*, 432–35.

22 If it is suggested that mutual conflict between communities is a natural model, then one may see an enforced 'precarious toleration', rather than a real harmony and coexistence. See Paul Hedges and Mohamed Imran Mohamed Taib, 'The Interfaith Movement in Singapore: Precarious Toleration and Embedded Autonomy', in *The Interfaith Movement*, eds John Fahy and Jan-Jonathan Bock (New York: Routledge, 2019), 139–56.

23 Kwame Anthony Appiah, *Cosmopolitanism: Ethics in a World of Strangers* (New York: W. W. Norton, 2007); and Ulrich Beck, 'The Cosmopolitan Society and Its Enemies', *Theory, Culture & Society* 19.1–2 (2002): 17–44.

24 See Paul Hedges, 'Should Interfaith and Interreligious Dialogue Include Atheists? Towards an Interworldview Perspective', *Interreligious Insight* 15.1 (2017): 38–47.

25 See Alan Race, 'Interfaith Dialogue: Religious Accountability between Strangeness and Resonance', in *Christian Approaches to Other Faiths*, ed. Paul Hedges and Alan Race (London: SCM Press, 2008), 155–72.

26 See Edward Kessler, *An Introduction to Jewish-Christian Relations* (Cambridge: Cambridge University Press, 2010), and the important Jewish 'Dabru Emet' statement (2002), available at http://www.jcrelations.net/Dabru+Emet+-+A+Jewish+Statement+on+Christians+and+Christianity.2395.0.html?L=3. This is not to say that all interreligious dialogue is positive or shows increasing understanding, and it may be engaged reluctantly, may add to tensions, or may see power dynamics from a dominant partner distorting the voice of the other side. See, in general terms, Hedges, *Understanding Religion*, chapter 14, and Hedges, *Controversies*, 94–102. Specifically on Jewish-Christian dialogue, see Alana Vincent, 'Convergence and Asymmetry: Some Brief Observations on the Current State of Jewish-Christian Dialogue', *Interreligious Studies and Intercultural Theology* 4.2 (2020), 201–23.

27 See Susanne Wessendorf, '"Being Open, but Sometimes Being Closed":
    Conviviality in a Super-Diverse London Neighbourhood', *European Journal of
    Cultural Studies* 17.4 (2014): 392–405.

28 Wessendorf, '"Being Open"', 394.

29 Max Bergholz, *Violence as a Generative Force: Identity, Nationalism, and
    Memory in a Balkan Community* (Ithaca, NY: Cornell University Press, 2016).

30 See Adam Seligman and Robert Weller, *Rethinking Pluralism: Ritual,
    Experience, and Ambiguity* (Oxford: Oxford University Press, 2012), 19–20.

31 For an excellent example, see the work of CEDAR as recounted in Adam
    Seligman, Rahel Wasserfall and David Montgomery, *Living with Difference:
    How to Build Community in a Divided World* (Berkeley: University of
    California Press, 2016). For their website, see https://www.cedarnetwork.
    org. On the principles, see Paul Hedges, 'Conceptualising Social Cohesion in
    Relation to Religious Diversity: Sketching a Pathway in a Globalised World',
    Interreligious Relations 16 (2020), available at https://www.rsis.edu.sg/
    wp-content/uploads/2020/07/IRR-Issue-16-May-2020.pdf.

32 These are not always included in reflection in interreligious ventures, but
    may be considered central for the nexus of issues key to interreligious studies,
    see Paul Hedges and Liu, Yue, 'Interreligious Studies and Law: Decolonizing
    Freedom of Religion and Belief', in *The Georgetown Companion to
    Interreligious Studies*, ed. Lucinda Mosher (Washington, DC: Georgetown
    University Press, forthcoming).

33 See, for instance, Najeeba Syeed and Heidi Hadsell, eds, *Critical Perspectives
    on Interreligious Education: Experiments in Empathy* (Leiden: Brill, 2020).

34 See Paul Hedges, 'Framing Cohesive Societies: Some Initial Remarks and
    Ways Ahead', in *Faith, Identity, Cohesion*, 191–202; Eboo Patel, *Interfaith
    Leadership: A Primer* (Boston: Beacon Press, 2016); and Hedges,
    'Conceptualising Social Cohesion'.

FURTHER READING

Chapter One: Dehumanizing humans: Prejudice, identity, and othering

Allport, Gordon, *The Nature of Prejudice* (New York: Addison-Wesley, 1954).

Anderson, Kristin, *Benign Bigotry: The Psychology of Subtle Prejudice* (Cambridge: Cambridge University Press, 2010).

Dovidio, John, Samuel Gaertner and Adam Pearson, 'On the Nature of Prejudice: The Psychological Foundations of Hate', in *The Psychology of Hate*, ed. R. J. Sternberg, 211–34 (Washington, DC: American Psychological Association, 2005).

Kite, Mary and Bernard Whitley, Jr, *Psychology of Prejudice and Discrimination*, 3rd edn (London: Routledge, 2016).

Chapter Two: The hatred unto death: When prejudice becomes killing and genocide

Bandura, Albert, 'Selective Moral Disengagement in the Exercise of Moral Agency', *Journal of Moral Education* 31.2 (2002): 101–19.

Kalyvas, Stahis, *The Logic of Violence in Civil War* (Cambridge: Cambridge University Press, 2006).

Levene, Mark, 'Genocide', in *The Cambridge World History*, vol. 7, ed. J. McNeill and K. Pomeranz, 420–41 (Cambridge: Cambridge University Press, 2015).

Malešević, Siniša, *The Rise of Organised Brutality: A Historical Sociology of Violence* (Cambridge: Cambridge University Press, 2017).

Interlude 1: What is religious hatred?

Hedges, Paul, *Understanding Religion: Theories and Methods for Studying Religiously Diverse Societies* (Berkeley: University of California Press, 2021).

Juergensmeyer, Mark, *Terror in the Mind of God: The Global Rise of Religious Violence*, 4th edn (Berkeley: University of California Press, 2017).

Chapter Three: The oldest prejudice? Christian antisemitism from the Gospels to the ghettoes

Cohn-Sherbok, Dan, *The Crucified Jew: Twenty Centuries of Christian Anti-Semitism* (Grand Rapids, MI: Eerdmans, 1997).

Kaufmann, Thomas, *Luther's Jews: A Journey into Anti-Semitism* (Oxford: Oxford University Press, 2017).

Miller, Ronald, 'Judaism: Siblings in Strife', in *Christian Approaches to Other Religions*, ed. Paul Hedges and Alan Race, 176–90 (London: SCM, 2008).

Ruether, Rosemary Radford, *Faith and Fratricide: The Theological Roots of Anti-Semitism* (New York: Seabury Press, 1974).

Chapter Four: Kafir and Turks: Christians and Muslims through history

Ayoub, Mahmoud, *A Muslim View of Christianity: Essays on Dialogue by Mahmoud Ayoub*, ed. Irfan Omar (Maryknoll, NY: Orbis, 2007).

Cardini, Franco, *Europe and Islam*, trans. Caroline Beamish (Oxford: Blackwell, 2001).

Griffith, Sydney, *The Church in the Shadow of the Mosque: Christians and Muslims in the World of Islam* (Princeton, NJ: Princeton University Press, 2008).

Thomas, David, 'Dialogue before Dialogue', in *Contemporary Muslim-Christian Encounters: Developments, Diversity, and Dialogues*, ed. Paul Hedges, 1–15 (London: Bloomsbury, 2015).

Chapter Five: Religious hatred as racial hatred: Enlightenment, citizenship, and racialization

Bethencourt, Francisco, *Racisms: From the Crusades to the Twentieth Century* (Princeton, NJ: Princeton University Press, 2013).

Hochman, Adam, 'Racialization: A Defense of the Concept', *Ethnic and Racial Studies* 42.8 (2019): 1245–62.

Meer, Nasar, 'Racialization and Religion: Race, Culture and Difference in the Study of Antisemitism and Islamophobia', *Ethnic and Racial Studies* 36.3 (2013): 385–98.

Nirenberg, David, *Anti-Judaism: The History of a Way of Thinking* (New York: W. W. Norton, 2013).

Interlude 2: Why did the Holocaust happen?

Lipstadt, Deborah, *The Eichmann Trial* (London: Penguin, 2011).
Michael, Robert, *Holy Hatred: Christianity, Antisemitism, and the Holocaust* (Basingstoke: Palgrave Macmillan, 2006).

Chapter Six: The West's eternal Jewish question? Politics, antisemitism, and Holocaust denial

Hirsh, David, *Contemporary Left Antisemitism* (Abingdon: Routledge, 2018).
Laqueur, Walter, *The Changing Face of Antisemitism: From Ancient Times to the Present Day* (Oxford: Oxford University Press, 2006).
Lipstadt, Deborah, *Denying the Holocaust: The Growing Assault on Truth and Memory* (New York: Plume, 1994).
Lipstadt, Deborah, *Antisemitism Here and Now* (London: Scribe, 2019).

Chapter Seven: 'Why do they hate us?' and 'Why do we hate them?': Contemporary Western Islamophobias

Alsutany, Evelyn, *Arabs and Muslims in the Media* (Albany: New York University Press, 2012).
Beydoun, Khaled, *American Islamophobia: Understanding the Roots and Rise of Fear* (Berkeley: University of California Press, 2018).
Green, Todd, *The Fear of Islam: An Introduction to Islamophobia in the West*, 2nd edn (Minneapolis, MN: Fortress Press, 2019).
Moosavi Leon, 'The Racialization of Muslim Converts in Britain and Their Experiences of Islamophobia', *Critical Sociology* 41.1 (2015): 41–56.

Interlude 3: Are antisemitism and Islamophobia connected?

Meer, Nasar, ed., *Racialization and Religion: Race, Culture and Difference in the Study of Antisemitism and Islamophobia* (Abingdon: Routledge, 2014).
Renton, James and Ben Gidley, 'Introduction: The Shared Story of Europe's Ideas of the Muslim and the Jew – A Diachronic Framework', in *Antisemitism and Islamophobia in Europe: A Shared Story?*, ed. James Renton and Ben Gidley, 1–21 (London: Palgrave Macmillan, 2017).

Chapter Eight: From People of the Book to enemies of Islam: Islamic antisemitism and Palestine–Israel

Donner, Fred, *Muhammad and the Believers: At the Origins of Islam* (Cambridge, MA: Belknap Press, 2010).

Firestone, Reuven, 'Muslim-Jewish Relations', *Oxford Research Encyclopedia of Religion* (2016), doi:10.1093/acrefore/9780199340378.013.17.

Tibi, Bassam, *Islamism and Islam* (New Haven, CT: Yale University Press, 2012).

Webman, Esther, 'From the Damascus Blood Libel to the "Arab Spring": The Evolution of Arab Antisemitism', *Antisemitism Studies* 1.1 (1997): 157–206.

Chapter Nine: Killing for the Buddha: Islamophobia in the Buddhist world

Fernando, Jude Lal, 'Buddhism, Nationalism, and Violence in Asia', in *Controversies in Contemporary Religion*, vol. 3, ed. Paul Hedges, 61–90 (Santa Barbara, CA: Praeger, 2014).

Frydenlund, Iselin, 'Buddhist Islamophobia: Actors, Tropes, Contexts', in *Handbook of Conspiracy Theory and Contemporary Religion*, eds Asbjørn Dyrendal, David G. Robertson, and Egil Asprem, 279-302 (Leiden: Brill, 2018).

Jerryson, Michael, *If You Meet the Buddha on the Road: Buddhism, Politics, and Violence* (Oxford: Oxford University Press, 2018).

Pradeep, Anuruddha, 'The Political Dimension of Buddhism in Sri Lanka', in *Buddhism in Asia: Revival and Reinvention*, ed. Nayanjot Lahiri and Upinder Singh, 261–89 (Singapore: Institute of South East Asia Studies, 2016).

Chapter Ten: Hindutva as hatred: Hindus, Muslims, and the fatherland

Jaffrelot, Christophe, *The Hindu Nationalist Movement in India* (New York: Columbia University Press, 1996).

Kakar, Sudhir, *The Colors of Violence* (Chicago, IL: University of Chicago Press, 1996).

Smith, David, *Hinduism and Modernity* (Oxford: Blackwell, 2003), 49–64.

Waikar, Prashant, 'Reading Islamophobia in Hindutva: An Analysis of Narendra Modi's Political Discourse', *Islamophobia Studies Journal* 4.2 (2018): 161–80.

Interlude 4: Can we regulate religious hatred?

Ghanea, Nazila, 'Minorities and Hatred: Protections and Implications',
International Journal on Minority and Group Rights 17.3 (2010): 423–46.

Gould, Rebecca Ruth, 'Legal Form and Legal Legitimacy: The IHRA Definition
of Antisemitism as a Case Study in Censored Speech', *Law, Culture and the
Humanities* (August 2018): 1–34.

Epilogue: The good news: Dialogue, civil rights, and peacebuilding

Hanh, Thich Nhat, *Being Peace* (Berkeley, CA: Parallax Books, 1996).

Hedges, Paul, 'Conceptualising Social Cohesion in Relation to Religious
Diversity: Sketching a Pathway in a Globalised World', *Interreligious Relations*
16 (2020), available at https://www.rsis.edu.sg/wp-content/uploads/2020/07/
IRR-Issue-16-May-2020.pdf.

Leirvik, Oddbjørn, *Interreligious Studies* (London: Bloomsbury, 2014).

Patel, Eboo, *Acts of Faith: The Story of an American Muslim, the Struggle for the
Soul of a Generation* (Boston, MA: Beacon Press, 2010).

Seligman, Adam, Rahel Wasserfall and David Montgomery, *Living with
Difference: How to Build Community in a Divided World* (Berkeley: University
of California Press, 2016).

Syeed, Najeeba and Heidi Hadsell, eds, *Critical Perspectives on Interreligious
Education: Experiments in Empathy* (Leiden: Brill, 2020).

INDEX

Abraham (patriarch) 55, 70, 158,
    227 n.14
Abrahamic 47, 48, 145, 165,
    227–8 n.14
academia (academic/scholarship)
    antisemitism in 62, 93, 111, 115–16
    freedom 115
    neutrality/power relations/reflexivity
        in 3–4, 182, 204, 211 n.11,
        276 n.5
    racism in 204, 236 n.26
    See also orientalism
Africa (African) 39, 68, 80, 81, 87, 89,
        90, 94, 108, 130, 149, 159
    ancestry and racial identity 84
    Ethiopia 68, 87
    Ethiopian Jews 135
    and Ham (biblical character) 237
        n.38
    Morocco 164
    and slavery 20, 87, 88, 237 n.38
    South Africa 87, 115
    See also Black, colonialism, Egypt,
        Fanon (Frantz), slavery
ahimsa 166, 167, 176, 206, 207
    in Hindu thought derived from
        Buddhism and Jainism 193
agency (human, for or against violence/
        prejudice) 41, 209
Akhand Bharat 184, 186, 189
Al Qaeda 31, 138, 162, 163
Al-Andalusia 75–6, 89, 234 n.52
Al-Husseini, Amin 155, 160, 163
Allport, Gordon 11, 12, 13, 14, 15–16,
        17, 22, 23, 24, 65, 84, 207
alt-right 108, 109, 112, 122, 194
analytical category (as compared with
        definitional category) 5, 34, 46
anti-racism. See racism

antisemitism
    in academic interpretations 62
    Arab Christian antisemitism
        152–3, 154
    in Buddhists 175
    Christian 51–65, 109–10, 143–4
    defined 6
    in Enlightenment 90–3
    in Hindus 187
    International Holocaust
        Remembrance Alliance definition
        118, 196, 201
    Islamic 46, 149–64
    modern Western 93–6, 107–9
    new (left-wing) 113–22
    not traditional in Islam 151–2,
        158, 164
    'polite'/socially acceptable 3, 142,
        145
    Semites 143–4
    untheorized (as prejudice and
        identity creation) 3; 4–5, 43, 83,
        145–6, 223 n.67
    See also Black Death, blood libel,
        Boycott, Divestment, Sanctions
        (BDS) movement, Christianity,
        deicide, dhimmis, ghettoes,
        Holocaust, Nazis, pogroms,
        Protocols of the Elders of Zion,
        racialization, Talmud, shtetl,
        Zionism
apartheid
    Israel as apartheid state 114,
        115, 119–20
    South Africa 87, 115
apes
    bonobos 29, 86, 217 n.10, 224 n.84
    chimpanzees 27, 29, 33, 34, 86, 217
        n.10, 224 n.84

humans as primates/apes 17, 27, 29, 86, 224 n.84
murder and violence 29, 33, 34, 41, 224 n.84
Appleby, Scott 45
Arab
  envisaged as Muslim 81, 135
  as Semite 144
  See also antisemitism, nationalism
Arendt, Hannah
  banality of evil 31, 219–20 n.34
  on Holocaust 37
Armenian Genocide 39, 152
Ashin Wirathu 176–7, 179
Ashoka 167, 184, 261 n.8
Augustine of Hippo 2, 55–6, 57, 59, 60, 72, 228 n.17
Ayodhya 181, 183, 184, 191, 199, 270 n.49, 271 n.50

Babri Masjid 181, 183, 190–1, 267 n.8
Bandaranaike, S. W. R. D. 170
Bandura, Albert
  humanization 203
  moral disengagement 30–1
Banu Qurayzah 156
Barth, Karl
  antisemitism in 103
Baumann, Zygmunt 35, 38, 40, 221 n.52
benign bigotry 16, 23, 186
  See also discrimination
Bergholz, Max 36, 209, 219 n.31, 222 nn.61, 62, 63, 225 n.86
Bernard of Clairvaux 59, 73, 231 n.21
Bethencourt, Francisco 85, 97
Beydoun, Khaled 132, 135, 204, 251 n.39, 253 n.71
Bharatiya Janata Party (BJP) 185, 186, 187, 188, 189, 190–1, 192–3
Bible
  as corrupted 71
  different versions 61
  endorsing genocide 38, 41, 247 n.63
  first and second Testaments 110
  Jewish and Christian interpretation 62
  usage/readings as antisemitic 51–3, 54, 61–2, 90, 110, 143–4
  usage/readings as racist/racialized 87, 119, 237 n.38
  See also Abraham, covenants, Ham (biblical character), Jesus, Paul
Black Death
  blamed on Jews 57
Black
  Black Americans and Jews 64, 93–4, 206, 207, 252 n.58
  Black Jews 135
  Black Lives Matter (BLM) movement 137, 213 n.11
  Black Muslims 135, 136
  Black women 16, 85
  civil rights movement 206
  as racialised marker 84, 86, 87–8, 96, 98, 234 n.1, 252 n.58
  and slavery 222 n.60
  See also Ham, racialization, racism, slavery
blood libel 56–7, 153, 154, 155, 162
Bosnia-Herzegovina 209, 222 n.62
  See also Srebrenica
Boycott, Divestment, Sanctions (BDS) movement 114–16, 117, 122
Brubaker, Rogers 20, 24, 84
Buber, Martin 203, 276 n.2
Buddhism (Buddhists)
  ahimsa in 166, 167, 176, 193, 206, 207
  as dhimmi 171
  justification for violence in 165–70
  Nalanda 171–2, 173
  sangha (monastic community/ monks) 165, 166, 168, 169, 170, 179, 261 n.10
  sasana, need to defend 165, 177, 263 n.25
  See also Ashin Wirathu, Dharmapala (Anagarika), Hanh (Thich Nhat), Myanmar, Sri Lanka, Thailand
Bunzl, Matti 142, 143, 144
Bush, George W. 130–1, 133, 136
Butler, Judith 115

Cameron, David
  good-Muslim-bad-Muslim trope 133
Cardini, Franco 68, 74

cartoons
  antisemitic 120
  of Muhammad (*Charlie Hebdo*) 127,
    139, 145, 255–6 n.21
Catholicism (Catholics)
  as heretics 73
  prejudice against 62, 88, 229 n.32
  reject Antisemitism 109–10
  See also antisemitism, Augustine,
    Bernard of Clairvaux,
    Christianity, Jesuits, Josaphat
    (Saint), popes
Charlottesville ('Unite the Right' rally)
    108, 109, 127
Chatterjee, Partha 5
Chinese
  Chinatowns 139
  prejudice against 22, 164
Christianity (Christians)
  and antisemitism 51–65, 90–1,
    92, 94, 96, 99, 100, 103, 108,
    109–10, 153–4
  and Islamophobia 67–81
  and racism 85–6, 87–8, 136
  as syncretic 45
  theological differences with
    Islam 69–73
  See also Bible, blood libel, Catholics,
    Church Fathers, covenants,
    Jesuits, Jesus, Luther (Martin),
    Protestantism
Christianophobia 151, 158, 197
Church Fathers
  and antisemitism 53–6
  See also Augustine of Hippo, John
    Chrysostom, Justin Martyr,
    Tertullian
colonialism (Western)
  anti-colonialism 154, 161, 164
  and antisemitism 153–4, 161,
    164, 175
  and (impact on) Buddhism 167–70,
    174, 179, 262 n.20
  colonial difference 20
  and genocide 36, 37, 39, 164
  and (impact on) Hinduism 185, 187,
    189, 194
  and Islam 76, 78–9, 130, 153,
    164

  and Islamophobia 167, 175, 185,
    189, 194
  and Marxism 248 n.76
  and Nazis/ Holocaust 154–5
  and racism 40, 85–6, 87, 174–5
  and religion/civilization matrix
    223 n.75
  See also nationalism, slavery
conspiracy theories 95, 96, 108–9,
    113–14, 119, 155, 162, 164, 180,
    243 n.6
  *See also Protocols of the Elders of
    Zion*, QAnon
Corbyn, Jeremy 113–14, 116, 117, 121,
    122, 246 n.54
Covenants
  biblical 55, 109, 110, 166,
    227–8 n.14
  Islamic 157, 166
  Jewish understanding of three
    covenants 55, 227–8 n.14
cows
  Buddhist protection of 176,
    264 n.47
  Dalits and 193
  Hindu perceptions of Christian and
    Muslim eating of 189, 193
  and Sikhism 264 n.47
  and vigilantism 192–3
crusade(s)
  against Cathars 40
  to Constantinople 59
  crusade(ers) and hostile aggression
    73, 130
  first 59, 73
  and Jews 65, 73
  modern invocations (Islamophobia)
    130, 133
  Muslim perception of 80, 81, 162
  rationales for 59, 73, 80
  second 59, 73
  See also violence

Dawkins, Richard 47, 131, 132
decolonialism/decolonization (critique
    of Western norms) 3, 4, 18–19,
    44, 122, 214–15 n.31, 248 n.76
  colonial difference 5
  postcolonial critique 18

See also Chatterjee (Partha), colonialism, Fanon (Frantz), Mbembe (Achille), orientalism, philosophy ('Western'), Said (Edward)

dehumanization 6, 7, 22, 30–1, 38, 39, 41, 203

deicide, charge of (Jews blamed for Jesus' death) 52, 55, 56–7, 110

deindividuation 21–3, 35, 52, 203

Dharmapala, Anagarika 169, 170, 175, 176, 179, 264 n.40, 264 n.47, 277 n.15

dhimmis (*ahl al-dhimma*) 46, 57, 69, 75, 151, 152, 157, 158–60, 162, 164, 171, 183, 257 n.28, 258 n.37

dhimmiphobia 151, 158, 164

dirt (filthy)
    other as 22–3
    See also disease, Douglas (Mary), pollution

discrimination
    Allport's usage 15, 16
    blatant or covert/subtle 23, 139
    defined as prejudiced behaviour 11–12, 14
    as gendered 4
    leading to violence 27
    majority-minority dynamics 21–2
    and racialization 98
    See also antisemitism, benign bigotry, *dhimmis*, Islamophobia, law, prejudice, women

disease
    and discrimination 57
    linked to antisemitism 95

Douglas, Mary 40
    'matter out of place' 23

Dreyfus Affair 94–5

Egypt 76, 78, 89, 130, 137, 247 n.63

Eichmann, Adolf 101–2, 219 n.34

Enlightenment (European)
    and antisemitism 90–4, 96, 99
    as defined herein 235 n.3
    and ghettoes 64
    posited link to genocide 40
    and racism 83, 89

Erasmus of Rotterdam 61

Esposito, John 79, 136, 179

Europe
    as arbitrary construction 129–30
    imagined in relation to Islam 68–9, 73, 74, 76–9, 80–1, 125, 129–30
    myth of white European civilization (philosophy) 88–90, 98, 173
    and racism 84, 86, 87, 91, 194, 222 n.60

fascists
    Brexit and fascist propaganda comparison 132
    British fascists and black shirts 113, 211 n.6
    influence on Hindu nationalism 187, 269 n.33
    Jewish and left-wing alliance against 113
    UK Conservative Party, alliance with 246 n.49

Fanon, Frantz 39, 93, 141, 146

Firestone, Reuven 52, 151, 156, 158

Foucault, Michel 30, 185

France
    antisemitism in 58, 94–5, 108, 111
    French Revolution 91
    Front National 108
    influence on Arab antisemitism 152–3, 154
    Vendée 40

freedom of religion and belief. *See* law

Freire, Paulo 4

Frydenlund, Iselin 180, 262 n.20

Galtung, Johan 28–9, 236 n.24

Gandhi, Mohandas Karamchand ('Mahatma') 184, 186, 206

Genocide
    begins with words 16, 36
    in biblical record 38, 41, 247 n.63
    definitions 27–8, 32, 33–4
    factors in 34–6
    and hate 17
    as 'natural' 30, 34–5
    origins of term 32, 36
    through history 36–41

untheorized 32–3, 34–41
   See also Armenian Genocide,
      Holocaust (Shoah), Rwandan
      genocide, Srebrenica
Germany
   antisemitism in 93
   Islamophobia in 149
   See also Hitler (Adolf),
      Holocaust, Luther (Martin),
      nationalism, Nazis
ghettoes 63–5, 101, 103
   in Papal States 64–5
   as theological concept 64, 65
   in Venice 64
   See also shtetl
Girard, René 24, 59, 101
good-Muslim-bad-Muslim binary 126,
   132, 133, 193
Green, Todd 125, 126, 128, 136
groupism 84, 215 n.35, 234 n.1

hadith 71, 149, 156, 157, 158, 161,
   233 n.45
   Hadith of the Rock 157
Hall, Stuart 21
Ham (biblical character) 87, 143,
   237 n.38
Hamas 121, 163, 207
Hanh, Thich Nhat 206, 276 n.6
Harris, Sam 47, 129, 131, 132, 251 n.32
hatred
   Allport's usage 13
   definitions of 16–19
   as 'natural' 17
   related to love 17, 65
   of religion 47–8
   religious hatred as human hatred 43,
      45–7, 48
Herzl, Theodore 118, 119
Heschel, Abraham Joshua 206, 207
Hinduism (Hindus)
   concept/identity of, and British/
      colonial/indigenous creation/
      influence 185, 187, 266 n.4,
      268–9 n.26
   'everyday' as counter to militant
      violent forms 267 n.11
   historical relations with
      Muslims 182–4

Hindu identity as not natural to
   Hindus 187
Hindu Islamophobia, rationale for
   term 2, 6
   See also Hindu nationalism, India
Hindu nationalism (nationalists)
   British influence on 184–5
   See also Bharatiya Janata Party
      (BJP), Rashtriya Swayamsevak
      Sangh (RSS), Hindutva, Vishva
      Hindu Parishad (VHP)
Hindutva
   and Hindu nationalism 185–9, 190,
      192, 193, 194
   as inclusive concept 186, 187
   Nazi influence on Savarkar/ Hindu
      nationalist concept 187
   Savarkar's definition 186–7, 189
Hirsh, David 107, 114, 115, 116,
   117, 122
Hirsi Ali, Ayaan 47, 128, 131, 139
Hitler Adolf 37, 96–7, 101, 102–3, 112
   Mein Kampf 97
Holocaust (Shoah) 25, 35, 36, 37, 39,
   40, 41, 99–104, 107, 196, 203,
   224 n.82
   antisemitic framing 116, 198
   Auschwitz 16, 35, 101, 103
   and Christianity 51, 60, 100,
      103, 208
   denial 111–13, 122, 123, 164,
      198, 201
   as Final Solution 37, 97,
      101–2, 102–3
   and Germany 99–100, 224 n.82,
      242 n.1
   and Nazi ideology/Hitler 37, 102–3
   as obligation 204
   resistance to 104
   and State of Israel 118, 120
holy war
   as Byzantine concept 69
   not meaning of *jihad* 69, 129, 136
Holy Week
   attacks on Jews during 56–7, 59
Hugh of Lincoln (little) 56
Hume, David 86, 88–9
Huntington, Samuel 67
   'clash of civilizations' thesis 136

iconography (art/images)
and prejudice 35, 221 n.55
specific images 82, 87, 132, 191
identity. *See* in-group out-group, social
identity theory
in-group out-group 13, 19–21, 22, 24,
63, 73, 84, 85, 98, 130, 187,
190, 194
violence, linked to 29, 35
India (Indians)
antisemitism in 163
Aryan invasion thesis 268–9 n.26
Indian nationalism 184
India-Pakistan relations 189, 190
Mother India 188, 190
as secular multicultural
democracy 185
See also Akhand Bharat, Hinduism,
Hindu nationalism, Modi
(Narendra), Moghul Empire
Indonesia 78, 81, 128, 136, 172,
220 n.39
Intergroup Contact Thesis 24–5, 207
intersectionality (intersectional) 16, 30,
59, 83, 93, 95, 98, 146, 163,
175, 213 n.16, 218 n.19,
252–3 n.58
Iran 137, 139
Ayatollah Khomeini 133, 139
Iranian Revolution 143, 161
Irving, David 111, 112
ISIS (so-called Islamic State in Iraq and
Syria, aka Daesh) 30, 127, 138,
144, 176, 219 n.22
Islam (Muslims)
alliances with Christian leaders
46, 76, 77
as Arab/Saracen/Turk in European
imaginary 69, 77, 81
imagined Islamic world 73, 80, 125,
136, 248 n.1
logic of conquest in 68
motif as threat/violent (Western/
orientalist/Islamophobic trope)
46, 47, 67, 68–9, 74, 127–9, 130,
133–5, 142
perceived as threat by Buddhists
171–3, 175–6, 177, 178, 179–80
perception of decline 78–9

religious tolerance in 68, 75
as 'securitised faith' 136–8
spread peacefully 78, 130, 172
See also antisemitism, *dhimmi*, jihad,
Islamophobia, Muhammad,
People of the Book, racialization
Islamism
as problematic term 134, 151
Islamophobia
in Buddhism 165–6, 172–3, 174–80
in contemporary Christianity 200
defined 6, 125
in Hinduism 182–4, 185,
187, 188–94
Islam as Christian heresy 72, 73
'Islamophobia Industry' 131–2,
133, 136
Runnymede Trust report 126
socially acceptable 142, 145
subtle Islamophobia 138–9
See also cartoons, good-Muslim-
bad Muslim binary, media,
orientalism, othering, pogroms,
racialization, terrorism
Israel-Palestine
antisemitism and criticism of 117–
22, 201, 246 n.57, 246–7 n.58
and biblical texts 144, 162
declaration of State of Israel 161
peace activism in 207
State of Israel, framing as
progressive or colonial 115, 162
usage herein 242 n.3
See also apartheid, Jerusalem,
Judaism, *Nakba*, Zionism

Jerusalem
crusader conquest of 73, 130
destruction of 56
Jesus and 53
Muslim conquest of 68
Muslims originally prayed
towards 156
temple 54
Jesuits
and antisemitism 57
Jesus
crucifixion and trial of 52, 57, 70,
226 n.1

historical aspects 53, 227 n.5
as Islamic prophet 69–70, 71, 158
as Jewish 51, 53, 60
Jewish denial of Jesus as Messiah as
    antisemitic trope 56, 155
Jewishness of, as obscure 53–4
See also Christianity, deicide, Trinity
jihad 129, 157, 160, 162, 230 n.6
    Islamophobic/Western
        misperceptions of jihad 69, 130,
        131, 133, 152, 256 n.3
    'love jihad' 177, 190, 265 n.53
    not meaning 'holy war' 129, 136
    'population jihad' 190
    See also militant neo-Islamic
        jihadism
John Chrysostom 55, 60
Johnson, Boris
    alliance with fascist parties 246 n.49
Josaphat (Saint) 173
Judaism (Jews)
    emancipation 64, 90–4, 97, 159
    legalistic, portrayed as 53, 55, 62
    Rabbinic 54, 61, 62
    spilt from Christianity 54, 55,
        227 n.10
    understood as orthopraxy 56
    See also antisemitism, covenants,
        Zionism
Juergensmeyer, Mark 45, 156, 245 n.47
Justin Martyr 54, 55

kafir 72
Kalyvas, Stathis 30, 222 n.63
Kant, Immanuel 86, 91, 224 n.82
Kendi, Ibrim X. 84, 85
King Jr., Martin Luther 206–7

Laqueur, Walter 55, 109, 243 n.5
law (legal regulation)
    and discrimination 23, 195–201
    freedom of religion and belief 92,
        171, 196–8
    and hate speech 16, 196, 200
    human rights 46, 89, 92, 115, 128,
        129, 130, 137, 174, 195, 197–9,
        201, 274 nn.11, 14
Lemkin, Raphäel 36
Levene, Mark 38, 40

Levinas, Emmanuel 25, 203, 204
Lewis, Bernard 136, 151, 152, 159
LGBTQI community 93, 115, 137
Likud 120, 162, 248 n.71
Linnaeus, Carl 86, 93
Lipstadt, Deborah 100–1, 107, 111,
    112, 114, 116, 117, 201
    Denial (film) 112
Luther, Martin
    and antisemitism 37, 60, 61–2,
        63, 91, 99
    and Islamophobia 76, 77–8
    On the Jews and Their Lies 60,
        61–2
    invoked in Nazi Germany 100, 103

Mahavamsa 168, 169, 170, 174, 179
Mahmud of Ghazni 182
Malaysia 163–4
Maldonado-Torres, Nelson 39
Malešević, Siniša 29, 40, 41, 224
    nn.82, 83
Mbembe, Achille 19, 38, 224 n.84
media
    and antisemitism 94–5, 116, 145
    Islamophobia in 47, 126, 127, 131,
        132–4, 139, 145, 176, 246 n.49,
        251 n.36
    See also social media
Medina 68, 149, 155, 156, 163,
    233 n.45
Mendelsohn, Moses 91
militant neo-Islamic jihadism 30, 134,
    152, 153, 161, 163, 176, 204
mimetic desire 24, 101
mirror neurons 29, 217 n.11
Modi, Narendra 181, 185, 192, 193,
    194, 272 n.65
Modood, Tariq 135, 268 n.16
Moghul Empire (Moghuls) 182, 183,
    187, 188, 194, 234 n.52
moral disengagement 30–1
Muhammad 68, 69, 70, 71, 75, 76, 155,
    157, 159, 160, 171
    European myth as heretic 72
    and Israelite prophetic lineage 156
    Luther on 78
    See also Banu Qurayzah,
        cartoons, *hadith*

murder
    as used herein 33–4
    See also violence
Muslim Brotherhood 151, 162, 163, 164
Myanmar 41, 167, 172, 176–9, 179–80,
    261 n.10
    See also Ashin Wirathu

Nakba 38, 161
Napoleon (Bonaparte) 76, 78, 93, 130
nationalism (nation state)
    Arab 153, 154, 155, 161, 164
    colonial influence 153, 154, 155,
        169–70, 184–5
    concepts/development of the nation
        state 38–9, 90, 91, 118
    German 39, 91
    Greek 91
    Jewish (also Jews as nation/Israel)
        38, 91, 118, 143
    link to genocide/violence 37,
        38–9, 40, 46
    Sri Lankan (Sinhala) 169–70
    Turkish 153
    See also Hindu nationalism,
        secularism, Zionism
Nazism (Nazis, National Socialism)
    antisemitic ideology of 37, 96–7
    and Holocaust denial 111, 112, 113
    influence on Islamic antisemitism
        149–50, 151, 154–5, 161, 164
    influence on militant *Hindutva*
        ideology 187, 269 n.28
    link to colonial genocide 39
    Neo-Nazis (contemporary) 107, 108,
        109, 112, 246 n.49
    See also Hitler (Adolf), Holocaust
        (Shoah)
New Atheists 2, 48, 131–2
    See also Dawkins (Richard),
        Harris (Sam)
9/11 (terror attack) 47, 119, 126, 127,
    130, 133, 134, 136, 137, 140
Nirenberg, David 59, 90, 91, 100, 102

orientalism (orientalist) 84, 129–30,
    132, 133, 134, 136, 138, 143–4,
    151, 164, 187, 268–9 n.26,
    269 n.30

othering (othered) 19, 21–3, 25, 35,
    52, 85, 101, 104, 203, 216 n.44,
    221 n.56
    and securitized identity 22
Ottoman Empire (Ottomans) 39, 76–7,
    78, 89, 91, 130, 152, 153, 154,
    160, 234 n.52
    millet system 152
    See also Turkey (Turks)

Palestinians 38, 64, 114, 115, 119, 120,
    121, 149, 161–2, 163, 242–3 n.3,
    258 n.41
    linked to Amalekites 38, 119
    See also Hamas, *Nakba*
Pandey, Gyanendra 26, 30, 191, 218–19
    n.21, 267 n.9, 267 n.11, 268 n.17
Patel, Eboo 204
People of the Book 69, 71, 151, 156–7,
    158–9, 164, 171, 173, 258 n.38
philosophy ('Western')
    genealogy of 76, 88–90, 130, 173
Pinker, Stephen 29
pogroms 15, 40, 59, 94, 99, 101,
    102, 160
    against Muslims 192, 193
pollution
    as trope in prejudice/discrimination
        22–3, 96, 101, 104
    See also dirt (filthy), disease, Douglas
        (Mary)
popes
    Benedict XVI, 110
    Gregory X (Pope): 'Letter on
        Jews' 57
    Paul IV: *Cum nimis absurdum*
        ('Since it is absurd') 64
    Urban II, 73, 231 n.18
    See also Catholicism (Catholics)
prejudice
    Allport's concept 11, 14–16
    antisemitism and
        Islamophobia as 4–6
    definitions/theories, of 11–14
    distinction of prejudice, stereotype,
        and discrimination 11–12, 23
    as 'natural' 12–13
    'polite'/socially accepted 23,
        142, 145

scale of 14–16
See also antisemitism,
   discrimination, hatred,
   iconography, Islamophobia,
   stereotypes
Protocols of the Elders of Zion 95, 97,
   117, 153, 155, 162

QAnon 109, 243 n.6
Qur'an
   contextual reading (in traditional
      Islamic scholarship, and need for)
      46, 72, 149, 157
   and Islamophobia 70, 132
   on Jews and Christians 71, 156–7,
      158, 161, 171, 230 n.4
   Luther on 77–8
   warfare/violence in 129, 136
   See also People of the Book
Qutb, Syed 151, 152, 153, 154–6, 157,
   161, 162, 163, 164
   Our Struggle with the Jews 154–5

racialization
   and Bible 87, 237 n.38
   Black and white 87–8, 93–4, 222
      n.60, 234 n.1, 236 n.40, 237 n.38
   concept 83, 84–5, 98
   of Jews 6, 83, 90–4, 96–7, 98, 99,
      115, 143–4, 150, 156, 157, 161,
      162, 164, 175, 197, 257 n.70
   of Muslims 7, 48, 83, 126, 134–5,
      143–4, 175, 197
   and Sri Lankan Buddhist
      nationalism 169, 175, 179
   See also racism
racism
   in academia 236 n.26
   anti-racism 114, 144–6, 209, 234
      n.1, 236 n.24, 245 n.47
   anti-racism and antisemitism 113–
      17, 121, 122
   Christianity, and 85–6, 87–8, 92
   colonialism/capitalism, and 85, 86,
      87–8, 248 n.76
   as fluid/malleable concept 83,
      84, 98–9
   as intersectional 98, 108, 163
   intra-white racism 88

learnt (in children) 84, 235 n.1
   as metaphysical principle
      (antisemitism) 4, 96, 97–8
   Muslims, and 3, 125, 126, 132,
      134–5, 138
   origins of modern 85–6
   not scientific 84
   theories of 84–5
   'one-drop' rule / 'blood lineage'
      ideology 85–6, 87, 96, 99
   See also racialization
Rashtriya Swayamsevak Sangh (RSS)
   186, 187–8, 190, 193, 269 n.33,
   272 n.70
religion (concept)
   as employed herein 2, 43–5, 46
   as having no agency/ speaking about
      2, 84, 260 n.1
   not inherently related to prejudice/
      violence 1–2
   See also hatred, sacred (as
      sociological marker), world
      religions paradigm
religionophobia 47
   hatred of religion 47–8
   See also antisemitism, Islamophobia
Renaissance 60, 61, 89, 130
   Hindu 185
   twelfth century 76, 89
Rohingya 41, 177–8, 179, 265 n.57
Romanies 22, 27, 97, 101, 111
Rothschilds 113
   Lionel de 92
   Mayer Amsched 113–14, 245 n.34
   'Rothschild Zionist' 109
Ruether, Rosemary Radford 59
Rushdie, Salman 139
Russia/Soviet Union
   antisemitism 119
   pogroms in 40, 94
   Stalinist antisemitism 113, 121
Rwandan genocide 40

sacred (as sociological marker) 45, 46,
   207, 245–6 n.47
Said, Edward 129, 143
   See also orientalism
Salafi 162, 173, 253 n.66
   See also Wahhabism

Santos, Boaventura de Sousa 18, 205
Saudi Arabia 128, 137, 162, 163,
    253 n.66
Savarkar, V. D. 186–7, 188, 189, 268–9
    n.26, 269 n.28
Sayyid, Salman 125, 126, 211 n.9
scapegoat (scapegoating) 23–4
    Allport on 23–4
    Girard on 24
    Jews as 24, 59, 65, 100, 101
    and ideological theory 24, 65
    and manufactured consent 24
secularism (secular) 3, 44, 45, 46, 47,
    79, 81, 90, 91, 92, 118, 119,
    128, 134, 139, 143, 144, 145,
    161, 170, 174, 185, 245–6 n.47,
    256 n.11
Shah-Kazemi, Reza 173
shariah 72, 129, 142
shifting third 81
shirk 70
shtetl 63, 64, 94, 239 n.69
    See also ghettoes
Sikhism (Sikhs) 12, 183–4, 185, 188,
    264 n.47, 272 n.65
    mistaken for Muslims 134–5
Singapore 128, 163, 172, 197, 199–
    200, 201, 250 n.20
slavery (slaves) 20, 44, 86, 88, 91
    and Christianity 87, 143
    and colonialism/modernity 39, 86,
        87, 222 n.60, 224 n.82
    and genocide 222 n.60
    and Islam 156
    as violence 28, 36, 224 n.82
social identity theory 19–21
    See also Henri Tajfel, in-group
        out-group
social media
    role in spreading/facilitating
        prejudice 108, 176, 178
Spivak, Gayatri Chakravorty 30, 204
Srebrenica 37, 41
Sri Lanka 128, 165–6, 167–70, 174–6,
    178, 179, 261 n.10
    See also Bandaranaike, S. W. R. D.,
        Dharmapala (Anagarika),
        Mahavamsa, Walpola Rahula
Stanford prison experiment 31

stereotypes
    internalization of 22
    as part of prejudice 11, 12–13,
        19–21, 84
    positive and negative 6
    stereotype activation 21
    See also antisemitism,
        discrimination, Islamophobia,
        prejudice
supersessionism 71, 110

Tajfel, Henri 11, 13
Talmud
    and antisemitism 61–2, 63, 100
Tamil Tigers 174, 175
terrorism (terrorists)
    antithetical to Islam 128, 129,
        133, 150–1
    conceptions of 121, 127, 128
    and freedom of religion 197
    Islamic (Islamophobic trope) 47,
        126–7, 128–9, 133, 136, 137,
        138, 176
    Jewish 115
    nuclear threat 218 n.18
    right-wing 127, 128, 249 n.12
    secular (nationalist) 127, 128
    suicide bombing 128, 250 n.18
    as violence 34
    See also Hamas, militant neo-Islamic
        jihadism, Tamil Tigers, war
        on terror
Tertullian 55
Thailand 167, 172, 178, 180, 261 n.10
Tibi, Bassam 151, 152, 153
Trinity
    in Christian-Muslim relations 70,
        71
Trump, Donald 120, 132, 134, 137,
    163, 181, 193–4, 201, 224 n.82,
    248 n.71
Turkey (Turks) 30, 39, 64, 128,
    153, 185
    as synonym of Muslim 77, 81
    See also Ottoman Empire

ulama 46, 72, 167
Umayyad dynasty 75, 159, 160,
    233 n.45

United Kingdom (UK), antisemitism in 111, 113–14, 116–17
  Islamophobia in 132
  racism in 23, 85, 92, 132
  See also Cameron (David), Corbyn (Jeremy), Johnson (Boris)
United States (USA)
  antisemitism in 92, 93–4, 108, 109, 110, 111, 201
  freedom of religion in 92
  as 'Great Satan' 161, 162
  Islamophobia in 108, 127, 132, 135, 136, 137–8, 139
  racism in 86, 93–4, 108
  violence against women in 128
  See also Bush (George W.), Trump (Donald)
Universal Declaration on Human Rights (UDHR) 195, 196–7, 274 n.11
untheorizing 4–6, 28, 32–6, 65, 146, 223 n.67, 224 n.82

vigilantes
  far-right 22
  Hindu 192–3, 70 n.272
Vishva Hindu Parishad (VHP) 187, 188, 190, 191
violence
  defined as direct, structural, and cultural 28–9
  development in human society/civilization/modernity 29–30, 39, 40, 224 n.82
  as a generative force 36, 209
  as normalized/ routine 28, 30, 36, 101, 175, 218–19 n.21
  outcome vs process of 30
  possible against both strangers and neighbours 32, 209, 220 n.39, 225 n.86
  as rational 30, 35
  related to prejudice 13, 14, 15–16, 27
  vigilantes 22

See also dehumanization, genocide, mimetic desire, moral disengagement, murder, pogroms, slavery, terrorism, women

Wahhabism 162, 163, 164, 173, 253 n.66
  Muhammad Ibn Abd al-Wahhab 162
  See also Salafi
Walpola Rahula 169
war on terror 80, 130, 133, 136, 176, 178, 180, 189
Webb, Alexander Russell 79
Weber, Max 40
Webman Esther 152, 162
white supremacy 87, 96, 127, 130, 133, 137, 234 n.1
  See also racism
Wiesel, Elie 98, 146
Wirathu. *See* Ashin Wirathu
women
  leaders 128, 131, 250 n.20
  seen as at risk 177, 190
  violence/discrimination against 4, 16, 31–2, 85, 91, 95, 115, 128, 135, 139, 158, 218–19 n.21, 221 n.56
world religions paradigm 43

yoga
  International yoga day 192
  See also Modi (Narendra)

Zimbardo, Philip 31, 103, 230 n.25
Zionism
  anti-Zionism (criticism of Zionism/Israel) 113, 107–8, 114, 118, 119, 120–1, 122, 201, 246–7 n.58
  as involving removal of Palestinians 38, 119
  militant religious Zionism 110, 119, 247 n.64
  secular vs religious forms 118–19
  varying definitions 118–19, 122